FEMINIST JOURNEYS

VOIES FÉMINISTES

Edited by / Sous la direction de
MARGUERITE ANDERSEN

Feminist History Society / Société d'histoire féministe
Ottawa

THE ONTARIO HISTORICAL SOCIETY

ISBN
978-0-9866478-0-2

EDITED BY
Marguerite Andersen

DESIGN
Zab Design & Typography Inc.

CONTENTS

> Prime Minister Lester B. Pearson
with members of the Canadian
Federation of Business and
Professional Women's Clubs,
July 1963

Archives of Ontario, F4526-2

> Le Premier ministre Lester B.
Pearson avec des membres de la
Fédération canadienne des clubs
de femmes de carrières libérales et
commerciales, juillet 1963

FEMINIST HISTORY SOCIETY

The Feminist History Society is committed to creating a lasting record of the women's movement in Canada and Québec for the period between 1960 and the year of the Society's founding, 2010. Our objective is to celebrate fifty years of activity and accomplishment by creating a written legacy for ourselves, our families and friends, our communities, students, and scholars. The beautiful books we publish, with membership support, will be as spirited and diverse as the movement itself, meant to stand together, and to encourage and challenge those who follow.

Members of the non-profit Feminist History Society receive an annual book at no extra charge, and may also purchase other books published by the Society.

Over the course of a decade, our goal is to publish two or three books a year chronicling different aspects of the movement from sea to sea to sea. The topics will be as diverse as our wide-ranging campaigns for equality through transformative social, economic, civil, political, and cultural change. We will make every effort to be inclusive of gender, race, class, geography, culture, dis/ability, language, sexual identity, and age.

We maintain an open call for submissions. There will be many different authors. Individuals and organizations who participated in the movement are all encouraged to contribute. There will be a variety of formats, including autobiographies, biographies, single- and multi-themed volumes, edited collections, pictorial histories, plays, and novels.

National co-editors for the Society are M. Elizabeth Atcheson and Constance Backhouse. Shari Graydon, Lorraine Greaves, Diana Majury, and Beth Symes are sharing their broad experience to move the Society forward. Mary Breen is overseeing the Society's administration. Dawn Buie has created the Society's web site, making it simple to join and contact us. Zab of Zab Design & Typography has created the visual identity for the Society, as well as the book design for the series. We offer our heartfelt thanks to all of the talented and committed women who are providing encouragement, advice, and support.

We urge you to join as a member, and to participate as an author, in the Feminist History Society.

http://www.FeministHistories.ca
info@feministhistories.ca
A project of Women's Education and Research Foundation of Ontario Inc.
Charitable Registration No. 889933669RR0001

LA SOCIÉTÉ D'HISTOIRE FÉMINISTE

La Société d'histoire féministe s'est engagée à dresser l'historique du mouvement féministe au Canada et au Québec pour la période située entre 1960 et l'année de la fondation de la Société, soit 2010. Ce faisant, nous voulons célébrer cinquante années d'activité et d'accomplissements en publiant cet héritage écrit, pour nous-mêmes, nos familles et nos amies, nos communautés, ainsi que pour la population étudiante et les universitaires. Les ouvrages que nous souhaitons publier, grâce à l'appui de nos membres, seront aussi inspirés que diversifiés, à l'image du mouvement lui-même, et visent à resserrer nos rangs tout en incitant d'autres adeptes à suivre le mouvement.

Les membres de la Société d'histoire féministe, société à but non lucratif, recevront chaque année un livre de la série, sans frais supplémentaires, et peuvent aussi, bien entendu, acheter d'autres publications de la Société.

Au cours de la prochaine décennie, notre objectif consistera à publier deux ou trois livres par année en vue de faire la chronique des différents aspects du mouvement et ce, de l'Atlantique au Pacifique jusqu'en Arctique. Les thèmes abordés seront aussi diversifiés que nos vastes campagnes pour l'égalité le furent par le biais de réformes sociales, économiques, civiques, politiques et culturelles. Nous déploierons le maximum d'efforts pour que nos publications soient les plus représentatives possibles, et traduisent la diversité des expériences vécues, selon le sexe, la race, la culture, la classe sociale, la situation géographique, les handicaps, la langue, l'identité sexuelle et l'âge.

Notre invitation à soumettre des textes en vue de leur publication tient toujours. L'éventail des auteures sera très varié dans la mesure où nous sollicitons aussi bien les particuliers que les organisations qui ont participé à ce mouvement. Les formats seront tout aussi diversifiés, puisqu'il s'agira d'autobiographies, de biographies, de monographies ou d'ouvrages à thèmes multiples, de recueils édités, d'histoires illustrées, de pièces de théâtre et de romans.

Ce sont M. Elizabeth Atcheson et Constance Backhouse qui assument en collaboration la direction éditoriale de la Société, à l'échelon national. Shari Graydon, Lorraine Greaves, Diana Majury et Beth Symes se chargent quant à elles, grâce à leur vaste expérience dans le domaine, de faire évoluer la Société. Mary Breen supervise l'administration de la Société. Dawn Buie a conçu et mis sur pied le site Web de la Société, facilitant ainsi les communications avec vous. Zab, de chez Zab Design & Typography a créé l'identité visuelle de la Société et se charge de la conception graphique de la série de livres. Nous tenons à remercier du fond du cœur toutes les femmes talentueuses et dévouées qui nous accompagnent par leur appui, leurs encouragements et leurs conseils.

Nous vous incitons vivement à vous joindre à la Société et à vous impliquer, en qualité d'auteure, aux projets de la Société d'histoire féministe.

http://www.FeministHistories.ca

info@feministhistories.ca

Un projet de la Women's Education and Research Foundation of Ontario Inc.

Numéro d'entreprise de l'organisme de bienfaisance : 889933669RR0001

> Demonstration, Parliament Hill, Ottawa

Archives and Special Collections (CWMA), University of Ottawa (P-X10-1-110)/Photographer unknown

> Manifestation, Colline parlementaire, Ottawa

FOREWORD

Marguerite Andersen

To compile this collection of feminist journeys has been a delight. First of all because I had the privilege of reading the stories of so many interesting women, but also because the work allowed me to tie the knot with my first feminist publication, *Mother was not a person (1971)*, a collection of feminist essays that had two editions and sold 6,000 copies. I hope *Feminist Journeys/Voies féministes* will follow or even surpass its example.

Le recueil présente plusieurs contributions en langue française. Why not? *Pourquoi pas, disait le macaron de 1975. Ces textes particulièrement significatifs sont des exemples de la lutte pleine d'énergie qu'ont menée les féministes québécoises de la deuxième vague du féminisme canadien.*

I must thank all the contributors for their patience with me. I often took quite some time to answer your e-mails or answered them collectively. I am glad we got it done.

I must thank Jean Hewitt and Karin Wilson who did the first editing of the individual texts, Karen Gelb who served as our copy-editor, Valérie Leclercq who served as translator for the foreword and introductory chapter, Martin Dufresne who served as our French copy-editor, and Margie Wolfe who generously shared editorial and publishing expertise.

Voilà. Vous m'avez permis une belle aventure; permettez-moi maintenant de vous en remercier.

INTRODUCTION

Constance Backhouse

FEMINIST HISTORY SOCIETY

Feminist Journeys / Voies féministes is the first book to be published by the Feminist History Society. Many of us have been part of the feminist movement during the exciting and challenging fifty years between 1960 and 2010. We want to preserve this history for posterity, before too many feminists of our generation die, and the others who were part of it forget what we did.

Feminism has a history that predates the 1960s and will continue long after 2010. Although some historians reject the concept of "waves," many have described the feminist campaigns for suffrage and temperance during the nineteenth and early twentieth centuries as the "first wave of feminism." The upsurge of feminist activism that began in the 1960s has often been characterized as the "second wave." We have begun in 1960, which witnessed the founding of the Voice of Women in Canada and Québec. The decade of the 1960s also saw the appointment of the Royal Commission on the Status of Women, and the creation of "women's liberation" groups across the country.

It was more than twenty-five years ago that I first learned about an earlier project to chronicle feminist history, undertaken by the "first wave" of feminists in the nineteenth century. The idea originated with the American suffragists Elizabeth Cady Stanton, Susan B. Anthony, Matilda Joslyn Gage, and Ida Harper Husted, and culminated in a publication of six, thick, hard-cover volumes, entitled *History of Woman Suffrage* (New York: 1881-1902, 1922).

The six volumes cover the years from 1848 to 1920. In 1985, the year my daughter was born, I treated myself to the purchase of a full set. The preface of volume 1 gives some idea of the editors' thoughts as they undertook to document their history.

> In preparing this work, our object has been to put into permanent shape the few scattered reports of the Woman Suffrage Movement still to be found, and to make it an arsenal of facts for those who are beginning to inquire into the demands and arguments of the leaders of this reform. [...] In giving the inception and progress of this great agitation, we who have undertaken the task have been moved by the consideration that many of our co-workers have already fallen asleep, and that in a few years all who could tell the story will have passed away. [...]
>
> To the few who, through ill-timed humility, have refused to contribute any of their early experiences we would suggest, that as each brick in a magnificent structure might have had no special value alone on the road-side, yet, in combination with many others, its size, position, quality, becomes of vital consequence; so with the actors in any great reform, though they may be of little value in themselves; as a part of a great movement they may be worthy of mention—even important to the completion of an historical record.
>
> [...] Those who fight the battle can best give what all readers like to know—the impelling motives to action; the struggle in the face of opposition; the vexation over ridicule; and the despair in success too long deferred. [...] As an autobiography is more interesting than a sketch by another, so is a history written by its actors, as in both cases we get nearer the soul of the subject.
>
> We have finished our task, and we hope the contribution we have made may enable some other hand in the future to write a more complete history of "the most momentous reform that has yet been launched in the world—the first organized protest against the injustice which has brooded over the character and destiny of one-half the human race."

The words spoke poignantly across the centuries. We took inspiration from the women who had preceded us, who had dared to imagine a world of equality, and who had devoted so much of their lives to campaigning for change. As I displayed my six volumes, given pride of place in my dining room library in London, Ontario, I thought about feminists having the foresight to write their own history as it unfolded. I knew we should be doing the same thing.

Somehow, the majority of us became too busy making history to actually write our own. I have always felt that was neglectful, even rash. As some of the founding mothers of our generation of feminism have begun to die, it serves as a wake-up call that this is a pressing task that can no longer be put off. Our movement is not at an end. In fact I think even those of us who were active from the early-1960s have many years of very useful activism left in us. But the third and fourth waves are upon us, and now is time to take stock of what we did and how we did it. To preserve our memoirs for posterity before we lose many other key players, or our memories begin to fail.

WHAT TO SELECT FOR THE FIRST BOOK AND
WHO TO EDIT IT?

Where better to start than a book on what provoked us to self-identify as feminists? All of us had "beginnings" in this movement. Indeed, that seemed to be an obvious foundation upon which to rest what will follow. Identifying as a feminist has never been easy. How many times do we hear the incessant "I'm not a feminist, but…"? Quite a number of women have also made very successful careers out of lambasting feminists and feminism. Yet countless of us have claimed the label, proud to wear this as a badge of honour. What prompted us to self-identify? Who and what inspired us? What did this new label signify to those of us who chose it?

It was Marguerite Andersen who first proposed to compile and edit a collection of short stories from feminists across Canada and Québec, describing how they "came to feminism." We leapt at the opportunity. How fitting it was that Marguerite, one of the path-breakers for our feminist era, should be the person to offer to do this. Indeed, Marguerite was one of the first to publish explicitly feminist work. Her marvellous compilation of essays titled *Mother was not a person* was acclaimed as the first Canadian feminist anthology of the era when it was published by Black Rose Books in Montreal in 1971. A professor of women's studies, French literature, and philosophy, Marguerite has taught at universities in Nova Scotia, Québec, and Ontario, and at the girl-centred Toronto Linden School. She has published a remarkable list of award-winning French and English novels, poetry, short-story collections, plays, and non-fiction. *De mémoire de femme* (Montréal: Quinze, 1982) won the prize of the *Journal de Montréal*. *La soupe* (Sudbury: Prise de parole, 1995) won the Grand Prize of the Salon du Livre de Toronto, and *Le figuier sur le toit* (Ottawa: Les Éditions L'Interligne, 2008) won the Trillium Prize and Le Prix des Lecteurs Radio-Canada 2009. Her website describes her as "an adventurer" who never became a "recluse in an ivory tower." It reminds readers that she is a mother of three children and a grandmother of seven. It displays photographs of her at the age of eight playing at the edge of the Baltic Sea, confronting the Montréal police during the student strikes in 1969, and receiving an honorary doctorate from Mount Saint Vincent University in 1999. Who else could possibly be better suited to edit a collection of stories from the unruly, eclectic, inspiring feminists who answered the call?

HOW THIS BOOK CAME ABOUT

The idea germinated in February 2008, when a group of about thirty women came together in Ottawa to talk about how we would go about creating the Feminist History Society. Marguerite's call for submissions went out via the feminist grapevine and untold email listservs the summer afterward. The call requested autobiographical texts under 2000 words, due in January 2009, describing how the writers came to feminism. Given our movement's well-earned reputation for punctuality, it should make some feminists smile to learn that the first deadline did not "take." The next reminder call that circulated sought texts between 1000 and 2000 words, due July 2009. Marguerite's gentle advisory added: "If July 31 seems impossible for you but you would like to contribute your story, please send me a note advising me at which date I shall receive your submission." The first snowflakes were falling in Ottawa in the late fall of 2009 and the final submissions were still sliding in.

So much for timeliness. Far more important, as we have always known, was the open-hearted reception that greeted the call. Over ninety writers crafted their individual reflections on how they came to identify with feminism. Collectively, their contributions were extraordinary in scope, depth, and breadth. The women who wrote ranged across race, class, disability, sexual identity, age, language, and geography. Some came to feminism in a memorable moment. Others inched their way through, slowly warming up to the identification over months, years, and decades. Still others could not remember any time when they had not self-identified as feminist. The factors that influenced the group were equally diverse: a montage of family, work, and educational experiences all made their mark. What was most exciting was that the voices told such moving and important tales. Taken together, the mixture of stories represents the remarkably variable nature of feminism in our era.

One of the women who volunteered to help edit this collection, Karin Wilson, put it well when she wrote: "This has been an amazing, and often moving, experience reading through all these essays — and I know I only have half of them. At times I laughed out loud, at other points I was moved to tears, and many times I couldn't help but think: will the current generation of women even believe some of this stuff? (I'm 48.) It's hard to fathom all the societal and personal changes we've all gone through."

HOW TO READ THIS BOOK

We have struggled with how to present the unruly and multifarious voices that these texts depict. We initially thought we might try to stream the essays by theme, sorting them into sections based on various descriptors or motivating factors. Yet the complexity of the stories defies streaming, with themes that occasionally parallel or overlap, often contradict, and more often stray in all directions. In the end, we reverted to the simplest, most democratic method we could adopt: sorting the essays by the alphabetical order of the names of the authors. We also decided to place the short author biographies at the end of the book, rather than at the end of each piece, in order not to break the flow of the narratives.

Each piece stands alone, reflecting one author's own individual history and story. With over ninety independently minded writers, there has also been some diversity in form and style. In the end, we had to abandon any desire for rigid stylistic conformity. Yet each piece adds a genuine voice to the understanding of how it was that so many women chose to claim their place within feminism in this era. In their divergences, they coalesce to create a many-textured whole that is all the richer for the disparities. Readers are invited to read from front to end, from end to front, or to pick this volume up anywhere and peruse it through a random selection. As a collection, these texts offer a kaleidoscopic picture of how a wave of feminism came to fruition over the past fifty years.

We hope you will find that the experience of reading this collection will offer a window into the origins of the strength and vibrancy of feminism in our time. And we hope that if you missed our call for submissions, or were one of those whose story came in just past the final, final, final deadline, that you will consider uploading your contribution onto the Feminist History Society website. This is *our* history. It needs your voice too.

INTRODUCTION

Constance Backhouse

LA SOCIÉTÉ D'HISTOIRE FÉMINISTE

Feminist Journeys / Voies féministes est le premier ouvrage publié par la Société d'histoire féministe. Nous avons été nombreuses à participer au mouvement féministe durant le demi-siècle, passionnant et riche en défis, allant de 1960 à 2010. Notre objectif consiste à préserver cette histoire pour la postérité, avant que ne disparaissent, hélas, un trop grand nombre de féministes de notre génération, et que celles qui en ont fait partie n'oublient ce que nous avons accompli.

L'histoire du féminisme date de bien avant les années 1960 et se poursuivra encore longtemps après 2010. Il est certes des historiens qui rejettent la notion de « vagues », mais nombreux sont ceux pourtant qui regroupent sous le vocable de « première vague du féminisme » les campagnes menées par les féministes en faveur du droit de vote et contre l'alcoolisme au cours du dix-neuvième siècle et au début du vingtième siècle. L'essor de l'activisme féministe amorcé au début des années 1960 a souvent été désigné comme la « seconde vague » du mouvement. Nous avons entamé notre militantisme en 1960, année où La Voix des femmes a vu le jour au Canada et au Québec. Durant cette décennie, la Commission royale d'enquête sur la situation de la femme au Canada a également été nommée, et on a vu des groupes de « libération des femmes » éclore dans tout le pays.

Voilà plus de vingt-cinq ans, j'ai entendu parler pour la première fois d'un projet antérieur, entrepris à l'instigation des féministes de la « première vague » au dix-neuvième siècle, dans le but de retracer et consigner l'histoire féministe. Ce sont les suffragistes américaines Elizabeth Cady Stanton, Susan B. Anthony, Matilda Joslyn Gage, et Ida Harper Husted qui en ont eu tout d'abord l'idée. Ce projet aboutit à la publication de six gros volumes reliés et intitulés *History of Woman Suffrage* (New York : 1881-1902, 1922), couvrant la période de 1848 à 1920. En 1985, l'année de naissance de ma fille, je me suis offert la série au complet. La préface du premier volume donne un aperçu de ce qui avait incité les rédactrices à entreprendre cette tâche.

> [TRADUCTION] En débutant ce travail, notre objectif a été de regrouper, sous une forme durable, les quelques comptes rendus épars du mouvement en faveur du droit de vote pour les femmes, et d'en faire un arsenal de faits pour ceux et celles qui s'interrogent sur les revendications et les arguments des instigatrices de cette réforme. [...] En décrivant les débuts et le cheminement de ce grand mouvement, nous avons été émues à l'idée que bon nombre de nos camarades avaient déjà disparu et que dans quelques années, toutes celles capables de narrer ce récit ne seraient plus de ce monde [...]

> Nous aimerions rappeler à celles qui, par une sorte de modestie tardive, ont refusé de relater leurs expériences, que chaque brique d'un imposant édifice ne présenterait aucune valeur intrinsèque si on la voyait isolée au bord du chemin, mais qu'en l'ajoutant à beaucoup d'autres, elle finit par revêtir, de par sa taille, sa position et sa qualité, une importance vitale pour l'ensemble. Mais il en va ainsi des acteurs et actrices de toute réforme majeure : même si à titre individuel, l'on n'apporte qu'une contribution modeste, lorsque l'on fait partie d'un vaste mouvement, on devient une personne digne de mention et même importante au parachèvement d'un compte rendu historique.

> [...] Ceux et celles qui livrent la bataille sont les mieux à même de donner aux lecteurs ce qu'ils veulent savoir — soit les motivations qui les poussent à l'action ; l'âpreté de la lutte face à l'opposition ;

l'humiliation d'être ridiculisées ; et le désespoir face à une victoire trop longtemps différée. [...] Tout comme une autobiographie est plus intéressante que le portrait peint par un tiers, ainsi en est-il de l'histoire racontée par ceux et celles qui l'ont vécue et qui nous livrent l'essence même du sujet.

Notre tâche est à présent terminée et nous espérons que notre contribution permettra à d'autres, à l'avenir, d'écrire une histoire plus complète de la « plus formidable réforme jamais entreprise dans le monde — soit le tout premier mouvement de protestation lancé contre l'injustice qui a pesé sur la nature et le destin d'une moitié de la race humaine ».

Ces mots continuent de résonner de façon poignante à travers le temps. Les femmes qui nous ont précédées ont été notre source d'inspiration, car elles ont osé, en leur temps, imaginer un monde où l'égalité régnerait enfin et consacré la majeure partie de leur vie à mener campagne pour ce projet de réforme. En disposant ces six volumes à la place d'honneur dans la bibliothèque de ma salle à manger à London, en Ontario, j'ai pensé à ces féministes qui avaient eu la sagacité de rédiger leur propre histoire alors même qu'elle avait lieu. J'ai su alors qu'il nous fallait en faire de même.

À un certain point, nous sommes devenues, pour la plupart, trop occupées à faire l'histoire pour avoir le temps d'écrire la nôtre, ce que j'ai toujours trouvé négligent, voire irréfléchi. Le fait que certaines des mères fondatrices de notre génération de féministes aient commencé à nous quitter retentit comme un avertissement qu'il devient urgent d'agir, que l'on ne peut plus remettre à plus tard notre devoir de mémoire. Notre mouvement est loin d'être moribond ; en fait je pense que même celles d'entre nous qui étaient actives dès le début des années 1960 ont encore beaucoup à apporter en termes de militantisme. Mais les troisième et quatrième vagues sont dorénavant parmi nous et le temps est venu de dresser le bilan de ce que nous avons accompli et de la manière dont nous l'avons fait. Il nous faut livrer de vifs souvenirs à la postérité avant que d'autres de nos compagnes de lutte ne disparaissent ou que nos mémoires ne deviennent faiblissantes.

QUE CHOISIR POUR LE PREMIER VOLUME ET À QUI EN CONFIER LA DIRECTION ÉDITORIALE ?

Quel meilleur point de départ qu'un livre décrivant ce qui nous a incitées à nous définir comme féministes ? Chacune d'entre nous a connu ses propres « débuts » dans ce mouvement. Cela semblait même une base évidente sur laquelle édifier ce qui allait suivre. S'identifier comme féministe n'a jamais été chose facile. Combien de fois avons-nous entendu l'incessant cliché « Je ne suis pas féministe, mais… » ? Un grand nombre de femmes ont même connu de fructueuses carrières en vilipendant les féministes et le féminisme. Nous avons toutefois été innombrables à revendiquer l'étiquette, fières d'arborer cet insigne. Qu'est-ce qui nous a incitées à nous identifier de la sorte ? Où et chez qui avons-nous trouvé notre inspiration ? Quelle signification revêtait cette désignation pour celles d'entre nous qui avons posé ce choix ?

C'est Marguerite Andersen qui, la première, a proposé de colliger et de mettre en forme un recueil de brefs récits de féministes de tout le Canada et du Québec, décrivant leur « venue au féminisme ». Nous avons sauté sur l'occasion, car Marguerite, en sa qualité de pionnière de notre ère féministe, nous a paru être la meilleure personne pour mener à bien ce projet. Rappelons que Marguerite a été l'une des premières Canadiennes à publier des travaux explicitement féministes. Sa merveilleuse compilation d'essais intitulée *Mother was not a person* a été acclamée comme la première anthologie féministe canadienne à sa publication par Black Rose Books à Montréal en 1971. Professeure en études féministes, en littérature française et en philosophie, Marguerite a enseigné dans différentes universités en Nouvelle-Écosse, au Québec et en Ontario, ainsi qu'à The Linden School, une école pour filles de Toronto. La liste de ses publications, en anglais et en français, maintes fois primées, est impressionnante, qu'il s'agisse de romans, de poésie, de recueils de nouvelles, de pièces de théâtre ou d'ouvrages de nature générale. *De mémoire de femme* (Montréal : Quinze, 1982) a remporté le prix du *Journal de Montréal*. *La soupe* (Sudbury : Prise de parole, 1995) s'est mérité le Grand Prix du Salon du Livre de Toronto, et *Le figuier sur le toit* (Ottawa : Les Éditions L'Interligne, 2008) a reçu le Prix Trillium et le Prix des Lecteurs de Radio-Canada 2009. Sur son site Web, elle se décrit comme une « vagabonde » qui jamais n'est devenue « une recluse dans sa tour d'ivoire ». On y apprend qu'elle est mère de trois enfants, qui lui ont donné sept petits-enfants. On la voit aussi sur des photos, à l'âge de huit ans en train de jouer au bord de la mer Baltique, puis lors d'une confrontation avec des policiers montréalais lors des grèves étudiantes de 1969, et à une cérémonie où la Mount Saint Vincent University lui décerne un doctorat *honoris causa* en 1999. Bref, Marguerite nous a semblé la mieux placée pour recueillir des récits véridiques auprès du groupe éclectique d'indomptables et inspirantes féministes ayant répondu à notre appel.

COMMENT CE LIVRE A-T-IL VU LE JOUR ?

L'idée a commencé à germer en février 2008, alors qu'une trentaine d'entre nous nous étions réunies à Ottawa pour discuter de comment mettre sur pied la Société d'histoire féministe. L'invitation de Marguerite à proposer des textes a fait, l'été suivant, son chemin auprès des féministes par le truchement du téléphone arabe et d'innombrables listes de diffusion. Marguerite demandait de lui faire parvenir avant janvier 2009 des textes de nature autobiographique de moins de 2 000 mots, où les auteures décrivaient ce qui les avait amenées au féminisme. Connaissant la réputation de ponctualité de notre mouvement, certaines féministes souriront en apprenant que cette première date limite n'a pas été respectée... Dans son rappel suivant, Marguerite a invité les auteures à lui soumettre des textes comptant entre 1000 et 2 000 mots, avant juillet 2009, en ajoutant aimablement : « S'il vous est impossible de me faire parvenir votre texte d'ici le 31 juillet, pourriez-vous m'aviser de la date à laquelle je pourrais le recevoir ? » Les premiers flocons de neige tombaient sur Ottawa, à la fin de l'automne 2009, alors que les derniers textes continuaient à rentrer.

Mais assez parlé de dates d'échéance. Le plus important, en fait, et de cela nous ne doutions pas, c'est la chaleureuse réception avec laquelle notre projet a été accueilli. Plus de quatre-vingt-dix auteures ont pris la plume pour exprimer leurs réflexions sur leur cheminement individuel vers l'identification comme féministe. Collectivement, ces contributions impressionnent par la profondeur, la portée et le souffle qui les animent. Ces femmes diffèrent de maintes façons : la race, la classe sociale, les handicaps, l'identité sexuelle, l'âge, la langue et la géographie. Certaines d'entre elles sont devenues féministes à la suite d'un événement marquant. D'autres ont cheminé à petits pas, suivant progressivement, au fil des mois, des années et même des décennies, les méandres du processus d'identification. Pour d'autres encore, il n'y a pas un seul jour de leur vie où elles peuvent se rappeler n'avoir pas été féministes. Les facteurs déclencheurs de cette identité sont tout aussi variés, en ce qu'ils relèvent d'expériences liées à la famille, la carrière et l'éducation qui, toutes, ont laissé leur marque. Entendre ces voix nous raconter ces expériences aussi prégnantes qu'émouvantes a été particulièrement inspirant, et la combinaison de ces histoires illustre bien la nature éminemment variée du féminisme de notre époque.

L'une des femmes qui se sont portées bénévoles pour nous aider à assembler ce recueil, Karin Wilson, l'a d'ailleurs très bien exprimé : « Lire ces récits a été pour moi une expérience fantastique, souvent bouleversante, — et je n'en ai lu que la moitié. Par moments, je riais tout haut, à d'autres, je fondais en larmes, et souvent je ne pouvais m'empêcher de me demander si la génération actuelle des femmes allait même accorder foi à certains de ces récits (j'ai 48 ans). On se fait difficilement une idée de l'ampleur des changements, sur les plans social et personnel, par lesquels nous sommes toutes passées. »

COMMENT ABORDER CE LIVRE ?

Nous avons longuement débattu de la manière de présenter les voix diverses et rebelles qui se pressent dans ce recueil. Au début, nous pensions classer les textes par thèmes, en les triant selon divers éléments descriptifs ou facteurs déclencheurs. Cependant, la complexité même des histoires relatées, combinée aux difficultés nées du chevauchement, des contradictions et de l'éclectisme de leurs thèmes défiait toute tentative de classification systématique. Nous sommes donc revenues à la méthode la plus simple et la plus démocratique possible : présenter les textes par ordre alphabétique d'auteures. Nous avons en outre choisi de placer leurs notices biographiques à la fin du livre, plutôt qu'à la fin de chaque texte, évitant ainsi de rompre le fil narratif.

Chaque texte se démarque de l'ensemble, reflétant la pensée et l'histoire personnelle de son auteure. Avec plus de quatre-vingt-dix femmes aussi indépendantes d'esprit, il fallait bien s'attendre à une grande diversité de style et de forme. Nous avons donc abandonné toute velléité d'imposer quelque uniformité stylistique. Et pourtant, chacun de ces récits authentiques nous aide à comprendre comment tant de femmes ont choisi de revendiquer leur place au sein du mouvement féministe de notre époque. De par leurs divergences, ces voix forment ensemble une matière opulente et multiforme, dont les disparités mêmes ne font que renforcer la richesse. Vous pouvez lire ce recueil du début à la fin, ou le commencer par la fin, ou encore le feuilleter en s'arrêtant sur un texte en particulier, au choix ou au hasard. Ensemble, ces récits dressent un portrait kaléidoscopique de l'évolution de cette vague du féminisme au cours des cinquante dernières années.

Nous espérons vivement que cette lecture vous livrera le secret de la force électrisante du féminisme de notre époque. Et nous espérons que, si vous n'avez pas reçu notre appel à propositions ou que vous avez raté notre échéance finale de remise, vous voudrez bien télécharger votre contribution au site Web de la Société d'histoire féministe et ajouter ainsi votre voix aux textes recueillis. Car *votre* voix fait aussi partie de *notre* histoire.

> Native Women's Association of
  Canada, Demonstration, Parliament
  Hill, Ottawa, 1993

  Archives and Special Collections
  (CWMA), University of Ottawa
  (PC-X10-2-91)/Anne Molgat

> Association des femmes
  autochtones du Canada,
  Manifestation, Colline
  parlementaire, Ottawa, 1993

RECOGNIZE ABORIGINAL WOMEN
WE ARE THE KEEPERS OF THE CULTURE

FEMINIST JOURNEYS

VOIES FÉMINISTES

1 | ROADBLOCKS

Marguerite Andersen

During childhood and teenage years, I made some declarations as to what I wanted to become: at age 4, the patient lady in the ever so clean public toilet on the Joachimstaler Platz, Berlin, near the Kurfürstendamm; at age 10, a gardener in a garden like ours, with flowers and fruit trees; at the time of braces, a dentist; as of age 16, an actor. My parents neither encouraged nor discouraged any of these choices. I don't think they even really commented. They must have thought that I would eventually find my way. Furthermore their idea of education, besides aesthetically pleasant surroundings, good schools, lots of books, fresh air, healthy food and civilized behaviour, was to let us be, my two sisters and me. The oldest had wanted to become a modern dancer; she studied with Mary Wigman, then, in 1935, emigrated to England where she married a German refugee. The second had wanted to become an opera singer, studied singing and violin, got pregnant and married her lover. By the time I got out of secondary school, where I had discovered my love for everything French, Hitler had closed all faculties of arts where I might have gone to study French literature. He had also thrown my father, member of the Landtag for the Deutsche Demokratische Partei and Assistant Deputy Minister of Education during the Weimar Republic, out of office. We became relatively poor.

To avoid military service, I married a German soldier, thinking that later I would be free to do what I wanted. I very quickly divorced when I discovered that I was expected to do as told. Exhausted by the war, I married an officer of the French army in 1946 and moved with him to Tunisia, again thinking that I could later do whatever I chose. Maybe I did not even think; I just wanted out of Germany. In Tunis, I had two boys, then divorced when I despaired that I wasn't "allowed" to do what I wanted: study, teach, and be free. I returned to Berlin.

I attended the Free University of Berlin from 1951–58, thinking I would later teach French and English in secondary schools. I soon discovered that this was not to be the case. I had lost my German nationality when I became a French citizen in order to be able to take a teaching job in Tunisia. In Germany, as in France or its then protectorate Tunisia, teachers were public servants and had to be citizens of the country where they wanted to teach.

While continuing at the Freie Uuniversität, writing an M.A. thesis on Proust, I taught at three different private schools to earn enough money to house and feed my two sons and myself. Sometimes, in the morning, I had to figure out where in Berlin I was going. Luckily, my mother paid for a weekly cleaning lady, while my sons' father paid for nothing. (The funny thing is that when he died in 2008, the French government decided I was entitled to a small pension for the years I had lived with him, allowing him to make a career. *Merci aux féministes françaises !*)

I emigrated to Canada in 1958, having accepted a contract teaching French for the Protestant School Board of Greater Montreal. I enrolled at the Université de Montréal to work toward a Ph.D. *en lettres françaises*, met and married a Dane, and quickly wrote his M.A. thesis so we could both go and teach French at the University of Addis Ababa. I gave birth to a daughter. We later taught at the University of North Dakota. I wrote my Ph.D. thesis on the great Paul Claudel, never finding out that he had a sister, Camille, who will remain famous for her wonderful sculptures, even though she was, as soon as her protective father had died, put in a lunatic asylum by her famous brother. Back in Montreal, the Dane and I both taught at Loyola College (later to become part of Concordia). At one point, I declared I was not going to write his Ph.D. thesis for him, whereupon he left to live with a probably more docile female student.

At this point, I was still not reflecting on feminism. But feminism was everywhere. My friend and colleague Katherine Waters, who taught English literature at Loyola, inspired me in 1970 to create and teach an interdisciplinary course in women's studies. She and I managed to get it accepted by the Loyola Senate; 55 students enrolled.

Teaching the course was a great learning experience for me. I read and read and read books about, for, and by women. The course resulted in the publication of a book entitled *Mother was not a person: Writings by Montreal women*. In fact, the book became a Canadian bestseller. In it, I had compiled essays from students registered in the course and academics coming to teach it.

Finally cured of marriage, I was doing what I had always wanted: studying and teaching while being in the company of women on the road to freedom. And something was adding itself to my life: writing, writing fiction and autofiction in French. I have done the three ever since.

2 | CHANGE IS NEVER GIVEN

M. Elizabeth Atcheson

I became a feminist on April 21, 1978, shortly after 8:30 a.m.

That was when the Honourable Dennis Timbrell, then Minister of Health for Ontario, said "no" to the Toronto Women's Health Clinic proposal.

It was the way he said no that did it for me.

In 1977–78, I was 25 and in my final year of law school at the University of Toronto. All through law school I had shared an apartment in the Beaches area of Toronto with Constance Backhouse. I was from Fredericton, New Brunswick, and she was from Winnipeg, Manitoba. We met in the late 1960s as members of the insurance-industry sponsored Canada Council of Young Drivers. It was our introduction to Canada, public affairs, and Ralph Nader-inspired advocacy, as we crisscrossed the country lobbying for safer cars, safer roads, and improved driver training for young people.

Just as I entered law school in 1975, Constance graduated, moving through her articling year and the then-required and much-disliked bar admission course in 1977–1978. It was the worst of years and the best of years in the bar admission course, as sexist observations made by a long-time instructor were publicly challenged by a group of feisty feminists, among them Constance, Diana Majury, Beth Symes, and Marilou McPhedran. They decided to put their legal training and advocacy talents to work on a bigger project, and I signed on too, to create the Toronto Women's Health Clinic. We wanted to create the first comprehensive care facility for well women in Canada.

It might not be obvious why a group of young lawyers would take on a health care project. Taking personal control of our health, sexuality, and reproduction was then, and remains now, at the heart of women's liberation all over the world. While some aspects of this control are private, others are very much in the public sphere. The women's health movement had significant public momentum by the 1970s in Canada, and our laws and institutions were under pressure to change. We wanted to end discrimination in public and private programmes relating to women's normal life events, including pregnancy and motherhood — these are neither disease nor sickness. We wanted informed and accessible health care facilities and providers, and inclusive health policy. We wanted full reproductive choice.

In health, as in other areas, there were law-based barriers pushing back on women's health reform. Yet law also offered a set of tools useful for breaching those same barriers. In this case, as in most, law was a necessary but not sufficient element. We would be joined by women doctors, and we would be supported by a broad community.

The clinic was to be a place where women seeking information could come, and they could find support in decision-making, or treatment for a specific medical condition. We wanted it to be expert in overall-health maintenance, female anatomy and physiology, nutrition, exercise, health habits, sexuality, venereal disease, reproduction, birth control, parenting, menopause, and aging.

We did not think that care that was both information and discussion intensive could be given adequately in a general hospital. Even in those days the cost of hospital beds was in the headlines and under pressure. As for public health clinics and doctors in private practice, there were limits on the degree to which they could specialize. We very much wanted to get outside traditional sex role stereotypes and cultural assumptions. A stand-alone clinic with a well-woman perspective was chosen because we believed it could do the job best. We had hoped that the Toronto Women's Health Clinic could be a prototype.

Our experiences as women, our feminism at that time, led us to three core elements for the clinic. These elements were implicit at the beginning, but they became more explicit as we faced challenges to our vision. The clinic had to be independent, women-run, and legal.

A big, open question for us when we started was what we could do, what we should do, about abortions. We were unquestionably pro-choice, whatever the different shadings of our individual positions. When we started, we did not think that it was possible to undertake abortions legally in a clinic setting, although we knew that there was a need.

Prior to 1969, both the dissemination of birth control information and abortions were illegal in Canada. A person performing an abortion was liable to imprisonment for life. The *Criminal Code* was amended in 1969 to legalize both birth control information, and abortions in limited circumstances. Abortions could be performed in a hospital, with the approval of that hospital's three-doctor therapeutic abortion committee, if the pregnancy was found likely to endanger the life or health (undefined, and therefore up to the therapeutic abortion committee) of a pregnant woman. Between 1969 and 1976, Dr. Henry Morgentaler was acquitted numerous times on charges of conspiracy to commit an abortion, putting the 1969 amendments in the political spotlight and creating legal confusion. Then, in 1977, the *Report of the Committee on the Operation of the Abortion Law* (the Badgley Report) was released with the key finding that only 20.1% of hospitals even provided abortion services.

When we looked at the 1969 amendments more closely, we learned that abortions could be carried out in "accredited" or "approved" hospitals. The clinic could never qualify as an "accredited" hospital, but, it might qualify as an "approved" hospital. That is, one approved for the purposes of the *Criminal Code* provisions by the minister of health in the relevant province. In this case, the clinic would have to be approved under the *Public Hospitals Act* by the minister of health for Ontario. We decided it was worth a go.

So there we were with the Honourable Dennis Timbrell on the morning of April 21, 1978. A former high school teacher, he was elected to the Ontario Legislative Assembly in 1971. He had been in the health portfolio for about a year when we met. We sat at a table with the minister at the head of the table. We were not the first group to seek the designation of an approved hospital under the *Criminal Code* provisions — a group working to open an abortion clinic with Dr. Henry Morgentaler had been before us.

Our goal was to use our brief time with the minister to state the merits of our proposal. To that end, we planned that we would decline coffee (a time waster!) and make no detailed presentation (all the detail had been provided in writing, in advance) but instead be blunt and go right to the heart of the matter from our perspective. We were going to offer a distinctive and comprehensive service, we had a detailed operational plan, we were seeking no government grants to do it, we had professional and public support. Would he recommend to cabinet that the clinic be designated a public hospital?

Very close to the beginning of the conversation, Timbrell stated that he had had lunch with the Roman Catholic Archbishop of Toronto, Emmett Carter (the next year he would be elevated to cardinal) during the previous week, and went on to talk about that conversation.

I felt at the time that the reference to the Roman Catholic archbishop was deliberate, and intended to be meaningful. To use the kind of idiom that was frowned on in feminist circles because of its roots in male conflict, it was "a shot across the bow." We were opponents. Timbrell had a position and he fully intended to hold that position. It was always obvious that he had the power and I was not naive about our chances of success. What surprised me was how openly Timbrell signalled who was inside and who was not, who had access and influence and who did not. The archbishop did, we did not.

As the meeting progressed, Timbrell first said that before a clinic could be established — even though we were requesting no public funds for the clinic — we would need to reach an agreement with a hospital to close obstetrical beds. We asked whether, if we met this requirement, he would recommend that the clinic be approved as a hospital, he said no. Timbrell stated that, due to his personal views, he could not "in good conscience" approve a free-standing clinic that would do abortions. There was no way forward but to affiliate with an existing hospital.

Ultimately, we abandoned the Toronto Women's Health Clinic proposal as there was no way it could be independent, women-run, and legal. To the great credit of those involved, who were prepared to take risks I was not, Dr. Morgentaler opened a Toronto clinic which was not an accredited or approved hospital. Dr. Morgentaler was eventually charged in respect to his work at this clinic. This time, when his case reached the Supreme Court of Canada in 1988, the law had changed. Relying on the new *Charter of Rights and Freedoms*, the court struck down the abortion law as unconstitutional because it infringed upon a woman's right to life, liberty, and security of the person. Abortions since have been regulated in the same way as any other medical procedure.

My involvement in the Toronto Women's Health Clinic moved me from having an interest in what concerned women to being an advocate for women. It is good to seize the moment, even if it feels like a shaky step. My New Brunswick roots were semi-rural and Baptist, dominated by the values of grandparents and parents who lived through depression and wars. It was not dour or sour, but it was focused on keeping out of trouble and building a more financially secure life. I was the first person in my family to go to university, which I started just as the changes of the 1960s were being digested. There were few women teachers, and they were just starting to have practical and theoretical influence.

I will be forever grateful to Gillian Thompson (at the University of New Brunswick) and Mary Eberts (at the University of Toronto) for their example, substantive strengths, and mentoring. As I gained in experience, I also learned to appreciate the tough road they themselves had walked as early feminist academics, like the road walked by so many of the women who came before me and made it easier and better for me. Between university programs, I spent a year as a Parliamentary Intern that happened to coincide with the International Year of the Woman. I was starting to see the dots, but

I certainly had not connected them until I stepped out of the role of observer and into the role of doer.

In the course of seeking supporters for the Toronto Women's Health Clinic, I soon found myself in a wonderful community of feminists. Corporate law was my vocation, feminist advocacy my avocation. With the Ontario Committee on the Status of Women, I worked on the implementation of the recommendations of the Royal Commission on the Status of Women that were within provincial jurisdiction. I came to know feminists across the country through our determined campaign to ensure that the *Canadian Charter of Rights and Freedoms* was strengthened, and could be used to address historic and systemic disadvantage. I am proud to be a founding mother of LEAF — the Women's Legal Education and Action Fund.

Along the way, a small number of things have become very clear. Women must make change, for change is never given. Change that benefits women also benefits families and communities. Our diversity and wonderful disputatiousness present short-term challenges for us, but are long-term contributors to our success. Even when we fail, we succeed, because we link to the women who have gone before and the women who come after. What strength, and what fun, to be part of that!

3 | I GOT THERE THROUGH WOMEN'S STUDIES

Betty Baba

My life as a feminist started with a personal conviction resulting from my cultural background. I hail from the traditionally patriarchal Igbo society, one of the largest ethnic groups in southeastern Nigeria, where men have more privilege than women. It was my reaction to this background that first started me down a feminist path.

When I left Nigeria to study in France, my ambition was to become a French teacher after graduation. However, as an undergraduate student, I was curious to learn more about women, and to understand the roots of the differential between women and men. I started reflecting on certain customs and practices in Africa, such as the Osu caste system in Nigeria; and Trokosi, the ritual servitude of virgin girls dedicated to religious shrines in atonement for alleged misdeeds of a family member, practiced in Ghana, Togo, and Benin; and genital mutilation, which occurs in so many African countries.

I also read a lot. I developed an interest in reading books on theories: Freud, de Beauvoir, the biological determinism research relating to the women's movement. I soon saw that patriarchal assumptions concerning the appropriate place for women in a "man's world" are seamlessly woven into the thought structure and social policies of most western cultures. They are so seamlessly interwoven that they seem to dictate the natural way for things to be. To quote Adrienne Rich:

> Women grow to womanhood in a world where it is assumed that women are a subgroup, that "man's world" is the real world, that patriarchy is equivalent to culture and culture to patriarchy, … that generalizations about "man", "humankind", "children", "blacks", "parent", "the working class" hold true for women, mothers, daughters, sisters, wet-nurses, infant girls, and can include them with no more than a glancing reference here and there, usually to some specialized function like breast-feeding.

Given all this new knowledge, I therefore decided to pursue my education in Women's Studies. My first research paper was on the controversy of abortion in the United States. Why did I choose this topic? Because abortion is considered a serious crime in Igbo traditional society. It is considered killing, which, unless demanded by the gods, is not in keeping with Igbo morals. In African society, marriage is always considered a fiasco if there are no offspring; the husband is advised to marry another wife. This has practical reasons: having many children increases the chance of being cared for in one's old age in a society where there is no social security.

Studying this topic really enlightened me on how women in Europe could terminate their pregnancies due to personal reasons.

I found this interesting, and wanted to continue learning and studying these topics. I continued my education, still majoring in Women's Studies. Having become interested in the topic of polygamy, I chose it as the topic for my doctorate. I started pondering on the issue of polygamy in Africa where social order and dignity are automatically associated with large families, even though accumulating women and children may lead to a lack of means of subsistence. Although this research was interesting, I found I was more concerned with the economic and social problems of the modern era.

Today, as a feminist, I see myself as a woman, mother, and wife still bent on working towards some of our unachieved goals. Women now have the right to vote, hold public office, have equal pay for equal work, have a career or own a business, and can choose to be childless, or unmarried, or married with children. Despite these gains, certain aspects of women's lives, like women's victimization, still occur with alarming frequency. I am sad to know that in certain countries unlawful practices, such as forced marriages, genital mutilations, human trafficking, and sharia — all opposed to international human rights legislation — are still being accepted and performed. My hope is that we continue to work toward eradicating these circumstances, and further advancing the quality of all women's lives.

4 | SEVEN HUNDRED MEN IN SUITS

Constance Backhouse

Seven hundred men in suits. The meeting room in the grand downtown hotel was jammed to bursting with them. It was a chilly morning in Toronto in the spring of 1976, inflation was spiralling out of control, Prime Minister Pierre Elliott Trudeau's "wage and price controls" had sparked furious controversy throughout the country, and the overflow crowd had turned out to attend a business conference on Canada's economic future. I was a newly minted lawyer, and had registered at the last minute at the door. A few minutes late for the opening session, I hesitantly tiptoed into the room. Then I noticed an empty chair adjacent to one of the only other women present. I gratefully slid into it.

The opening speaker was John Crispo. He was a business professor from the University of Toronto and an influential media columnist, touted as an expert in political and economic issues. I did not know at the time that he also fancied himself a "Rebel without a Pause" and a "Canadian Maverick," phrases he would adopt for the title of his autobiography years later. If his remarks that day were radical or unusual, I did not notice. I was too angry. For Crispo, whose presentation was underway already, had apparently taken a leaf from the speakers' manuals that advised humour as a way of warming up an audience. He had launched into a stream of appallingly sexist jokes, provoking deep guffaws from the suited men around the room. I held my breath thinking surely this would pass and he would get on with his substantive speech. But no. A full twenty minutes later, he was still in full sail, regaling the assembled conference goers with story after story about blonde bimbos, sexpot secretaries, and nymphomaniacs.

I was acutely embarrassed. I may have grimaced. Possibly I groaned. And then I noticed that the woman beside me looked similarly upset. We struck up a whispered conversation. I learned that the stunningly beautiful woman beside me was Leah Cohen, a businesswoman who worked at IBM. Her sarcastic commentary on Crispo's misogynistic remarks caused both of us to break out laughing. We continued to whisper back and forth, and soon gave up all pretence of listening to any of Crispo's lecture, or any of the presentations that followed. Our conversation ranged widely, as we moved quickly beyond introductions, to in-depth discussions about our jobs, the challenges facing women at work, and the evidence of deeply-embedded sexism in society. Oblivious to the disruption we were causing, we conversed continually throughout the morning's panels, and then all through the conference lunch.

Leah Cohen spoke with impressive intelligence, pride, and self-confidence about feminism and its ideals, and her optimism that radical change could bring gender equality into being. I marvelled at how much she knew about the women's movement — its dreams, goals, strategies, and accomplishments.

Up to that morning, I would not have claimed feminism publicly. I had grown up in a family where women were encouraged to think beyond traditional gender barriers in education and occupation, and I had chosen to study law in an era when women were only beginning to enter the profession in substantial numbers. But I had avoided identification with feminist law students, naively assuming that equality was within personal reach. As I had started to become better acquainted with the world of practice, in the law school clinic and as an articling student, I slowly began to recognize sexism more clearly, and to chafe at the difficulties that beset women lawyers — the skeptical clients, the paternalistic male lawyers, the mocking court officials. Yet I had never thought much about the women's movement or my potential role within it.

I was fascinated by Leah Cohen's inclusive characterization of feminism. She welcomed me to the women's movement with open arms. She was so positive about the potential of feminism to transform women's place in society. Her buoyant sense of humour was infectious. Before the conference ended, she had invited me to brunch the next Sunday at her High Park apartment. I was hooked.

In the years that followed we became inseparable. We devoured all of the wonderful books that were emerging from the burgeoning feminist publishing houses. We recruited other women to join us in a variety of feminist activist projects. We forged exciting connections with Canadian and American feminists who were gathering forces to mount campaigns to eradicate inequalities. After Leah taught me how to turn my university-essay writing style into something more accessible, we co-authored a series of feminist magazine articles. Our personalities and our thinking had become so intertwined that we often finished each other's sentences.

Quite by happenstance, we both lost our jobs because of coercive sexual overtures, and we spoke at length about how we might turn our misfortunes into transformative change. We used our time-out from the paid labour force to do research into the problem that had only recently been given a name, and we co-authored *The Secret Oppression: Sexual Harassment of Working Women*; in 1979 it was the first book on the subject to be published in Canada. The notoriety from that publication catapulted us into public attention, and we travelled the country speaking to feminist groups, business and labour organizations, educational institutions, and countless radio hosts, newspaper reporters, and television talk show MCs.

In the decades that followed, feminism enriched my life immeasurably. I cannot begin to imagine how much poorer I would have been without the enduring friendships, interconnected communities, inspiring ideas, and life goals that feminism offered to all of us who took up its cause.

And I wonder, if I had not slid into the empty chair beside Leah Cohen that morning, whether it all might have passed me by. Would I have dismissed Crispo's malevolent sexism as yet another intermittent irritation that deserved no further attention? Perhaps if Leah had not come into my life, I would have met some other captivating feminist who offered sure-footed leadership and guidance. Perhaps my feminism might have ignited all on its own. Certainly those were the years when feminism was blossoming on every corner.

Yet I remain quite certain that meeting Leah was pivotal. Her brilliance and wicked sense of wit gave my initiation into feminism its distinctive flavour and its mesmerizing influence. I have proudly claimed feminism as my life mission ever since. Whatever I have managed to accomplish is, in large measure, attributable to her initial infectious energy and the hopes that she engendered in so many that our world could be improved dramatically. Leah Cohen captured for me the glorious exuberance that was at the heart of feminism in those wonderful decades.

Leah Cohen died on May 10th, 2007. She is greatly missed.

5 | NO FIXED RULES, PLEASE

Clare Beckton

I believe I was born a feminist. At an early age I rebelled against the imposed lines of responsibility drawn between my brothers and me. I was blessed with three brothers, so I had early role models about how men were supposed to behave. My mother believed that her role was in the house; she refused to do work on the farm that she considered to be man's work. I, however, wanted to be able to do the same things as my brothers and often followed them around on the farm and imitated their play. I resented it when my parents would allow them to wander farther afield than me.

In our small town in Saskatchewan, in the '50s and '60s, the role models for young women were farm wives and mothers, teachers, bank tellers, nurses, and women who worked in the local restaurant or pub. Only a few women from the community ventured to institutions of higher education. However, the farm women I knew were amazing; the work could not have been done without them. They provided sustenance for the family, working long hours to make gardens grow, to preserve produce, make meals, wash clothes, look after the children, and the chickens, and the geese and participate in the life of their communities. Many helped out with the farm work as well.

I never saw women in governance roles. While I was aware of the power imbalance, I had no one to speak to about it because it was just the way that things were done in rural communities. The men gathered to speak about politics, the weather, and the crops of grain, and the women gathered to share news about their lives. My father was different from other men in the community. He was much older than my mother and believed in higher education, something that he had always wished for himself. He also wanted his daughter to be able to support herself should something happen to her husband.

Somehow I never really fit into this small town life. While I loved the community I knew I was not destined to be a farm wife, or teacher, or nurse. I disagreed with my mother over the division of labour in the house. I developed a strong sense of fairness and the appropriate use of authority, and a strong dislike for fixed notions of roles. At a young age law captured my imagination. I watched law enforcement shows on television and courtroom dramas. I would have chosen to be a police officer but the forces had height requirements that were difficult for women to meet. And there were no female role models. However, at university, a very progressive associate dean of law encouraged me to enrol in law school after I had done my undergraduate work. At that time women constituted only 10% of the law classes, so it was a challenge. At that time I saw law as a powerful tool to support appropriate use of authority and to enable me to take on a role different from those traditionally occupied by women.

I started university at a time when rebellion was everywhere. The Vietnam War protests were alive and "flower power" was the buzzword. Some feminists were burning their bras, blaming men and their power structures for all the problems that women faced. Irrespective of the feminist approach espoused, there was a sense of freedom and possibility for all women. We felt that we could have both a career and a family; many of us chose to enter university. The Royal Commission on the Status of Women was established, and published its report outlining many of the challenges that women faced. I remember being impressed with the fiery politician Judy LaMarsh, who was a strong voice for women, and demonstrated that women could attain elected office despite the challenges in getting there. I also met other young women full of promise who hoped for a different future than that of their mothers. Many of us believed, rightly or wrongly, that our mothers would have liked something different.

Reality hit again when I started teaching law. In my first class I encountered a young man who said to me, "I have never had a women professor and I do not like it." My male colleagues had no idea how to treat me as I was the first full-time woman faculty member. No role models existed for them or me. Some treated me like a sister, some tried to date me, and some made life difficult. A small number treated me with the same respect as all of their colleagues. I felt that I had to work harder and try harder to obtain my promotions. It was also at this point in my life that I really began to understand not only the societal inequalities between men and women but also the legal structures that supported this inequality. I realized that it was important to get more women into positions to change these structures, so I promoted hiring more women to the faculty of law and in the broader university community.

My view was reinforced through the implementation of the equality guarantee in section 15 of the *Canadian Charter of Rights and Freedoms*. I joined the federal Department of Justice in 1984. My role was to align federal laws and policies with section 15 and to support the minister to seek changes where required, including initiatives to enable women to enrol in the combat arms of the Canadian Forces, and the recognition of common law relationships. At that time, we knew that legal guarantees and mechanisms were essential in moving toward equality; we now know they are not enough to achieve equality.

In the ensuing years I have come to the realization that equality for women is vital not only as a fundamental human right but to ensure long term prosperity for Canada or any other country. Women bring to the table skills and perspectives that are so important in facing the multi-faceted problems of today; when they are left behind everyone loses. Achieving equality requires multiple interventions across the spectrum of women's lives. We Canadians have made considerable progress in our journey toward equality since I was growing up in rural Saskatchewan, yet plenty of work still remains.

6 | A JOURNEY FROM PATRIARCHY TO POWER

Monique Bégin

Born in Rome in March 1936, to a French Canadian father and a Belgian Flemish mother, I was raised in Paris until we had to escape the German invasion. On June, 1940, we joined the columns of refugees on the roads of France, to arrive a few years later to a very modest Notre-Dame-de-Grâce flat in Montréal: father Lucien and mother Marie-Louise, with four children. Three more were to follow.

A self made man who had become a sound engineer in the movie industry, having married past forty after an adventurous life in different countries, my father had cast himself in the role of the family patriarch, absolute monarch of this restricted circle, requesting total obedience and compliance. He had cast me in turn in the role of the eldest child; that I was a daughter did not disturb him a bit. Loving justice and tolerance, valuing cultural differences, a stranger to nationalisms of all kinds, a man of total integrity, a humanist and a scientific mind with a broad culture, brilliant and funny, my father was also authoritarian, argumentative and stubborn, at times quite violent with words and even with sticks. Although I recall praying for him to die when I was a teenager, I would never have changed him for the fathers of my friends, who I found rather boring.

At home, besides love and affection and the balanced presence of mother, we had great principles, great culture and great food, and not much more. Friends were absolutely forbidden in our apartment. So was the outside world in general. Radio, newspapers, magazines, phonograph, even the telephone, were banned from home. We had lost everything during the war and, starting in 1947, the nine of us would live for 20 years in a rented five room flat, with no furniture other than a table, chairs, two bookcases and army bunk beds, and lots of orange or butter crates turned into whatever else was needed as furniture.

For many years, I sincerely believed that I had been brought up in an egalitarian family, in a totally non-sexist fashion. I felt a free spirit as a young girl. It was true in terms of domestic roles: both parents were great cooks; father could iron perfectly; he had taught me carpentry work; and the boys had to do their beds and help with the dishes.

It took me literally decades to understand the most subtle and pernicious "intellectual" sexism father preached at home in his speeches to us, especially to me, the eldest. His repeated quotes from the Old Testament, St. Paul, St. Augustine, St. Thomas Aquinas, the Fathers of the Church and other sources, even his dear Léon Bloy, reveal a profound philosophical and theological contempt for women, very much in the tradition of the history of ideas of the Western World. It did not have so much to do with equality in daily life but with a Catholic Church vicious prejudice of women as either the Virgin Mary or Marie Madeleine the prostitute, and, at another level, with the deeply rooted but rarely expressed view that women could never be great artists or scientists.

I always argued with my father, challenging his preachings on how to conduct one's life while not putting it into practice. These arguments ended quite dramatically when, after a grand scene, he threw me out of the house the day of my 21st birthday, in 1957, on the grounds that I was "undermining his paternal authority."

I had always wanted to study but there was no money to pay for the "collège classique," the sole point of entry to a university in Québec. I had started teaching in 1955, also registering at the University of Montréal adult evening classes, earning a B.A. in August 1958. In September, I became a regular student in the Department of Sociology M.A. program. For ourselves and a small network of friends from other faculties, I organized a series of cultural anthropology films, the "Cinanthrope," where we learned of Margaret Mead, Ruth Benedict and Oscar Lewis. We also organized weekly seminars where we discussed controversial authors. Our first book was Simone de Beauvoir's *Le deuxième sexe*, finally available in Montréal ten years after its publication in France. Her thesis came as a revelation to me. I easily related to the book on the grounds of justice and equality, but felt uncomfortable with its dogmatic dimension. I had no idea that seven years later I and others, under Thérèse Casgrain's leadership, would co-found the Fédération des femmes du Québec.

During my years of studies and even when I started working as a social scientist, I was not interested in joining associations. I did not think of calling myself a feminist in the early '60s. My first feminist involvement came about in 1963 when I accepted to participate as a volunteer on a committee of the Montréal Catholic School Board, devising retraining courses for married women re-entering the paid labour market. For me it was a utilitarian initiative, something practical to do for women from an economic viewpoint. Finally, in 1964, pressed by a good friend, Yvonne Raymond, I became a member of l'Association des femmes diplômées des universités (University Women's Club) specifically to participate in the preparation of a feminist brief and recommendations to the Parent Commission on Education.

Women's associations in Québec were also busy preparing documents and recommendations for changes to family and property law surrounding the celebration of the centennial of the Québec Civil Code, in 1966. We founded the Fédération des femmes du Québec in April 1966, inspired by the enthusiastic celebration a year earlier under Thérèse Casgrain's leadership of the 25th anniversary of women's right to vote provincially. Nevertheless, causes still made me uncomfortable because of their emotional and dogmatic aspects.

Finally Fernand Cadieux, an exceptional sociologist and an

unsung leader of the Quiet Revolution, for whom I was working, pushed me into the great feminist adventure. The Fédération des femmes du Québec (of which I was the first vice-president) joined forces, early in September 1966, with English Canada's Committee for the Equality of Women, a re-grouping of 32 anglophone women's organizations under the leadership of Laura Sabia, demanding a Royal Commission of Inquiry on the Status of Women in Canada. Pressure began to bear on the federal government, and, within six months, the commission was created. I was appointed its Executive Secretary.

The rest, as far as my life is concerned, is history. As of then, I acted as a feminist as often as I could — I would say always — and kept looking at situations as opportunities to promote simple justice and social change in favour of women.

On September 15, 1976, still a backbencher (I had first been elected to the House of Commons on October 30, 1972), I refused Prime Minister Trudeau's offer to be appointed Minister Responsible for the Status of Women. Although I was excited by the idea of a new challenge, my first reaction was negative: I would be the first woman, and moreover an identified feminist, to receive this junior ministerial position, but I would also be the first minister to be named without the benefit of a regular portfolio, that is, without budgets, legislative and executive powers and the usual body of public servants. Furthermore, I knew we were about to enter a recession and that there would surely be no more money for women, and this after the International Year of Women (1975) had created great expectations in women's associations. Also, the Badgley report on abortion was about to be released and I already knew from the private presentation to Trudeau of the Report of the Royal Commission on the Status of Women in Canada (1970) that he would never budge on the subject.

I was angry and hurt that a prime minister like Trudeau would resort to what seemed to me a gross electoral tactic that would surely, in time, have a boomerang effect against the government. After explaining my reasons to the Prime Minister, I refused his offer, thanked him while stating my frustration, and left. That same night, he called me and asked if I would possibly accept the position of Minister of National Revenue. I was sworn in the next day and thus became a full cabinet minister.

I joined the ranks of academics in September 1984 and found it even more compelling to call myself a feminist, for knowledge — education and research — as well as the institutions of higher learning and of advanced research, are far from being gender-neutral. I am convinced that every discipline taught is seriously distorted when it comes to understanding the gendered human nature, including, in a very pervasive way, biology, medicine, and sciences. In addition, the milieu and the institutional culture of each discipline and faculty, including the institution itself, reproduce to a greater or lesser degree the machismo of the surrounding society.

To call myself a feminist is to state many things at the same time. It is a personal statement about injustice, inequity, waste and plain stupidity. And it is also a political statement acknowledging my participation in one of the two greatest revolutions of the 20th century, the other being the decolonization of the world.

7 | POOR, BLACK, AND FEMALE

Wanda Thomas Bernard

In many ways my life was pre-scripted for me because I was born poor, Black, and female, in a rural segregated Black community in Nova Scotia. But pivotal moments throughout my life helped me to change the script and write my own story.

I was the middle child of 12 children raised by our parents. The first pivotal moment in adjusting the script of my life occurred in my early childhood; it was the sudden death of my father when I was 12 years old. My mother was left a widow at the age of 39. Her oldest child was 18 years old, the youngest 18 months; both were sons. The evening of my father's death, my mother's very special aunt came to visit us at our home. She expressed amazement at the sight of me, barely tall enough to reach the table, preparing the evening meal for the family.

I realize now that this was when I began my journey to feminism. Although I was not the oldest child, as one of the eldest female children, by age 12 I was experienced at preparing the family meal for 14 people. This experience, and the story of it, became a part of our family folklore. It framed the way people in the family saw me, and it also framed the way I began to see and define myself. Most importantly for me, it started my questioning of the taken-for-granted assumptions about sexist gender roles and norms. But of course, at that time, I did not have the language to critically analyze what was happening to me.

A few weeks after my father died I entered an integrated high school. I was in grade 8, and in the mid-1960s streaming students in schools was normalized. I was streamed into class 8A, and although approximately 50% of the students in the school were African Nova Scotian (ANS), I was the only one in class 8A. There were two streamed into 8B, perhaps fifteen in 8C, and streams 8D and 8E were at least 85% ANS. This was the first time in my life that I became fully aware of racism. Racism was palpable in my school, but I had no way to name it or address it, and there was no language to define or describe it.

Questioning the racism I experienced in school led me to the civil rights movement, both in Halifax and in the United States. I became involved in youth programs led by our local community development worker, and began reading about Dr. King's work. I was in school when Dr. King died. We were so traumatized, and angry, that we organized a protest the next day; a group of Black students marching through the hallways of our school demanding an end to the racism we were experiencing. This "outburst" eventually led to a class action human rights complaint against our high school and the school board.

In the story of my awakening to racism, I also recall that the civil rights movement did not embrace the feminist movement, and perhaps was even threatened by it. I recall feeling very conflicted as I was painfully aware that both sexism and racism framed my reality. But forced to choose, I chose the fight against the oppression of racism.

Another pivotal moment in my life that enabled me to change the script and rewrite my course occurred when a white man, the late

Captain Don Denison, used his power and privilege to get my sister and me into post-secondary education.

My sister Valerie, my cousin Connie Glasgow, and I were the first people from our community to go to an institution of higher learning. We graduated from Mount Saint Vincent University, and each went on to postgraduate studies in our respective fields. Connie became an educator and administrator in the public school system. Valerie became a nurse and health educator and later opened a home health care agency in Chicago. I became a social worker, then a professor, then a researcher and administrator. Throughout my career, I was an advocate and community activist—always fighting for change, and primarily addressing issues of race oppression.

My journey to thinking differently about sexism, feminism, and other forms of oppression began after I graduated from the Maritime School of Social Work (MSSW) at Dalhousie University. I had continued my involvement and engagement as a community member of the MSSW Committee on Racial and Ethnic Affairs (COREA). It was at a COREA meeting that a former faculty member, Dr. Bessa Whitmore, talked with me about doing doctoral studies and considering a possible career in teaching social work. While the thought of doing research and becoming a university teacher was of definite interest to me, I could not see how I could do it, given my family and other responsibilities.

In 1989, the MSSW had a faculty member retire and decided to hire someone from the equity seeking groups. This was considered an important step for the school as it had an Affirmative Action in Admissions Policy in place since the early 1970s, specifically targeting Black, Mi`Kmaq, and Acadian students (persons with disabilities were included in 1996, and sexual orientation in 2009). I was encouraged to apply for this position, and was the successful candidate. This phase of my academic career at Dalhousie began on January 1, 1990. My contract stipulated that in order to be considered for tenure I had to complete coursework toward a Ph.D. within the first seven years of my appointment. I received my Ph.D. in 1996, from the University of Sheffield. I have been Director at the School of Social Work at Dalhousie since 2001, currently completing my second five-year term.

Today, I would say that I have been a feminist since my childhood.

I embrace an Africentric feminist perspective. My Africentric feminist lens allows me to embrace all of who I am, to facilitate change, and to work with allies in fighting oppression.

8 | STEP BY STEP

Jane Bigelow

I grew up in Toronto during the depression, WWII, and Kate Aitken's *Art of Homemaking*. Even as a young girl, I felt clearly that life was unfair: boys had more freedom and privileges. I complained about this, often, but was always told: "That's life Jane, there's nothing you can do about it." Even so, I was privileged and was sent to a girls' school (St. Clements), thus avoiding much of the boy/girl teenage angst. The expectation at school, although not at home, was that all of us would go on to university.

At the time that I was preparing to go to university, there were no role models and no school counsellors with whom to review programs. I had once mentioned to my father that law might interest me, but he told me that I wouldn't want to be a lawyer: "Women who are lawyers never get married." While reviewing other course options, I discovered a course in Physical and Health Education in the University of Toronto calendar. Since I was competitive and athletic, I thought it would be a good fit and enrolled.

After I graduated, I went on to complete teachers' college. From there, I moved to Ottawa to begin my teaching career. It was my fortune to meet there another teacher who expressed many of the views and opinions about the world, particularly about women and politics, that I had been silently questioning. In Ottawa, I cast my first vote and it was for Charlotte Whitton. My second vote was for the CCF in a federal election. My political life had begun!

Two years later I moved to Hamilton to teach. Another woman, who had graduated the same year as me, had applied for the same job: she mentioned she was getting married, I didn't. As a result

I obtained the full-time position and she the part-time position. And I got married too.

After my husband obtained his Ph.D., we travelled to Copenhagen where my daughter was born. I delivered in a birthing center: ten days of rest and care for the mother and child! After moves to New York, and Tallahassee, we settled in London, Ontario, by then with two babies. My interest in politics had not gone away. A month after we arrived in London, a federal election was called. I was excited to find that our riding's NDP candidate was a woman, Pat Chefurka. I connected with her and before I knew it, my political life was coming into being. I became involved not just in an election, but also in politics within the party structure. Locally I became a member of the riding association executive and was active in the Women's Committee. At about that time, there was a reference in the newspaper about the formation of the Royal Commission on the Status of Women. I brought forward to the committee the idea that we should study the participation of women in electoral politics. And so we did; we prepared a brief that was presented to the Commission.

By the end of the decade I had become Vice President of the Ontario NDP.

I returned to university at the University of Western Ontario to study part-time towards a Master's degree in Urban Studies. At the same time I became active in the local movement working to make changes in the way in which citizens participated in the decision-making process at city hall. Over five years of growing success, and the recognition that they had common community interests, community associations came together and formed an umbrella organization: the Urban League. As a member of the University Women's Club I made sure I was present to defeat a motion to censure Laura Sabia who had threatened to use violence as a tactic if the government did not set up a commission on women's rights.

As part of my community work, I helped to establish the first St. Leonard's House in London, modelled after the very first one in Windsor. I also worked with the London Council of Women. While the council was working to make positive changes for women, many of the women members themselves did not want to be mentioned in the newspaper under their husbands' names, as they feared their husbands might be embarrassed. The women on council wanted to use their maiden names when written about in the newspaper. However, we were told that this could not be done. When I asked the editor "why not?" he told me that no woman was "allowed" to use her own name unless she had done something important.

In December 1969 a municipal election was called. Since my activism had a broad base across the city, I decided to run for a citywide position on the Board of Control, a position unique to London. I was elected one of nineteen members, and I was the only woman. The night of the election I was asked by the media what was going to happen to my children. In response I asked them why the men were not asked the same question.

During my second term on the Board of Control, I received the highest number of votes; this made me Deputy Mayor. Within three months the new Mayor had to resign because of ill health and I was elected by council as Mayor. A woman mayor; a first for the city of London. I quickly discovered that I enjoyed the public platform unique to the position. It was a powerful lever for promoting communities' interests and concerns, not just locally but provincially, federally, and even internationally.

My feminism expressed itself in many ways: I pushed for greater access to child care, the hiring of women in administrative positions, eliminating discriminatory practices affecting female applicants and female employees, bringing women into the police force, and encouraging women and advising women who had an interest in politics and who wanted to get elected. I made many speeches and particularly enjoyed the ones given to men's groups, who mostly wanted to know just what it was that women wanted. Moreover, I solved a problem of sexual harassment at city hall before sexual harassment even had a name.

It was important for me to keep connected and remain supportive of the changes other women were bringing to our community in order to improve women's lives. I worked to support those who were struggling to find ways to help women who had been raped or were battered; those who were attempting to ease financial access for women through the Women's Credit Union; and those facilitating counselling and support for women entering the workforce. Of course, I also supported a wide range of other issues: I promoted bike paths and was outspoken about the need for public support of the arts community.

I was defeated in the election for the 1980 council and decided to take a year off from everything. Then, I joined the public service and started doing community development work in the area of unemployment. At the same time, I joined the Board of Directors of the Women's Community House. Later, when an opportunity arose for me to work for the Secretary of State as the manager for the South Western Ontario District, I took the position, although it required a move to Hamilton.

While in Hamilton, I volunteered as a crisis-line counsellor at the Rape Crisis Centre and later joined the Board as Treasurer and Chair. Returning to London upon retirement, I joined the London Sexual Assault Centre, again holding a variety of positions on the Board. The only volunteer work I do now is with My Sisters Place, a day program for homeless women and women at risk of becoming homeless. When I phoned to see if they needed volunteers — not for the Board of Directors — they asked if I could I sew. Well, yes, I can sew and now work with the sisters on sewing projects, helping them to do some of their mending, teaching them to use a sewing machine, and just talking.

In London, some of us decided that the history made by women — the second wave feminists — should not be lost or forgotten. We are collecting archival material from women active in changing the lives of women between the years 1960–2000. Also of interest to us are the archives of the feminist organizations that were established during that period. The collection will become a permanent part of the University of Western Ontario Archives. We are known simply as the Women's History Group.

On reflection I don't think there was any one thing that prompted me to begin living and working as a feminist. I think my political interests and experiences provided the momentum. Feminism took my activism en route and kept me grounded.

> Voice of Women, Demonstration, Parliament Hill, Ottawa, September 25, 1961

Duncan Cameron / Library and Archives Canada / PA-209888

> Voix des femmes, Manifestation, Colline parlementaire, Ottawa, le 25 septembre 1961

NO NUCLEAR ARMS
FOR CANADA
PAS D'ARMES
NUCLEAIRES
POUR LE CANADA
Of Women

9 | MON FÉMINISME À MOI

Josée Bouchard

Simone de Beauvoir l'a très bien dit : « On ne naît pas femme, on le devient. » L'influence sociale définit en majeure partie notre identité. Ce n'est qu'assez tard dans ma vie, en fait lorsque je suis devenue professeure de droit, que j'ai commencé à m'identifier ouvertement comme féministe. Je n'étais pas encore conscientisée aux concepts et aux théories féministes, mais, sans trop le savoir, je vivais déjà mon féminisme dans mes émotions, dans mon monde intellectuel et dans mes actions politiques.

Mon identité féministe s'est d'abord façonnée dans le giron familial. Je viens d'une famille traditionnelle canadienne-française catholique, avec un père professionnel et une mère chargée des responsabilités familiales. Dans ce cadre peu féministe en essence, mes parents m'ont pourtant inculqué un grand sens de l'indépendance et de l'autonomie et une estime de soi en tant que femme. Grâce à eux, j'ai acquis une conviction profonde de l'égalité des femmes. J'ai toujours été convaincue que je ne dépendrais jamais d'autrui et que je poursuivrais mes propres ambitions. Dans mon parcours ultérieur, j'ai fini par rejeter les structures institutionnelles paternalistes, telles que le système religieux dans lequel j'avais été élevée.

C'est en 1989, après mon arrivée comme professeure à la Faculté de droit, Section de common law de l'Université d'Ottawa, que je me suis sensibilisée au féminisme et que j'ai commencé à clamer mon appartenance à ce mouvement. S'identifier publiquement, à cette époque, comportait tout de même certains défis. Je craignais par exemple de ne pas être à la hauteur de mes collègues féministes, que j'admirais profondément, de ne pas être assez féministe à leurs yeux. Je craignais aussi que l'identification ne mène à la stigmatisation. N'allait-on pas dire, avec dédain, *elle est féministe*…

Malgré cette confusion initiale, j'ai embrassé pleinement le féminisme. On m'avait initiée à l'œuvre de Simone de Beauvoir qui, dès les années 40, parlait de la réalité de l'Autre, de la réalité féminine, et à Catharine MacKinnon, qui avait publié son livre sur la théorie de l'État et influencé l'évolution du droit en matière de harcèlement sexuel aux États-Unis. C'est à cette époque que j'ai commencé à adopter une approche féministe dans ma recherche et mes écrits. Les juges Wilson et L'Heureux-Dubé siégeaient à la Cour suprême du Canada ; les articles 15 et 28 de la *Charte des droits et libertés* étaient en place pour garantir l'égalité des droits et libertés aux hommes et aux femmes; et les décisions *Morgentaler* et *Robichaud,* notamment, avaient été rendues en faveur des droits des femmes. Il y avait, pendant cette période, de l'optimisme dans l'air. Il y aurait de quoi écrire une thèse sur l'évolution des droits des femmes depuis cette période et sur l'à-propos de cet optimisme, mais ce n'est pas pour aujourd'hui : il s'agit de raconter ma venue au féminisme.

En 1989, le mouvement féministe se faisait sentir au sein de la faculté. La masse critique y était et j'étais entourée de femmes féministes et courageuses. Celle qui, dans mon cas, a joué le rôle le plus important était la professeure Michelle Boivin, de la Section de droit civil. Michelle a été tout au long de sa carrière une féministe engagée ; elle a laissé sa marque dans le monde juridique. En tant que mentore, elle m'a suivie durant mon parcours de juriste et est toujours présente dans ma vie. Ses conseils quant à mon cheminement académique et professionnel, nos échanges intellectuels et personnels, ses commentaires sur mes ébauches de textes et nos sorties sociales, familiales et professionnelles me sont toujours indispensables.

Nous nous sommes connues en participant à des rencontres entre féministes francophones des Sections de droit civil et de common law. Nous avons pris de bons repas arrosés d'excellents bordeaux, tout en discutant de sujets intellectuels, comme les concepts d'égalité, le critère de la femme raisonnable victime de harcèlement sexuel et la réalité des femmes francophones en milieu minoritaire. Nous discutions aussi de sujets plus personnels, comme nos relations familiales, sociales et professionnelles.

Michelle était ma plus grande critique, celle qui notait mes ébauches de textes à la plume rouge, sans hésiter à proposer des modifications radicales et des conseils constructifs. Ses commentaires, toujours réfléchis, justes et bien mérités, m'ont aidée dans ma carrière. Michelle m'a fait comprendre qu'il faut avoir une pensée critique pour réussir, mais qu'il faut aussi savoir utiliser les critiques d'autrui pour grandir. Grâce à nos discussions intellectuelles et à notre relation personnelle, elle m'a inculqué une confiance indispensable en notre féminisme. Les années se sont écoulées, Michelle a rangé sa plume rouge, et son mentorat est devenu notre amitié.

Nous nous sommes rapprochées davantage avec la naissance de mes trois filles. Michelle avait alors deux garçons adultes et elle était ravie de devenir la pseudo-tante de mes filles. De mon côté, je profitais bien des conseils experts d'une mère. Et voilà que la sagesse féministe passait d'une génération à l'autre. Michelle a maintenant trois petites-filles, toutes belles et brillantes, qui ont hérité de la force de caractère de leur grand-mère. Encore une fois, le féminisme se propage et se répand.

Aujourd'hui, mes sources d'inspiration sont mes trois filles, Camille, Emmanuelle et Nicola. Elles sont nos nouvelles ambassadrices et, comme d'autres jeunes de leur génération, elles sont prêtes à relever les défis et à travailler dans le but de redresser les inégalités qui, hélas, subsistent encore.

10 | LA FIBRE FÉMINISTE

Sophie Bourque

Dès la première année du primaire, Lise, notre mère, répétait comme un mantra, sans relâche, à ses « trois petites chattes » : « Les filles, éduquez-vous, devenez des professionnelles et ne dépendez jamais d'un homme. » Si dans certaines familles l'entreprise familiale se lègue de père en fils, chez nous la fibre féministe est la première tranche de l'héritage.

En plus d'être élevée avec deux sœurs, j'ai passé mon cours secondaire dans une école de filles, dirigée par les Dames de la Congrégation Notre-Dame, une école qui faisait la promotion de l'excellence académique et encourageait toutes les aspirations professionnelles. Aucune limite n'était imposée à nos rêves et nous étions persuadées qu'il en serait toujours ainsi.

Mon arrivée au collège me révèle une autre réalité. Il me semble dès les premiers mois que les gars occupent l'essentiel de l'espace public et qu'insidieusement, les filles se trouvent reléguées au second rang. Je ne comprends pas. Je commence alors à militer au comité femme du collège. La fin des années 1970 est l'époque des grandes revendications, dont le droit des femmes à la libre disposition de leur corps et l'abolition de toutes les formes de discrimination. Belle école que celle des grandes manifestations, celle de tous les espoirs ! En même temps, on milite pour l'accès à l'éducation libre et gratuite et pour les prêts et bourses ; le féminisme s'accommode mal des autres formes de discrimination.

Première idée de carrière : devenir historienne pour écrire l'histoire des femmes au Québec. Mais ayant aussi, par pure bravade, fait une demande d'admission à la faculté de droit de l'Université de Montréal, j'y suis admise. Je choisis le droit. Je ne l'ai jamais regretté. Une chance d'ailleurs puisque, quelques années plus tard, le Collectif Clio s'est chargé avec brio de rendre aux femmes leur histoire.

Pas de comité femme à la faculté de droit mais, encore là, la portion de l'espace occupée par les femmes me semble congrue. Je suggère à différents professeurs de nous rendre plus présentes, en parlant par exemple de créancières ou de présidentes de conseil d'administration. Que de réactions, un vrai florilège : du rire gras enrobant un « Mais certainement, ma p'tite dame » à l'accueil chaleureux, « J'ai quatre filles et c'est avec plaisir que je vais m'y appliquer. »

Reçue au Barreau, je m'implique dans mon milieu professionnel. En 1987, je siège au conseil d'administration de l'Association du jeune Barreau de Montréal. Cette association centenaire regroupe les avocats et avocates de 10 ans et moins de pratique. Je découvre que le congé de maternité est quasi une chimère dans le milieu des cabinets d'avocats. Le choix de l'hôpital pour l'accouchement semble même parfois dicté par sa proximité avec le bureau ! Lorsque je soulève en réunion qu'il y a là un sérieux problème, quelqu'un me répond qu'accoucher et élever des enfants est une affaire privée qui ne regarde pas le cabinet pour lequel l'avocate travaille. Heureusement, mes autres jeunes collègues reconnaissent d'emblée que les choses doivent changer. Une étude sur la conciliation travail-famille est commandée au Conference Board du Canada. Publiée en 1988, elle sera la première au pays à traiter de cette réalité dans le monde juridique. Dans la foulée, l'AJBM met sur pied un comité travail-famille et réunit les associés principaux des grands cabinets pour ouvrir le dialogue. Celui-ci persiste et les principes des congés parentaux entrent dans les mœurs.

De 1991 à 1993, je fais partie du groupe de travail sur l'égalité des sexes dans la profession juridique mis sur pied par l'Association du barreau canadien (ABC). Ces deux années seront marquantes. Si je connaissais le pouvoir des mots, elles m'ont appris celui de sa jumelle, l'écoute. Une avocate autochtone nous a d'ailleurs dit : « Vous n'avez pas besoin d'avoir vécu toutes nos expériences pour faire votre travail, en autant que vous nous écoutiez. Après, nous vous faisons confiance. »

Les travaux sont dirigés par l'honorable Bertha Wilson, première femme juge à la Cour suprême du Canada, qui vient de prendre sa retraite. Après deux ans d'études, de rencontres avec des avocates et de rapports d'experts, le groupe de travail dresse un constat des obstacles que les femmes affrontent dans la profession, que ce soit en milieu académique, en grands ou petits cabinets, en entreprise, au gouvernement ou à la magistrature. En 1993, le rapport intitulé « Les assises de la réforme : égalité, diversité, responsabilité » est déposé. Il comprend plus de 200 recommandations qui proposent des solutions afin d'éradiquer les inégalités.

Le dépôt du rapport suscite des débats parfois houleux au conseil de l'ABC lors de l'adoption des recommandations. La leçon de l'écoute s'avère utile pour parvenir à des consensus.

Par la suite, je siège au comité permanent sur l'égalité, dont le mandat est de voir à l'implantation des recommandations adoptées par le conseil. J'en assume la présidence de 1996 à 1998.

Certains constats sont dressés lors d'un colloque tenu à l'Université d'Ottawa en 2003 à l'occasion des 10 ans du rapport. Depuis 1993, beaucoup de chemin a été parcouru, mais beaucoup reste à faire. De fait, quinze ans plus tard, plusieurs considèrent toujours ce rapport d'actualité.

Par ailleurs, si à l'époque le sexisme dans la profession avait été évoqué du bout des lèvres, le racisme est encore un plus gros tabou. Très tôt, le groupe de travail est confronté à l'existence de la double discrimination vécue par celles appartenant à une minorité visible. Comme l'a dit si bien une avocate noire : « Si une avocate blanche dans son cheminement de carrière peut rencontrer un plafond de verre, une jeune femme noire frappe une porte de fer dès l'accès à la profession. » Il a fallu un deuxième groupe de travail pour s'atteler à cette tâche.

En 1991, je suis devenue membre du comité sur les femmes dans la profession du Barreau du Québec. Le mandat de ce comité, créé la même année, est de faire le point sur la situation des femmes dans la profession, de sensibiliser la communauté juridique aux problèmes rencontrés par les avocates, de proposer des solutions et de voir à leur mise en application. Je suis présidente de ce comité en 2005 lors de ma nomination à la magistrature. Parmi ses réalisations, la mise sur pied en 2003 d'un Programme d'assistance parentale pour les travailleurs autonomes membres du Barreau du Québec. Ce programme, financé par l'ensemble des membres du Barreau, permet aux avocates et avocats travailleurs autonomes qui deviennent parents de bénéficier d'une aide financière pour absorber une partie de leurs frais d'exploitation durant les premiers mois d'un congé parental. Unique au Canada, ce programme a permis à des dizaines de jeunes avocates et avocats de maintenir une pratique déjà affectée par l'arrivée d'un enfant.

Soulignons qu'en 2006, à la suite de l'insistance du comité sur les femmes dans la profession, le Barreau crée un poste de conseiller à l'équité, dont le mandat est de promouvoir l'égalité de ses membres dans les milieux de travail et de le soutenir dans ses objectifs d'égalité dans ses pratiques, processus et fonctions. Le Barreau du Québec est le seul ordre professionnel au Québec à s'être doté d'un tel poste et l'un des six barreaux au Canada à l'avoir fait.

Je ne peux terminer sans embrasser ces femmes à qui je dois tant. Ma mère Lise, mes sœurs Marie-Claude et Ariane, mon amie Gloria Di Francesco, Cecilia Johnstone, cette femme exceptionnelle aux qualités rares de cœur et de tête et qui nous a quittés beaucoup trop tôt, Mélina Buckley, une source constante d'inspiration, Patricia Blocksom qui se déplace maintenant en Afrique pour aider ces femmes qui en ont tant besoin, l'honorable Bertha Wilson qui a fait la démonstration éclatante que pour juger il faut comprendre, et que pour comprendre il faut connaître, Jocelyne Olivier à qui les avocates du Québec doivent tant, Louise Mailhot, mentore généreuse s'il en est une, Sylvie Grégoire, preuve de la force tranquille de la volonté et de la bonté. Il y en a beaucoup d'autres. J'espère qu'elles accepteront un salut discret mais affectueux.

11 | I JUST KNEW

Laura Brandon

I think feminism crept up on me unaware. I did not set out to be a feminist, nor did I seek out feminist causes. Rather, I just knew that, eventually, life would disappoint me if I did not look at, and live in, the world as a feminist. I do not consider myself an activist, but I do place the utmost importance on living a professional and personal life that places women at its centre.

I grew up surrounded by some powerful women, including my mother, my two aunts, and their friends. They were variously artists, professionals, volunteers, and homemakers. I was also aware of some notable antecedents including, in particular, my great-great-great grandmother who founded a home for women in Toronto. I do not think a single one of these women considered themselves feminist, which may account for my lack of early interest in feminism. They did believe in education and work, but consistent with the cultural mores of their times, perhaps disappointingly, they also believed that these activities should be relinquished when marriage and children entered the picture.

Upon completion of my B.A., I tried teaching, worked in advertising, married, and moved from England to Canada, from where my family came. When I could not find a job in Canada, I chose to start a family and stayed home to raise two children. Throughout this period, I was aware that this was not what my university friends were doing. And even though I enjoyed my domestic life, from early on it was clearly not enough to satisfy. I was always a freelance writer, teacher, curator, arts volunteer, and advocate; but only after I had looked after my family responsibilities.

In 1981, I started working laboriously on a biography of Canadian artist Pegi Nicol MacLeod. I found her story compelling, and empathized with her domestic challenges as an artist and mother. However, I could not find a publisher for my book; I filed it away and got pregnant again. It seemed easier somehow.

At age 40 my life changed. I knew of a man who had nearly died at 40, and I realized with new clarity that if my husband were to die,

I could not support our family. I also recognized that I could not get the work I enjoyed without more education. So, I went back to school and got my M.A., with the help of a legacy from my father.

Shortly after I graduated in 1992, my husband encouraged me to apply for my current job as war art historian at the Canadian War Museum. When I got the job, my family moved from Prince Edward Island to Ottawa. Looking back on this period, I realize that I needed and received a lot of mentoring and support, largely from men. At this stage in my life, it was not forthcoming from anywhere else. Because of the field I work in now, which is overwhelmingly masculine, men have continued to play a significant and much appreciated role in my professional life. In fact, the absence of women in my work has led me to write about missing women war artists and the influence of men on museology as it pertains to war museums. Over the years, it has become clear to me that the study of war marginalizes women, except where their activities mirror men's, or are understood in terms of their relationships with men.

In 2005 the successful publication and reception of my biography of Pegi Nicol MacLeod accelerated me in a feminist direction. With this, one might argue that my life changed once more, at age 50. From age 40 to 50, I was a feminist-in-training. Since Pegi, I have identified myself as a feminist. This book enabled me to move from the confines of the war museum to the world of women scholars and curators in a way I had not been able to do before. Now, my support structure is as much female as it is male.

How do I practice my feminism? First, the mentoring I received from men, and more recently women, has led me to position the mentoring of women as artists, writers, scholars, or curators very high on my personal agenda. Support can make a world of difference in someone's life. I do not support these women simply because they are women, but because their work introduces and enlarges feminist perspectives in areas that are broadly and traditionally understood from only male perspectives. Second, in my own work as an art curator and writer I struggle to keep feminist perspectives in view. I refuse to write out or curate out women and their points of view from my work; I try to ensure that their contributions are recorded.

Finally, I am a feminist because I believe being one makes

a difference. The difference may well be microscopic, but an accumulation of such differences eventually becomes visible and, I believe, has an impact and leads to change.

12 | JE NE SUIS PAS NÉE FÉMINISTE, MAIS PRESQUE

Claire Brassard

Je ne suis pas née féministe, mais presque. Simone de Beauvoir écrivait *On ne naît pas femme, on le devient*. Eh bien, d'accord, je suis devenue féministe, probablement en devenant femme. Du plus loin que je me souvienne, le seul souvenir de ma mère est un souvenir des premières expressions du féminisme. Ma mère était mère de six enfants et travaillait à l'extérieur de la maison parce que le salaire de mon père était insuffisant. Elle a poussé ses deux filles, ma sœur aînée et moi, à s'instruire pour être indépendantes : « Ne comptez jamais sur un homme pour vous faire vivre. Ne comptez que sur vous-même. » Le message s'est très bien rendu. Nous nous sommes instruites et avons toujours été indépendantes financièrement.

Cet état naturel étant, il y a quand même eu un déclic décisif en matière d'engagement féministe au tout début des années soixante-dix. Issue du mouvement étudiant, je me suis retrouvée, au hasard de rencontres, dans un groupe de femmes faisant la promotion de la légitimation de l'avortement et la contraception libres et gratuits. Ce groupe était constitué d'étudiantes de l'Université McGill, en médecine et en biologie, et de jeunes femmes issues comme moi du mouvement étudiant.

Nous avions en commun d'avoir été associées aux mouvements de contestation de 1968 et de 1969 contre la guerre au Vietnam, pour la protection de la langue française au Québec — McGill français —, pour la libération des prisonniers politiques membres du Front de libération du Québec, le FLQ, et pour les droits des femmes.

Nous étions socialistes plutôt que communistes, comme nombre d'autres groupes qui émergeaient à l'époque, et nous n'étions pas particulièrement indépendantistes. La justice sociale et la défense des droits des femmes étaient pour nous prioritaires, avant la question de l'indépendance politique du Québec qui recueillait par ailleurs un très large appui parmi la jeunesse québécoise en ébullition et en quête d'identité. D'ailleurs, nous nous méfiions du mouvement indépendantiste qui nous apparaissait, à raison, très traditionaliste, du type « Travail, Patrie, Famille » et plutôt sexiste.

Le groupe de McGill avait produit un formidable document d'information sur la contraception, instrument exceptionnel d'éducation et d'émancipation pour les femmes, et nous l'avons distribué avec enthousiasme pendant des années après l'avoir traduit en français.

C'est ainsi que nous avons pris conscience de la condition des femmes face à la sexualité et à l'avortement et que, par la suite, nous avons mis sur pied le « Comité de lutte pour l'avortement et la contraception libres et gratuits. » Pendant ce temps, le Centre des femmes de Montréal publiait un journal féministe et socialiste, *Québécoises Deboutte* !, qui avait un tirage de 2 000 copies, une troupe de théâtre féministe se mettait sur pied, Le Théâtre des cuisines, et enfin une maison d'édition, Les Éditions du remue-ménage, commençait à publier. Le mouvement était en grande ébullition de 1971 à 1978.

En 1979, j'ai été à l'origine du magazine *La vie en rose,* revue franchement féministe et progressiste que j'ai dû abandonner rapidement, compte tenu que je commençais une pratique en droit du travail qui m'a complètement happée.

À la même époque se développaient un peu partout en régions des « Centres de femmes » qui s'affichaient carrément féministes. D'autres groupes féministes mettaient sur pied des garderies, un autre magazine, *Les têtes de pioches*, et une autre maison d'édition, La pleine lune. Ces derniers groupes étaient davantage radicaux et pas nécessairement socialistes.

Pendant mes études de droit, j'ai mis sur pied le Groupe de recherche et d'action sur l'exploitation des femmes (GRAEF), réunissant des étudiantes dont les travaux académiques portaient systématiquement sur des enjeux féministes. Je me rappelle notamment l'analyse que nous avions faite des derniers jugements en matière d'aliénation d'affection, recours que seuls les hommes pouvaient instituer contre les présumés amants de leurs épouses, sans devoir d'ailleurs prouver qu'il y avait eu relation sexuelle, hommes qui invoquaient que leurs épouses avaient été victimes de séduction dolosive par le prétendu amant. On se serait cru au 18ᵉ siècle ! Nous étions encore à l'ère de l'ancien Code civil napoléonien, qui fut révisé en 1994. Le GRAEF a existé à l'Université du Québec à Montréal (UQÀM) de 1973 à 1977.

Pour ma part, la lutte pour les droits des femmes a toujours été étroitement liée à la lutte pour la justice sociale, et je me suis rapidement associée au mouvement syndical quand j'ai terminé mes études de droit.

En tentant de me résumer pour répondre à la question « Comment êtes-vous devenue féministe ? », je pense que dans la mouvance du mouvement de contestation et d'émancipation de la fin des années soixante (pensons à Mai 1968 en France, aux tristes événements du campus de l'Université Kent en Ohio et des manifestations contre la guerre au Vietnam un peu partout dans le monde), j'étais moi-même éprise de justice et de liberté et ne me distinguais pas de la jeunesse de l'époque. Mais dans cette mouvance, j'ai senti que les femmes risquaient de faire les frais de certains abus, notamment des abus sexuels. Il devenait parfois difficile de distinguer la véritable libération sexuelle d'une certaine forme d'exploitation. Ajoutons à cette confusion floue, mais néanmoins réelle, les grossesses non désirées et les filles enceintes abandonnées à leur sort, et nous retrouvons là les germes de ce sursaut féministe des temps modernes. Les jeunes femmes d'alors se sont solidarisées et il s'est créé un large mouvement de réelle émancipation élargissant ses revendications à l'égalité dans les conditions de travail, aux garderies gratuites, à l'égalité en éducation, etc.

Et nous avons en grande partie réussi ! L'*empowerment* des femmes a été extraordinaire parce que les féministes ont réussi à faire bouger beaucoup de choses. En me rappelant ces années de militantisme aigu, je ressens toujours ce même sentiment de grand accomplissement. Au Québec, nous avons obtenu des avortements dans les hôpitaux avant l'abrogation de la loi, nous avons protégé la clinique du Dr Morgentaler, nous avons obtenu le premier réseau gouvernemental de garderies, nous avons défoncé les portes des tavernes réservées aux hommes seulement, nous avons obtenu des lois sur l'équité salariale, des programmes d'égalité des chances, des programmes d'action positive, des standards d'habillement plus confortables et d'autres que j'oublie.

Tout est toujours à refaire, je sais. Mais nous avons appris ensemble, les femmes, à nous organiser, à nous sentir plus fortes et plus capables et cela, c'est inestimable.

C'est un acquis que nous transmettons à nos filles et à nos garçons qui continueront ce dont nous avons nous-mêmes pris le relais, soit la lutte de bien d'autres femmes avant nous pour le mieux des femmes en société et donc, pour le mieux-être de la société entière ! Aujourd'hui, le « Nouveau combat des femmes » comme l'écrit Gisèle Halimi, c'est la juste représentation des femmes partout où les décisions se prennent, notamment dans les gouvernements de tous les niveaux. J'y pense.

Et pourquoi pas faire de la politique à soixante ans ? On commence à être à notre meilleur à cet âge ! Et il y a encore tant à faire !

13 | MY MOTHER DIDN'T PLAY BRIDGE
Mary Breen

My mother didn't play bridge. I think that's how it all started for me, back in 1968. We moved to Etobicoke, then a very suburban part of Toronto, because my dad didn't want me crossing busy streets when I started kindergarten that fall. My parents had married late, and I was an only child. My mum was 38 when I was born, which was pretty unusual for that era. More unusual still, by that point she had already spent 17 years as a bacteriologist at the Hospital for Sick Children.

In her postgraduate science program at McGill in the 1940s, my mum had been one of only two women. At my mother's funeral, the other woman in her program at McGill, who had not had children and had remained a bacteriologist, said it was a loss to the hospital when my mum left to raise me. She had set the standard in the lab.

When my mother landed in Etobicoke and didn't play bridge, she was a social pariah. Nearly all the women on our sidewalk-less street with big green lawns were mothers. All of them got together weekly to play bridge — and probably to drink gin — but my mother did not. This was enough of an issue for her to mention it often when I was older; but not enough of one for her to learn to play.

My mother hated cards, but she loved science. She also loved fashion, and designed and made all of her own clothes as a young woman. She had wanted to become a fashion designer, in fact, but her father thought that was a frivolous career, so she didn't follow that path. I still have her portfolio full of beautiful yellowed sketches. I'd say the world of art and design suffered a loss when that door closed too.

So much talent squandered over so many generations.

As a kid, I was impressed that my mum could open jars with her baby fingers, thanks to years of dexterity involving test tubes. But of course I didn't realize what she'd had, and what she'd given up, to be a mid-century middle-class wife and mother. What she'd given up for me.

She never could bring herself to leave my father, partly because she felt she wouldn't be able to cope with the guilt (he was mentally ill), and partly because she was afraid she'd end up in poverty in her old age. As it turned out, she didn't get to old age. She died at 64. But the money she'd saved helped save me from poverty when I also found myself rather ill-equipped for motherhood, but for very different reasons.

Despite feminism, because of feminism, or regardless of feminism, I became a mother at 23. I didn't have to; I wanted to.

My mother and I had become feminists by then, mostly via the peace movement that engaged us both in the struggle to end the nuclear arms race. It was the Voice of Women that drew my mother in, and gave her a whole new group of friends and the sense of belonging she'd sorely lacked on that terribly lonely street in Etobicoke.

I have made almost entirely different choices than my mother, with one notable exception: we both had children with very smart, very troubled men. (Funnily enough, I chose my husband because he was a feminist.) My mother stayed in her marriage because my father threatened to kill himself whenever she got too close to leaving. I left my marriage, and my husband took his own life. But I was in a better position to accept that the former didn't cause the latter. My mother bore all *but* the financial burden of raising me, while I bore the entire financial burden of raising my daughters, which baffled my father. He helped as best he knew how until his death, ironically at a ripe old age.

Sometimes I wish I could tell my mother, "You didn't have to do that." About ending her career, about keeping her marriage, about all of it. But of course the sacrifices and ensuing changes that she and her generation made allowed me and my daughters to lead lives full of risk, and that's invaluable to me.

I continue to make life decisions based on passion. I have entered my middle years as an out lesbian. I've had several careers, and ended up an entrepreneur in the arts. What will my experiences teach my daughters? Well, they're not afraid of change or financial hardship, which makes them terrifically resourceful and adventurous. They may have learned never to rely on men, which might turn out to be a shame, or might stand them in good stead. I hope I'll still be around to find out, when they're old enough to reflect back on how *they* became feminists.

14 | ME, THE RADICAL FEMINIST

Alice Brona

I can recall three events that initially awakened my consciousness. The first was when Pat Dewdney, a librarian at the London Public Library, gave a talk in 1970. She was describing the women's movement. At the time, I was still unmarried and had a pretty good life. I stood up and said that in ten years I had never had trouble getting hired for a job. Twice, I had bought cars with no one co-signing for me, I could live where I chose, I had my own apartment, had some savings, and did some travelling. She responded, "It's people like you that kept the Blacks in slavery so long."

My second defining moment came during the '70s. Now married, I attended a lecture at the University of Western Ontario given by Rosemary Brown, a woman, a politician (NDP), from western Canada. A Black woman and a social worker, she spoke of her personal story of growing up in Jamaica. She told of her aunt, a social worker, who went about telling people it was not their fault that they were poor, explaining how oppression kept them that way. Rosemary Brown followed the example of her aunt and became a social worker. She later wrote her autobiography, *Being Brown*, recounting personal experiences of discrimination. It is a story of perseverance.

The third defining experience came when my marriage ended after ten years, and I joined a Catholic divorce group. (Doesn't that sound like an oxymoron?) This was a support group for male and female Catholics who had experienced divorce. One evening the group discussion was about communication. The theory being presented was that couples who talk to each other will stay together. I made the point that marriage is not an equal relationship: one partner has the power. A male doctor from Spain took offense at my remark and said, "Well, we all know you are a radical feminist." Name calling, labelling, a common method of silencing. I had never been called a feminist before and was surprised at the remark. A friend said to me, "You poor thing, I would have burst into tears." No doubt that was the desired effect. But I considered his words, and decided to take them home and try them on. They were a good fit, and I have worn them for many years since.

During the 1980s and 90s, I was an Associate of the Holy Cross Centre for Ecology and Spirituality, in Port Burwell, Ontario. This meant that I went there not only for retreats, but that I was an occasional staff person. I grew to love the place, and it was the Centre that led me toward ecofeminism.

Perhaps this part of my journey has something to do with my affinity for water. I was born under the sign of Aquarius and I am very drawn to water. I love to gaze at water and can walk for hours along a beach. My mother was born somewhere along the St. Lawrence River, and my father was born on an island. I was born a stone's throw from the Welland Ship Canal (later the St. Lawrence

Seaway). As a child, I watched ships from all over the world pass through our town. The ships climbed the mountain, by passing through the twin locks, while our family enjoyed a Sunday picnic. During my years at boarding school, I had both sight and sound of the mighty Niagara Falls from the bedroom window. We were told that Niagara Falls was one of the wonders of the world. When I returned to visit years later, I realized how I had been marked by these magnificent cataracts. I have crossed the Atlantic by ship three times, and I have lived on the Pacific coast, with the ocean at my doorstep. Water, cool, clear water, I love water.

Over the years, and in connection with the Holy Cross Centre for Ecology, I learned a lot about ecology and spirituality. I learned in conversation with others, from the writings of Thomas Berry, from the latest books in the library, from watching videos of the annual colloquium, and from other speakers at the Centre. Last one up, I'd turn off the lights and step outside into the pitch black night. It was so dark you could walk into a tree. The clear sky was full of bright shining stars. I was absorbing knowledge without any effort on my part. It was almost a Theology degree by osmosis. I liked what I was learning. I was very much in agreement with what I heard, but I could not have explained it to anyone.

While at the Centre for Ecology, I made this contribution to the *Sextant*, the Centre's newsletter, and it continues to ring true today:

The mission statement of Holy Cross Centre was "Toward a Caring Earth Community." I have come to believe this goal is essential for the survival of all of us. Thomas Berry says, before making any decision whether it be business, education, medicine, or government, we need to ask how will this impact on the environment? When we are connected to the Earth, we care about it like kin. What harms the Earth, harms us. When we are cut off, or out of touch with nature we become dispirited. Ecofeminists note the similar way women and the Earth have been subdued, dominated, exploited and raped. The essence is respect for all of Creation. We are all inter-connected in the web of life.

15 | COMING TO FEMINISM

Kim Brooks

STARTING YOUNG

My love for coffee started early in life, as did my embrace of feminist values. In fact, they started so early that both seemed like a natural part of being human. For me, feminism is rather like a good cup of coffee. I anticipate a lively conversation with feminist colleagues and friends the way I anticipate a cup of coffee in the morning. I feel more awake when I've had one. And each feminist is unique in her (and on the rare occasion, his) own way: with her own convictions, passions, idiosyncrasies, and commitments.

I was born in the early 1970s. My parents had a child rearing philosophy that seems to have been based largely on treating my sister and me as though we were (for the most part) equal members of the family. Generally speaking, if my parents did something, we were allowed to do it too. This became an early litmus test for me, and meant that I did not see my parents have a glass of anything containing alcohol for years. But their inability to rule out coffee consumption meant that my sister and I were born into a caffeinated state. Certainly by three years of age we were drinking coffee (albeit weak and milky) with our morning cereal.

Our commitment to feminism was a similarly inherent part of our childhood. The feminist politics of my childhood were marked by *Roe v. Wade*, a decade of *The Feminine Mystique*, Millett's *Sexual Politics*, (Canadian-born) Firestone's *The Dialectic of Sex*, the Combahee River Collective, Angela Davis' autobiography, and the Royal Commission on the Status of Women. The Report of the Royal Commission was one of many books on the bookshelves of my childhood, inscribed from my father to my mother in celebration of one of her birthdays. Feminist perspectives underscored our everyday life, and you could see that clearly in various day-to-day occurrences and in the conversations and topics explored on special occasions or school events.

GIRLS' THINGS AND BOYS' THINGS

My sister had a penchant for selling her toys and other personal effects. From time to time, she would be inspired to put some of her valuable possessions into a plastic basket and wander around the house with the basket slung over her arm peddling her wares. On sale might be any number of things: books, Tonka trucks, dolls, clip-on earrings. On one of her rounds, by the time she reached my father much in the basket had already been purchased by my mother or me. My father, who was working at his computer in his office, was interrupted by my sister. When he said that he was willing to see what she had, my sister gave her remaining treasures a good look. She then commented, out loud, that there was nothing appropriate left for my father, since she had only "girls' things." Without missing a beat, and with a straight face, my father picked out two clip-on earrings and a necklace from the basket. He pronounced that there was no such thing as girls' things and boys' things and put them on.

THANKSGIVING AND WOMEN'S WORK

I've been to a number of Thanksgiving dinners over the years. They aren't identical, but they have a familiar structure. Generally speaking, someone, almost always a woman (sometimes it is a couple of women), spends the better part of the day in the kitchen making dinner. Making Thanksgiving dinner seems to involve extensive physical effort, stamina, motivation, and skill. It involves lifting a 10 pound bag of potatoes, scrubbing, cutting, boiling and mashing them; washing, stuffing, and at regular intervals basting a 20 pound turkey; making gravy — not to mention preparing vegetables, soup, salad, and appetizers, setting the table and serving drinks!

One year we all sat down to the Thanksgiving table after my mother had laboured in the kitchen all afternoon with minimal help from the rest of us. My father positioned himself in front of the turkey getting ready to carve it. At that precise moment my sister asked: "Have you ever noticed that women do all the behind-the-scenes work at Thanksgiving, including lifting the turkey and other labourious tasks, and yet when it comes time to simply handle a knife to cut into it, the time when the work is actually being observed, the men take the public role and do the carving?"

SCIENCE IS FOR BOYS

As a consummate nerd, two of my favourite times in the school year were the annual public speaking contests and the annual science fair. While some people imagine that an appropriate topic for a public speech for someone in elementary school is their pet, or baseball, or their grandmother, my parents urged us to take on serious issues of the day. Hence, my speeches were on the rights of the child, the threat of nuclear annihilation, and the symbolic meaning of the explosion of the space shuttle Challenger, among other gripping current public affairs topics. The science fairs were taken similarly seriously, especially by my mother, who insisted that girls should do math, science, computers, and gym throughout their education. So, for science fair projects, instead of getting to create models of the planets, I found myself building a motor to see how magnetic fields would affect its operations, and testing the effect of oxygen on the photosynthesis process.

YOUNG WOMEN AND FEMINISM

In spite of the keen sense of the importance of gender equality instilled by our parents in both my sister and me, I didn't engage in any serious way with organized feminist activities until I was in university. Probably the most formative experience for me was with the China-Canada Young Women's Project. This project was started by Kimberley Manning (the Canadian connection) and Liu Dongxiao (the Chinese connection). The goal of the project was to bring the voices of young women to the United Nations 4th World Conference on Women. To that end, the Canadian chapter organized workshops with high-school aged women; we attempted to document their issues with the aim of having them take their messages to the conference.

The experience of working with a committed group of young feminists, and of engaging with them on topics of importance, was inspiring. I learned that feminists rarely agree on anything; that having a sense of humour and some humility about one's own views is critical for group organizing; that we all articulate the way we see the world around us in slightly different ways; and that listening is a highly undervalued skill.

About a year ago or so, I was sitting in my parents' living room with my son, my parents, and a friend of my father's who is getting close to 60 and who has three daughters of his own and several grandchildren. When I realized that I needed to go and change my son's diaper, I said to him: "Let's go change your diaper." To that, my father's friend said: "I have never changed a diaper."

My father's friend is wonderful with his kids and grandchildren: he plays with them regularly, carries them around on his shoulders, buys them treats, and dotes on them. But he does not change diapers.

Diaper changing could easily be used as an equality litmus test in child rearing. Other litmus tests for family life include who does laundry or cleans up the kitchen. That's not to let feminists off the hook of course: women really should be able to change a tire. And, naturally, everyone should know how to make a good cup of coffee.

16 | PERHAPS I ARRIVED AT THE BEST OF TIMES

Gail G. Campbell

My feminism has always been more personal than public, and my activism more reactive than proactive. For me, there have been no epiphanies, no transformations, but rather an evolution and a gradual awakening to responsibility, to other people — especially to young people — beyond my own immediate circle of family and friends.

My parents, with few resources beyond their lively intelligence, raised their six daughters to be independent thinkers, and my story begins in that unconsciously feminist household. As the youngest child, I observed my parents' and sisters' responses to implicit and explicit systemic discrimination. In 1951, having completed grade 12, my sister Audrey, a first class student, announced her plan to enrol in a commercial course rather than going on to grade 13. Dad urged her to take her grade 13. "Keep your options open," he said.

Our parents had high expectations for their daughters, and taught us to have the same. All six of us pursued professional careers. Although my older sisters came of age in an era of commonly accepted male privilege, we were not raised to accept such norms. In the early 1950s, when my sister Eileen was passed over for promotion in favour of an unqualified man, she refused to train him, choosing resignation rather than complicity in the face of blatant discrimination. Well before I had completed grade 13, both Eileen and Audrey had become teachers in a system that gave privileges to men. Male teachers received an allowance for coaching extramural sports teams while women did not; Eileen, an outstanding athlete, refused to become involved in coaching unless she received an equivalent allowance. More significantly though, women were not eligible for the same insurance benefits as their male colleagues. Women teachers, especially married women teachers, were divided on the issue of equal status for women. But the majority favoured equal status, and, because the majority of teachers were women, they won the day.

By 1964, when I became an elementary school teacher, times had changed, and I could, like many young women in today's world, remain blithely unaware of the more subtle systemic discrimination both inside and outside the public school system. Thus, I did not particularly notice that throughout my post-secondary education I had not even one female professor — not during the time when I was taking courses towards a B.A. at the University of Western Ontario, nor later, when I decided to pursue an M.A. as a full-time student.

At the same time, I knew that as an elementary school teacher earning as much as my male colleagues and receiving the same insurance benefits, I was in a privileged position. I was aware of a number of ongoing feminist issues. My sister Muriel, then the manager of a credit union, had written letters to the editor of the local newspaper publicizing and protesting the fact that, under the Canadian income tax system, married women working outside the home were disadvantaged in comparison to their common law counterparts. And I had lively conversations with Gayle Stucke, a childhood friend, who was, at the time, teaching at the secondary school level and was frustrated by the attitudes of the young women in her classrooms, the vast majority of whom expected to marry and saw no real need to think seriously about career options. But these conversations did not lead to broader discussions about feminism and feminist issues.

Not until I entered the Ph.D. program in History at Clark University in 1977 did I meet a feminist who engaged me in intellectual debate about feminist issues. Lisa Phelps, the only other student to enter the program that year, not only identified herself as a feminist but also taught a course in the newly established Women's Studies Program. Occasionally, the founders of that program organized gatherings, sometimes with invited speakers. These were interesting events, but what I most remember are the endless conversations with Lisa. And yet, despite my intellectual engagement with the issues, I did not take a course or write a single paper on a women's history topic. Nor did my doctoral dissertation, which focused on 19th-century voting behaviour, touch on women in any way.

Nonetheless, when I arrived at the University of New Brunswick (UNB) as a postdoctoral fellow in January of 1983, I was delighted to discover a community of feminist women. Gillian Thompson, the only woman in the History Department at that time, was central to that community. She had been named Advisor to the President on the Status of Women, and, in that capacity, had a budget to sponsor women speakers and initiate discussion among women on campus. Talks were always followed by a reception, and the dialogue often continued even after the food was gone and the wine bottles empty. A downtown Women's Centre drew in women from the broader community, hosting occasional evening events. It was there that I first heard economist Joan McFarlane talk about her hands-on research approach to the study of women's work in New Brunswick fish packing plants, joining the women on the line. On campus, women students also sponsored events, culminating in a conference at which Mary Daly was the featured speaker.

Perhaps I arrived at the best of times. I have not experienced such active interest in women's issues in any other place or at any other time. As I am a political historian, it is scarcely surprising that my first scholarly articles on women, and my first public activities on behalf of women, focused on the role of women in politics. In 1987, I represented UNB on the planning committee for a New Brunswick women and politics conference. And during the 1991 provincial election campaign, I served as moderator in an all-candidates debate on women's issues. Perhaps interest in women and politics peaked during the decade following the promulgation of the *Charter of Rights and Freedoms*, which, through women's intervention, was revised to include recognition of women's right to equal status in Canada.

My own feminist activities have focused increasingly on the University community. In 1998, with the support of the other women members of my department, I called a meeting to show solidarity with women students at a time when reports of incidents of sexual violence against women on campus had alarmed students but not, apparently, the administration. That meeting, which brought together women faculty, staff, and students, resulted in the appointment of a task force to recommend ways to achieve more positive learning environments. I decided to do what I could as an individual and became a sexual harassment advisor. Although I have not been overwhelmed with requests for advice or help, each year one or two women on campus do contact me, and I am there to hear them.

Feminist issues continue to shift and evolve, changing in time, just as my feminism does.

17 | FROM THE AGE OF FOUR

Margaret Conrad

I was a feminist from the age of four. Well, I am not certain that I was precisely four when the light dawned, but it was very early in life when I overheard a neighbour telling my mother that it was a great pity that a newborn child in the community was a girl. I took exception to that comment then, just as I do now.

In my home in rural Nova Scotia, gender roles were sharply defined. My father engaged in a variety of occupations to make a living for our family: working in the forestry industry, driving a truck, keeping a garden to grow much of the food we consumed, and cutting wood to provide the energy for heat and cooking. Meanwhile, my mother worked inside the home, a place that included two other women: my grandmother and me. We cooked, cleaned, canned, knit, sewed, quilted, and performed most of the health care any of us received. I was vaguely aware that my father had more power in the family, but my mother handled the money. She also kept us on a straight and narrow path, defined by her strong Baptist faith, which included, among other things, a strong commitment to social justice.

Since I had no brothers against whom to measure my condition, I had little personal sense of the double standard as it applied to boys and girls. Even my early schooling was mercifully gender neutral. I attended a one-room school for the first five grades, where every student was needed to make up two teams for softball. In high school, boys took Industrial Arts while girls were streamed into Home Economics. But, for the most part, we took the same courses and competed on equal terms — multiple choice exams, common at the time, made it difficult to discriminate. In 1963, I graduated top of my class, propelled by the goal of besting my closest male rival. My competitive spirit owes much to being a child of working class parents who wanted a better life for their only child. The arrival of television in our home in 1955 when I was nine years old — this before we even had indoor plumbing — had added daily fuel to my unarticulated desire to embrace the good life as defined by North American mass consumer culture. Education was my only route to that goal.

Like many young women at the time, I had no ambition to "be" anything. Later in life, I submitted myself to aptitude tests used in the counselling office at Acadia University to see if they were biased. The results suggested that I was most suited to being either a lawyer or a historian. When I graduated from high school in 1963, few women were lawyers. Indeed, women had only just been granted the right to sit on juries, and quotas limited the proportion of women and minorities admitted to major professions to 10 per cent.

I gradually settled into history at Acadia University, which I attended as a scholarship student from 1963 to 1967. The head of the History Department, Harry MacLean, liked women (he had two exceptionally bright daughters) and actively promoted his best female students. Having taught in the United States for many years, MacLean was aware of the debates on the status of women that were percolating south of the border. I was oblivious to the larger context in which my undergraduate career unfolded, but my sense of injustice was greatly enhanced during my years at Acadia. As a "freshette," I was confined to residence three nights a week, which was a real handicap for diligent female students; no such restrictions were imposed on "freshmen." Maids cleaned the rooms and changed the bedding for male students; female students were denied these services. Although men in campus housing were allowed to have cars, we women were not. I still bristle thinking about these small slights.

It was MacLean who ensured, through the award of A pluses in his courses, that I graduated with the university gold medal in 1967. He was also instrumental in having me apply for a Woodrow Wilson Fellowship to support my graduate studies. By the mid-1960s, the National Organization of Women in the United States was calling into question the gender bias in scholarship competitions and thus I found myself a Woodrow Wilson Fellow courted by many universities in North America. While MacLean was determined that I go to Yale, I stubbornly insisted on remaining in Canada. Somewhere along the way I had become a feisty Canadian nationalist. I opted for the University of Toronto.

In Toronto, my feminist consciousness began to develop more substance. I was deeply offended when one of my professors suggested that, since I was the only woman among fifteen men, my presence threatened the male bonding that he promoted in his class. He suggested that I might be "happier" in another seminar. History was then, and to some extent still is, defined as a masculine discipline — women are better suited to literary studies, don't you know?

Like many other women in this period, I was encouraged to do the shorter D.Phil. rather than a Ph.D. I did neither. I married in 1968 and took a job at Clarke Irwin Publishing where I worked as editor for a textbook aptly titled *The Story of Western Man*. With my marriage quickly falling apart, I was taken under the protective wing of senior editor Norma Pettit, who has been one of my most influential mentors. Among the activities she suggested we do to take my mind off marital miseries was to audit an evening course taught by Alan Borovoy, General Counsel of the Canadian Civil Liberties Association. His class helped me to develop a political framework in which to "see" the injustices perpetrated on Aboriginal peoples, minorities of all kinds, and women. This was empowering stuff.

In the summer of 1969, Harry MacLean asked me to teach at Acadia after someone had abruptly opted out of a contract. I agreed. The challenge was an enormous one — teaching large, year-long classes in Western Civilization, British Empire, and Canadian History — but I survived the ordeal and the many slights I experienced as a young female faculty member. Invitations to campus events came addressed to "Mr. Conrad," the "faculty" washrooms and gym facilities were for the use of men only, and most people assumed that I was a secretary.

Of course, secretaries and female physical plant workers at Acadia suffered from the lower wages paid to women. And so, to my surprise, did I. When Nova Scotia's pay equity legislation went into effect in 1972, my salary jumped a whopping 18 percent. Secretaries and physical plant workers were not so fortunate.

In my early years at Acadia, two energetic colleagues, Lois Vallely and Lorette Woolsey-Toews, proved valued mentors. Not only did they have a firm grasp on the burgeoning women's movement, but they were also on the edge of academic developments in what was emerging as a whole new field of intellectual inquiry. With their encouragement, I offered my apartment as the site of a consciousness-raising group, and became involved in the activities of a community women's centre established in Wolfville. My male colleagues began complaining that I was losing my femininity!

In 1972–73, I took a year's leave to pursue a Ph.D. at the University of Toronto, where my feminism was further honed by courses and conversations. Meanwhile, my allies at Acadia made plans to launch the university's first interdisciplinary course, Women in the Modern World. In the fall of 1974, Donna Smyth, a new hire in the English Department, enlisted us in the cause of founding *Atlantis: A Women's Studies Journal*. It was launched in 1975, International

Women's Year, a busy time for me and other feminists who were called upon to explain ourselves, often to hostile audiences. Now a tight alliance, Acadia feminists lobbied against unfair practices in the university, pressed for a provincial inquiry on the status of women, supported the unionization of the faculty, and, in 1978, produced the first report on the status of women on campus. By the early 1990s, five of us (Dianne Looker, Donna Smyth, Hilda Taylor, Lois Vallely-Fischer, and I) were so persistent in our demands for justice that we were dubbed "the five feminists from hell," a label that we wore proudly. I also took my feminist sensibilities into research on Canadian women's history and to formal positions as head of the History Department, as president of the faculty union, and as a member of a variety of national organizations. In many of these venues, I think my presence made a small difference.

18 | NOT JUST WORDS

Maeve Conrick

To select one single event (or person) that led me to becoming a feminist would be an impossible task. My views and beliefs about feminism, and about being a feminist, are the result of myriad experiences covering three decades and three countries: Ireland, France, and Canada. However, as is probably true for most women, my mother was a particularly formative influence. Though she herself would never have dreamt of describing herself as a feminist, she succeeded in transmitting clear messages to her five daughters about the importance for women to achieve and maintain economic independence, in particular by having a professional career. She herself had been obliged to give up her own career as a senior nurse in a hospital in Ireland in the 1940s, when a "marriage bar" was in place, which meant that once married, women lost the right to continue in their posts in public service sectors and had to resign.

This discrimination was always a matter of deep resentment

for my mother, and I remember being very conscious, while I was growing up, of the negative effect this professional frustration had on her. The marriage bar was eventually abolished in the 1970s, in time for me to have the choice to get married and at the same time continue my career as a university professor. However, elements of discrimination remained, which steeled my resolve to work to eliminate discrimination against women, especially in the professional arena.

In the mid-1970s I left Ireland to go to France to study for a Ph.D. in General and Applied Linguistics at the Université de Provence, Aix-Marseille 1, at a time when the feminist movement was at its height and the subject of much popular as well as academic debate. I was exposed to much of the academic side of the debate through discussion with another Ph.D. student, Margaret Moriarty, who was researching a thesis on *féminité* in the work of the French novelist Georges Bernanos. Margaret Moriarty subsequently went to live in Canada (she is now an academic administrator at the University of Ottawa), and it was largely through her influence that I became interested in and acquainted with feminism in Canada.

When my son was born in 1981, maternity leave was not readily available to women academics. A report on maternity leave for academics published by the Irish Federation of University Teachers in the 1980s had as its title "Women Academics Don't Have Babies." The title came from a phrase reputedly used by a university administrator in reply to a question put to him about what maternity leave provisions were in place in his university. How could one not be a feminist in the face of such evidence?

My work in the context of feminism in Canada builds on my background as a linguist, which provided me with the tools to carry out various studies on the representation of women in the French language in Quebec and in French Canada generally. I began work on the feminization of professional titles in French (*la féminisation*) in the mid-1990s, initially as a professor visiting the Centre for Canadian Studies at the University of Ottawa, then under the direction of Professor André Lapierre. Subsequently, I secured support for my research from various funding sources, such as the Canadian Government Faculty Enrichment Program and the Prix du Québec. My research involved collecting and analyzing primary data from print media (including newspapers such as *La Presse, Le Devoir, Le Droit,* and *l'Acadie nouvelle*) and from internet sources.

For me, one of the most compelling aspects of research into *la féminisation* is the evidence it provides of the leadership that Quebec and Canada have demonstrated internationally by highlighting instances of linguistic discrimination in French, and suggesting ways in which such linguistic discrimination might be remedied from a feminist point of view. Canadian and Quebec feminists challenged the linguistic authority of bodies such as the Académie française, which continues to be fiercely opposed to modernizing French vocabulary and grammar to take into account the changing professional roles of women. Despite this opposition, however, the use of feminized forms of professional titles, such as "la professeure," "la ministre," "l'ingénieure" and "l'avocate," has now become the rule rather than the exception in Canada, thus increasing considerably the visibility of women in the full range of professional contexts.

Even more notable is the fact that this feminist linguistic reform has influenced the use of the French language in many other francophone countries and regions, such as Belgium and Switzerland. This linguistic reform is even apparent in France, where women government ministers are now systematically referred to as "la ministre." This is indeed a measure of the success of Canadian, and especially Quebec, feminists in bringing about change.

In terms of my professional life, I consider the work I have published in this area to be among the most important academic contributions I have made during my career to date. I continue to work and publish on the feminization of professional titles in French, and I still find plenty of interesting material, as well as many lively debates, to which I am happy to contribute. As a university professor in the French Department for almost thirty years, I have had the privilege of coming into contact with several generations of students (of which over 90% are female). In my capacity, I am in a position to sensitize them, on the basis of real world examples, to the challenges women of my generation faced, as well as the challenges that still remain.

In discussions with students about their views on what the most important contemporary issues are, one point that continues to arise is that the terms "feminist" and "feminism" have acquired particularly negative connotations in recent times. Though some might perceive this as nothing more than a minor, purely terminological, issue, it reveals a lot about contemporary attitudes and concerns. Many young women take the gains of generations of feminists for granted, and take the view that gender equality has been achieved; that there is no further need for a feminist movement and that being a "feminist" is an outdated concept. There is a fear that ours might be the last generation for whom the term "feminism" has positive value; that we might be the last generation who are proud to describe ourselves as "feminist."

Much remains to be done if the gains of the past 40 years are to be maintained and consolidated.

19 | DADS HANGING DIAPERS OUT TO DRY

Sharon Anne Cook

It seems strange to me now that so much of my personal history with feminism has been deeply intertwined with men. On the other hand, living in a household with three males and having worked the early part of my career primarily with men, perhaps it isn't so strange after all. There were women in my story, but as I look back on my experiences now, I seem to have always had the goal of winning over men with whom I lived, worked, or taught.

My introduction to feminism — and the first image of recall — was through consciousness-raising groups in the late 1960s in Ottawa. I remember a group of earnest young women sitting on various living room floors, talking about injustices that feminism would right. I had very recently arrived in town, newly married, and feeling disoriented. I recall finding the group sessions intensely interesting, but also feeling awkward and out of step, rather like the "country cousin" (I was from the west after all). But I suppose that was precisely the point of the sessions: to make one aware of inadequacies and to spur study and reflection.

I had originally been invited to these consciousness-raising groups by an old high-school friend from Calgary, Frances Wright (who later founded the Famous Five Foundation). And it was Frances who asked in a note several years later if I had read the Royal Commission Report on the Status of Women. I was ashamed to admit that I had not, and ran right out to get a copy. By that time, 1972, we were living in Kingston and I had recently given birth to our first son. Sitting up through the night, nursing the baby and reading the Report — that is the second image I recall. I was furious with myself that so much was new to me.

Later that year, I found a teaching position in Ottawa and became the breadwinner for the family, with my husband staying home with our first, and then with our second son. Having been raised by a warm and nurturing father, my husband took to the role of house-spouse naturally. I have a clear memory of driving into our housing project one winter evening behind a male neighbour. My husband was hanging diapers on the clothesline. I almost hit the car ahead of me when the man suddenly stopped, got out, and staring in disbelief at my husband shouted "What the f*** are you doing?"

There weren't a lot of dads hanging diapers on the line in those days.

I had the good fortune to land my first teaching position in an extraordinarily talented and committed Department of History in an upper-middle-class high school. When I began there, I expected I would have been one of few to identify as a feminist, but I felt no censure or opposition during this formative period. Everyone was reading Margaret Atwood and marveling at her insight and skills. We had some female students who questioned why there was so little material about women in our history courses. I tried to change this, using whatever materials I could find.

I knew how very lucky I was to be a part of that intelligent staff, and to be so strongly supported in my early years. I had a series of positive mentors during that period: fair-minded men and women who delighted in debate. This is yet another image I carry with me. I recall most Friday afternoons sitting in the history office with my colleagues. During these many after-school discussions, I learned a huge amount, and I suspect that some of the knowledge we shared influenced others too. After a few years, I was named a department head at another school. I loathed administration. However, over the intervening thirty-five years, I continued as an administrator there and at the university level. This shows in part my definition of feminism — leading even when you would rather not: better to be in charge of the ship, actively using feminism, than to be subject to others' orders.

In my next two schools, I encountered very different cultures amongst teachers regarding feminism generally and women's roles in particular. In one school setting, I had no sooner joined the staff than the Principal named me the Department Head, over a competent man who had been in that school for some years. I remember how shocking the principal's act was for all of us; I was embarrassed and considered rejecting the post. My image of that period is one of realizing one day after school that all of my colleagues had disappeared. Wandering the halls, I saw them meeting in a classroom — without me. The next morning in the prep room one of the "old boys" approached me and very formally announced, "We discussed you at length yesterday, and we have decided to give you a chance." I was immediately struck by his choice of words: they discussed *me*, not the situation. One could not fail to personalize a crisis of this type. We learned to live with one another.

When I moved to the university level in the late 1980s — again almost immediately into an administrative position — I encountered far more resistance. I, along with the first wave of women who had completed doctorates, entered the academy into a teacher education program previously the preserve of men. Faculties of Education had first been incorporated into the university system in Ontario in the 1970s, so the old hierarchy remained from the Teachers' Colleges, and that hierarchy never admitted women, except possibly as Deans of Women. These men stood to lose status and authority to the younger, better educated, and overtly feminist women of my cohort. They did not take the demotion easily, waging a protracted war of memos, personal slights, and endless strategizing with their few sympathizers. I have a picture engraved in my brain of these men making furious speeches at meetings, in the hallways, in offices to try to turn back the tide of energetic women.

But we women had each other. That was what saved us: we mobilized to protect each other, arranging lunches to debate and bond, creating committees, and infiltrating the structure of the organization by requesting discussions about gender equity. As a group, we created the first women's association within the Canadian Society for Studies in Education: the Canadian Association for Studies of Women in Education (CASWE), which thrives to this day. These were heady times.

And then, the Montreal Massacre. Every feminist in Canada must have that day inscribed in a special, painful compartment of her brain. As a mother of sons I felt an enormous responsibility for raising young men who would follow feminist principles in their lives, and who would defend those principles. I had a lot of confidence in our sons' decency and intelligence — but as a feminist, I wanted more than that. I wanted them to advocate for feminism.

So I was not prepared for the table discussion on December 6th, 1989. I was gobsmacked to hear one of my sons insist that such an act was only possible from a madman, and that feminism had little to do with it. His brother agreed. I understood their need to defend men at such a time, but I had worked hard at pointing to systemic injustice and this showed that I had failed in my mission. As I struggled to keep my composure, my husband took up the debate, and on and on it went. I could do nothing but cry — not exactly the best feminist position to take. I picked up my plate and cutlery and ran upstairs to my study (thank you, Virginia Woolf), and wept in private.

Finally, hours later, both lads tapped on my door and apologized for the distress they had caused, promising to rethink their position; I continued weeping, feeling that I had guilted them into the statement.

We talk about that evening fairly often, and neither son recalls it clearly. Both are good men, and both define as feminists today. Did that evening make a difference? Perhaps not consciously to them, but it certainly made a deep impression on me. It forced me to confront how far we have yet to go in understanding male rage against women, especially but not exclusively against feminists. It frightened me, and still does. It forced me to recognize the systemic dangers faced every day by our young female teachers — both by structures and by wrong-thinking people. And it caused me to reflect on the burden I was insisting my sons — and all sons — carry.

That burden increases as they age. Tim is now a committed and loving father to three glorious little girls, all (I hope) feminists in the making, and his challenge, and that of his quite remarkable wife, has become even greater with their arrival. As for me, I know that I will continue to influence the next generations, but the real work will be shouldered by our children now. I'll be watching the next phase of this revolution with great interest; I'm hoping that the tears are behind me.

20 | STILL WAITING FOR TRUE EQUALITY
Honourable Sheila Copps

"I am woman, hear me roar." These lyrics, penned in 1972, have been characterized as the theme song for the women's liberation movement. But for me, the road to feminism was hardly a roar. If liberation were a song, my music started with a lullaby.

I entered adulthood, lulled into the mistaken impression that the battle for equality of the sexes had already been won. After all, American tennis star Billie-Jean King had whipped Bobby Riggs in 1973 in three straight sets after he bragged about his superior male sporting abilities. And more than a decade had passed since Betty Friedan wrote the definitive treatise on the second wave of feminism.

My first hint of how far we still had to go in the quest for equality came when I secured a full-time job as a junior reporter in 1977. The *Hamilton Spectator* editor who hired me, welcomed me to the team with the statement, "I hope you realize we are exceeding our quota of women by hiring you." Thankful to have the job at all, I merely smiled and thanked him profusely. In those days, one would not think of filing an official complaint. It was almost expected that companies would apply quotas in their hiring of women. After all, only twenty-eight years earlier my mother had been fired from her secretarial job simply for the offence of getting married. In her generation, nobody thought twice about a company policy that permitted the firing of females simply because of their marital status.

As young women, we were socialized into believing that our lot in life would be to find a man who would support us. When I entered university, I had some revolutionary ideas. I quickly got active on student council at my alma mater of the University of Western Ontario. As vice-president external, I helped organize a demonstration against nuclear testing off Amchitka Island on the Pacific Coast. We managed to get 10,000 student activists to the Sarnia Bridge, closing the border that links the province of Ontario with the state of Michigan.

However, even with my revolutionary bent, I actually believed that life after university would probably involve working for favoured social causes for free, while my future husband would be the breadwinner. I mulled over an application to law school, but a friend convinced me not to apply, since I would be competing with a man who needed the job to support his family. I still shake my head today when I reflect on how gullibly I supported the socialized stereotypes defining the roles of women and men. Quotas, no problem. Glass ceilings, no problem. I was just happy to be working in what turned out to be a world dominated by men.

I believed in my own capacity to work hard and succeed. But I didn't realize how much my personal ambitions had been tempered by societal expectations. The newspaper business was a man's world. To get along, you did your job, laughed at their jokes, and tried to do your best to fit in. The same rules applied when I switched from covering the news to making it, running for elected office for the first time at the ripe old age of 24. I was elected at 28, and got my first dose of sexism up close and personal within a few weeks of arriving at Queen's Park as the newly minted Member of Provincial Parliament for Hamilton Centre.

After posing a question in the legislature, I was told by the minister and another member of parliament to "get back to the kitchen." Weeks later, members of the government were running bets on how much I weighed. A fellow member of parliament actually sexually assaulted me while we were touring northern Ontario communities studying the issue of spousal abuse.

That early experience with the stark reality of discrimination based on gender was extremely difficult. If I attacked my critics, I would quickly be labelled a bitch. If I did nothing, I would be seen to support sexism.

That fine line continued when I was elected to the House of Commons in 1984. During my early years, I was met with a barrage of sexism. I was called everything from baby, to slut, to whiner, simply for doing my job. Media coverage of male politicians focused primarily on their ideas. Media coverage of me focused on what I was wearing or whom I was dating. When I proposed legislation to protect gays and lesbians in the Ontario Human Rights Code, I was attacked as being a closet lesbian. When I asked tough questions in the House of Commons, I was accused of being strident. The pitch of my voice and the cut of my hair were both subjected to much media discussion.

My early years in the working world shook me to the core. My naïve belief that sexual discrimination was a thing of the past was shattered by the reality of a concrete ceiling. By the time I reached the age of 30, I was convinced that the only way for women to achieve real equality was by sticking together, and by understanding that we are not the problem.

Helen Reddy was right. In her liberation song "I am woman, hear me roar" her music showed us what is needed for women to liberate ourselves. We need to roar. And we need to stick together. If a farmer is elected to parliament, she or he has no problem in identifying herself as a voice for farmers. A westerner or Quebecer is determined to carry the message of their region to Ottawa. But even in 2009, many women are still afraid to identify themselves as feminists in support of the fight for equality.

We passed laws guaranteeing equal pay in 1952. That was the year I was born. I fully expected that by the time my daughter reached adulthood, the only place we would find discrimination was in the history books. When my daughter graduates from university this year she can expect to earn 15% to 20% less than young men in her class, simply because of her gender. In the past 25 years, women have streamed into the labour force at unprecedented rates. It is no coincidence that during that period, Canadians' real earning power has increased by only $50. We are currently ranked 48th in the world in the election of women to our national parliament — we rank behind Rwanda, Uganda, Eritrea, and Pakistan, just to name a few.

I was lulled into complacency in my youth. While I crept into feminism in my third decade, now, I am ready to roar. In 2010 we celebrate the 40th anniversary of the groundbreaking Report of the Royal Commission on the Status of Women in Canada. I only hope the testimonials of other women in this book will encourage readers to embrace feminism as the key to equality. We can't wait 40 more years for true equality.

21 | BRED IN THE BONES

Ann Decter

In the rambling house where I grew up, feminism was a constantly ringing phone and sweeping pronouncements on equality, as canned soup heated on the stove and a cigarette dangled dangerously above. It was the notion that my sisters and I were the intellectual equals of our brothers. Our family sprang from the union of two beliefs: that education held the power to change a life and ideas held the power to change the world. One of those world-changing ideas was feminism. While other mothers in our neighbourhood knit mittens, scarves, and thick Icelandic sweaters, my mother knit feminism into our bones.

My mother's earliest organizing was women's peace activism against the threat of nuclear war. Galvanized by the brinkmanship of the Cuban missile crisis, women like my mother and Carole Geller in Winnipeg, Muriel Duckworth in Halifax, Kay Macpherson in Toronto and many, many others across the country were compelled into action in the belief that together, women could make peace where men would fashion war. The white dial phone in our kitchen rang constantly; many a night the living room was filled with plotting, smoking mothers. Telegrams from the Voice of Women flew to Ottawa and back, letters were fired off to editors, and Mother's Day was a vigil for peace at the Cenotaph. A peace tour of Soviet women

— including the mayor of Moscow, a woman — crossed the country. I still have pictures of the day they visited our house in formal suits, beehive hairdos, and formidable state-issue glasses.

As students and hippies exploded against the American war in Vietnam, the Royal Commission on the Status of Women was struck. Women's peace activism flowed into women in electoral politics. In our house, feminism was named explicitly. In our prairie city, women demonstrated for much-needed family law reform, and Otto Lang became two four-letter words. Rosemary Brown ran for NDP leadership and on her campaign, we — I was now fully enlisted — wore t-shirts that read "A woman's place is in the House of Commons." Rosemary Brown lost that 1975 leadership race, and it wasn't until almost a generation later, in 1989, that Audrey McLaughlin became the first woman to lead a national political party in Canada. By then, my mother had died, and after a rebellious rejection of her belief in political activism, I found my own feminism.

In my early twenties, I stepped away from the path my mother had cleared. Writing became my tool for seeking truth and understanding, and community development suited me better than electoral politics. I was a feminist in my personal beliefs, but not an activist. Feminism was mostly about feeling very free to transgress — for example, training with a men's water polo team — and objecting to individual men's behaviour. I can still remember a male friend saying derisively, "At least you're not like those feminists." To his surprise, I answered, "I am a feminist," in a quiet voice. Apparently, it didn't show.

After years of working part-time in community programs and writing on my own, I began to seek formal outlets. Suddenly, I was in a writing workshop and working in the publishing industry. An interview for a job at Women's Press in Toronto led to an opportunity to volunteer there. I leapt at it. In women's writing and publishing, it all came together; I made sense. My writing was deeply infused with the beliefs of my childhood, beliefs that feminism had bred into my bones. A thriving community of women debated ideas and strategies, argued over the meaning and direction of feminism and the theory needed to move forward. I moved in a world where women passionately discussed the power of narrative, the structure of stories, how a sentence lay on a page, even where to break a line of poetry. It was like coming home after a very long walk in the cold.

In one way or another, feminism has always been a journey of coming home. Coming home to my childhood, coming home to community, coming home to those truths that reveal themselves again and again, like stripping away a layer of soil, only to find another layer beneath. And layer after layer, until finally, bedrock. It was a sustaining force, a world view, a mission and a perspective. Drawn from that place of women's power Audre Lorde described as ancient, deep, and dark. Adrienne Rich posits the question, "What behooves us?" and I find that my life is lived out in the answer, a deep liberating engagement with the world as it is.

As bones structure a body, what's bred into them structures a life. In the comfortable house where my daughter is growing up, feminism has seeped into the next generation. At 13, she sees the slant of social relations, complains about gender roles, and argues with her classmates about homophobia. She backed Hillary through the primaries, and celebrates Obama now. Feminism is in her bones, as surely as Beyoncé is in her IPod. Bred there, mother to daughter. A world-changing idea.

22 | LE FÉMINISME : UN CHOIX DE PARCOURS

Francine Descarries

Proclamer mon adhésion au féminisme et le revendiquer comme choix de vie s'imposent à moi comme le reflet de pratiques et de convictions profondément intégrées qui s'inscrivent dans l'histoire de ma vie. Le féminisme est pour moi une « manière d'être » et de dire qui je suis, mais c'est aussi un choix de parcours, une manière d'établir mon rapport au monde, mes idéaux d'égalité, de démocratie et de justice sociale. Le féminisme est pour moi une matrice de perceptions et d'actions, un habitus dirait Bourdieu, une « présence agissante » de tout le passé dont il est le produit.

Féministe de conviction et de métier, assez paradoxalement, il m'est impossible de répondre avec précision à la question : comment êtes-vous devenue féministe ? J'aimerais pouvoir dire que je « suis née féministe. » Ou encore, que c'est en lisant le livre culte de Simone de Beauvoir, *Le deuxième sexe*, que j'aurais entendu l'appel à l'adolescence. Mais non. Certes, le fait que j'ai dû à seize ans abandonner l'ambition de poursuivre des études postsecondaires après la mort de mon père, en 1958, pour que mon frère puisse continuer ses études en médecine a suscité chez moi une certaine conscience de l'injustice subie, une certaine révolte, mais une révolte d'une amplitude néanmoins insuffisante pour que je conteste le bien-fondé de la décision familiale ou que j'adhère de façon militante à la cause féministe.

Mon engagement féministe relève plutôt d'une lente progression, non nécessairement consciente ou linéaire, qui résulte d'un faisceau d'éléments conjoncturels et personnels. L'ambition de me réaliser à travers un projet de vie professionnel a toujours été présente chez moi, en dépit de l'omniprésence du modèle de la « bonne mère » qui constituait encore la norme ; mais je ne savais pas, à l'époque, que cette ambition était redevable des luttes menées par les pionnières et s'inscrivait dans la mouvance féministe en émergence au Québec.

Dans mon cas, deux événements sont à l'origine de ma prise de conscience féministe. Ayant interrompu mes études à l'âge de 16 ans pour les raisons familiales déjà mentionnées, je suis revenue aux études dès que l'occasion m'en a été donnée, soit à l'âge de vingt-sept ans, quelques semaines après la naissance de ma deuxième fille. Je savais depuis toujours que je voulais faire autre chose de ma vie que d'être une mère de famille à la maison. Mon retour aux études m'a confirmé que je n'arriverais pas à me réaliser sans prendre une part active à l'effervescence sociale d'alors. C'est donc au Cégep, sans que je sois pour autant capable d'en identifier l'élément déclencheur, que j'ai commencé à m'intéresser à la situation des femmes et particulièrement à l'intensification de leur participation au milieu du travail, qui constituait alors un trait marquant de la période.

Au cours de mes études universitaires, la lecture de *La femme mystifiée* de Betty Friedan (1963) a mis des mots sur le malaise que je ressentais. C'est toutefois l'essai décapant de Benoîte Groult (1975),

Ainsi soit-elle, qui me révélait l'existence de la misogynie de la société et de discours, normes et pratiques, élaborés dans des temps et des espaces différents, pour maintenir les femmes « en servage » et les exclure de la vie en société. C'est dans ce livre également que Benoîte Groult lève le voile sur l'incommensurable cruauté de l'excision et de l'infibulation. D'autres importants éveilleurs de ma conscience féministe ont été les traductions de l'étude d'Elena G. Belotti (1973), *Du côté des petites filles,* et celle de *La politique du mâle* de Kate Millett (1971) qui m'introduisait au concept de patriarcat. Collées sur ma réalité québécoise, l'étude de Mona Josée Gagnon (1974) sur *Les femmes vues par le Québec des hommes* et celle de Michèle Jean (1974), *Québécoises du 20ᵉ siècle,* ont alimenté mon indignation en me sensibilisant aux conditions de vie des femmes québécoises, à leur confinement dans l'espace domestique et au dénigrement, sinon au mépris, dont elles ont été l'objet de la part des autorités politiques, intellectuelles et religieuses.

Mais c'est mon contact avec la pensée féministe matérialiste française, telle que développée par les Christine Delphy, Nicole-Claude Mathieu et Colette Guillaumin et diffusée à travers la revue *Questions féministes,* qui m'a offert le registre d'analyse dans lequel je voulais situer ma réflexion féministe, a nourri mon engagement féministe et a suscité le désir de m'engager dans l'observation et la théorisation de la réalité des femmes comme acte militant. J'aimerais souligner ici l'importance du rôle joué par les Comités femmes des syndicats dans la diffusion de cette problématique au cours des années 1970. Je pense aux documents *Condition féminine* qui présentent un colligé des travaux menés au cours des années 1973 et 1974 par le Comité Laure-Gaudreault de la CEQ (Centrale des enseignants de Québec) et au rapport présenté par le comité de la condition féminine de la CSN (Confédération des syndicats nationaux), *La lutte des femmes, combat de tous les travailleurs,* au congrès de juin 1976.

Sans doute plus militante que théoricienne à l'époque, je n'ai d'ailleurs pas hésité à clamer haut et fort sur tous les toits la nécessité d'abattre le système patriarcal et le besoin pour les femmes de se libérer. Inutile de dire que l'étiquette de « féministe radicale » m'a rapidement été accolée, marquage dont je n'ai pas cherché à me départir depuis.

De ce féminisme militant et intuitif, je suis passée à un féminisme plus théorique et mieux intériorisé lorsque, après avoir écrit mon mémoire de maîtrise sur la reproduction sociale de la division sociale des sexes, *L'école rose … et les cols roses* (1980), j'ai donné en 1978 avec deux autres collègues étudiantes, Zaïda Radja et Isabelle Lasvergnas, le premier cours de « Sociologie de la condition féminine » à l'Université de Montréal. Faut-il le dire, mes collègues et moi ne disposions pas alors de beaucoup plus de connaissances, ou d'outils conceptuels et théoriques, que nos nombreuses étudiantes. C'est sans doute notre seule volonté de porter un regard nouveau sur les rapports de sexe, de « dénaturaliser » la question « femme » et de comprendre les mécanismes à l'œuvre dans la reproduction de la division sociale des sexes qui nous aura permis de passer à travers l'expérience.

Bref, je suis devenue féministe, d'une part en m'interrogeant sur ma propre vie et celle des femmes autour de moi, parce qu'il m'était impossible d'accepter l'idée que les rôles, places et positions qui étaient réservés aux femmes dans la société étaient surdéterminés par leur sexe et que la maternité était la seule dimension à travers laquelle me définir et me valoriser. D'autre part, c'est au cours de mes études universitaires en sociologie — où la question « femmes » ou la critique de l'androcentrisme des sciences humaines n'étaient absolument pas à l'ordre du jour — que se sont déployés le questionnement et les apprentissages qui m'ont amenée au féminisme. S'est alors progressivement imposée à moi l'idée que le désir de comprendre et de contribuer à « expliquer les causes et le fonctionnement, le pourquoi et le comment de l'oppression des femmes en général ou d'un de ses aspects particuliers » (Delphy, 1977) deviendrait le moteur de ma vie intellectuelle et militante.

> Take Back the Night March, Montreal, August 2, 1980

Archives et collections spéciales (ACMF), Université d'Ottawa (PC-X10-93-50)/ Monique Bertrand et Dominique Malaterre

> Marche La rue la nuit Femmes sans peur, Montréal, le 2 août 1980

23 | ON NE NAÎT PAS FÉMINISTE,
ON LE DEVIENT

Nathalie Des Rosiers

Toute personne cherche à lutter contre les injustices qu'elle rencontre sur son chemin. Mais il y a en tant qu'il faut choisir…

Dans ce court texte, j'explore si c'est le féminisme qui m'a choisie ou si c'est moi qui l'ai trouvé. Est-ce par hasard que je me suis intéressée aux questions de prescription pour les victimes de violence sexuelle ? Étais-je prédestinée à réfléchir sur l'apport des théories féministes au droit de la responsabilité civile, ou s'agissait-il d'un choix rationnel et soupesé ? Est-ce la rationalité ou le destin qui a soudainement fait qu'un débat social nous a propulsées vers l'action ? Simone de Beauvoir disait qu'on ne naît pas femme mais qu'on le devient. Si on ne naît pas féministe, est-ce qu'on le devient ou est-ce qu'on choisit de le devenir ?

Le mouvement était déjà assez bien entamé lorsque j'ai commencé à m'y intéresser sérieusement. Mes années d'études chez les religieuses et mon éducation familiale très libérale m'avait bien préparée pour un mouvement qui valorisait la contribution des femmes et dénonçait les inégalités. Par la suite, les opportunités d'actions et de reconnaissance d'injustices se sont présentées tout à fait naturellement.

Le mouvement féministe offre énormément d'occasions de réflexion et d'action : c'est un projet intellectuel ambitieux, mais c'est également un projet pratique qui impose des connotations éthiques profondes. C'est un projet idéal où inscrire une contestation des injustices et des abus systématiques de pouvoir, un projet qui permet la cohabitation entre la critique intellectuelle et l'action communautaire. C'est une superbe méthodologie d'analyse de la société pour vaincre les inégalités endémiques, un projet intellectuel ancré dans une action éminemment pratique.

Le féminisme juridique invite à une réévaluation des nombreux réflexes du droit, réflexes souvent peu testés. Des principes de Wigmore de dépréciation de la crédibilité des femmes à la critique de la défense de provocation, de la sous-indemnisation des femmes à la dénonciation du voile de silence sur les agressions sexuelles imposé par les règles de la prescription ou aux inégalités fondamentales dans le calcul des contributions en droit de la famille, le féminisme impose une imputabilité aux règles de droit : protègent-elles *tous* les membres de la société ?

Intellectuellement, le féminisme est un terrain riche de recherches qui permet de jeter un regard critique sur le droit existant et sur les principes qui tentent de le justifier. Le féminisme exige de définir de nouveaux concepts et un nouveau vocabulaire qui soit plus inclusif et de trouver *Les mots pour le dire,* selon Marie Cardinal.

Il s'agit de s'exercer à apporter un regard critique sur les règles, leurs effets et surtout les métaphores utilisées par le droit pour se faire comprendre. *Écoute ma différence,* de Marielle Righini (1978), était le premier livre féministe que j'ai lu et il me semblait que le projet intellectuel féministe visait à réfléchir sur cette différence et à trouver une meilleure expression pour celle-ci au sein du droit contemporain.

Selon moi, le projet féministe cherche surtout à permettre à *toutes* les femmes de faire entendre leurs différences et de trouver les mots pour le dire. C'est un projet intellectuel d'interrogation : il ne s'agit pas de remplacer un vocabulaire hégémonique par un autre, mais bien de tenter de s'obliger à mieux comprendre les multiples réalités des femmes, leurs craintes et angoisses, la maternité, la non-maternité, la marginalisation la disparation des femmes autochtones, la violence conjugale, l'inceste, la traite des femmes, la discrimination contre les lesbiennes, le harcèlement au travail, le plafond de verre, la tentation de la « superwoman », les dettes transmises sexuellement, les inégalités salariales, la distribution des tâches familiales, l'expérience de la diaspora…

Le projet intellectuel féministe est infini et se nourrit constamment de la problématique inégalitaire dans toutes ses dimensions. C'est également un projet éminemment pratique.

Le féminisme invite à une réflexion sur notre propre rôle dans la hiérarchisation des pouvoirs. Tant de méthodes féministes m'ont été utiles pour réfléchir sur les moyens de mieux habiliter les autres à participer. Je me souviens d'un exercice où chaque participante avait une série de jetons qui devaient être déposés lors de chaque intervention : l'idée était de permettre à tous de prendre la parole et ainsi de limiter la domination du discours par quelques participants. C'est un exercice auquel je réfléchis souvent pour tenter de modérer mes tendances à prendre la parole trop souvent.

Savoir reconnaître les rapports de pouvoir dans toute situation et surtout réfléchir sur son propre pouvoir et rôle… Le féminisme est un rappel constant de la tentation du pouvoir et de la nécessité de toujours devoir le contrôler. Si on ne naît pas despotique, on peut le devenir. Le féminisme est un rappel à l'ordre : un avertissement constant que les rapports de pouvoir s'exercent dans les moindres gestes et dans toutes relations sociales. Le féminisme demande de réfléchir profondément et de façon pratique sur la façon dont on exerce le pouvoir et les limites et les mécanismes d'imputabilité que l'on s'impose.

Je me souviens d'avoir découpé une caricature de The Far Side qui me semblait très féministe : '*Stop looking for the perfect employee, try being the perfect employer.*' D'une certaine façon, le féminisme invite à réfléchir sur l'exercice de toute tâche. Selon moi, la discipline de recherche et d'examen de son propre pouvoir est un élément primordial d'un leadership moins tyrannique et davantage habilitant. Si je ne suis pas née féministe, je suis heureuse de tenter de continuer de le devenir.

24 | *WHY NOT?* ASKED THE BUTTON
Dianne Dodd

Historians often call the 1970 Royal Commission on the Status of Women the launch of second wave of feminism in Canada. Yet growing up in that era, I don't remember the Commission. I do, however, remember the United Nations International Women's Year in 1975. I had all the posters and buttons, and anything else I could get my hands on. "Why Not?" this, "Why Not" that... it became my slogan.

Like many people, I first learned about feminism in my family, or to be more precise, I first learned about patriarchy in my family, which in turn led me to feminism. I grew up in a large working class family: my parents married young, just after the Second World War. My father was a policeman and my mother a housewife — well, at least until the inflation of the 1970s collided with the growing needs of a growing family. Then she worked in a store for a while. In that sense they were typical. But my parents were atypical in that they had seven children, all born within nine years of each other! My parents had tried various forms of the largely unreliable birth control methods available in the 1950s and 1960s, clearly with limited success. They lived in a small town in Northern Ontario, where the only hospital was Catholic. Thus my mother couldn't get a tubal ligation and I don't know if they did vasectomies back then. I was the third child. There was an older sister and brother, and my arrival seemed to mark the beginning of a series of contraceptive failures. Soon I had a sister eleven months younger than me, followed by a twin brother and sister thirteen months after that. That was not the end. Another boy was born two years later; he had asthma, bronchitis and — just for good measure — projectile vomiting as well. Exhaustion may have taken over as a perverse form of natural birth control; there were no more babies after that. All of this may explain why, when I later became an historian, I chose to write about the birth control movement.

Like many families, particularly where resources were limited, my parents placed their hopes on the eldest son. Acknowledged as my parents' "favourite," my older brother was both resented and adored. He had musical talent, and despite the financial challenges entailed in raising seven children, my parents talked about sending him to university and, for the most part, managed to find the money for his piano lessons. He played beautifully — hearing his music fill the house was one of the happier memories from a somewhat chaotic childhood. Still, it was clear that my older brother was more important than I was, and that it was because he was male.

Growing up, my parents didn't show much interest in what I did, which in some ways was a blessing. They were preoccupied by the problems of my two younger siblings, especially my youngest brother, who had what we'd now call learning disabilities. The experts sent from the Toronto school board called it "dyslexia" but it perplexed my father, who tried so hard to teach his youngest son to read that his frustration often boiled over into screaming fits. This would send the whole household into a tailspin, my mother trying to wipe away the tears while the rest of us just hid. My sister, one of the twins, had worse problems reading and writing than my brother, but my father ignored her. I guess he was in keeping with prevailing views in his assumption that she wouldn't need an education as much as the boys would. Then again, perhaps he was just frustrated that the son who was named after him seemed to be such an idiot.

My family hardly ever read books and I don't remember reading much when I was young. As a high school student I thought that university was for rich people, and of course for my talented older brother. However, I did find a niche. I was acknowledged as the family rebel, who annoyed and sometimes amused people by asking variants of the question, "Why Not?" — although at that time the posters weren't out yet. Sometimes I tried to engage my father in debate on questions of the day, such as women police officers. He couldn't imagine that working. A well-meaning family man, he made an uncharacteristic dirty laugh when he suggested it would be improper for a man and woman to be on patrol together at night. Apparently it was okay in the day, though.

Increasingly unhappy, I left home a few weeks shy of my 18th birthday, without finishing grade 12. I guess I thought I'd get a job but didn't really have a plan. I worked for a year in Winnipeg, doing clerical work, and got really interested in feminism. It gave me a way to channel my growing anger at the injustice and waste of human talent that sexism created and endorsed. Or maybe I was just trying to find a better niche. I used to get into arguments with people, mostly men. One guy who worked in the warehouse at my workplace told me that ambitious women had too many male hormones and of course, a deficiency of female ones. Yeah, that was me!

In the meantime, my cherished elder brother died in a car accident. He had been groomed to study piano and my parents had been prepared to mortgage the house to pay for his studies. Shortly after his death, I moved to Calgary and worked as a secretary in an oil company. Spending some of the money that flowed in those boom years, the company sent all the secretaries to a "conference" associated with National Secretary's Day. But the joke was that we had to go on Saturday, presumably because the bosses couldn't manage a day without us. Heavens! They might have to make their own coffee, or look up a file themselves!

The irony was not lost on us. There was plenty of grumbling about giving up a Saturday for work. We all agreed that the guys would never consent to do this. There was a speaker who told the assembled multitude of Saturday scholars that the average IQ of secretaries was well above the national average. She assured us this was a good thing and that we were putting our superior intellect to good use in life and in business — or something to that effect. I took a different message from her talk. It occurred to me that all these above-average intelligent beings were being underutilized in pouring coffee and typing memos. Taking my cue from my beloved posters I asked: if these women were so smart, why not employ them in more challenging work?

Why not?

This was kind of an epiphany moment for me. It was at that point that I decided to finish my high school education in order to go to university. I'm certain I wouldn't have come to this decision without feminism — it was feminism that assured me I was indeed worthy. So, I enrolled in night school and started to discover a new me. Previously I had been satisfied with average grades, and although teachers had often told me I could do better, I never really understood what they meant. In my first term I took two courses, each two nights a week, working all day and attending classes four evenings a week, Monday to Thursday. I started with English and History and got marks in the 80s. It went so well that the following term I took two more, and added an additional course on Saturday mornings. I finished in eight months.

Going to university was a culture shock and an adventure all at the same time. Like all students, I discovered a new world of learning, including new friendships, amazing libraries and facilities, and new ideas among other things. But I also discovered that a working class, mediocre student from a small town could learn to read, write, think critically, understand the world, and even find a place in it doing something more challenging than typing. Feminism helped me to think past the working class culture that focused its limited resources on elder male children, and had nothing left for females. At university I discovered women's history, which gave me a real connection with the feminist movement and to academic analysis of the world around me. So much was happening in the field in those days, it was really exciting. I had pioneering professors — Marilyn Barber and Deborah Gorham at Carleton and later Ruth Roach Pierson at OISE. They were still fighting for the acceptance of women's history in the academic sphere, having to deal with male colleagues who laughed it off as a fad, and railed against the sudden incursion of noisy, demanding feminists into their quiet, academic domain.

No one in my family had gone to university. My mother thought I was crazy to give up what she considered "a good job" as a secretary. Nursing school she could have understood, but university! How would that get me a job? When I changed courses after my first year, my father thought I was mentally unstable. He didn't understand my strange passion for learning, for writing, or for researching. My siblings found some subtle and not-so-subtle ways to punish me for stepping outside their social domain. They made fun of the "women's libber," and worried aloud that I might think I was too good for them once I'd finished university. When I was going through my "poor student" phase, they especially relished ridiculing my diet of soup and Kraft dinner. Fortunately, new social networks opened up at the same time. The Women's Centre at Carleton, tucked away in a little corner on the 5th floor of the University Centre became my oasis. It was the place where I could go and vent about sexist students, professors, and debate everything from homophobia to women in the military. We debated whether feminists should decide everything by consensus or whether that was just being too nice. We went to protests and had potluck dinners.

By the time I went on to do my Master's and Ph.D. I was married and had children, eager to prove that women could do both, of course. There were times, trying to manage childcare along with writing a thesis, that I was truly afraid of never finishing. But the children proved wonderful distractions that often kept me sane, and "settling down" was something my family approved of. When I published my first article, they wanted a copy to show off to their neighbours and relatives. No doubt they ignored the feminist tone of the article, maybe they didn't even read it, but it was nice to see they'd injected some pride into their earlier dismay at my academic pretensions. Sadly, my parents died before my convocation — I think by then they would have liked to come.

Today I work in public history, where women's history is still not as readily accepted as it now is in academia. I write research reports and plaque texts for the Historic Sites and Monuments Board of Canada and Parks Canada. I feel I have justified the world's investment in educating this female, middle child of undistinguished origin, because my work helps to make ordinary women — who might not realize that women did important things in the past — feel some pride, a pride that might help them connect to their hidden talents.

> Buttons

Archives and Special Collections (CWMA), University of Ottawa /Artists unknown except for Sunday Harrison, "IWD, Women Say No to Racism, 1986, March 8th Coalition"

> Macarons

25 | TWICE BORN

Diane Driedger

I became a feminist twice. The first time it crept up on me in childhood. The second, it hit me over the head during a worsening of my disability, fibromyalgia.

In 1970, when I was ten years old, I noticed that things started to change in the house where I was growing up. My mother had just read Betty Friedan's *The Feminine Mystique,* and being a stay-at-home mom at that time, the book resonated with her experience. All at once, Mom divided up domestic tasks and my father, my brother, and I began to help around the house. We realized that Mom was not only there for our comfort, and she soon went back to the administrative work of her pre-child days.

My mother was an early champion for women's equality. So, although feminism was never a question for me, it was in grade 10 that my own position was solidified. It was 1975, International Women's Year. One girl friend handed out "Why NOT" buttons, while another discovered Ashley Montagu's book *The Natural Superiority of Women* and shared it with me. According to Montagu, women actually had more physical stamina than men — a new concept to us at the time. My English teacher self-identified as a feminist and some of the boys in class did not like this. Indeed, in her class we studied Margaret Laurence's *The Stone Angel* and *A Jest of God* within a feminist framework. This process provoked boys in the class to say things to my teacher like: "You only listen to what the girls have to say. You don't listen to us boys!" At the time, I thought, "Yeah, so what?" To me, the world was unfolding as it should.

Everything became political for me after high school. I had been studying the writings of the feminist and American civil rights movements, and I thought that I myself had missed the chance to be involved in all the major social movements for change. However, in 1980, I found the disability rights movement. As a non-disabled ally, I watched as women with disabilities began to assert their right to representation in Disabled Peoples' International, an international self-help organization spearheaded in 1981 primarily by men. Indeed, women pushed for representation in the organization and wanted the issues of women to be taken seriously. In Canada, in the mid-1980s women with disabilities formed the DisAbled Women's Network (DAWN) Canada. Many women felt that men in the disability movement were not taking their concerns seriously. Men tended to view issues around childcare and violence against women as "add-ons," not core issues.

During that same time, my own interpretation of feminism meant that I had to be better than men on the work front, and at that time, in order to achieve this goal, many women were trying to operate like men to advance in the work world. This did not work well for me. I found myself leaving behind many of my "feminine" creative pursuits and my emotional life, as I thought that these did not fit into a male world. I pushed my poetry and my visual art deep down inside, trying to focus only on the work at hand.

And then a catalyst arrived. My marriage ended and I experienced a workplace injury that would lead to an ongoing disability. During that period, I relied on work more than ever to feel valuable as a person. But when my work life was in jeopardy I came to realize that I had left part of myself behind. I reintroduced poetry and writing into my life, and started to reignite those "feminine" pursuits I had pushed aside for quite a while. At the same time, my workplace injury evolved into fibromyalgia, a kind of arthritis of the muscles. I think that this was formerly known as "rheumatism." As a result of the fibromyalgia, all of a sudden it was hard to be political in the ways that I had been before; it was hard to go out and participate in the disability movement, to participate in women's organizations that held endlessly long meetings that I no longer had the stamina to sit through. I wondered, what was wrong with me?

Some years later, in 1996, I was born a feminist again when my fibromyalgia worsened. The extremely cold winters of Winnipeg had taken their toll on my muscles — I experienced full body pain and fatigue. I spent evenings lying down in my apartment alone. I needed a place to "thaw out" my muscles, to regain health. I was still trying to do everything, and realized that I could not continue this overachieving lifestyle in the hopes of being like some "superman." This stance had cheated me. I came to realize that *all* people are equal and all have talents. There are not just one or two things that are valuable to life, such as workplace performance and academic grades. Many, many more things have value and meaning.

Indeed, I discovered this when I volunteered with the DisAbled Women's Network of Trinidad and Tobago for three winters. I had been working with this organization in my former job as International Development Officer for the Council of Canadians with Disabilities (CCD). During those three winters in the late 1990s, I taught a self-esteem and body image course for the women there. I realized, almost for the first time, that we all had talents in different areas, each woman had something to offer to the group. I too had something to offer, even if I could not work long hours tirelessly. Even a little bit was enough.

This realization continues today in my involvement with the DisAbled Women's Network (DAWN) Manitoba. At the 2008 Christmas party, one of our members was asking each woman, one at a time, if she needed a hug. Several others were organizing and warming up the potluck food, and another was organizing the gift draw — all talents, all needed in our group. Indeed, to me, my new definition of feminism recognizes that all persons are equal to one another, and that all talents and all lives are worthy and required in our society.

26 | COMMENT JE SUIS DEVENUE FÉMINISTE

Micheline Dumont

Les mamans restent à la maison; les papas travaillent au bureau. C'est ce que la vie m'a appris dans l'enfance. Mais parce que ma mère jugeait que l'école, c'était trop important, j'étais libre de toute tâche ménagère durant l'année scolaire. Toutefois, l'été venu, je suis initiée à toutes mes futures tâches en compagnie de mes six sœurs. Mais je ne joue pas à la poupée : je lis, je me déguise dans des pièces de théâtre, je fais du vélo, de la natation.

À l'adolescence, je découvre progressivement que filles et garçons suivent des chemins différents. Les garçons de mon âge qui poursuivent leur éducation au-delà de la petite école doivent fréquenter un collège classique où le programme dure huit années. Pour nous, les filles, c'est le pensionnat et le cours Lettres Sciences qui dure quatre années. Je suis jalouse ! Découvrant par la suite qu'il me serait possible de bifurquer vers le cours classique après mes quatre années, je me bute sur le refus de mon père. Je dois rester à la maison et il espère qu'une année sans l'influence des religieuses va avoir raison de mes ambitions intellectuelles. Plusieurs adultes de ma famille m'expliquent que le mieux pour une fille, c'est vraiment de devenir secrétaire, « car Churchill et Roosevelt ont épousé leur secrétaire. » Cet argument ne me convainc guère. Un journal étudiant s'intéresse à l'orientation professionnelle. Il n'y est question que des professions masculines. Cela m'enrage et j'écris une lettre de protestation au journal, sous un pseudonyme, car je crains de formuler mes idées en public. La lettre est publiée en première page du numéro suivant. Le texte est intitulé « Ta, ta, ta, ma fille ! » C'était en 1953.

Je lis et je vais au cinéma, enfin accessible depuis que j'ai 16 ans. J'ai droit à une petite allocation en échange des services ménagers que je rends à la maison. C'est trop peu pour mes désirs de cinéma, de livres, de disques. Je souhaite travailler durant la saison estivale. Nouvelle interdiction. Les sœurs de mon père, qui sont célibataires, n'ont pas le droit de travailler non plus. J'occupe alors mon temps en travaillant bénévolement pour la Jeunesse Étudiante Catholique, un mouvement de l'action catholique. J'y apprends beaucoup de choses : l'engagement social, l'habileté à parler en public, l'art de défendre ses idées, l'enthousiasme pour l'idée de changer le monde !

À cette époque lointaine, le moyen de transport favori des jeunes est le *hitch-hiking*. Les garçons peuvent en faire impunément, pas les filles. Pas étonnant que dans mon journal intime, je formule parfois le souhait impossible : « Que j'aimerais être un garçon ! »

Je me présente à un concours organisé par Les femmes universitaires (aujourd'hui : Femmes diplômées des universités) pour gagner une bourse qui me permettrait de faire mon cours classique. Je suis parmi les finalistes mais je ne gagne pas. Toutefois, les autorités d'un collège de filles écrivent à mon père pour l'informer que je pourrais obtenir une bourse du collège. L'interdiction est levée et j'entreprends le second cycle du cours classique en septembre 1953. Entre-temps, la situation financière de mon père s'est améliorée et j'obtiens par la suite facilement la permission de poursuivre mes études à l'université. J'ai ainsi ouvert la porte pour mes sœurs : elles sont toutes passées par l'université.

Je choisis la Faculté des Lettres. Me voici dans des classes avec des garçons. Ils m'intriguent. Mais je découvre rapidement que pour eux, je demeure « juste une fille. » Ils veulent bien discuter avec moi (quelques-uns me disent « mon vieux », oubliant alors que je suis une fille), mais pas question de sortir avec moi. Les garçons de ma classe cherchent des femmes sans aucune ambition intellectuelle.

Durant cette époque, je fais partie d'un groupe de lecture. Nous lisons *Le Deuxième sexe* de Simone de Beauvoir, et ce livre provoque chez moi un éblouissement. Pourtant je ne me sens pas le courage de renoncer au mariage et à la maternité, comme l'auteure. Sans fiancé comment faire ? Je trouve par la suite un poste de professeur d'histoire dans une école normale et je poursuis mes études universitaires. Je serai une femme de carrière !

À la surprise générale, je me marie en 1964. Pour l'époque, c'est tard, car j'ai 29 ans.

Au printemps de 1965, les femmes du Québec participent à un colloque organisé pour l'anniversaire du droit de vote. Moi, je n'en ai même pas connaissance. Je suis toute à la joie de donner naissance à ma première fille. Nous partons pour Paris : mon mari fait un doctorat en sociologie. La carrière universitaire, ce sera pour lui, moi j'y penserai lorsque mes enfants seront à l'école. Je ne remets nullement en question les modèles sociaux.

En 1966, les Québécoises sont mobilisées par la fondation de la Fédération des femmes du Québec, en 1967, par la Commission Bird. Je suis loin de ces événements : je suis en France !

Or, la Commission Bird me rattrape pour rédiger un texte sur « *L'histoire de la situation de la femme dans la province de Québec.* » Je suis plutôt mobilisée par la nouvelle orientation de ma vie : on m'a offert un poste à l'Université de Sherbrooke. Il y a déjà deux femmes dans mon département : n'est-ce pas un signe que la situation est réglée pour les femmes ? J'enseigne la didactique de l'histoire : c'est donc dans ce sens que je dirige mes lectures, mes recherches, mon enseignement.

Cependant, l'actualité m'interpelle. Je lis *La femme eunuque*, de Germaine Greer; *La politique du mâle*, de Kate Millett. J'entends vaguement parler de *Women's Lib* aux États-Unis, du MLF de Paris, des *Québécoises deboutte !* de Montréal. Je trouve toutes ces jeunes femmes un peu survoltées, mais en même temps, ma belle conviction que, pour les femmes, la situation est réglée, qu'il est possible de tout faire, commence à s'effriter dangereusement. La publication de mon étude pour la Commission Bird en 1971 me vaut plusieurs demandes de conférences et je découvre que l'histoire des femmes est mobilisatrice.

En 1975, avant de prendre l'autobus pour Sherbrooke, je passe dans une librairie et j'achète le nouveau best-seller, *Ainsi soit-elle !*, de Benoîte Groult. Je commence le livre au terminus et je le termine en arrivant à Sherbrooke. Je ferme le livre et… je suis devenue féministe. En deux heures, toutes mes lectures, toutes mes expériences prennent un nouveau sens : je comprends ce qui m'est arrivé, je vois le fil conducteur de ma vie. Dès l'année suivante, je commence à enseigner l'histoire des femmes, et depuis cette date, je n'ai pas encore épuisé les remises en question de l'épistémologie féministe. Oui, vraiment, je suis devenue consciemment féministe en deux heures, car quatre décennies d'altérité, pour reprendre le concept beauvoirien, avaient préparé le terrain.

27 | IT TOOK ME A LONG WHILE
Mary Eberts

I was seventeen years old when I realized that being female was connected to experiencing discrimination. The realization came as a palpable *Ms.* magazine type "click."

The September that I started grade nine, I went to the commencement exercises at my new high school. One of my neighbours, J.D., took many prizes; he had graduated the spring before, and that September had started studying architecture at the University of Toronto. J.D. and his older sister M. had played with me when I was very small, and it made me so proud to see him celebrated for his achievements.

One of the awards he won was of particular interest to me. The Paul Davis Award was given in recognition of achievement in both academics and athletics. J.D. had stood first in his graduating class, and had been the quarterback of the football team. He was a natural for the award. Seeing him receive the award, I decided that I too wanted that award when I graduated from high school, and from then on, set my course to earn it.

The academic part was relatively easy. I stood first or second in my year throughout high school, and in the important grade 13 year, managed to best my usual competitor for first place. The sports part, however, was very difficult. My only athletic activities before high school were non-competitive swimming, riding my bicycle, and the enforced playing of baseball every spring at my elementary school. Baseball was agonizing: we had to wear our jeans to school on the day of the games, and mine were always unfashionable, as well as way too revealing of my less than "ideal" figure.

Sports did not get easier for me in high school, but I participated in them with an application that I have not since matched. Achieving a first-place standing in an intramural sport earned one a "bar" to sew on the sleeve of a blazer; so did participation on an intercollegiate sports team. Earning enough bars in enough years produced an athletic letter. I managed to earn several bars in track and field, volleyball, badminton, and basketball, and against all expectations, achieved my athletic letter in grade 13.

All summer, I waited for the school to notify me that I had won the Paul Davis Award. Nothing came. Perhaps, I thought, they were going to surprise me with it. I went to the commencement exercises at my old high school in September of my first year in university, 1964. I was prepared to give my valedictory address, and proud that I had won many academic awards and scholarships, without which I could not have afforded to attend university. However, I still had no news about the Paul Davis Award.

Imagine my surprise upon opening the program for the

commencement exercises. There had indeed been a winner of the Paul Davis Award, but it was not my name under the title of this much anticipated prize. The winner of the Award had stood eleventh in our graduating class, and served as the "trainer" for the boys' intercollegiate basketball team (he was in charge of oranges, chocolate, towels, and water). Although not in top standing in academics or athletics, he did, however, satisfy that one all-important requirement: he was male.

The description of the Paul Davis Award given by the Principal at commencement made it clear that it was to honour a male student for outstanding academic and athletic achievement. These days, the Award is now open to both male and female graduates of my former high school, but I will always remember my commencement exercises, at which so many of my real accomplishments had been recognized, as the moment when I learned that being born male was an accomplishment in itself.

That was my first "click," but it was not my last.

Central as this experience was to my awareness of discrimination, it did not make me a feminist; in 1964, I had not even heard of feminism. Nor did I become a feminist during my undergraduate and legal education at the University of Western Ontario. Although, in law school, where I was one of six women in my class, the "clicks" were now occurring daily. Only years later, upon reading Constance Backhouse's work on the chilly climate at Western, did I realize that almost all of the legendary women professors at Western during my time there had themselves suffered pronounced discrimination. Though I knew most of them personally, and took comfort from their presence at the university, I was unaware of the backstory of discrimination: they did not make an issue of it, and neither did anyone else.

It was not until I was at graduate school at Harvard in 1971 and 1972 that I took my first steps as a feminist. There were so many women at the law school that we filled the whole of the student dining room at the introductory reception given for us; for the first time in four years as a law student, I did not feel like a freak of nature because I was a woman studying law. There was no doubt, however, that these women at Harvard Law were a transitional generation. My roommate, for example, had attended Yale as an undergraduate in the first year women had been admitted there.

While Harvard Law School was a welcome respite from the sense of isolation and exceptionality that I experienced in law before and after graduate school, it was my extracurricular experience at Harvard that played the major role in awakening me to feminism. It was there that I joined a consciousness-raising group of five women, which met weekly. We discussed Friedan, Greer, Firestone, de Beauvoir, Perkins Gilman, Mill and Taylor Mill, Wollstonecraft, and our own lives. I was the only Canadian (and only law student) in the group. We were all white, and all heterosexual; two of us were working class, the other three middle class. Not a boldly diverse gathering, to be sure, but each of us had experienced, or embraced, marginality in different ways. In those discussions, I became aware of myself as an agent, an actor, and not just as someone upon whom others acted. In those discussions I began the long and winding journey of trying to live a feminist life.

28 | DES MOTS À L'ÊTRE, DE L'ÊTRE À LA FEMME

Nathalie Fave

Combattre l'injustice et les inégalités. C'est le credo initial auquel j'ai adhéré inconsciemment et qui m'a projetée dans le monde des femmes. Je crois qu'il a pris ancrage en moi quand j'avais six ans, alors que je découvrais les formes géométriques et autres hiéroglyphes que j'apprenais laborieusement à tracer, petite fille, sur le banc d'une école française. Ces formes, des MOTS. Une étincelle s'alluma en moi. Je sus que de leur bon usage pouvait jaillir une infinité de mondes et de messages.

Plus tard, guidée par une insatiable soif de savoir et d'apprendre, je suis allée voir le monde. Avec mes livres. J'appris la lumière et la blessure de l'Afrique. Tahar Ben Jelloun, Frison Roche et Le Clézio. La richesse du patrimoine oral et le relief de la lumière. Kourouma.

Je partis à la découverte de Tombouctou en avalant les récits de voyage de René Caillé. J'appris l'aberrante réalité de l'apartheid et le courage de l'engagement. Merci André Brink. Je compris le choc des cultures et les enjeux de la colonisation grâce à Amadou Hampaté Ba; les combats contre l'esclavage, grâce à Schoelcher; le poids des traditions sur les épaules des femmes, merci Mariama Ba.

Je compris la nécessité du syndicalisme grâce à *Germinal*, de Zola, et la lutte des classes grâce à Stendhal et son roman *Le Rouge et le Noir*. Des mots de Gabriel García Márquez, *cent ans de solitude* s'ouvrirent à moi dans l'ampleur d'un relief historique sud-américain. La dépression qui ronge la vie, je la connus grâce à Hemingway. L'âme slave se révélait grâce à Tolstoï et Dostoïevski, la dictature par le biais de Neruda. Des anthropologues américains, comme Jared Diamond, j'appris l'évolution des sociétés. Les mots ont nourri ma révolte et développé mon sens de l'engagement.

Au Sénégal, j'ai longtemps peuplé ma vie de la Négritude parce que l'oppression du peuple noir me brûlait l'âme ; un documentaire, *Négritude,* en est ressorti. Selon Fanon, *on ne naît pas nègre, on le devient* ; Senghor disait sur cette lancée : c'est *le Blanc qui fait le Noir*, autrement dit, le racisme naît d'une différentiation entre les peuples en fonction de leur couleur.

La portée universelle de cette condescendance raciale à l'encontre des Noirs me questionna progressivement sur ma propre réalité de femme. Les mécanismes de l'oppression des Noirs me semblèrent similaires à ceux que les hommes employaient vis-à-vis des femmes.

J'ai longtemps été aveugle, parce que dans ma cellule familiale l'approche genre était proscrite. Nous étions une tribu d'enfants, considérés sur un pied d'égalité. Nous étions bel et bien soumis aux mêmes lois, frère, sœurs, père et mère. Mes tantes avaient des métiers. Ma mère, femme au foyer, avait autant de poids dans la gestion du portefeuille familial que mon père. Aveugle, et par conséquent démunie d'instruments de combat, je tombai au cours de ma vingtaine dans le chaudron de la violence et de l'oppression comme un chaton perdu et effrayé.

C'est le trajet de ma trentaine, qui s'exprima au travers de la Négritude et du combat pour une civilisation de l'Universel respectueuse de sa diversité, qui aboutit en fin de compte à mon plongeon dans le monde des femmes, entamant un lent processus de compréhension féministe. Oppression des Noirs, oppression des femmes. Je ne fis que changer mon fusil d'épaule, mais dans les deux cas, il était clair que j'avais cessé de tirer des balles à blanc… Mon combat initial reprenait sens, je devais lutter contre l'injustice, coûte que coûte. Il m'avait donc fallu près de dix années pour comprendre les racines de l'iniquité tout en armant mon cœur et mon esprit aux défis qui m'attendaient. Je repris de plus belle le chemin de ma plume. Pour panser mes plaies grâce à l'envol dans des mondes parallèles, la poésie fut un remède efficace. Et pour témoigner et hurler, essayer de réveiller le monde et peser du poids de ma rébellion têtue, la prose, les chroniques, les romans, nouvelles, essais ou conférences feraient l'affaire.

Le Canada m'appelait. Une fois encore, mon combat commença par une autre guérilla. Celle de la francophonie en milieu minoritaire. De là, je participai au dialogue franco-métis et partis à la découverte de l'histoire autochtone dans les Prairies, en Saskatchewan et au Manitoba. Je revins naturellement dans le giron des femmes, offrant des services de conseillère, puis me vis confier la direction d'un organisme de revendication politique en péril, soumis aux coupures budgétaires en vogue dès lors que les instances fédérales canadiennes avaient décidé d'engager un bras de fer avec le discours féministe.

Nombreuses sont les jeunes femmes qui aujourd'hui embrassent un discours selon lequel les femmes auraient remporté tous les combats, acquis une pleine reconnaissance de leur rôle, une parfaite équité dans leurs droits. Cependant, même dans la plupart des pays occidentaux, les femmes, à niveau de qualification égal, continuent de gagner un tiers de moins de ce que gagnent les hommes. Au Canada, il est aisé de constater que les choix politiques des dernières années pénalisent fortement les femmes, en particulier quand on voit que le déficit effarant de places de garderie les obligent souvent à renoncer à une carrière… donc à l'autonomie, à la liberté de choix.

Je finis par atterrir à Toronto dans un organisme offrant des services aux femmes francophones. Là, je fus happée par une autre dimension, par d'autres enjeux. Dans une communauté francophone multiculturelle, j'arrivai, encore imprégnée par mes dix-huit ans d'Afrique, porteuse de mon approche universaliste. Je débarquai dans un organisme qui reflétait cette diversité, pour mon plus grand bonheur initial. Enfin, pensais-je, allais-je pouvoir affirmer une approche concertée d'universalisme et de genre. Je voyais avec confiance se côtoyer parmi la vingtaine d'employées du centre des citoyennes du monde, issues de tous les continents, de tous les pays de la francophonie. J'abordais ce travail sans préjugés de race, de couleur, ni de tendances sexuelles. Mais je dus constater que mon discours ne pouvait être compris ni intégré d'emblée dans cet environnement pesant, que je devais montrer patte blanche en fin de compte. Je m'étonnai d'entendre parler des communautés ethnoculturelles. Par ces termes édulcorés, je compris que l'on refusait d'aborder les défis frontalement. De même, la catégorisation suspecte des arrivants séparait, par les mots et les concepts, les immigrants des réfugiés, comme si ces derniers n'appartenaient pas à la première définition... Était-ce une façon de diviser pour mieux régner, pour mieux catégoriser les arrivants en strates subtiles ?

Dans ce contexte de discrimination, le discours féministe semblait parfois secondaire. En partant du général au particulier, il s'agissait d'abord de prendre en compte le cadre traditionnel de la communauté francophone en milieu minoritaire, incluant le poids de l'oppression langagière, le déni de la spécificité culturelle d'un peuple fondateur possédant une religion différente de celle de la majorité ; la seconde strate consistait à cerner la dynamique de la confrontation culturelle entre les immigrants d'ailleurs, confrontés à une communauté traditionnelle : comment cette francophonie éparse pouvait-elle interagir au contact des Canadiens-français qui avaient adopté des stratégies de défense et de survie propres à leurs enjeux ? Comment ce peuple pouvait-il avoir conscience de l'importance de l'afflux de francophones d'ailleurs pour renforcer le maintien de sa langue ? Parmi ces problématiques, la dimension de genre arrivait comme un troisième facteur, et les traumatismes des femmes s'additionnaient aux deux premiers facteurs de fragilisation. Il apparut que le féminisme devait être repensé en intégrant les enjeux des femmes issues d'autres cultures... et que celles-ci avaient seules le pouvoir de redonner un nouveau souffle à une cause qui mobilisait peu la relève canadienne.

La compréhension de ces paramètres m'a permis de prendre du recul. Il n'en demeure pas moins que, au-delà des sources de tension jaillissant de ce contexte en mutation, j'ai l'immense bonheur de diriger une structure qui offre des services souvent vitaux aux femmes francophones et que cette mission me donne des ailes.

Quant à moi-même, je continue également mon chemin sur et par les mots, tentant de conquérir l'essence de l'humain au travers de moi-même et de semer mot après mot ma touche de femme, militante et rebelle au-delà des terres abordées.

29 | YES, WE CAN
Louise Henrietta Barton Forsyth

Growing up in Saskatchewan — born in Regina, with much time spent with my pioneering grandparents north of Swift Current — gave me the advantage of being surrounded by strong women who set their own objectives and never hesitated in their determination to achieve them. This was their precious gift to me — a gift of vision, energy, love, and ethical integrity — that has been the driving force carrying me on the exhilarating paths of my life. My mother's wonderful name, Marvel Alpha, continues to symbolize this gift for me. Following their example, I have aspired to live a life of radical commitment to fairness and respect for all women as well as others who have been, and continue to be, disadvantaged and victimized by misogyny, racism, homophobia and too many other manifestations of discriminatory social values, practices, and discourse.

My childhood during World War II was not marked by family loss due to the devastation of war. Yet awareness of this devastation and its impact on our living circumstances was always present in our lives. A particularly important aspect of what the war meant in my life was the gathering around me of a group of mothers — including my own mother and three of her sisters — with their children. All their husbands were away in the armed forces. My aunts cared for me and my cousins, while my mother, like Rosie the Riveter, worked in a munitions factory (she repeatedly expressed her pleasure at learning, after the war, that not a single bomb from that factory had been exported to the killing fields). There was something very special about exploring my childhood in the company of strong, loving women; that something special has remained with me over the course of my life.

Despite what is said about the fifties as an age of flaccid conformity, it was a decade of exciting growth and discovery for me. Looking back on those years, I am overwhelmingly aware of the important role that committed and risk-taking teachers had in my life: the doors of knowledge they opened for me and the unconditional permission they gave me to explore my ideas, body, feelings, tastes, relations, in the many contexts of the world I was discovering around me. It was in high school and then in university that I learned that all taboos can be challenged and should, at the very least, be critically examined. Resistance to received ideas and adoption of oppositional stances proved to be exhilarating. As a result, I was ready for the counter-cultures, protests against the war in Vietnam, hippie movement, and opposition to racism that burst onto the scene in the sixties. I soaked it all up.

At the same time, I must have been quite conflicted. I saw myself as a free spirit floating on the exciting wavelengths of these powerful new movements while I was simultaneously living in the suburbs of London, Ontario, with a husband and four children — the epitome of conformism!

While I never doubted my love for the children, I had to face the fact that I was having terrible nightmares where I was hurling the children off stormy mountain-tops into endless space. Inner voices were telling me that I was in danger of abusing them, that I had to change something to nurture my spirit. The traditional norms of motherhood were proving dangerous to me and my children. So I returned to university to complete an M.A. (1963) and Ph.D. (1966) in French Studies. This entailed myriad strategies and innumerable sleepless nights at a time when daycare and student loans were still unknown.

My graduate research was on seventeenth century writer of comic theatre, Molière, thanks to whom I learned to value humour, view men's blatant abuse of power with a scornful and critical eye, and love the theatre for its power to show the darkly comic underbelly of human folly.

The shift that transformed me into a radical feminist occurred in the mid-1970s, when several things came together to raise my consciousness. I was co-author of a report on the status of women at the University of Western Ontario. Since our mandate was to report on the status of all women (including faculty, limited term instructors, students, support staff, and so forth) we took full advantage of the opportunity to interview and solicit input widely. The personal stories shared with us proved traumatic for me as they revealed the abuse, exploitation, inequities, and humiliation suffered by women. Particularly painful were the accounts received in women's washrooms offered by women who had recently immigrated to Canada (these women were afraid of retaliation in the form of union discipline or loss of employment if they attended the meetings we organized or put anything in writing).

An important spinoff of the preparation of the status of women report at Western was the almost immediate formation of new friendships with women. We revised curriculum and created programs, organized events, addressed specific issues, and demanded change. We read all the exciting books and articles that were being published and we created a women's caucus. A group of us formed a militant, fun-loving book club, the Hags and Crones, that still exists today. We boldly addressed the chilly climate, and we did not hesitate to be outrageous.

At the same time that I became fully aware of the sexist practices of the university where I was employed and the society in which I lived — where I was increasingly feeling like a member of a dynamic community of engaged women — I shifted the area of my teaching and research specialization to Québec literature and culture, particularly Québec women's writing. During the Quiet Revolution in Québec, in the 1960s the long-simmering but quite passive anger of Francophones against Anglo domination radically transformed into an irresistible, proactive force. Rather than waiting for the anglophone majority of Canada to do the right and equitable thing, a young generation of Québécoises and Québécois emerged determined to take their destiny into their own hands. Their slogan was *On est capable*, which I would translate as "Yes we can." Their medium was the French language, particularly as it flourished in songs, poems, plays, movies, novels, comics and speeches at rallies.

While Québec women artists rarely espoused nationalism and

certainly never spoke out in favour of violence, they captured the highly charged energy that pervaded Québec society in the sixties, seventies, and eighties. The constantly renewed and incredibly bold innovation they displayed was inspiring to me. Yes indeed, I felt then, and have never since stopped feeling, as a woman, feminist, citizen of Canada and specialist in Québec writing in the feminine: *on est capable!*

My career as a feminist and scholar continues to be rich and rewarding. My exhilarating paths have taken me to places where I have been a teacher, researcher, graduate student supervisor, department head, dean of graduate studies and research, president of the Canadian Association for Theatre Research, and president of the Canadian Federation for the Humanities and Social Sciences. In all of these places, I have worked with many others to try to meet the demands of the position while not compromising my feminist convictions nor my ongoing commitment to justice and equity. It has not always been easy to accomplish this juggling act in universities, still very much repositories of the master's powerful tools, his discourse and ideas. Still, I remain convinced that writing and education offer some of the most powerful tools available to give witness, communicate news of struggles to new generations, organize for change, and move a little closer to fairness for all.

30 | FLASH YOUR FEMINIST BLOOMERS
Barbara M. Freeman

It was on one of those lazy, warm summer afternoons, relatively rare in St. John's, Newfoundland, when my mother handed me a copy of Betty Friedan's *The Feminine Mystique*. I took to it immediately, perhaps because Friedan was one of the few voices that challenged the postwar idea that all women needed to do to be happy was to marry a nice guy and become suburban wives and mothers. At age 16 or so, I was no longer included in baseball games with the boy buddies of my childhood, but wasn't all that keen on courting any more romantic intentions, either. I did not want to have a boyfriend, get married, and have babies. I expected, and so did my mother, that I would become a career woman instead, a choice that was just beginning to become a respected alternative for college-bound young women my age. Anyway, what was one more book to devour for a dedicated bookworm like me?

Friedan's book certainly engaged my mother, a full-time homemaker who subscribed to *Chatelaine*, watched *Take 30* on CBC television, read newsmagazines and nonfiction, and was therefore quite aware of current events and the latest trends, including the liberal feminism of the sixties. Reading widely was also her way of engaging intellectually with my businessman father when he came home from work, which was as important to her as wearing lipstick, dressing well, and never letting him see her in hair curlers (one of her cardinal rules). Few of her attempts to encourage me to become more interested in my own appearance had taken any effect. I hated dresses, I hated lipstick, I wanted my freedom — and I got intense crushes on girls. But I couldn't talk about that to anyone.

Years later, my mother told me that it had occurred to her, when I was about 12, that I might be gay, a frightening insight for any parent at the time. "I suppose I knew then, but I didn't want to think about it," she told me, when I finally came out as a lesbian to her and my father when I was 30. All during my childhood and teenage years, my poor parents were torn between encouraging me to become more feminine, thereby keeping me socially safe, and giving me a certain amount of measured freedom, so as not to squelch my adventuresome spirit altogether. My father veered between amused affection and exasperation, not sure whether to take me go-karting or tell me to put on a dress. He did both, in fact, but mercifully not at that same time. Bringing me up was always an uneasy balance, especially given our background. Our family was considered "upper middle class," and we were Roman Catholic, which amounted to a double-bind in terms of social and moral expectations of my behaviour. Once, a nun witnessed me vaulting athletically over the railings in the church parking lot, flashing the navy blue bloomers under my school uniform. "Mrs. Freeman, how unladylike and immodest is that!" she complained to my mother over the phone.

To be fair to the nuns, some were fine teachers who encouraged us to do well in school, although it seemed that every lesson, from English to math, was laced with pious admonitions about proper Catholic behaviour. I had no sense of being sinful because of my attraction to girls, however. I was so innocent I did not imagine doing anything with a girl beyond kissing her. Only during my teenage years in a Catholic boarding school in Montreal was I painfully made to understand that "special friendships" with other girls were to be discouraged if you did not want to risk losing your sanity. When, at 17, I took up tennis, dating guys who shared my passion for the sport seemed like a workable compromise for all concerned, including me, who was by then frightened "straight."

At age 20, I entered journalism school at Carleton University in Ottawa. I successfully persuaded the managing editor at the *St. John's Evening Telegram* to assign me to general news, rather than the women's page, for my summer internship. To my surprise, he agreed and I became one of the few women in general news in Canada. Female journalists and broadcasters struggled for acceptance then. Many of the men resented us, although we had our supporters, too. During my subsequent career in Ottawa, at the CBC and in private radio, I regularly bent the ears of a few, sympathetic male colleagues, hating the fact that so many others dismissively called women in the business "bitches," "broads," or "chicks," sexually harassed us, or allowed others to do it, or simply refused to assign us to interesting news stories.

As a radio reporter, I did make it to City Hall, and also served as an on-air news reader, but there were still few women regularly assigned to Parliament Hill. One of the most inspiring women I met at the time was Marion Dewar, then Mayor of Ottawa and a strong feminist and social justice advocate, who believed that women could accomplish anything. I looked up to the journalist and broadcaster June Callwood, who also did not hide her politics when she wrote or was on the air. I was always a left-leaning liberal journalist, never a socialist or radical feminist, although I was sympathetic to some of their arguments. As it was, I was having trouble reconciling my own brand of feminist politics and my journalism, and in the end I compromised on the question of "objectivity." I would not join a feminist organization while I was working as a reporter, because that would be a conflict of interest, but I would certainly make sure to actively cover women's issues as best I could. That would be my contribution to the cause.

Feminism, with its goal of strengthening women, also gave me the courage to finally be myself in my personal life. In 1971, I had married a broadcast journalist whom I met in England, despite the fact that I had secretly continued to be strongly attracted to women, a tendency I tried to dismiss in my own head as inconsequential to my "real" life. Four years later, I fell intensely in love with a straight woman who could not reciprocate my feelings, leading me to realize that I needed to explore my gay side with women who loved other women. I did so by attending the weekly lesbian drop-in evenings at the local Women's Centre, occasions that usually led to secret excursions to a well-hidden gay bar. After an agonizing summer for me and my husband, I came out as a lesbian and left my marriage, although at that point, I was not openly gay to anyone beyond close friends and family because I did not want to risk my job. At the time, gays and lesbians had very little in the way of legal protection from discrimination, and former spouses, especially husbands, tended to be most unforgiving, which added to the risks of exposure. To give him his due, my husband never threatened me that way and eventually came to terms with my lesbianism. We became friends again before his untimely death a few years later.

For a number of years afterwards, my personal life continued to be a struggle. And again, it was feminist influences that most helped me. The tension of not being out as a lesbian contributed to an equally closeted alcohol dependency that, in 1986, I managed to overcome with the help of Amethyst, a women's addiction recovery agency in Ottawa. My Amethyst counselors, who were strong feminists, believed that substance abuse affected women differently than it did men, and treated us accordingly. My time there not only strengthened me in every way, it led to opportunities to put my feminism to good use as a volunteer.

At that point in my career, I had already spent a few years teaching radio journalism at Carleton University, my feminist consciousness in tow and my lesbian identity still under wraps. One of my first self-assigned projects was to completely rewrite the school's radio news manual, using more inclusive language and providing anti-sexism guidelines. Aside from a few colleagues, my main supporters then were the feminist professors and classmates I met as I studied part-time for a Master's degree in Canadian Studies, and later a Ph.D. in History. There were other colleagues who were suspicious of my politics, however, and I suffered professionally to some degree. For example, I was first hired as an instructor on contract for several years, and despite all my hard work, I was initially refused a promotion to assistant professor with tenure because, I learned, I did not have enough support on the male-dominated committee. I appealed to our fair-minded dean, and she overturned that decision.

My academic career progressed without too many glitches after that. In 1994, I was able, despite lingering opposition in some quarters, to introduce a new course to the Carleton curriculum, a seminar now called, "Gender, Diversity and the Journalist," in which I challenged my students to think carefully about those hot-button issues when they cover them in the news. I have also published articles and books with a focus on history, women, and journalism.

While I never did discuss my personal life in class — that's not the place for it — I gradually stopped hiding who I was. It helped that over time, we won stronger legal protection as gays and lesbians, and the faculty and students became far more open-minded than they used to be. For instance, one of my grad students warmly offered congratulations after I explained to her, when she asked, that the recent photo on my office shelf was of me and my female partner of over 25 years, taken on our wedding day.

Our wedding ceremony was performed by a good friend, a retired Unitarian minister, whose very liberal and open congregation has since welcomed me as a member. It is a humanist, non-denominational church, chock-full of feminists and progressive men devoted to social justice, with a stated commitment to making gay, lesbian, bisexual, and transgender people feel welcome and appreciated. As I write this article, I am helping to organize the annual Pride church service, which, needless to say, will be a far cry from the patriarchal Sunday Masses of my childhood.

I have been really fortunate to live my life during a time when transition and self-definition for women, including lesbians, have been possible — although not universal, certainly not perfect, and not attained without a great deal of struggle. I have been able to accomplish a lot because of feminism, and it remains important that younger women today continue to flash their feminist bloomers.

31 | MOTHER PASSED IT ON

Veronica P. Fynn

It all started with one woman: my Mama. Maybe this is my mother's story as much as it is mine. Whether it is hers, mine, or our shared story, here it is with gratitude, appreciation, and honour.

I was born in Liberia in the 1970s. As I remember it, Liberia was a peaceful, care-free country. This Americanized colony wanted to be like America. It shows in our flag, our capital city (Monrovia, named after James Monroe), and our politics. In fact, it was only recently, in January of 2009, that I found out that there was a Whig Party in America. Until then, I had only known it as the ruling party in Liberia. It did not surprise me that for over a century Liberia existed as a one-party state, governed by what was known as the True Whig Party, mimicking the US in full swing. The True Whig Party — led by "freed" black slaves who had resettled in Liberia —subjugated and oppressed the natives of Liberia even though they had also endured similar hardships through slavery in America. How convenient!

As young children, my mother would gather us around and say: "Mama loves you very much, but she wants you to be very good children. For as long as you are under my roof and I am feeding you, I am in control here. Otherwise, you will have to leave my house, because I do not have men and women under my roof, only children."

Amongst my siblings, I had always been the toughest of kids. At the age of thirteen, after I first met my biological father, I remember asking my mother: "Mama why do you have to take care of us all alone? Why isn't papa helping you?" She did not answer. Life was difficult as Mama was our major source of support for many years. So much so that Mama could not afford fifty cents for transportation to school on a daily basis.

From first grade to tenth grade Mama was the center of my life. Daddy (my stepdad who had looked after me since I was about three years old) was also quite instrumental in my development, and my subsequent interest in mathematics and science. But later he would repeat the exact same mistake my biological father made: leaving my mother for another woman. This left my mother with a total of eight children to fend for. Many days I watched Mama get up at 2 a.m., with me and my two older brothers, to make pastries, sandwiches, and confections to take to school and sell. Mama claimed that I was considered the lucky one. "Patience is the lucky one. She always sells everything given to her and even returns home with the correct change," my mother would snap at my brothers who did otherwise. Of course, I did not like to sell. For me, sales from Mondays through Fridays meant I would not play with my friends during recess. And on Saturdays, when most kids met to play on the field or in the park, I could not, because I had to sell everything before I could play. This is not to say that I did not have a happy childhood. In fact most of my formative years were spent in Bardnersville Estate and those were the best days of my childhood.

Through these times, one thing I came to appreciate of my mother was her ability to raise all eight of her children equally. I remember my mother making schedules every month for house chores. It was rotational, including cooking, sweeping and cleaning the house, and washing dishes and clothes. To her, we were all equal, and it was very important that we learned to do everything so that no one would say, "Your mummy didn't train you well." In fact, my mother embarrassed me on many occasions when my friends were around. She would say, "Patience does not know how to cook, her brothers cook much better than her." She was not lying. I simply preferred going to school more, and on most occasions I got away with it because my mother would support us if, and only if, what we wanted to do was linked to our education. So, rather than staying in the kitchen to cook, I would ask for permission to go to school with my friends to work on an assignment or something of the sort.

As if poverty and the absence of a father in our lives were not enough hardship, Liberia's bloody civil war erupted in 1989. Mama became sick and my brothers went missing, leaving me to manage my family between 1990 and 1992. I suddenly realized that there was no man in our family apart from my two younger brothers who were between 6 and 9 years old. My three younger sisters all looked up to me to find food and up-keep the family. I will not go into details here because these were very painful and difficult times, but one thing always kept me going, the hope and trust that Mama had embedded in us all from a very young age that hard work does pay off. She always said: "The education I never got, you will get it. If I have to eat rocks and sand to make sure all of you acquire education, I will." She put even more emphasis on me as her first daughter, "Patience, do not end up like me. I want you to take your education very seriously so that you can one day have your own house, car and live a life free of my suffering."

I listened to Mama. In fact I listened so well that when she saw me in 2005 after we had been separated for over thirteen years, she could not say anything but cry. She realized that her labour had not been in vain. Seeing her child so educated (I am currently in law school, working on my fifth university degree), never having married, having no children, and physically well, she knew she had done her job, and an excellent one too.

By now, it must be clear why I have told my story in this way. It has not been one single factor that has led me to feminism, but many factors over the course of my life. The absence of my father, being raised without any emphasis on gendered roles, seeing Mama struggle so much all by herself to make sure we had food and education, the war in Liberia, and my life as a refugee without my family for over nine years, have all influenced my view of myself as a woman.

In Ghana, where I lived as a refugee from 1992 to 2001, I endured so much trauma; in fact, those were the worst years of my life. My determination to fight for the cause of women, especially refugee women, started to sharpen during these traumatic periods. No doubt my childhood was very challenging, but at least I had my family around me. Living as a refugee all by myself, and becoming a single immigrant to Canada were the two major turning points in my life that heightened my level of feminism.

Barely one month after I had acquired my third academic degree, I found myself in Geneva, Switzerland, as a young Canadian professional working with the International Organization for Migration. My motivation to go to law school and continue my cause for forcibly displaced women and children in Africa started on that trip to Geneva. When I visited the UN Palais and realized that ninety per cent of all UN representatives were men, it saddened me. I constantly questioned why refugees and displaced women and children — making up seventy-five per cent of the world's refugee population — were not being represented. Why are refugee and displaced women not given equal opportunities with the UNHCR? I think it is time that a woman with a refugee experience becomes the High Commissioner for UNHCR.

I know that my mission has just started.

32 | LIFTING WEIGHTS

Carolyn Gammon

Totally unprepared for feminism, I was born in 1959 in Fredericton, New Brunswick. I was a jock: Female Athlete of the Year at Fredericton High, and varsity athlete in field hockey and basketball at the University of New Brunswick (UNB). In a country-wide fitness contest, with events that included running up the CN tower, and pulling a car, I was declared "Canada's Fittest Female." The next year, while attending Université Laval, I was "discovered" in the weight room. "That weight you're lifting," said my soon-to-be coach, "is a Canadian record." In 1983 in Birmingham, England, my sports career culminated when I came 4th in the world in women's power lifting.

I had no need for feminism. I was strong — stronger than most men! I was a high achiever academically and athletically. If women did not achieve, I figured, it was because they did not pull themselves up by the boot straps (jock straps?). In these pre-conscious days I had a feminist friend in Fredericton; I thought she was weird. I couldn't understand why she would protest a Lady Godiva ride: an annual event sponsored by the UNB Engineers where a naked woman posed on the hood of a car and was driven through campus. What was there to protest? A harmless prank. I did not understand.

It was my lesbianism that eventually led me to consider feminism. All through sports I had been surrounded by wonderful, exciting women, who were both leaders and care-takers. I would defend to the last breath that they were NOT lesbians. Most of them were. Despite a fairly liberal upbringing, I had imbibed the idea that lesbians were abnormal, strange…and somehow dangerous. But, I loved women.

Today I can trace my feelings back to early childhood. I had crushes on my coaches and co-athletes. I never dated a boy. One sports trip as I lay on a school bus rumbling through the New Brunswick countryside after a game at night, a boy was thrown on top of me and we were forced to kiss. In retrospect, I realize they had thrown the gay basketball star on top of the lesbian one in a ritual of compulsory heterosexuality. Later I would force myself through hetero-sex numerous times in an attempt to be "normal."

Although I was surrounded by lesbians, no one felt they could speak to me openly.

I finally found my own way, far far away from New Brunswick and the prying eyes of my hometown. After the world championships in power lifting in England, I worked and travelled in Europe for a year. When I first slept with a woman, the dam broke. I cried for weeks. Every part of my body, newly touched, set off a wave of shame. My lover kept asking, "Are you sure?" "Is this what you want?" Bawling, I assured her it was. One night I had a flashback to a black and white film clip: the silhouette of a lesbian hanging. As a young girl my mother had sat me down in front of a film with Audrey Hepburn and Shirley MacLaine about two women running a girls' boarding school; they are accused of being lesbians. Although they have no relationship, when one of the women faces her true feelings for her colleague, she hangs herself. The film was called *The Children's Hour.* I guess my mother thought it was a TV hour for children.

For the next three years of my life I lived with a woman. We kissed inside the entrance of our house before leaving, knowing we would not be showing affection in public.

Although it was lesbianism that drew me to consider feminism, it was not sex with a woman, but activism, that brought me out of this pre-feminist limbo. Accompanying my old feminist friend from Fredericton days, I started going to Ontario Coalition for Abortion Clinics (OCAC) meetings. I sat through exciting but confusing meetings with acronyms flying around my head. These sometimes strident, sometimes gentle, powerful women (like Judy Rebick or Carolyn Egan) inspired me. We set up human chains around the Morgentaler clinic so women entering would not be physically harassed. We plastered the city with posters. I interviewed older women about backstreet abortions in a project to document that terrible past. I wasn't quite sure what lesbians had to do with abortions but I loved the energy of the women at OCAC.

Then, I was horizontally recruited by a Trotskyist at one of the meetings—my first big love. I joined the Young Socialists and learned about the oppression of women from a Marxist perspective. We met young members of the still forbidden African National Congress. The International Women's Day marches were a highlight—to be out on the street proclaiming one's affiliation with women and, yes, finally, feminists. As a child I had rushed to the next door neighbour's to see the Santa Claus Parade in Toronto on TV (she had colour), and now here I was in my own parade, celebrating women!

Along with activism came women's culture. The poems of Adrienne Rich, the "Twenty-one Love Poems," and her vital analysis of compulsory heterosexuality; finally I had words and concepts to understand my battle with self-hatred. The overpowering music of Rita MacNeil and Ferron; we danced to "Rise Up" and "Free Nelson Mandela." I was learning how women's rights, gay and lesbian rights, and Black rights, go hand-in-hand. Audre Lorde's "The Master's Tools Will Never Dismantle the Master's House" was a vital lesson we all tried to live by. And by the time I left Toronto for Montreal in 1986, I had come out with a vengeance.

Although I signed up for an M.A. in Creative Writing, I really did Lesbian Studies. I instigated the Lesbian Studies Coalition of Concordia. When we were dismayed to learn that our Women's Studies courses at the Simone de Beauvoir Institute were not

> Rally, Convocation Hall, University of Toronto, International Women's Day, 1987

Archives and Special Collections (CWMA), University of Ottawa (PC-X10-1-1200)/ Johanne Pelletier

> Rassemblement, Convocation Hall, Université de Toronto, Journée internationale des femmes, 1987

necessarily attending to lesbian content or lesbian students, we lobbied for the integration of lesbian content. We invited speakers who reflected the diversity of our group. To address our own "isms" we held workshops on unlearning racism and anti-Semitism. These were heady times and slowly but surely that shame and self-doubt that encased me began to peel off like the skins of an onion. I wrote and performed my own poetry, came out big with my first book: *Lesbians Ignited*. I embraced feminism with a bear hug and never let go.

I have lived in Berlin, Germany, since 1992. My main work is with Holocaust survivors and my most recent book, *Twice Persecuted*, is the story of a survivor. I live in a legal partnership with Katharina Oguntoye—one of the founders of the Afro-German movement. Together we run Unlearning Racism workshops across the country. We have been together 18 years and our beautiful son, Noel, is ten. My feminism was hard-earned. I wish I could say I had an "aha!" epiphany, but in truth, it was a process of decades. It seems every step of my life from Fredericton to Berlin was paved for me by feminism. It prepared me for the work I now do, and for my life-partnership. And I am still lifting weights, feminist weights I like to think, because being and becoming a feminist is a life-long workout!

33 | A LONG PROCESS
Joan Gilroy

How did I become a feminist? It was a long process nurtured through reading critical texts alongside my involvement in both university and community-based feminist groups during exciting times: the so-called second wave of the women's movement.

In the 1950s, I obtained an undergraduate degree in liberal arts at Dalhousie University and a graduate degree in social work at the Maritime School of Social Work (later part of Dalhousie University).

My early practice of social work sensitized me to differences of many kinds, but it was feminism that helped me to make connections among difference, inequality, and injustice. There was no eureka moment in my becoming a feminist, only a gradual accumulation of reflections on my experience. The colleagues and students in social work that I met over many years, in Canada and other countries, inspired me to continue on my journey toward feminist goals.

In common with most of the women in my class, I came into social work to "help people" but I had a rather vague and limited notion of who needed what kind of help. At the time, social work operated primarily on a charity model: seeing problems as arising from individual or family inadequacy or misfortune — rather than being rooted in systemic inequalities. People experiencing problems were believed to warrant at least temporary help, under specific conditions. Feminism helped me to see that social inequalities were neither inherent nor natural. Further, feminism taught me that social workers had a part in reproducing and maintaining oppressions and that we could instead promote equality and justice.

In the early 1960s I joined the faculty of the Maritime School of Social Work (still not yet part of Dalhousie University) as a field instructor and student advisor. Toward the end of my first year, I vividly remember personally experiencing discrimination. The Director told me that two men and one woman were being hired, and that the men, because they were married and had children, would be paid more than the woman was being offered, and more than I was earning — even though the Director recognized that our qualifications and experience were roughly the same. This was common practice at the time. (It was assumed that women would marry, leave their careers or make them secondary to family responsibilities.) At the same time, I learned that my new male colleagues would teach academic courses, while the women would supervise students in required field practice in social service agencies. Since I was at least as qualified to teach as the men, I was disappointed. My women colleagues and I talked among ourselves about the differences in salary and work assignments, but we more or less accepted them as normal.

In the early 1970s, I took a graduate degree in criminology at the University of Toronto and wrote my thesis on problems faced by women being released from prison. In this program I read critical sociological texts, including feminist critiques of the treatment of women in conflict with the law. Finally, my readings and experiences connected. Difference often meant inequality, something that was not natural but rather social, created by people in specific relations of power. I do not remember if I called myself a feminist when I began this degree, or even when I finished a year later, but regardless of the label I knew I would make women's issues the focus of my work.

My teaching greatly shaped my feminism. In International Women's Year (1975) I attended a conference of the Canadian Research Institute for the Advancement of Women. I came away from this conference inspired to mobilize female colleagues. I invited all the women at our school, including students, to come together and talk about feminism and how we could use it in our program. I also circulated any articles I could find about women's issues and feminist perspectives in social work, and we began to introduce feminist content in courses.

Across Canada, my colleagues and I were pioneers in feminist social work. In the 1976–1977 academic year, we formed a women's group at our school that included all female employees, faculty, administrative and secretarial staff, research officers, and the librarian. We called ourselves a women's group because we wanted to be inclusive. Some colleagues worried that the terms "feminist" and "caucus" might scare some women away. We strove to incorporate feminism into the curriculum, and alter some aspects of our working conditions, guided in our work by ideas of collectivity and caring practices drawn both from social work as well as our new-found feminism.

During the same year, twelve graduate students organized a student women's caucus. They invited Helen Levine from the Carleton School of Social Work, the leading radical school in Canada at that time, to meet with women students and faculty in our school. Helen amazed me with her feminist critique of professional practice in mental health, and by sharing her experience as a mental health consumer, a definite no-no in helping professions at that time. Helen Levine became my feminist social work mentor, colleague, and dear friend. Later we invited her and Rosemary Brown, a

Black social worker, politician, and feminist activist, to the school as visiting faculty. The faculty/staff women's group and the student women's caucuses in my own school were essential in developing a feminist core in our curriculum, and were a source of support and stimulation for me.

Encouraged by our own experience, the work at Carleton, and Gillian Walker's Status of Women Report for the Canadian Association of Schools of Social Work, the Maritime School's Women's Group organized a national women's caucus in social work at the 1977 meetings of the Learned Societies. We wanted to share information and experiences as women working and studying in Canadian schools of social work, support each other in adding feminist perspectives to curricula, and change the marginal position of women in the national academic and accrediting body. To facilitate communication, we began a newsletter. We were able to keep this caucus active for over twenty years, despite minimal resources.

Volunteer work also shaped my feminism. For example, from 1975–1980, I chaired a feminist community-based organization working with women in conflict with the law. We not only worked with individuals directly but tried to involve them in social change activities directed toward improving their living conditions at home and in prisons; increasing opportunities for education, training, and jobs; finding accessible child care; and help for addictions and mental health issues. We tried to apply feminist principles in our work and learned how difficult it was to implement ideals such as equal pay for work of equal value — which meant paying the bookkeeper, case workers, and director at the same rate — because federal, provincial, and other funding sources insisted on differential pay.

Several other events in my life helped shape my feminism. In 1980, I went to the Ontario Institute for Studies in Education (OISE) to do graduate work in sociology in education and women's studies. At OISE I was privileged to be one of a wonderful group of graduate students studying with feminist scholars such as Dorothy Smith, Mary O'Brien, Margrit Eichler, Ruth Roach Pierson, and Alison Prentice. I was exposed to theories of oppression based on class, gender, race and sexual orientation. The ideas were mind boggling! At the same time we were educated and exhilarated by feminist musicians, poets and artists of all types, lectures from feminist scholars from many countries, and by participating in marches for social justice. I went to OISE as a feminist and left strengthened and enriched in my feminist knowledge and values.

In 1990, I became the Director of Dalhousie's Maritime School of Social Work — the first female Director since the School's founding in 1941. I found it more difficult to work as a feminist administrator faced with complex and challenging issues and realities such as decreasing resources, increasing regulation, and centralization of decision making. I took an early retirement in 1998. I continue my association with the university as an adjunct professor, at present exploring the history of feminism in social work education and how feminism and social work education have evolved.

Reflecting on this history, I can say with certainty that feminism has enormously enriched my life and work. I am proud to be a feminist, proud of our accomplishments in planting feminist values and theoretical perspectives in social work education, and thereby challenging traditional academic and professional notions of learning and practice in our field. Inherent in all of this work was the belief that feminism in its diverse forms could transform the world, that it could create more radical social work education and practice, that is, social work committed to equity, social justice, and community.

34 | HEMLINES WERE ALREADY TOO SHORT

Charlotte Gray

In London, England, in the mid-1970s, the women's movement had made little headway in the circles in which I moved. This was partly because we weren't very interested in politics, but also because it was hard to spread the idea of sisterhood in British society, where to this day social class is a bigger divide than gender. The feminist magazine *Spare Rib* first appeared in 1972, but it was too earnest for me. Angry polemics by radical feminists would be followed in the next issue by acrimonious rejoinders from socialist feminists. I preferred to read, in public, *The New Statesman*, and in private, *Tatler* or *Vogue*.

I was working at the *Daily Express* at the time, where one of my jobs was to select readers' letters for publication. Most of the letters came from elderly colonels in the Home Counties, complaining about slipping standards. Food, manners, pronunciation, service... everything was slipping, according to these *Express* readers. The only exceptions were women's hemlines. They were already too short.

As time went on, the inequities in my workplace began to irritate me. Most of the women journalists were confined to the Women's Page, sat in an open plan area, and fetched coffee. Men had offices with doors which opened only when the coffee had arrived. I started reading Fleet Street's best women columnists, such as Katherine Whitehorn in *The Observer*, who challenged her readers' assumptions in such witty, graceful prose that nobody felt threatened. Attitudes began to change — even amongst *Express* readers. My favourite correspondent became a woman who always began her letters: "I'm no bra-burner but..." I found myself adopting this formula when making my own increasingly subversive comments. It was the classic British humour trick — use irony to protect yourself from looking like a ranter. That way, you say what you want to say at the same time as you distance yourself from the statement.

Fast forward to my emigration to Canada in 1979. It was like shifting from first gear to overdrive, because I arrived in a country where second wave feminism had already had an impact. Thanks to the Royal Commission on the Status of Women, governments had been grappling for nearly a decade with issues like violence against women, the wage gap, and the lack of women in senior ranks of the public service. A Liberal government was in power: it was accepted wisdom that women should play a larger role in public life, and be appropriately rewarded for it. *Chatelaine*, the most popular women's magazine in the country, encouraged women to get involved in campaigns for pay equity, adequate childcare, and more women MPs. I recall the first dinner parties I attended in Ottawa, where words like "misogyny" and "patriarchy" were flung around. Women and men who were out of step with this powerful social movement retreated to the sidelines. Wimpy little starters like, "I'm no bra burner but…" were lost in the fierce deluge of certainty.

At one level, I was completely comfortable with this. Why not? These campaigns could only improve all women's lives.

But at another level, I was more ambivalent. While certainty does result in a clear focus, it also generates intolerance. I remember one woman newspaper columnist, at a dinner organized by a feminist organization, insisting that women who stayed home to raise their children would have only themselves to blame when they discovered they had inadequate pensions. A few activists voiced such rage about institutionalized sexism that they appeared to have no sense of history, or comprehension of the way societies evolve and change. It wasn't just male dinosaurs who had closed minds. Polemicists and demagogues can create social change, but they can also get right up some listeners' noses. I frequently found myself grabbing a Kleenex, and thinking wistfully about the "I'm no bra-burner but…" days.

And then, in 1989, twenty-five-year-old Marc Lépine walked into the École Polytechnique in Montreal, armed with a semi-automatic rifle. After shouting that he hated feminists, he murdered fourteen young women and injured ten more. In a suicide note, he blamed feminists for ruining his life.

For about a week after this horrendous event, I resisted the idea that the massacre was more than an isolated act of a madman. After all, there have been random acts of violence within schools, coffee shops, and city streets as long as there have been guns. Lépine was a seriously screwed-up young man who had been abused as a child and then abandoned by his father. To label the massacre as a symbol of male violence against women looked like exploitation of the grief of the victims' families. It also seemed to put the blame for Lépine's actions on all men, including those who were as eager for social change as feminists. Just as I had found the idea of "sisterhood" difficult back in England, so I now found blaming a homogeneous "patriarchy" equally exasperating.

But after a week, I began to rethink my resistance. The issue of violence against women was bigger than Lépine, but he had drawn the lesson from the culture around him that such violence was, if not permissible, accepted. Yes, he was seriously disturbed, but he got his ideas from somewhere. Suddenly, "I'm no bra-burner but…" began to smack less of irony to me than of denial. Perhaps the extremists among feminist leaders were short on common humanity, but on the other side of the argument, Lépine reflected a murderous male anger. He did not represent all men, just as the angry feminist leaders did not reflect all women. But his actions did have a wider implication than his own psychosis. These implications are visible year after year, in stories like that of Robert Pickton, the Vancouver pig farmer convicted of killing six women and probably guilty of the deaths of far more; or the murder of young Muslim women by their fathers and brothers, if they step out of line with Sharia law; or the predicament of teenage girls in Bountiful, BC, who are forced into polygamous marriages with their community's leaders. These are the extremes of misogyny, but misogynist assumptions still ripple through our society and contribute to some women being treated as second class citizens. In 1989, I accepted that, if I was truly committed to gender equality, I had to wear the label "feminist" with true conviction.

35 | I WAS A SLOW LEARNER
Shari Graydon

My turning point as a feminist was like the slow but inevitable veering off the straight path — a misguided bowling ball heading into the gutter. The direction of my life definitely changed as a result of missing all the pins, but I figure the view of the bowling alley from the gutter is actually more interesting: you're not travelling so fast, you get to look around along the way, and you can see more clearly the futility of smacking into a set of phallic objects that are immediately set up again by some invisible and relentless automatic force.

The telling moments began early and accelerated as I grew older, but I was a slow learner. During my teens and twenties, I worked my way through blind ignorance, initial outrage, and resigned acceptance; by 30, I was ripe for conversion. And it was then that

I was projected irretrievably down the alley of feminist activism. Twenty years later, my mother is still shaking her head, trying to reconcile her image of her sweet-tempered fun-loving daughter with the stereotypes she bought of shrill bra-burning man-haters. Which is ironic, as she was the one who started me on the trajectory of no return.

I was 13 when she went on strike. Not because she belonged to a union. In fact, she was a self-employed businesswoman who brought home about as much bacon as my dad. The trouble was she cooked most of it, too — and cleaned up afterwards.

The walkout occurred on a Saturday morning. She calmly announced that she would not be doing any laundry, housework, or meal preparation for several days. Nor would she be available to answer questions pertaining to any of said activities. My two older sisters, my younger brother, and my father and I would simply have to figure things out for ourselves.

I wish I could say that the incident inspired me to make like June Cleaver and haul the vacuum cleaner out of the closet on a weekly basis, unasked. Instead, my mother's small act of rebellion instilled in me an early antipathy toward the prospect of one day having to divide my own waking hours between a full-time job *and* washing other people's dirty socks. And yet, what I experienced as a smack-upside-the-head was completely forgotten by my two older sisters. They both grew up to take their husbands' names and give birth to beautiful children while bringing home bacon and washing socks. So it's quite possible that I came into the world pre-programmed with a feminist gene, just waiting to be triggered.

My grade 10 art teacher, Miss Reid, deserves some credit. For our seasonal craft assignment, she distributed blocks of wood and carving tools to the boys, and cardboard cones, styrofoam balls, and spray paint to the girls. Those blessed with a Y chromosome were invited to chip away at their block to reveal whatever their twisted imaginations could conceive. In contrast, we double-Xers were required to fashion near identical "angels" by gluing the balls on top of the cones and spraying them with paint.

Having successfully completed a similar assignment in grade 2, I was much more interested in the infinite possibilities residing in the block of wood. But good girl that I was, I fulfilled the angel assignment before risking the future of my untutored fingers by hacking away at a small plank I rescued from the reject pile. Incensed at my insubordination, Miss Reid would not even look at — let alone mark — the wood carving so enduring that it's survived dozens of move-inspired purges to remain hanging on my office door to this day. Incensed myself, I abandoned my allegiance to visual art and switched my elective to theatre the following year.

Waiting tables during university proved an effective means of funding my education and collecting propositions from soused middle-aged men, but I was stunned to discover that some restaurant jobs were closed to me by virtue of my gender. In the late 1970s, the ritziest eating establishments — while they may have hired women at lunchtime — reserved the more lucrative evening hours for male servers. (I believe this was due to the voice of authority that naturally issues forth from men's throats when they're asked what kind of wine one should consider pairing with the puréed livers of force-fed geese.)

During this period, my ultra-competent mother, a registered nurse who'd abandoned bed pans and thermometers to build a successful career representing high-end furniture companies, got put out to pasture at the age of 50. In the face of her stellar sales record and the universal respect of her clients, some myopic manager 2,000 miles away decided that a guy 20 years her junior with a family to support could do better. When he drove the business she'd built up into the ground in less than two years, she had a moment of bittersweet vindication, but it still sucked.

Meanwhile, back at the University of British Columbia's theatre department, I was collecting the kind of disappointments that help prepare you for the real world: mine centred around the joys of competing for one of the two or fewer female walk-on parts typically included in most classic and contemporary plays peopled largely by complex and compelling male characters. As an energetic student who reliably showed up at rehearsals, my three years there gave me the opportunity to play a pushy landlady, a put-upon maid, an obedient pupil (who gets raped), the girl next door (also raped), and a rich bitch. During the same period, my male peers played kings and criminals, patriarchs and professors, writers and revolutionaries.

Because this was apparently not discouraging enough, during

my last semester, my acting professor, Charlie, took it upon himself to inform me that despite the A's I'd consistently earned, I'd likely never make it in the business. "Frankly," he told me, "you don't have the commercial look." Few 21-year-olds appreciate being informed that they're not pretty enough to flog dishwashing soap, but I was too stung to protest that even Cinderella features two ugly sisters and an evil stepmother, so surely I'd have options.

I graduated with a Bachelor of Arts in 1980. As I began my search for career-potential employment, my father recommended I take a typing course and work my way up. This was not advice he would ever have given my brother under similar circumstances, but it reflected his perspective on how women got ahead in business. When I entered the corporate world in 1985, the stakes got higher but the attitudes did not. A year after I joined an international public relations firm at an entry-level position with a salary to match, I experienced a little sisterhood from one of the secretaries. She informed me that the agency's newest hire — a man who couldn't write a news release to save his life — was being paid $8,000 a year more than me. She also confided that he'd cleverly found an opportunity to reveal to her that he didn't wear underwear.

When he was fired twelve months later for incompetence, if not regrettable hygiene and incipient harassment, I was rewarded with a nominal salary increase and a fancier title. Perhaps it was this minor triumph that emboldened me.

The agency's head office in Toronto had a contract to promote powdered coffee. I was assigned the task of generating earned media from radio stations in western Canada. My Toronto colleagues' strategy had been to hire a young model, dress her up in small strips of stretchy fabric, and send her out to chat up DJs with a tray of parasol-decorated glasses of instant coffee and ice cream. The bikini babe approach had apparently been a big hit in central Canada, but I indulged my nascent feminist sympathies by informing my colleagues that the west was more enlightened, and such sexism wouldn't fly. Miraculously, they believed me.

I commissioned the creation of the "World's Largest Coffee Bean in Bermuda Shorts," a massive papier mâché affair equipped with outsized sunglasses and Hawaiian print boxers. The talented improv artist I hired to wear the thing managed to get on-air mention of the client's product in dozens of radio stations. As subversive acts go, it wasn't exactly worthy of a chapter in the annals of the Second Wave, but I felt the kind of triumph normally reserved for toppling the state.

And then, significantly, after winning a professional award for my work managing the multi-dimensional PR needs of a growing forest company, I was forbidden to participate in the competitive business pitch to a mining company. This, my boss assured me, was not because he doubted my ability to do the job, but because he was certain that the prospective client would be unable to see past my small frame and curly blonde hair.

I was startled to discover my unnatural attachment to exercising my flak and shill skills on behalf of miners. But the time I'd spent hanging around sawmills in northern British Columbia was to blame. Hosting special events in lumber yards and interviewing men felling trees had allowed me to trade my panty-hose and pumps for cotton pants and rubber-soled boots.

The boots represented a no-going-back revelation. They connected me to the planet in a remarkably liberating way. I could easily run five blocks or level a well-aimed kick at a would-be-attacker if I had to. I felt like Wonder Woman – better, in fact, because my clothes kept me warm and comfortable, whereas hers made her look like a cheerleader on steroids.

So I kicked off my heels and became self-employed. And a year into my freelance career, I discovered that even charging half the rate the agency had billed for my time, I could still earn twice as much as they'd paid me, so I went back to school part-time. And a pivotal event happened while I was auditing a first-year course on the social dimensions of advertising. Although a more perceptive person who'd spent three years in the world of image manipulation might already have woken up to the impact of sexist portrayals in advertising on women's real life experiences, I was still in denial.

Enter Suzanne Strutt, then executive director of MediaWatch. She arrived at the lecture theatre with a sheaf of print ads she'd torn out of some magazine. She more than compensated for the low-tech nature of her display with the scorching condemnation of her analysis. The light bulbs exploded in my head, and when she was done, I rushed to the front of the room.

Within a year I had become the BC representative to Media Watch's National Committee, and nine months after that, I was elected president — confirming the fact that there are no glass ceilings in under-funded, non-profit women's groups relying on volunteer labour.

Two decades later, my identification as a feminist remains a core aspect of how I see myself. And if, as recent research suggests, it's helped me to have a more satisfying marriage and better sex, that's more than enough compensation for the occasional hate mail or personal attack suffered along the way.

36 | THE POLITICS OF HOUSEWORK

Lorraine Greaves

My emergence as a feminist came early. It concerned the most important, universal, economically vital, but often dreary, of life's activities: housework. I was seven, and my parents were into assigning their children "chores." One day, I was instructed to "wash the dishes," and my brother was instructed to "take the garbage out." I simply asked "why were the jobs assigned that way?" and unknowingly ignited a discussion with my family that persists to this day. Who does what, and why, to support the business of living? And further, is it fair?

The answer I received was decidedly unsatisfactory to my seven-year-old mind, setting off a lifelong search (and career choices and moves) for answers to the fundamentals of role assignments, gender, tradition, relationships, economics, culture and health. It is fair to say my life's work has wound itself around these questions, whether teaching, doing research, advocating for change, starting women's organizations, or making health policy. It has led to a life of questioning practices of sexism, discrimination, and violence, unravelling the economics of women's labour, the politics of housework, the health costs of roles, and the ongoing pressures of societal expectations on women, across the globe. I somehow felt that the personal was the political from the outset.

Selma James was among the first group of overtly feminist authors I read, or at least recognized as such. I was in England for a long stay after graduating from university. She had released a publication entitled *Power of Women and the Subversion of the Community* (authored with Mariarosa Dalla Costa) that launched the "wages for housework" campaign, leading to arguments that caring work and women's work should be economically valued and counted. Her material and related writings were part of the British feminist second wave. It sat alongside other authors, such as Betty Friedan and Germaine Greer, who, from very different standpoints, were also trying to unravel the problem of domesticity, women, and social control. The project of women's liberation was full on.

The personal aspect of this debate within my family was crystallizing in my relationship with my mother. My father simply saw my ongoing questions as evidence of intelligence that ought to be encouraged, but he, perhaps, had less to lose. My mother, however, was a grateful participant in 1950s domesticity, embracing the rules completely. This was undoubtedly a welcome change after spending her teen years making munitions in a Northern England factory, living on rations, and pinning hopes of a better future on, not only war's end, but a wartime marriage and aspirations of peace and prosperity.

Moving to Canada embodied that change, and occurred with the 1950s in full swing. Women who were mothers did not work (!) and were very clearly supporters to male ambition, male career development and, nominally at least, fully in charge of the home front. In my family's case, the home front was peaceful and prosperous, but years later, the second wave (re)learned and republicized the issues of power sharing, domestic violence, economic dependence, and mental and physical health costs that were simmering below the surface. These were temporarily unnamed problems, hidden for a while from public view, while post-war economic and cultural rebalancing took place.

There had been other phases of articulating women's lot in European societies and our second wave was in a proud line of such movements. Each country has a story, but within and across it there are themes of similarity. Who were the politicians, the people behind the monuments, the "leaders"? Who were the professionals, the authorities, the favoured ones? Men and boys, and more specifically, particular groups of men and boys who were also privileged by class, lineage, and history.

As a sociologist, the more important question for me became, "who got to define what was real, or important, or remembered?" This is perhaps the most important question of the second wave. But back to Mom. It became clear that if I was right about feminism, then she was wrong about accepting being a 1950s domesticated woman. She felt that axiom, and so did I. How to resolve that one? What was consciousness and how were we to share it? Was I matronizing her?

She wanted to understand me, but my early and crude grasps of emergent ideas, and my unrelenting questioning of assumptions often spurred painful reflection or defence on her part. I hated my role in this, but saw no other route. We were engaged in this dynamic for a long time. Secretly, though, I decided that the best thing to do was to make her proud, by taking my own path, and somehow proving myself.

It was years later, on the occasion of publishing my first book (with a decidedly feminist message) that we clicked. She held a fresh copy of it in her hands one spring day on the deck at the cottage, and simply said "I can't believe my daughter did this, and I am so proud." In that moment, I could see our conflict for what it was — a tableau against which I could play out my evolution as a feminist. She had provided the opposition to my ideas, the yin to my yang, the contrasting choices to mine, the resistance to my aggression, the critique to my politics, the other side, so continuously and personally, that she made me who I am.

She died a year later, prematurely, but we were at peace.

At the same time, my search for a proper feminist education in post-secondary institutions was fruitless. I got an education, but not the one I wanted. I was an undergraduate student in a sociology department in the late 1960s with only two women professors out of 35 (and they were on limited term contracts). The most influential professors were American men who had dodged the draft, so I ended up knowing a lot about Black Pride, racism, and the civil rights movement, but nothing about women. And absolutely nothing about Black women.

I entered (or should I say, tried to enter) the teaching profession but realized that the tiny group of men in my Education degree cohort were already handpicked as successors by the (entirely) male principals in the schools where we were practice teaching. We women were going to be line workers, no matter how ambitious, or smart, or strong. One day, during a stint of practice teaching in a classroom, I was shocked to hear the male principal's voice come out of the public address system (he had been surreptitiously listening in to my lesson). In that instant I realized I could not teach in such a paternalistic, male run system, especially when most of the workforce was female. It felt utterly objectifying, almost like science fiction — a world that was weird and controlled by disembodied male voices. As a woman, I would be forever ignored, controlled, condescended to, and unrecognized. I went back to school.

As a graduate student I ended up having to choose between social work and sociology, having been accepted to both in the same week. I realized the former would give me a job, but it felt too limiting. I had questions that needed answering in a broader way. So I re-entered the Sociology Department, with two women out of 35 professors. However, half the graduate students were women. Even though it was now the mid-1970s, there was no real way to cut through the male dominance of the department, despite the fact that feminist ideas and texts were pressing in from the outside. After I graduated with a Master's degree, I went to teach in post-secondary, thinking that this would give me more respect and freedom. It did, to an extent. Ideas were freer flowing, and I could design my own curriculum, but ultimately I left the system because of my own ambitions. Again, the administrators were mostly men, and upward mobility or leadership roles for women were few and far between. I tried to ascend numerous times, or to construct leadership roles or new projects, but felt tolerated, sometimes indulged, but never rewarded.

I realized none too soon that my real education was going to be elsewhere. It would consist of a different reading list, and would be in a different setting. I co-founded a wonderful feminist reading group, called the Hags and Crones, which is now over 30 years old.

I remember the first meeting, 15 women gathering to talk about a pivotal book, and to explore argument, debate, and ourselves. Finally, I had a setting, a reading list, a debating club, a touchstone, lifelong friends, and access to ideas and materials that would, quite simply, change my life. We read everything from Kate Millett to Dorothy Dinnerstein to Betty Friedan, to Virginia Woolf to Adrienne Rich to Starhawk to Diana Russell to Gloria Steinem, and on and on.

We started by reading Mary Daly's epic, *Gyn/Ecology: The Metaethics of Radical Feminism*, and we had to read it in six instalments as it was so profoundly dense. I can say that in 425 pages, Mary Daly changed my life. Her most important contribution was to link various atrocities against women, and the systems behind them, from across the globe and over time. She linked suttee, genital mutilation, gynecological practices, myth-making, witch burning, and foot binding in a riveting tome that left no culture out. She defined, for me, the pervasiveness and global nature of women's oppression, but gave hints about the strength of female friendship, and reminded us of a history of female intellect, resistance, and strength. She suggested sparking and spinning, and counselled continued movement.

She also had a comment on mother–daughter dynamics: "Radical feminism means that mothers do *not* demand Self-sacrifice of daughters, and that daughters do not demand this of their mothers." This helped to frame my own life, my time with my mother, my own journey. As I write this, a tiny column in the *Globe and Mail* informs me that Mary Daly, theologian, has just died, aged 81. She was remembered solely as the feminist professor who barred men from her classroom at the Jesuit-run Boston College.

Why is it still so hard to get a feminist education?

37 | I FELL INTO EVERY TRAP

Shirley Greenberg

How did I become a feminist? Did the fact that, while growing up, I fell into every trap laid for women have anything to do with it? Maybe. (One major trap: expecting one's life to be complete with the addition of a man (husband)). The fact that I read Simone de Beauvoir in the '50s (*The Second Sex*) and Betty Friedan in the '70s (*The Feminine Mystique*) and both really resonated, also had something to do with it. Then along came the newspaper reports of various doings of feminists in the United States and in Toronto. Feminists like Gloria Steinem, Ti-Grace Atkinson, Bella Abzug and other Americans were well publicized internationally, and I felt they were speaking directly to me.

In Ottawa, the first public stirrings were led by NDP women who were primarily of the WAFFLE section. I attended a few of their meetings, but the group did not stay together very long. Their major concerns at the time were day care and abortion rights. In fact, they established a referral service in the late '60s to help provide information to women seeking an abortion (unavailable in Ontario at the time). Not long after the WAFFLE women stopped meeting, a few women began gathering together on Monday nights at the Quaker Meeting Hall on Fourth Avenue. I'm not sure who initiated the first meeting, but Alma Norman was among them. I attended the third meeting and hardly missed one from then on.

Around the same time that this was happening in Ottawa, some of the women in Toronto who had been involved with the Report of the Royal Commission on the Status of Women, formed a group intended to maintain pressure on the federal government to implement the recommendations of the Report. This new group was known as the National Action Committee on the Status of Women. Some of the women from Ottawa joined in. Amidst all of the growing action and enthusiasm, the Women's Liberation Meetings soon transferred from the Quaker Meeting Hall, which was now too small, to a building off Lewis Street in Ottawa Centre. At each of these Monday night meetings we would take up one issue to discuss, and we would pick a different issue each week.

Who came to these meetings? As word spread, more and more women came, all of whom had some strong link to the issues we were concerned with. Each brought energy and ideas. I was happy to be in the thick of all this. Every meeting was exciting and energizing. Each meeting was really a giant consciousness-raising event. Small consciousness-raising groups were formed from the beginning: we each had things to learn, sometimes such things as how to stand on our own two feet! We were teaching each other.

A favourite slogan at the time was, "The personal is the political."

Over time new issues surfaced and decisions had to be made regarding what actions needed to be taken. It was here that the decisions were made to form a Rape Crisis Centre, a Women's Career Counselling Service, and a house of refuge for abused women and children. And it was following a discussion of the legal status of women that I decided to apply to law school.

My timing was very fortunate. During my second year at law school, in 1974, the women of Windsor Law School held the first major conference to discuss women's issues. A few of us gathered together to form the National Association of Women and the Law, with a caucus of this group at each law school. The law school at the University of Ottawa, which I was then attending, became a leader in feminist activity for the next few years. We held meetings, some of them open to the public, to discuss issues; we disseminated information; and we obtained government grants to fund students while they researched and wrote articles on the state of the law and how it affected women. We formed a speakers' bureau and addressed many organizations in our local area.

At the time, reform of family law was a major issue in every province, and especially Ontario. We examined the draft amendments to the law and made our own critique. We arranged for a member of the caucus to attend meetings of the Legislative Committee at Queen's Park, in Toronto, to address the issues. We passed the hat to raise the necessary money for bus fare to send our colleague to Toronto! (We really worked on pennies in those days.) We lobbied whatever government was sponsoring legislative change affecting women, federal and provincial.

Eventually I graduated from law school and opened my own law practice in Ottawa, with associate Catherine Aitken. Catherine was new to Ottawa but had become known as a feminist, so it was a natural thing to link up with her. When it came to opening my law practice, I had very fortunate timing once again. The first major reform of family law was implemented on June 1, 1978, and that is when the doors to my practice opened. Through our careful examination of the law during its formulation and passage through the legislature, and as a result of our lobbying, I felt very familiar with it and not that handicapped by being new to law practice.

Catherine and I both practiced family law and soon became well known in the community. When I began practicing law there were only ten women lawyers out of a thousand in private practice in Ottawa, and only a few of these practiced family law. So Catherine and I were very much in demand from the beginning. However, the number of women practicing doubled every year, and there is certainly no shortage any more.

I remained in practice for a very challenging fifteen years. I left during a recession when lawyers were finding it hard to find work if they were newly called to the Bar, or seeking articling positions. Many women were in practice, there was no shortage, the laws had been quite satisfactorily improved for family matters, and I felt my services were not really needed, so I retired.

The world has certainly changed for the better for women, although much still needs to be done. Now I try to help by contributing funds to those organizations trying to make a difference. I am happy to be identified as a feminist and very pleased to have been part of the movement that has improved conditions of life for all women in Canada.

> Women's Protest Tea Party, Rideau Club, Ottawa, 1972

Duncan Cameron/Library and Archives Canada/PA-211369

> Tea Party de protestation des femmes, Rideau Club, Ottawa, 1972

38 | SPACE TO FIT A FOUR-LEGGED WOMAN

Nancy E. Hansen

Where to start? That's a difficult question really. I am now in my fifties, and no matter how it is framed, rights issues have always been a fundamental part of my life. Growing up in Ottawa, at an early age my parents underscored the importance of equality for my brothers and me, involving us in discussions about poor housing conditions in First Nations' communities, and the need for change. I remember sitting in my high school political studies course in the mid-1970s and quietly questioning the South African Ambassador's explanation of his country's racial segregation policies when he spoke to our class.

I have always had a mobility disability, using crutches to move around. I have always been proud of who I am: a person (a woman) with a disability. It was an attitude reinforced by a strong network of family and friends. Over the years I kept wishing that society in general would grow-up with regard to their attitudes about disability, and start to see potential, instead of deficit, just as my friends and family had done. Strangers seemed to be amazed that I enjoyed living my life doing everyday things. Why was it so different or interesting that I would want to participate fully in daily life?

I finished high school and went on to university, and in December 1980 I started work as a clerk with the federal government. It was there that one of my co-workers said, "It's your year next year."

1981 was the United Nations International Year of Disabled Persons. It was an exciting time, a pivotal period in my life. Finally, disability issues were on the map. There was official recognition that people with disabilities existed; our concerns were discussed and debated in the public domain. Recognition of disability issues on an international scale provided the stimulus for federal and provincial governments to (finally) develop and implement substantive legislative changes to building codes and employment and transportation policies, all facilitating access for people with disabilities. With these legislative advances came the passage of the *Canadian Charter of Rights and Freedoms* — and the *Charter* was the first constitutional document to formally recognize the rights of disabled people.

At this point I came to see the law as a means to getting significant social change for all women. I attended a fundraiser for the Women's Legal Education and Action Fund (LEAF), and it was there that feminism came to the fore for me. The LEAF philosophy seemed to be a good fit; it still does. I have been a regular LEAF supporter from the beginning. In my experience, LEAF was the first mainstream women's organization that tried to practice inclusiveness. I felt welcome there, and I really enjoyed attending the various fundraising events and meeting other women who truly supported equity issues.

I demonstrated on Parliament Hill, supporting a woman's right to choose, really choose, what happens to her body. As a woman with a disability the right to choose was, and still is, doubly important. Disabled women were often not perceived as *women,* let alone sexual beings, or mothers. To this day, it is still the only large-scale demonstration that I have ever participated in, as large crowds do not work well for four-legged women. The jostling and compact space involved in demonstrations require a level of heightened awareness to maintain one's balance while standing on crutches and avoiding being toppled over.

Returning to study at Carleton University in the late 1980s was a difficult period for me. At that time Women's Studies courses did not include content about women with disabilities. They were remote and theoretical. Disability was nowhere to be found. However, in the midst of this turmoil I did meet some great women — a dear friend, and some great professors.

A real turning point for me came while taking a women's health policy course with Monique Bégin. Other professors had talked about having space, but this was the first time it really existed for me. Professor Bégin talked about the everyday activities of women, in real terms, not dogma. In such a truly inclusive place, I felt it was okay to be close to the subject matter. Prior to this course, I had not believed it was possible to discuss subject matter that cut close to the bone in an academic setting. But there was space for everyone in that class. It was the first time I found a space that really "fit" me. It felt natural, I was not the "other," I did not feel like an outsider consigned to the margins.

It was like a dam bursting. For the first time, I spoke and wrote about disabled women's issues. My knowledge and experience had value and I could articulate my pride in being a disabled woman. It was a watershed that changed my life and I have not looked back. I have gone on to find a rewarding career in the academy. A place that fits.

39 | COMPETENT WOMEN IN AIR-RAIDS
Jean D. Hewitt

I was one of those young women who grew up blithely assuming that women's liberation was a fait accompli. Hadn't we achieved the vote and the chance at myriad career choices, thanks to the likes of Emmeline Pankhurst and Susan B. Anthony? My early years provided no experiences to challenge this view. As a child born in an air-raid shelter during WWII, my world was full of competent women: they drove ambulances, went off to factories, and kept things ticking over. Many were larger than life, like my Aunt Vi, in her WAF uniform, smoking cigarettes and tackling anything a man might do.

Of course, there were men around during this time, but they were the older ones who worked as fire wardens and policemen. Our fathers existed only in the conversations of mothers and aunts. When the war was over, many did not return. Others, mine being one of them, came back, could not adjust to family life, and left. I did not meet my father again until I was in my thirties.

My rather innocent view of where women stood in society remained intact as I headed off on a scholarship to a prestigious girls' grammar school at the age of ten. There, I learned about suffragettes, and downtrodden women in "backward" countries. However, I saw nothing downtrodden about the accomplished women who taught me. Our headmistress, an unmarried Quaker, made it clear that marriage was a relationship, not a career. I took this lesson seriously. I stayed in school, completed my post-secondary education, and planned a career overseas. However, because everyone else was doing it, I also got engaged. In 1961, when a job I had obtained in Nairobi was put on hold because of Mau Mau terrorism, I got married and headed with my new husband to Canada.

During those first years of teaching in Ontario, I cannot say I was unaware of inequities. I noticed that school boards were reluctant to hire young married women, and that the moment they became pregnant they had to resign. I saw that all the positions of responsibility in school systems were held by men. I noticed that when the principal left to go to a meeting, the older, much more competent female teachers were overlooked as supervisors in favour of young male teachers. I noticed that I was not allowed to teach the senior grades of the elementary school, in spite of the fact that I had been a secondary teacher. It was believed that only men had the authority to keep good discipline. I saw all these things, but I did not grasp their relevance. I was caught up putting a husband through university, holding down a full-time job, taking upgrading courses at night and, of course, doing all the household work too. I was a typical, sixties do-it-all superwoman, although I didn't realize it at the time.

As I reached my turning point in 1968, I could best be described as a complacent feminist. I had no doubt in my own mind that I was equal to men, but had no idea how controversial this would be as the second wave of twentieth century feminism took shape.

My feminist awakening came in two quite distinct steps that stand out clearly in my mind, over forty years later. The first moment occurred when I went with a friend to one of the public hearings being held by the panel working on the Royal Commission on the Status of Women. As I listened to the speakers and read their handouts, I was astonished to find out how much blatant discrimination against women was occurring in all areas of Canadian society. I left the hearings determined to do something.

The second incident gave me a greater sense of how much there was to be done, and galvanized my resolve. At a party, I broached my concerns about discrimination against women with two highly educated, thoroughly modern, male friends. I expected support and stood speechless as they both casually dismissed the work of the Commission as "a lot of fuss about nothing." They then had the gall to assert that women had neither the desire nor aptitude to do much of the work men did. Life for me was never the same.

The following years were spent in a frenzy of catching up. I read Simone de Beauvoir. I read Betty Friedan. I read Germaine Greer. I became active in the Status of Women Committee of the Federation of Women Teachers. I began to link with other like-minded women in the community and to challenge the status quo. We talked about our female experiences, often late into the night. Our cars sported bumper stickers: "Uppity Women Unite" and "Women Make Policy Not Coffee." I wrote papers. I wrote letters. I became exactly what one radio interviewer rather disparagingly called me — an activist.

During my graduate work in the late sixties, I wrote a research paper on the influences on the vocational choices made by gifted females. I defended my paper in front of a class made up almost entirely of men, many of whom had difficulty with what I said. One of the men in the class asked if I was a "Women's Libber." I said that I was. A week later, the same man asked me if I would come and speak to his Kiwanis Club about women's liberation. This was the first of hundreds of presentations I gave on various aspects of feminism over the next decade. I spoke to all kinds of men's service clubs and to many other groups gathered in churches, synagogues, high schools, college and university classrooms, and library meeting rooms.

It would be good to think that all that was accomplished by Canadian feminists over the last fifty years was sufficient. It was not. Discrimination, subtler yet just as pervasive, still exists. For me, feminism is a life's work.

40 | UPSTAIRS AND DOWNSTAIRS
Audrey Hozack

My recognition of the inequality between men and women began in the early 1950s at the University of Toronto. Encouraged by government grants to cover tuition, veterans of WWII were enrolling in droves; the campus was overcrowded and exciting. There was a spirit of optimism and a determination to put the war behind us and enjoy life and everything that it had to offer.

At the time, I did not know anything about feminism, but I did know that it was not fair that I should have to quit my job at the university simply because I was going to be married to a fellow employee. We were both very happy in our positions, he as Manager of the Hart House Theatre, located in the bowels of the building, and I with the Students' Administrative Council, then housed on the upper level of the building.

The university Personnel Department assured me that I did indeed have to leave my position upon marriage. This regulation was in full force. But, they did point out that part-time work didn't have any status, and therefore was not restricted due to marital circumstance. So, once married, I left the Students' Administrative Council accepting a beautiful, engraved, silver-plated tray as my farewell gift. Immediately I followed up on the idea of part-time work at the university and, lo and behold, there was a part-time position available in Hart House as secretary to the Graduate Secretary. I had found my opening, and shortly thereafter I was back at work at the university.

In the late '50s, my boss was offered a tempting position with the National Ballet that he couldn't refuse, and suddenly I found myself doing his work. After meetings with the Personnel Department and discussions at the Board of Stewards (the governing body of Hart House) approval was ultimately granted for me to take over his position. I took on the full position of Graduate Secretary; I had become a full-fledged member of the Hart House staff, the first time a woman had risen above the role of secretary. Despite the title though, I was still unable to use the dining or athletic facilities, and

I was certainly not mentioned in the 1969 publication *An Uncommon Fellowship:The Story of Hart House.*

In the early 1960s I was invited to attend a meeting (because my husband was not available that evening) about the possibility of fundraising for the arts in Toronto. Those in attendance were men from trust companies, banks, and large corporations plus Vida Peene, a big-time donor to the arts. As far as I was concerned, she was the only one present who appeared to have any idea how to go about organizing anything, and I came home raging about the apparent inefficiencies of the assembled executives.

A professor friend of mine was amused by my remarks and encouraged me to get into a new course at the university in Business Administration — a forerunner to Management Studies. He said that the time had come for women to take their place in the business world. So there I was, in the mid-'60s, prepared to take on the world of business while still, of course, working full-time. There were only three other women in the course, and we all loved the challenge. It took a couple of years of intense study but I graduated from this course, first in the class and with a couple of awards and scholarships. Onward and upward!

I took my diploma to the Warden of Hart House and asked for consideration for an administrative position. He apologized, while telling me that there was no opportunity for advancement in Hart House. The Personnel Department had the same story: there was no category for employment of women in the administrative area in the university. It just so happened that as I was leaving the Personnel Department, I bumped in to Joe Evans who had just been asked to form an Alumni Association. Joe commented that he had just been told that he would not be able to hire a woman for his new department because there was no category for women in administration. When I told him that I had just been told the same thing, he invited me back to the newly established Alumni House, which he had recently equipped with a couple of desks, telephones, and empty file cabinets ready to begin his mandate to bring alumni support to the university.

We talked over our individual problems and it was serendipity — I wanted advancement and he wanted a woman to assist him. Fortuitously, we had both known the President, Claude Bissell, since his student days. Accordingly, when Joe phoned him and asked for an appointment to discuss "a serious matter," we were invited to come in the next day. The President listened to our stories and admitted that it didn't make much sense not to have an employment category that would give women the opportunity to advance, especially in light of the new business administration program offered at the university, and open to women. He took immediate action and the employment category was added to the roster. It didn't take long before I was installed in Alumni House as Associate Director.

The news soon spread throughout the staff that there was now a new employment category for women. Something the Staff Association had been trying to get in place for many years. Did we recognize this as a feminist victory? Or even feminism? I don't think so, but in retrospect it was.

In 1971, the deed of gift of Hart House was being changed so that women, who had been clamouring for equal membership, could finally be accepted as full members. When the position of Assistant Warden (Administration) was advertised, I applied immediately. Because there was doubt that a woman could handle the facility, the finances, the food services, and the personnel that had by tradition been the responsibility of a man, I was interviewed by not one, but two Vice-Presidents of the university. After a grueling interview, one VP decided that I could do the job; the other VP expressed his regret but he didn't think a woman would be able to deal with all the responsibilities. However, after a little more time he changed his mind. He called me the next day to say that he felt he had made a mistake and, yes, I had his approval. So in 1971, I moved back to Hart House in anticipation of the admission of women as full members in the fall of 1972.

As pleased as I was about my position, there was still one more battle to fight: I insisted that the salary for the positions of Assistant Warden (Administration) — my position — and Assistant Warden (Programs) — my office mate's position — be the same. After more difficult negotiations, I succeeded; we would have the same salary!

Initially two male members of the staff were very difficult. They both announced that they had no intentions of being supervised by a woman. But eventually they decided they would rather accept the situation than resign. There was also some resistance from the female staff, until they came to understand that some of the knowledge I brought with me gave them more responsibilities. Also, they no longer had to do personal errands for their bosses.

The last thirteen years of my working life were spent in a happy atmosphere, and my persistence for equality had paid off. At each step I was looking after my own interests, but I like to think that it helped many other women in the university get the jobs for which they were well qualified.

Is the battle for equal rights over? Don't bet your money on it. I enjoy life now, in a building where the women still serve the coffee and the men are aghast at the idea that they might be asked to do this simple task.

41 | SOPHIE SNODGRASS ON CBC RADIO
Sylvia Hughes

My mother was named Sylvia after Sylvia Pankhurst, and so was I. My grandmother fought for the vote. Long before the official liberation movement, I was raised with the politics of equality for women. That, along with my mother's mantras of "Men are Swine" and "Marriage is Hell," totally conditioned me for the Gloria Steinems and the Germaine Greers of the liberation movement. It really felt as though the world had finally caught up with me.

But had it?

Early on, I realized that, along with liberation, women were being allocated more work. So I created a character for CBC Radio — Sophie Snodgrass, the Over-Liberated woman. She loved liberation, as she told her listeners:

Before liberation all I had to do was clean the house, raise the children, cook the meals, do the laundry, and leave everything ready for the morning. But now that I'm liberated I have to clean the house, raise the children, cook the meals, do the laundry, pick up the beer, shovel the driveway, change the oil in the car, take out the garbage and, of course, leave everything ready for the morning. Isn't liberation wonderful?

Sophie Snodgrass got mail from all across Canada from women who were finding liberation a lot more work than they had imagined. Gloria and Germaine made it sound so logical, so plausible. But what about the night of freezing rain, after which your husband hands you an ice-scraper and expects you to take care of the car? Well, this was the flaw. Some jobs are just naturally gender-related. Liberating women actually meant un-liberating men. Women who proudly announced that they could open doors for themselves, thank you, blanched at the thought of changing a tire on a snowy night. Who wanted to be liberated then?

And so the great struggle of who-does-what started, and it is still going round in circles today. This is because many men were raised by a mother who believed in liberation as a principle, but never taught her son to separate the colours from the whites, or how to load the dishwasher. And so many men, raised by women who considered themselves "liberated," still expected to enjoy most of the privileges dad had. Like sitting down and reading the paper after dinner. For women to achieve real liberation, they had to start by un-liberating men.

At the same time as writing and performing Sophie, I was writing cartoons for *Redbook* magazine, all depicting domestic chaos at various levels. A woman challenges her husband, saying, "Well, if I have to thank you for doing the dishes, will you send me flowers for doing the laundry?" Or, addressing the twin freedoms of social and sexual liberation, picture a couple in bed: The woman is sitting up and the husband complains, "When you said you had something new and different to do in bed, sorting laundry never even entered my mind."

Again, mail arrived, mostly from the US, with women asking "How do you know my husband so well?" I had a standard reply: "There's only one — we each just get a different version of him."

I collected nearly a hundred of these cartoons and tried to sell them as a book entitled "We Sure Liberated the Hell Out of You" — the cover showing a woman totally exhausted, surrounded by a smiling, well cared for husband and kids.

No interest at all.

In my marriage I continued my own campaign of independence. I had a career. And when children came along, I hired nannies. And when my career prospered and involved business travel, I had housekeepers take over the household. And I didn't feel the slightest twinge of guilt. My mother had a career. My grandmother had her own business till she was eighty-four. I worked 24/7, but I had my own life. My own career. My own money. My kids were well-adjusted and healthy. I did it. I proved that a woman can have it all. Can be independent. Can really be liberated.

Sure she can, if she's lucky enough to have a successful two-income marriage, a great career, well-spaced children, and a co-operative husband. Apart from objecting to me taking a job with Air Canada ("you'll have to work shifts"), my husband was pretty easy-going. His twin brother was anything but, and I saw his wife — a bright (as it turned out MENSA-material) woman — stuck in the suburbs, seething with resentment and not understanding why, all the while criticizing me for my choices. I however, felt I had it licked.

Except...

During the day our lives were full and rewarding. But at night, if my husband didn't want to go out, then I didn't. If I wanted to go out alone, he wasn't pleased. And if I wanted to go out and leave him alone to babysit, it wasn't happening.

I realized that in spite of all my rhetoric I was actually, at best, semi-liberated.

Just about this time I met a man who was to change my life. His name was Joe. He was gay; he was my hairdresser's partner. A New Yorker, he moved to Canada to be with John, who was himself Australian and couldn't get a green card in the US. Our relationship was magnetic. As soon as we met, we talked, we laughed, we found we had a lot in common. He hated Rogers & Hammerstein, and loved to entertain. Joe and John became part of our lives, in spite of my husband's objections, in spite of my in-laws' horror and gossip, in spite of everything, they became part of my extended family. And they changed my life.

Because they were gay my husband had no logical reason for jealousy. Because they were gay, they improved our lives immeasurably. Joe and his mother turned me into a gourmet cook. Joe and John taught me to have style. They improved my self-image, which increased my confidence. When I was considering an abortion, because I felt that at 39 I was "too old," Joe's comment was wise and wonderful. "Your mother's always old," he commented. His mother had been 40 when he was born and his buddy's mother had him at 18, and to the kids, the mothers were the same age: Old. So I had my daughter, and the boys became her Godfathers.

When she was about four my daughter whispered to me, "Daddy says you were a good wife till you got involved with these *homiesexuals*." That's when it hit me. I realized that I had carved out a whole new freedom with my new friends. We went to singalongs in gay bars, shopping trips to Buffalo, movie and theatre nights — just the three of us. My husband was always wrapped up in his work. And it was my daughter repeating the phrase "a good wife" that showed me exactly how I had fallen from grace, and how much I had changed. I no longer sought permission for anything, I would invite my husband along and if the answer was "no thanks," then I went anyway. I was no longer a "good wife," I had become a liberated woman.

I had enjoyed taking advantage of my full liberation, without actually recognizing it. And it took an indiscreet four-year-old to open my eyes!

42 | IT TOOK TWO MOVEMENTS

Tracy Isaacs

My mother raised me on feminist orthodoxies, the way others might raise a Catholic. The message came to this: You can be anything you want when you grow up but not a secretary or a nurse or a housewife or anything else servile, and by no means be dependent, and for God's sake do not drop math even if you think you won't need it. She and my dad had abandoned all that they knew to come to Canada in 1967 because all that they knew were the restricted circumstances of being Coloured in apartheid South Africa.

With the racist policies of our homeland behind her, and a mind accustomed to taking note of inequality, my mother came to Canada as a young doctor's wife with two small children and a third on the way. Life without apartheid was immeasurably better. My parents could almost forget about oppression. Almost.

My mother read *The Feminine Mystique,* and a little later, *The Female Eunuch,* and issues of *Ms.* magazine that had made the rounds among the other suburban wives who were her friends.

Every day she made dinner for me, my two brothers, my father, and her own father. We ate together as a family. So, we were all together that evening in 1980, eating generous helpings of curry and rice, when she slammed her fist down on the dinner table hard enough to make the plates jump and said, "I'm fucking serious." This from a woman who, though not quiet, did not slam fists or swear. Just before that, one of my brothers had chuckled — it was a nervous chuckle, perhaps masking disbelief — after she had announced, in a voice shrill yet firm, that she would not do our laundry anymore because we were now old enough to do it ourselves.

That was the first time I experienced the palpable force — the courage — of a woman taking a stand against patriarchy. Right there in the family kitchen. Our family kitchen. My forty-three year old mother. I was fifteen.

Just a few months before that, those issues of *Ms.* that circulated through suburban homes started making their way into my hands. My mother left them out where I'd be sure to see them. I always turned straight to the "No Comment" column near the back of the magazine. It reprinted offensive ads sent in by readers — most depicted women in sexualized, sometimes violent, and objectifying or belittling scenes that had little or nothing to do with the product being sold. Sometimes people submitted examples in which domestic violence was portrayed as a matter of course. My heart used to race as I flipped ahead, ready to be outraged and rendered speechless by the blatant sexism. How could they think that was okay?

That one page of *Ms.* a month made me see the world through new eyes. But I didn't think to turn those eyes back on myself. I had all the right feminist ideas; I didn't like women to be objectified.

The National Film Board's classic anti-pornography film, *Not a Love Story*, shocked me, especially when it flashed the image of the *Hustler* cover that depicted the woman's body going through a meat grinder. I thought of marriage and love and motherhood as traps to be avoided. Women should have careers, be self-sufficient, and not let old-fashioned ideas hold them back. All of these things I believed.

But I hadn't yet fought for the cause.

The fighting kind of feminists scared me. Could we not just quietly claim what was rightfully ours? I believed that's what I'd done in the pursuit of my career as an academic. The voices of these louder feminists occasionally tugged at my young conscience, but more often I thought they were holdovers from earlier times. Looking back, if I'd had the word I might have called myself a "post-feminist," the kind of young woman whom I worry for because she doesn't yet know that the path ahead is still littered with debris.

In 1992, I started my professional academic career as a philosophy professor in a tenure track position, still convinced that I'd gotten by on my own merits, that I'd never faced any sexist discrimination, and that I would automatically command the same respect as my male colleagues. A more senior, tenured male colleague befriended me. Other women had warned caution; he was known to turn on people, especially women. He himself told me once, conveying a story about someone with whom he'd fallen out, that he held grudges with relish. I missed the warning, feeling overly secure in our friendship.

In my second year of teaching, this colleague and I were on a departmental hiring committee together. New positions were scarce in the early nineties; the stakes in hiring for tenure track positions were high; they resulted in colleagues for life. The appointment grew contentious because it struck up a battle over territory. The ground began to shift just slightly away from the old guard, of which my friend was a part. The new direction would build strength in research areas more likely to attract female applicants. I liked that.

The day before the committee was to take a vote, my friend asked me to meet him for a drink. I explained how I intended to vote. "If you vote that way, it will affect our friendship," he said.

"You're not serious?" I said. He had a smile on his face, a self-satisfied smile like many men tend to have when they feel themselves exerting their influence. I remembered his proud disclosure: *I hold grudges.*

The next day, his camp lost the vote. The friendship faltered, as promised. We endured a decade of willful and cold silence, neither of us acknowledging the other's presence with so much as a glance or a greeting. Two weeks after the meeting I borrowed a copy of the film, *The Chilly Climate for Women Faculty at Colleges and Universities*, made at my institution the year before I arrived, by the very women who scared me, the women whose feminist fortitude pricked at my conscience. I watched the film alone in my living room and listened to story after story of exclusion so subtle you might think you were crazy to think anything of it: "They all went out for lunch every day and never, ever invited me. If I invited myself along, everything changed. It was like we were out on a date." "I asked a question at a talk and the speaker just looked right past me and said, 'Are there any other questions?'"

They spoke of the chill, the deep freeze, even permafrost in their workplace. In the thirty minutes it took to watch the film, I had started to cry, first quietly, then heaving sobs, as one experience after another — my own, not someone else's — fell into place. My academic career, from undergraduate philosophy major to tenure track assistant professor, was re-framed. Feminism wasn't just about sexist advertising and pornography and what happened to other women less fortunate than I. We could not just quietly claim what was rightfully ours. I finally understood this about the academy: the men didn't want us here as peers at all. Their lives would be an order of magnitude easier if we weren't here. Female faculty members who expect to be colleagues are…inconvenient.

I immediately began to re-tool so I could teach feminist philosophy. I got more active as an executive member of my institution's Women's Caucus, ultimately serving for two years as its President. Instead of finding myself busy every Wednesday, I attended the regular Wednesday Feminist Lunch on campus so I could connect with the other women. In that moment, watching that film, I decided I wanted to become one of the women on campus who used to scare me. And so I did.

43 | BOOKS DID IT

Linda Kealey

There was no sudden "light bulb" or click moment for me, but rather a slow process of reading and digesting various books that tackled themes of inequality — books such as Betty Friedan's *The Feminine Mystique*, de Beauvoir's *Second Sex,* the novels of James Baldwin, and the classics such as *To Kill a Mockingbird*, and *Black Like Me*. As a young woman growing up in northern United States I became aware of inequality along racial lines first. Though I was, through books, dimly aware of gender inequalities, it wasn't until the 1960s and early '70s that I began to fully grasp the unequal laws, customs, and practices that defined most women's lives, even the most privileged.

Growing up in the '60s and moving to Toronto for university certainly raised my awareness of the gaps between races, classes, and the sexes (as we used to say). I wanted to help make the world a better place and was searching for avenues that would result in change.

As for many young women, university meant making my own decisions, and shaping my own future. As part of the new cohort of university students from less affluent backgrounds, I knew that I was the first in my family to attend higher education and explore beyond the normative pattern for women: to work for a time, find a spouse, and have children. I enrolled in Sociology not knowing exactly what sociology was — I thought it related to social work and doing good, and that was enough to entice me. It was during those years at university that I met my life partner; we married when I was 21 (and he somewhat younger). After graduating from the undergraduate program at the University of Toronto I went to Library School for a one-year program.

It wasn't until sometime later that I decided that women's history would be my life's work. I began reading women's history in the late 1960s, mostly American and British publications. These readings led me to think about graduate study, something that was encouraged by women at the University of Toronto, particularly Jill Ker Conway, with whom I studied until she left to become the first woman President of Smith College in Massachusetts. As a graduate student at the University of Toronto, I also benefitted from the comradeship of other women in the graduate program in History.

Those years in the late 1960s witnessed the emergence of the women's movement. In Toronto I became involved in New Left politics, which meant a lot of discussions of current issues such as the war in Vietnam, the oppressive nature of the capitalist system, student politics, and much more. There were demonstrations against the war, demands for more democratic student government and university practices, as well as disruptions of classes taught by right-wing professors. Women involved in New Left politics began to question the male leadership and women's secondary status in political groups supposedly dedicated to eradicating inequality.

We wrote our own manifesto critiquing male-dominated left wing politics. Very quickly this work became more organized and evolved into more conventional forms, though at the time we considered its content "radical." By the early 1970s the Canadian Women's Educational Press in Toronto had published *Women Unite*, a collection of essays and poetry on women's struggles; more books followed that would remedy the absence of material by or about Canadian women. In 1974, for example, the Press published *Women at Work: Ontario 1850–1930*, one of the first works in Canadian women's history, and winner of the City of Toronto Book Prize. The first women's history course at the University of Toronto was launched by historians Jill Ker Conway and Natalie Zemon Davis.

Although my plans to write a thesis on women's history with Jill Ker Conway did not work out, in my subsequent work at Memorial University of Newfoundland — where I taught from 1980-2002 — I was able to redefine myself as a historian of Canadian women. As a new faculty member, I not only taught but I also had a two-year-old daughter to care for. I remember the struggle of trying to finish my thesis in the midst of teaching and family life; without daycare it would not have been possible. As is often the case with women academics, I did not really consider having any more children as I was focused on teaching, and research, and academic and professional life in general.

I became involved in the initial stages of Memorial's Women's Studies Program, which began in 1983, and remained involved in the later development of its Master's in Women's Studies. During the 1980s I was also active in the early stages of the Canadian Women's Studies Association, serving as president in 1983-84, and as a board member and English language editor of the Canadian Research Institute for the Advancement of Women.

I continued my involvement in various organizations over the years; this enabled me to stay connected with ongoing changes, and supportive of progressive developments. In 1989, I authored a report on the Status of Women in History; and in the 1990s I served on a number of boards including the Canadian Historical Association. In the 1990s I also took on the roles of board member, then co-editor, of the *Canadian Historical Review*. When I lived in St. John's I also served on the board of the St. John's Status of Women Council, a community organization, and edited *Pursuing Equality: Historical Perspectives on Women in Newfoundland and Labrador* (1993, 1999).

Since moving to Fredericton, New Brunswick, and situating myself at the University of New Brunswick at the end of 2001, I have also given considerable time to the Aid to Scholarly Publishing Program — a part of the Canadian Federation of the Humanities and Social Sciences — reading manuscripts and serving on the Board of Management and as a board member and co-editor of *Atlantis: A Women's Studies Journal*. From 2003-2005, I served on the board of the International Federation for Research in Women's History. In addition, in the last few years I have spent a considerable proportion of my time working on the history of nursing in New Brunswick, partnering with the Nurses Association of New Brunswick and the New Brunswick Nurses Union which has allowed me to interview dozens of nurses active in their profession and union.

I am now embarking on a new facet of life as the academic convenor of Congress 2011, the annual meeting of humanities and social science associations which will take place in Fredericton. While my teaching duties have been reduced in recent years, I plan to continue to supervise graduate students whose work I highly value as they are producing the new research that keeps the fields of Women's History and Women's Studies vibrant.

Strong role models, mostly women, but some men, have been

influential in my life: grandmothers, my mother, high school teachers (nuns), women historians, feminist activists, and those radical women and men who challenged the status quo, often at great personal cost. I have been privileged in my life and hope that what I have contributed matters.

I dedicate this short autobiography to one of the greatest achievements in life as I have known it, my daughter, Caitlin.

44 | GENETIC PREDISPOSITIONS

Janice Kennedy

I was waiting for it. In the 1960s, when feminism barged into polite society with its badass ways and kickass appeal, I was ready. The new movement may have been considered the Second Wave, but it was the first for me. And I couldn't wait to dive into it.

That is, as an early baby boomer growing up in Montreal, one whose childhood and adolescence were shaped by the 1950s and early '60s, I had already experienced what felt like a lifetime of gender-related rigidity: white gloves for young ladies; no shorts, jeans, or slacks downtown; lacy mantillas for churchgoing. Relationships conducted under the straitjacket dictates of role-defined etiquette. Femininity models plucked from a pop-cultural pantheon dominated at one end of the spectrum by June Cleaver, and, at the other, by the Bunnies at Hugh Hefner's hip Playboy Mansion.

By the time I emerged from my teens, I was chafing, questioning and, given the Cleaver–Bunny paradigm, on my way to developing a well-defined sense of inadequacy.

Then along came feminism.

At least, that's the way I remember it, as a single surge into my life. I know the actual wave broke more gradually, that there were gutsy and articulate women — Simone de Beauvoir, for instance — who had been preparing the way while I was searching for white gloves to wear downtown. But to me, as I entered my 20s, feminism was a brassy character in a fabulous play, and it was making one heck of a grand entrance.

I was ready, in other words, when all the buzz started swirling around names like Friedan, Gurley Brown, Greer, Millett — and the iconoclastic views they tossed about. I was ready when Gloria Steinem (who had so vividly, and so sassily, exposed the rot in the foundation of Hef's mansion) launched *Ms.* magazine, to which I subscribed from the beginning. I was ready for the Women's Studies classes that started proliferating, and for which I signed up for the pure subversive joy of them. I burned no bras (did anyone, really?), but I was ready for the heady discussions sparked by the explosion of seditious ideas flung out there by thinkers like Shulamith Firestone and some of the convention-be-damned contributors to Robin Morgan's *Sisterhood Is Powerful*.

I was ready — but not in a new-convert kind of way, suddenly afire with rebellious philosophies and radical perspectives. It was an exciting time, and the exhilaration was not lost on me. But I was gripped not so much by revolutionary zeal as by a vast exhaled sigh of relief. Finally, I thought. Finally, it had happened. Finally, what I had always known, what I had been brought up with, what had been imprinted generations earlier on my DNA — finally, it was getting airplay and even (hesitantly at first) a growing chorus of approval.

Women? Equal to men? Without reservation?

Today, such phrasing sounds almost quaint, which may be some small measure of progress (at least in those parts of the world where the fate of women is not in the hands of fundamentalist chauvinist males). But in the late 1960s, it was far from quaint. This was a time when I could watch CBC and be treated to a little satire by cartoonist Peter Whalley called *Big Sister Is Watching*, a paranoid and cliché-ridden commentary on the new Royal Commission on the Status of Women. Without fear of repercussion, the national broadcaster could also shrug as host Gordon Donaldson indignantly wondered about uppity new feminists, noting that while "generations of domesticity may have hobbled her mind," today's woman was nonetheless "demanding equal rights in the labour market while retaining the special privileges of a lady."

There was a kind of bred-in-the-bone quality to the assumed conviction in (male-dominated) society that women were all very well, but just not quite the equals of their fathers, brothers, husbands, and sons. In the early '60s, I remember my brother telling me about his male political science professor at a Montreal university — a man who went on to a career in media and federal politics — criticizing Diefenbaker cabinet minister Ellen Fairclough with a breathtaking swipe at her gender. Fairclough, said the prof about Canada's first female federal cabinet minister, was such an incompetent woman "she couldn't even bear children." That he was wrong on both counts never registered as even a ripple on the smooth surface of his self-assured maleness.

The early second-wave feminists spoke of equality, and calibrated it against a male measure of the world, precisely because this equality was a principle that had languished for so long, so far from universal acceptance.

Except in my family. In my family, which never seemed to march to exactly the same beat as everyone else's, there was never a scintilla of suggestion that the girls were less than the boys, that their behaviour should be different, that their paths toward adulthood had to lead down more constrained avenues of expectation. There was never any sense at all that society, which assumed vast gender differences and which casually accepted a staggering gender imbalance, had got that part of things right.

It came from my mother's side.

There is a telling anecdote involving my grandmother, my mother's mother. A peppery blend of Scottish and Loyalist strains, she did not suffer indignities gladly, her own or others'. One of the more colourful times this was evident, according to my mother, was when, back in the early 1930s, she and my grandmother were on a Montreal streetcar. All of a sudden, the conductor at the front started loudly berating a cowering woman who, it seemed, had committed the unpardonable act of being both poor and having insufficient funds for the fare. As the yelling continued, my grandmother rose from her seat, marched to the front of the streetcar and demanded, "How dare you speak to this woman like that?" She made a few comments about bullies and people who abuse their authority, and promised that, if he didn't stop immediately, she would report him. According to my mother, who felt the kind of squirming mix of embarrassment and pride that only a young daughter could feel, he stopped.

It may be a small story, but it hints at a spirit not constrained by artificial gender niceties, particularly when such constraints were the rule. My mother, in a much less peppery way, was no slouch as a feminist either, both before and after the word became common currency. As we were growing up, she worked outside the home (she was a teacher), managed the household money (because she was so much better at it than my father), and never, ever let my sister or me set our sights lower than she knew they could be. She was the gentlest, and strongest, person I have ever known, and I think that fact has subconsciously informed my feminism — which I have tried to shape to be less about unproductive anger than about righteous resolve.

So the wave of new feminism that broke over the world in the 1960s was not entirely new to me. It felt more like an unlocking of something already there, an airing of family tradition.

And it brought a kind of pop-cultural pizzazz to it. As a young teacher in a large Montreal high school, I abandoned the "Miss" designation early and happily embraced "Ms." I experienced the liberation of relationships no longer dependent on outdated role-playing. When I moved in with the man I married in 1975 (during International Women's Year, which I didn't see as ironic then and still don't, given that the man in question has always been as committed to equality as I am), I gave him a gift I had ordered from the back of *Ms.* magazine, right near the ads for decals proclaiming, "A woman without a man is like a fish without a bicycle." It was a sturdy cotton apron, encouragingly emblazoned, "Share the shitwork."

Much of this was pretty superficial stuff, of course. By the heady days of the '70s, feminism had become culturally cool, and some degree of superficiality was probably unavoidable. And yet, I believe the pizzazz was useful. I believe it eventually and inevitably led to something deeper, both for us older feminists today and the younger women who have taken the spirit and enriched it with more breadth and more depth. Our concerns now are both global and more serious, in many cases. Outrage at some man's denunciation of the "Ms." honorific pales significantly beside news of a Sudanese woman threatened with the lash for wearing pants in public, or young women murdered for the "honour" of their families.

For such broadened outlooks, we offer much thanks to the women of the Third Wave. But I think it worth observing that their achievements happened because they were able to take what my generation contributed and then build upon it. Feminism has always been a healthy continuum.

Which is how I see it in the context of my own family.

My mother was a liberated spirit. She inherited much of that from her mother, both on Montreal streetcars and off. My grandmother's mother, widowed with three young children to support, declined family offers of help and moved from small-town English Brockville to big-city bilingual Montreal, where she got a job and raised her sons and daughter — a determined single mother at the turn of the last century. In 1835, my grandmother's grandmother, also newly widowed, moved (lock, stock, barrel and kids) from a genteel life in Scotland to the Lake Simcoe wilderness, where she both ruled the roost and thrived.

From what I can see, I have at least four generations of liberating uppitiness running in my veins. For me, that is heartening evidence that the spirit of feminism is bound by neither place nor time — whether first wave, second, third, or umpteenth — since it is obvious the struggle is clearly an ongoing one.

It certainly has been in my own family. I have two grown daughters whose feminism is so strong, so assured — so organic, really — it's taken for granted. This is who and what they are, with or without the label.

My elder daughter is a new lawyer. In fact, despite being a single mother of two with financial challenges, she was encouraged to go to law school by her grandmother. My mother knew her granddaughter's potential and gently voiced her support while the rest of us expressed our practical qualms. My mother died just weeks later, but it was obvious to me, as I sat in the great hall of the National Arts Centre in Ottawa in June 2009, emotionally watching my daughter being called to the Bar of Ontario, that my mother's spirit was abundantly present.

The new lawyer is fiercely committed to principles of equality and keeps the proclamation of the *Canadian Charter of Rights and*

Freedoms up on her workplace wall. My younger daughter, who has chosen a path in business, is no less fierce in beliefs that entwine rights, freedoms, and feminism. She conducts her life, domestic and professional, with those principles at its core.

I do not usually think of life as something neat and symmetrical. I do not generally believe in cosmic full circles. Except once in a while. It happens at those times when I let my mind drift to the grandmother I knew through my mother, to the mother I knew through the greatest good fortune, to the daughters I know through a benevolent grace that has blessed the world with their presence.

Once in a while, I understand that what goes around comes around, generation after generation, wave after wave. And that is a good and hopeful thing.

45 | AHA! MOMENTS

Cathleen Kneen

My first political act, at age 18, was to join the Campaign for Nuclear Disarmament, and I became deeply involved in the student peace movement as it morphed into social justice with the formation of the Student Union for Peace Action. I met my husband, Brewster, at a meeting in New York State that was designed to link the Canadian and US peace and social justice movements, and introduce student activists to the previous generation of radicals — all men. Back in Canada, I could not help noticing that many of the leaders in the peace movement were women — Voice of Women, Women Strike for Peace, Women's International League for Peace and Freedom. And indeed, looking at the likes of Ursula Franklin, Muriel Duckworth, Kay Macpherson, Betty Peterson, Peggy Hope-Simpson, and so many others, I developed a firm belief that when I had grey hair and wrinkles, I too might become really powerful. (The jury is still out on whether or not I was right.)

One of my first "aha!" moments in coming to feminism came

when we had our first child, whose early baby photos show him breastfeeding, or sleeping, at various meetings. Having experienced for myself the radical shake-up in relationships that occurs when a new person (a child) enters the family, I joined the natural childbirth movement to help other women prepare to work through this process. It seemed to me at the time that this was a good tool to help women think differently about their roles, as well as to think more positively about their bodies.

When Brewster and I, along with our two children, went to Nova Scotia in 1971 and started farming (sheep and cattle), a group of us young women quickly formed a women's consciousness-raising group. In International Women's Year (1975), when the Secretary of State provided some funding, we found a woman doctor and ran periodic pap smear clinics throughout our county. This led to the formation of the Pictou County Women's Centre, which became a safe space for women-identified women and a hub of feminist activity, women's self-help health, and rural women's outreach.

One cold March night, at around 3 in the morning, there was a knock on our farmhouse door. Two student nurses had been offered a lift home from the bus station in the nearby town, and instead had been taken to the woods and raped. They had escaped and made their way through the woods to our place. We sat them down, gave them hot drinks, and called the police. But it turned out, in the end, that the culprit was an off-duty policeman and the case was dropped.

What sticks in my memory of that night is the damp patch left on the kitchen chair where one of the women had been sitting. Yet another "aha" moment.

In our consciousness-raising group, we had all experienced some form of sexual assault, but for most of us it came in the form of what we understood to be "the usual date-rape experience." Recognizing this shared experience was a mobilizing insight into systemic violence against women, and along with other such stories led the Women's Centre to start a rape crisis line, and shortly thereafter, a transition house for battered women. All of this women-centered activity had a mixed effect in our personal lives. For the lesbians among us it was a lifeline. But for others it posed real challenges: we were no longer the women our husbands had married, and several marriages broke up. The men simply couldn't cope with these new, invigorated wives. I was one of the lucky ones: Brewster's response was along the lines of "you go, girl!"

While Brewster and I were full partners on the farm, it is also true that our roles were pretty traditional: he did all the machinery work and I did the subsistence part. I had a huge garden out of which I fed the family, and I did the canning, drying, freezing and cold storage for the winter. I raised pigs and chickens for meat and eggs. I milked a cow and made butter that I sold at the farmers' market along with the garden surplus. I made pottery and sold that too. I was also active in 4-H and farm organizations. One day I had another "aha!" moment when I realized that in many other places in the world I would be described as a farmer — but in Canada, I was a farmer's wife.

Meanwhile, on the farm we were reducing inputs as much as possible, for financial rather than ideological reasons — the organic agriculture movement was just getting underway at the time. We were also organizing among fellow sheep farmers, and in the process engaging in analysis of the food system ("how come New Zealand can land lamb here cheaper than we can raise it?"). We started writing a more-or-less monthly newsletter of food system analysis, *The Ram's Horn*, which we continued writing even after our children grew up and we left the farm.

All of these experiences and aha moments came together for me in a realization that the industrial mode of food production is inherently violent — think "breaking the virgin prairie" — and patriarchal. Like violence against women, it is all about control, and this is hidden deeply behind a facade of beauty and health. It is also profoundly destructive of relationships of respect and mutuality. The industrial food system is about forcing Mother Nature to do what *we* want; with chemistry and now biotechnology we can plunk our production system down anywhere in the world and make it happen. Never mind traditional knowledge; forget the critical role of women as seed-keepers; and ensure that skills, from wild harvesting to food processing, are displaced by products touted as "quick and easy." It is really little wonder that the movement for food security and food sovereignty in which I now spend most of my energies has so many women leaders — rather like the peace movement, come to think of it.

After all, the care of children is a women's issue. The health of the family is a women's issue — and, famously, fat is a women's issue. Women are still the ones who do most of the shopping, cooking, and often also the gardening and certainly, to the extent that it's still going on, the preserving. So I think it may be easier for women to see the "seamy side" of the food system, from underneath, rather than the seamless garment it presents publicly. From that perspective, feminism for me is a way in which I can be in solidarity with Indigenous peoples and other marginalized and colonized peoples, in a common effort to build sustainability and justice.

Aha!

46 | I TOO WAS A WOMEN'S LIBBER

Penney Kome

I took over the Woman's Place column at *Homemakers* magazine early in 1976. Soon after, I wrote a column called, "I'm not a women's libber, but..." which described all the ways that women tried to disassociate themselves from the movement while at the same time asserting that they believed in feminist values such as equal pay, daycare, and community property in marriage. By the time I finished writing the column, I realized that I too was a women's libber. So began twelve years of covering women's issues, meetings, conferences, demonstrations and other events, in Toronto and nationally.

In those halcyon days, magazines could afford to pay expenses for travel and for lunching with interview subjects. *Homemakers'* editor, Jane Gale, encouraged me to attend events like the National Action Committee on the Status of Women annual meeting in Ottawa. I found column topics and sources in workshops, and inspiration from the longtime activists such as Kay Macpherson and Laura Sabia, as well as the few women who served as MPs, including Pauline Jewett and Flora MacDonald. At that time, you could count the number of women in Parliament on both hands. Later, during the women's constitutional fight, the women's washrooms turned into venues for all-party strategy sessions.

Political activism was not new to me. I grew up in a neighbourhood full of atomic scientists and, as a result, started marching for abolition of nuclear weapons when most of the placards were taller than I was. Along with most of my peers in Hyde Park, Chicago, I also marched for civil rights and against the war in Vietnam — until, perhaps inevitably, I left the States as a protest against the war. The women's movement introduced me to a new kind of political analysis, as well as new ways of organizing.

As columnist, I covered a multilayered network of volunteer and government organizations devoted to promoting equality for women — from women's centres and shelters to university student groups, from union committees to the Association for Women Executives, from women's health collectives to Henry Morgentaler's abortion clinics. Back then, self-improvement was about much more than hairstyles or make-up. We were determined to rise *with* our gender, not *despite* our gender.

Economic inequality was glaringly obvious; I wrote about women and poverty, women and domestic violence, women and pensions, women and disabilities, women and food banks. Women's financial dependence on male breadwinners left them vulnerable to every kind of abuse and neglect. Employers had all kinds of reasons not to pay women the same wage as men doing exactly the same work, let alone doing work of equal value. As a way to get at the amount of unpaid work that women do, which often undermines our earning power, in 1978, I published a tongue-in-cheek 62-question survey about housework in my column, with help and advice from Professor Margrit Eichler. To the amazement of *Homemakers'* staff, we were swamped with about 3,200 replies, some of them long, handwritten letters.

Obviously, there was enough material for a book. I landed an Explorations grant from the Canada Council to pay for compiling the survey responses, as well as for me to travel across Canada from PEI to Victoria, BC. I collected 31 in-depth interviews with housewives, for what eventually became *Somebody Has To Do It: Whose work is housework?* (McClelland & Stewart, 1982). Those connections served me in good stead in 1980, when the Trudeau government pushed to repatriate the Canadian constitution, and to entrench a new Charter of Rights and Freedoms, under which (for the first time) courts could strike down laws. The Charter wording was weak; women's concerns were ignored; there was a national uproar, and by the time the shouting died down at the end of November 1981, Canadian women had won an Equal Rights Amendment (two, actually) just at the time that US women were losing theirs.

Former *Chatelaine* editor Doris Anderson was at the centre of the storm, "riding the cyclone" as she said. As President of the Canadian Advisory Council on the Status of Women, she had commissioned research on the wording of the proposed "non-discrimination" clauses, which showed them to be woefully weak. However, government interference cancelled her proposed conference where women could study the Charter and make resolutions about it.

I watched as volunteers stepped forward to stage the conference anyway. I knew most of the committee members, and I believed they could make the event work. Young lawyer Marilou McPhedran was a central figure, with other women lawyers like Mary Eberts and Beverley Baines in the background. Nancy Jackman (now Senator Nancy Ruth) provided strategic counsel as well as financial support. The organizers planned for 200 women to step forward. Instead more than 1,300 women from across Canada turned up at the conference held in the House of Commons on Valentine's Day 1981.

In the end, five key members — Marilou McPhedran, Rosemary Billings, Pat Hacker, Linda Nye and Tamara Thompson — worked until the government adopted a new Section 28 interpretive clause for the Charter. The clause states that "Notwithstanding anything in this Charter, the rights and freedoms referred to in it are guaranteed equally to male and female persons." The same group of women spearheaded a national feminist rebellion against including Section 28 in an agreement that the provincial premiers cobbled together, that would have allowed any province to override some equality clauses. Premier by premier recanted, over a one-week period.

It was a stunning political victory, followed quickly by the first appointment of a woman Supreme Court Justice, Bertha Wilson, in the spring of 1982.

Women's organizations began enjoying the unaccustomed (and as it turned out, brief) sense of having political power, stemming from their victory in that one-week national battle over Section 28. Not only did the federal Liberals pay attention to NAC (National Action Committee) and NAWL (National Association of Women and the Law) and the new LEAF (Women's Legal Education and Action Fund) but so did provincial governments. After a legal challenge, Yukon changed its "Married Woman's Name Act." Ontario scrapped the "man in the house" rule for welfare mothers. The federal government negotiated with the First Nations and arrived at a compromise revocation of the Indian Act's infamous Section 12 (1) (b), which stripped women of Indian status if they married a non-native man, but allowed men to confer Indian status on their wives.

By 1984 we were coming up on another election. I attended the Liberal leadership convention where John Turner stumbled in every speech, and Pierre Trudeau refused to shake his hand. Both were bad omens for my theory that the Liberals were bound to win again, because of support from women. John Turner didn't entirely throw away the election when he patted party president Iona Campagnolo's bottom on a public platform, but then he continued to act like a male WASP in power — alienating not only women, but also immigrants and other groups that traditionally supported his party. The Liberals lost, and Brian Mulroney's Conservatives took power. Feminism quickly became the "F" word, not to be spoken in Ottawa.

One benefit from the election was that the number of women in Parliament doubled, a trend that continued through the 1990s. All parties exerted themselves to recruit women candidates — often in ridings where other women were running — and the net effect was that more women won. In fact, Mulroney had a lot of trouble because some candidates who were intended to be token candidates actually became MPs, and weren't prepared for the job. As Mulroney's Conservatives took hold in Parliament, feminists fell out of favour. Pitching feminist stories to newspaper and magazine editors became more and more difficult. Some interest did revive after the December

6, 1989 massacre at the École Polytechnique demonstrated the true costs of sexism. I wrote a tribute on the first anniversary in my biweekly "A Woman's View" column that ran in the *Calgary Herald* from 1990-94; Sydney Sharpe and I alternated weeks.

Then the *Herald* fired us along with the other feminist columnist, Nancy Millar, all at the same time — just about the time that Conrad Black and Paul Desmarais gained control of what was then the Southam newspaper chain. Black's 1998 relaunch of the *Financial Post* as the *National Post* included an open declaration of war, in the form of a stable of anti-feminist reporters and columnists, led by Donna LaFramboise. Mulroney's government also stripped away funding for women's groups, nationally and locally. Paul Martin's Liberal government continued the policy, and Stephen Harper's Conservatives completed it. The multilayered network of activists has dwindled drastically. Most women's political action groups must operate as mainly volunteer organizations again, with constant fundraising for basic supplies.

Despite the backlash, the second wave of feminism did gain ground. Young women have advantages that my generation could only dream about, including access to birth control and abortion. More than half the students in medical, law, and journalism schools now are women. The Supreme Court ruled that sexual orientation is a prohibited ground of discrimination, and that gay-bashing is a hate crime. We did that, and much more.

Now it's time to look for the silver lining. The election of President Barack Obama (and Michelle Obama as First Lady) in the US brings renewed hope that feminists and other progressives can reclaim our place in politics and help create a peaceful, sustainable, just and equal world for all.

Andrée Lajoie

Je ne suis pas du tout certaine de mériter le titre de féministe, puisque je n'ai jamais milité dans aucun groupe pour défendre publiquement les droits des femmes. Mais puisque l'on me demande de participer à cet ouvrage, c'est sans doute que l'on considère que, dans ma génération, le seul fait d'exercer ses droits bien qu'étant femme et de publier sur le sujet nous situe parmi les féministes.

Tout d'abord, il faut dire que ce n'est que tard dans ma vie que j'ai expérimenté les deux incidents de discrimination qui m'ont fait prendre conscience de la situation des femmes dans notre société. Au départ en effet, fille unique et par conséquent non soumise à des comparaisons avec des frères, j'ai eu la chance d'avoir été élevée par mes parents à considérer que je devais gagner ma vie et ne jamais dépendre de personne.

J'ai fait mes études classiques, j'ai voulu devenir journaliste. Naïvement, j'ai cru que pour cela il fallait étudier en lettres, mais mon père m'a amenée à rencontrer un de ses amis directeur du journal *La Patrie*, Oswald Meyrand, qui m'a dit et je m'en souviens mot à mot : « La petite, si tu ne veux pas finir — pire qu'aux chiens écrasés — aux pages féminines, il faut aller en droit. »

Sans pouvoir saisir tout de suite l'ampleur du problème, j'ai entrepris mes études de droit à Montréal — nous étions 7 filles sur 135 étudiants — tout en travaillant déjà comme journaliste à *Vie Étudiante,* un mensuel pour étudiants, pour ensuite continuer en sciences politiques à Oxford (où il y avait encore des collèges séparés pour les filles, mais là encore, je n'ai pas compris…) et tout en étant correspondante à Londres pour l'émission *Commentaires* du réseau français de Radio-Canada. De retour à Ottawa, où mon mari d'alors était apprenti diplomate aux Affaires extérieures, j'ai continué de travailler comme pigiste à Radio-Canada et même au réseau anglais de CBC.

C'est alors, à l'été 1960, que Marc Lalonde — qui avait fréquenté la faculté de droit en même temps que moi et qui était devenu chef de cabinet de Davie Fulton, ministre de la Justice dans le gouvernement fédéral — se vit offrir de reprendre le cabinet d'avocat que Paul Gérin Lajoie quittait pour devenir ministre de la Jeunesse au Québec dans le gouvernement Lesage. Il me demanda si j'étais intéressée à le remplacer au cabinet de Fulton. J'ai évidemment accepté et Fulton, satisfait de mon C.V., me convoqua à son bureau pour une entrevue qui devait mener à mon engagement. Mais en m'apercevant, il s'écria : « *Mais vous êtes une fille ?* » (mon prénom Andrée se prononce de la même façon que le correspondant masculin, André, et sa connaissance du français ne lui avait pas permis de saisir la différence…). Et il continua : « *Je ne peux absolument pas vous engager : que dirait-on si je descendais avec vous un matin d'un train dans l'ouest pour un point de presse ?* » Là, j'ai vraiment été insultée et j'ai commencé à comprendre la situation des femmes dans notre société.

Pourtant, cela ne m'empêchait pas de continuer mes activités comme journaliste. Mais peu après, mon mari fut nommé troisième secrétaire à la Mission canadienne aux Nations Unies, ce qui faisait de moi ce que l'on désignait alors comme *an External Affairs wife*, spécialisée il va sans dire en petits fours et babillage dans les réceptions quotidiennes auxquelles je devais participer (j'en ai compté 79 entre septembre et Noël 1961), sans salaire il va sans dire… Si j'avais fait du journalisme culinaire, j'aurais peut-être pu continuer mon métier, mais pour les commentaires politiques dans un « pays hôte », c'était prohibé…

C'est ainsi que Jean Beetz, alors directeur du Centre de recherche en droit public nouvellement créé, vint à mon secours lors d'une rencontre à Montréal ; il m'engagea comme chercheur ; j'y suis encore professeure émérite.

Comme je l'ai indiqué au début de ce texte, je ne peux pas dire que cela m'ait amenée à militer comme féministe, mais je puis dire que j'étais dès lors vraiment alertée quant à la situation des femmes dans notre société occidentale, que j'ai continué à exercer mes droits et à veiller avec vigilance sur ceux de mes assistantes, et, bien sûr, ceux de ma fille.

Dans mes recherches subséquentes, j'ai analysé le discours judiciaire de la Cour suprême du Canada sur la fausse minorité que constituent les femmes (qui sont de fait majoritaires dans notre société, mais traitées comme une *minorité*). Le résultat en fut

Quand les minorités font la loi (2002, Paris, Presses Universitaires de France). Mes conclusions, dont je reproduis ici une courte synthèse, n'étonneront personne :

> Non seulement le clivage entre ce qui est acceptable à la minorité dominante masculine passe-t-il par l'argent (le redressement des inégalités économiques, notamment en matière de travail ou de fiscalité, n'en fait pas partie), mais aussi par le pouvoir politique (l'inclusion des femmes dans le processus de décision politique n'en fait pas partie) et social (l'inclusion des femmes dans les cercles où se transigent les affaires importantes n'en fait pas partie). Il s'arrête également au seuil de la sécurité procédurale : devant les tribunaux, la parole de l'agresseur sexuel continuera de valoir autant que celle de la victime à propos de situations où les preuves directes sont impossibles à fournir.
>
> Bref, les femmes peuvent mener leur vie privée à l'abri de la violence familiale, sexuelle et même symbolique, pourvu que les droits procéduraux des hommes n'en souffrent pas, et la Cour les protégera même contre les dangers que les grossesses non désirées font courir à leur santé psychologique. Mais pour l'argent et le pouvoir, on repassera : dans la sphère publique, ni l'égalité économique, ni la participation politique ou sociale significative ne leur sont accessibles, surtout si, en plus d'être femmes, elles ont le tort supplémentaire d'être Autochtones…

Je pose l'hypothèse que cette situation ne se reproduit pas nécessairement dans ce qui a été conservé ici de la société autochtone, ce qui m'a amenée à concentrer mes travaux actuels sur la place des femmes (et des aînés) dans la société autochtone au Québec.

Tant mieux si ma vie professionnelle et ces recherches me classent parmi les féministes, mais je continue de considérer que ce titre convient mieux à celles qui ont mené les batailles qui rendent maintenant improbables des incidents comme ceux que j'ai vécus.

> Women's March Against Poverty, Parliament Hill, Ottawa, June 15, 1996
>
> Archives and Special Collections (CWMA), University of Ottawa (PC-X10-2-93)/Nancy Adamson

> Marche des femmes contre la pauvreté, Colline parlementaire, Ottawa, le 15 juin 1996

48 | DEVENIR FÉMINISTE DANS LE QUÉBEC DES ANNÉES '70 :

MISER SUR LE TEMPS LONG

Lucie Lamarche

Je suis née à Montréal en 1955 dans un quartier ouvrier de l'Ouest de l'Île, aussi multilingue que multi *tout le reste*. Ceci semble tenir de l'anecdote, mais au contraire. Car à vrai dire, je garde un vibrant souvenir des stratégies de nos mères, toutes langues et cultures confondues, et qui étaient destinées à survivre aux grèves et aux pertes d'emploi menées et subies par nos pères. C'est ainsi que j'ai découvert le marxisme avant le féminisme. Il faut dire que le quartier ne manquait pas de mentors ! Et que parfois, le taux d'alcoolémie était directement proportionnel au tonus des discours auxquels on ne pouvait échapper, vu la proximité des cuisines. Chez nous, les mères travaillaient pour survivre et non pour s'affirmer. Ceci dit, le travail leur conférait un espace d'autonomie et un pouvoir sans précédent.

Mon adolescence s'est inscrite dans la droite ligne de celle de la première génération des jeunes Québécoises pour qui tout était permis, à condition de ne pas trop s'égarer du chemin de l'école. Évidemment, ma mère veillait au grain… et les Dames de la Congrégation Notre Dame aussi ! Rétrospectivement, je me dis que ces dernières comprenaient tout à fait les enjeux en cause, malgré leur air de supériorité alors qu'elles œuvraient *chez les pauvres*. Combien je me souviens de leur mantra : *vous n'avez aucune excuse de ne pas poursuivre vos études !* C'était un moment politiquement exceptionnel : on formait la première génération universelle de Québécois et de Québécoises capables de prendre les commandes.

Entre nous, les combats se sont donc rapidement révélés. Et au premier chef, l'accès à l'avortement et la lutte contre les violences faites aux femmes se sont imposés à notre génération. Il fallait des vigiles, des militantes, des diffuseurs d'idées, des bénévoles pour ouvrir discrètement la porte des refuges pour femmes … Entrecroisé avec les luttes ouvrières et celle de l'indépendance, tout ceci avait du sens et plus encore. Alors qu'aujourd'hui on encourage les étudiantes à faire don de leur temps, j'apprenais à poser des affiches et à répondre à des appels nocturnes de détresse ! Faut-il ajouter que nous n'avions aucune ambition de faire paraître de telles disponibilités dans nos CV !

Nous nous méfiions des bourgeoises, disons-le franchement. Et parmi celles-ci on comptait bon nombre de juristes un peu plus âgées que nous. Ainsi, dans le contexte québécois, le droit ne fut pas a priori identifié comme un terrain de lutte féministe. Cela explique le fait que nous ne sommes encore aujourd'hui que relativement sensibles au rappel de l'acquisition tardive du droit de vote. Droit essentiel, certes, mais…

C'est probablement la croisade du Docteur Morgentaler au fil des décennies 70 et 80 qui a changé la donne. Car plus le droit opprimait Morgentaler, plus la mobilisation était importante. Une sorte de conséquence négative, en définitive. C'est aussi le dossier des violences domestiques faites aux femmes qui nous a alertées : qui étaient ces magistrats qui décrétaient que nous avions ou non encouragé la violence dont nous étions victimes ?

Dans ce contexte, bon nombre d'entre nous se sont retrouvées sur les bancs de la Faculté de droit de l'Université de Montréal entre 1970 et 1980. Soyons honnêtes. Plusieurs d'entre nous aurions préféré les arts ou le voyage, mais classe sociale oblige… il fallait un boulot et nous n'étions pas trop bêtes ! Ce n'est que bien plus tard que l'utilité de cette formation se révélera.

Fait intéressant, ce lieu physique et intellectuel a très peu servi de repère identitaire pour les féministes. Il y avait peu d'espace… Et peu d'intérêt de notre part dans un contexte ou nul n'attendait de la Faculté qu'elle supplée au vibrato politique de la société civile, fort mobilisée par un ensemble de projets, dont l'indépendance du Québec, le marxisme et le féminisme. La majorité d'entre nous menions donc une vie parallèle : les études… et autre chose. J'exclus évidemment de ce diagnostic ceux et celles qui s'étaient déjà donné comme mandat principal, voire exclusif, l'indépendance du Québec et qui à cette fin, comptaient sur les lieux universitaires de pouvoir.

Ainsi, et bien que la Charte des droits et libertés de la personne au Québec ait été adoptée en 1975, je ne me souviens pas que cet événement majeur ait particulièrement mobilisé la communauté féministe.

Bref, lors de l'obtention de notre permis de pratique du droit, rien de particulier n'est réellement survenu sinon que nous avions acquis le droit légitime de participer comme acteur expert à la judiciarisation de certaines luttes politiques qui déterminaient plus que jamais les enjeux et les luttes féministes.

Ce parcours est à la source d'une différence importante, selon moi, entre le féminisme québécois et canadien : le féminisme québécois n'a jamais sacralisé les expertes juristes. Et ces dernières, dont je suis, se sont toujours d'abord reconnues comme féministes plutôt que comme juristes. L'accessoire suit le principal... Et ce dernier est le fruit d'une délibération politique. Bref, les féministes juristes québécoises ont l'habitude de ne pas avoir le dernier mot... ce qui remet le droit et les droits à leur place !

J'estime que l'illustration la plus percutante de cet énoncé réside dans l'affaire *Chantal Daigle* (1989). On se souviendra de cette affaire ou un père prétendait pouvoir interférer dans la décision d'une femme de se faire avorter. J'étais à la Cour suprême au moment précis où l'avocat de Madame Daigle a dû informer les juges du fait que celle-ci avait eu recours aux services d'une clinique new-yorkaise afin d'obtenir un avortement et ce, malgré la saisine de la Cour. Et je n'ai jamais douté de la sincérité du procureur qui prétendait n'en rien savoir. Toutefois, la séquence des faits m'a convaincue que le féminisme québécois avait une confiance limitée dans le droit. Le droit n'a pas paralysé Chantal Daigle !

Ainsi, le féminisme québécois a toujours remis le droit à sa place. Et la contribution de ce dernier au premier demeure somme toute peu déterminante, malgré les gains législatifs enregistrés. Fait intéressant, j'estime que cette limite est la première garantie de la longévité du féminisme québécois, qui n'est ni un féminisme expert, ni le résultat d'une militance d'abord soumise au droit et à la règle de droit.

Au Québec, le marxisme est passé mais le féminisme est resté. Certes, il encaisse des contrecoups et vit ses moments difficiles. Mais il y a peu de risques que le droit ne dispose *in abstracto* de ce qui importe aux Québécoises. Il n'en a pas le pouvoir ! Voici pourquoi le féminisme québécois peut se payer le luxe de *miser sur le temps long !* Il est inscrit dans le patrimoine des luttes sociales. Et j'aime croire que ma génération y est modestement pour quelque chose !

49 | ALWAYS A CONTRARIAN
Michele Landsberg

Looking back, I'd have to say that God had a lot to do with my becoming a feminist. It was a moment of epiphany. I was five years old, standing in our dim hallway next to the guppy tank (flick, flick, red stripe, blue stripe), looking up at my beautiful mother with her soft black curls and hazel eyes. Recently, I'd been sent to "Sunday school" at Holy Blossom Temple, the Jewish Reform synagogue, and there I had heard puzzling concepts. "Mummy," I asked solemnly, "Do you believe in God?"

My mother was sweetly conventional and eager to do right. "Why, yes dear," she said, with only a fraction of hesitation in her voice. "Of course I do. God made everything in the world…"

Thunderstruck, I stared up at her with a shocking new thought: Mummy, the fountain of all beauty, grace, and goodness; Mummy, the wise and gentle; Mummy…believed something so stupid.

So far as I can remember, this was the beginning of my being a contrarian. Not outwardly, of course — in the 1940s in Toronto, adults had unimpeachable authority and the concept of dissenting opinion was unheard of. I was a law-abiding child, wore smocked dresses on special occasions, and attended much-loathed ballet lessons. At age nine I stole a half-eaten and abandoned candy stick from another child and was sick with miserable guilt and remorse for a week, until I finally threw it out uneaten.

And yet, inwardly, despite my veneer of obedience and conformity, a kernel of resistance had been planted with that astonishing revelation that adults believed in God the way Christian children believed in Santa. My skepticism was further nourished from the time I began school. There was just so much about received opinion that was palpably wrong. Most of my fellow students, for example, knew and declared loudly that Jews were dirty. Chants of "dirty Jew!" were especially popular at Christmas and Easter, along with taunts about how we had killed Jesus. Given my mother's devotion to modern hygiene, mandatory hand-washing, scrubbing of vegetables, and injunctions about wiping from front to back, I knew absolutely that Jews were not dirty. And I knew that no one in my community had killed Jesus.

Our forced participation in daily Christian prayers and seasonal Christian hymns and carols at public school was, ironically, another useful wedge driven between me and my peers. It was such a grotesquely painful struggle to mouth those alien words and sentiments, such a wrenching betrayal of my parents (or so I felt), that an invisible shield of non-belonging formed around me. (This was all during World War II, and although adults did not speak to children of what was happening to Jews in Europe, there was a constant atmosphere of secrecy, fear, and embattlement about being Jewish in anti-Semitic wartime Toronto, at least in our family.)

What a piece of good luck that "non-belonging" was. I was impervious to what "everyone knew" and "everyone believed." At the age when gender stereotypes were driven hourly and daily into every child's brain — it would be another twenty-five years before women dared to throw away their girdles — I quietly stocked up my contrary opinions. I observed. I watched my macho father tie a frilly tea apron around his waist and wash the dishes one night to help my overburdened mother. To defend his masculinity, he spent the time declaiming women's inability to drive cars as well as men. Silently, I formed my own opinion.

Without conscious intent, I scoured the library for books in which girls played an active role. At Holy Blossom, I seized on the (exceedingly rare) examples of Jewish women who claimed a place in history. I was so swept away by Emma Lazarus that I memorized her entire poem inscribed on the Statue of Liberty: "Give me your tired, your poor, your huddled masses yearning to be free." A Jewish woman wrote that! Any scrap of female possibility was thrilling to me.

There was not a shred of daily life that wasn't ruled by gender. My well-meaning mother, anxious to bring her children up to succeed in mainstream, gentile society, drilled the rules into us at every opportunity: "Little ladies must never whistle." "Boys will be boys." "Girls should know better and try to keep their brothers out of trouble." "Ladies cross their ankles, not their legs." "All-white underwear…" "Girls may not play outside after supper." At the dinner table, my brother was exhorted by our proudly beaming parents to eat more, take second helpings, to grow big and strong! I was scolded away from the potatoes — as a child actress, I must watch my weight.

Language meant so much to me that by the age of 12 I became deeply troubled by the innate sexism of English. I spent hours scribbling poems and essays on the backs of my father's order forms (he was a travelling salesman in women's "shmattes") and I recall the intellectual seriousness I brought to the task of explaining on paper that the masculine pronoun "he," used universally, excluded me and was unfair.

Around this time, I stumbled across the name of the book *The Second Sex* by Simone de Beauvoir. I can't imagine where I saw the reference in my white-bread suburban setting, where I was still not allowed to have an adult library card. But I knew I had to read that book — the very title alone spoke to me, spoke of the secret knowledge I had about the unfairness of the world. On my regular rounds of libraries — I visited two or three each week on my bicycle, to avoid the only-three-books-at-a-time rule — I realized that the main adult library on St. George Street was attached to the Boys and Girls House. I could drift into the adult section unobserved. The first few times I tried to get my hands on the book, the librarian indignantly refused to loan me *The Second Sex*, which was kept behind the counter. One lucky day, I saw a dewy-fresh student librarian on duty. With nervous nonchalance, I pushed the request slip across the desk. Without a blink, she fetched the book for me.

Lightning bolts! Thunder! My heart actually raced as I read hungrily, chapter after chapter. So much of it was miles beyond my comprehension. And there were passages that were deeply disturbing: this wonderful woman, this author who was naming with brilliant clarity all the injustices from which women suffered, also seemed to hate women's bodies. (I was too young to understand ironies). She seemed to find childbirth disgusting and to detest motherhood. Nevertheless, here at last was a public voice to affirm my inner one. Here was the first person I had ever heard, met, or read who rejected the same limiting stereotypes that so angered me.

Reading Simone de Beauvoir, however half-comprehendingly, set the seal on my feminism. She gave me permission to turn my unspoken instincts into core beliefs.

By 13, at high school, I knew that I not only rejected the strangling prissiness of 1950s femininity, but that I was surely a loser in that game anyway. It just was not in me to simper, flirt, giggle and gaze adoringly upon those lumpen high school boys. I did not care to admire their sweaty and oafish team games. They certainly did not care to admire me, with my defiant pigtails (worn in explicit rejection of bouffant curls) and wearing my brother's fly-front jeans.

Now, from the perspective of having recently become a septuagenarian, I can see that I was always out of sync with my generation. Even at university, I met with a blank wall of gender discrimination and stupidity, especially on the part of the all-male professoriate. If several of the other female students harboured feminist sentiments, they were careful to toe the gender line and keep silent.

Throughout the late '60s, as the movement surged into life and a whole wave of younger feminists sprang up behind me, I was at home knee-deep in babies, snorting derisively at Betty Friedan ("Simone said this 15 years ago, and better!") and missing the entire phenomenon of consciousness-raising. It was exhilarating, a few years later, to come back into the work world at *Chatelaine* magazine, with feminists both much older than I (Doris Anderson) and much younger. Seven years after that, I was, finally, exactly the right age to reach a huge readership at the *Toronto Star*, a readership eager to seize a feminist analysis to make sense of their lives.

Feminism gave me a way to understand the world and a way to fight back — and it gave me the deep happiness of knowing that I was part of an era that changed the world for the better.

50 | L'ENSEIGNANT N'AVAIT PAS RAISON

Louise Langevin

1975. Année internationale de la femme. Je suis en IVe secondaire dans une polyvalente dans un milieu (défavorisé, je le réalise bien maintenant) des Basses-Laurentides au Nord de Montréal. J'ai 14 ou 15 ans. Dans mon cours de religion (classe de filles seulement), nous avons des présentations sur la sexualité. L'enseignant (dans la quarantaine) nous distribue une feuille qu'il nous dit de garder bien précieusement toute notre vie. Il s'agit de ses réflexions sur le sujet.

C'est comme s'il nous distribuait la vérité sur papier. Le document, présenté en deux colonnes, porte sur les qualités des femmes et des hommes. Les hommes sont décidés, ne sont pas peureux, ne sont pas émotifs, et sont capables de vivre seuls et ils sont débrouillards. Les femmes ne peuvent pas vivre seules, ne sont pas capables de prendre des décisions, sont peureuses et émotives et sont dépendantes des hommes. Il y avait d'autres « qualités » énumérées, mais je me souviens de celles-là.

Quel choc en lisant ce document ! Je connaissais des hommes et des femmes qui étaient différent-e-s de ce qu'il y avait sur cette liste. Du haut de mes 14-15 ans, je ne me sentais pas dépendante des hommes. Je me demandais comment cet enseignant en était arrivé à ses conclusions. J'ai compris qu'il pensait que les hommes étaient supérieurs aux femmes. Ce n'était pas la première fois que je recevais ce message au cours de mes études secondaires. Je ne me sentais pas inférieure aux étudiants masculins. Certes, je n'étais pas bonne en sport ou en mécanique et pas forte physiquement, mais j'étais dix fois plus intelligente qu'eux. Et j'allais le leur prouver. J'avais déjà compris que la meilleure façon d'assurer mon avenir était par l'éducation et non le mariage.

Je ne me souviens plus s'il y a eu une discussion en classe au sujet de cette liste de « qualités. » Je n'ai pas dit à cet enseignant qu'il était un gros porc macho. J'aurais dû. J'aurais été quitte pour une suspension. On était pourtant à l'époque du « savoir-parler », compétence que le ministère de l'Éducation voulait développer avec le « savoir-lire » et le « savoir-écrire. »

Je n'ai pas conservé ce document. L'enseignant de religion est aujourd'hui décédé. Je ne sais pas pendant combien d'années il a distribué ce document à ses classes et ainsi continué à propager ses idées sexistes et à faire des ravages. Je ne sais pas s'il était plus ou moins sexiste que les autres enseignants. Tout autant, je suppose.

Je n'ai pas suivi ses conseils. J'ai continué mes études contre vents et marées. Au cours des années, j'ai rencontré d'autres enseignants au collège, professeurs à l'université et collègues de travail qui pensaient (et pensent encore) que les hommes étaient (et sont) supérieurs. Je ne les ai pas crus (et je ne les crois toujours pas). J'ai aussi rencontré des femmes et des hommes convaincus du potentiel des femmes.

Aujourd'hui, lorsque j'enseigne, je suis toujours surprise de remarquer que les hommes prennent la parole beaucoup plus souvent que les femmes, même s'ils sont très peu nombreux dans le groupe, et peu importe le sujet. Pourquoi parlent-ils toujours ? Veulent-ils limiter la liberté d'expression des femmes ? Comment faire pour que les femmes s'expriment ?

Ce n'est que des années plus tard que j'ai réalisé que cet événement (avec d'autres bien sûr) avait contribué à faire de moi une féministe engagée pour l'atteinte d'une plus grande justice sociale. J'ai aussi réalisé le rôle important que jouent les enseignant-e-s dans le maintien des stéréotypes sexistes. Mes filles de huit et onze ans me disent que leur jeune enseignant d'éducation physique regarde toujours les exploits des garçons et pas ceux des filles, et donc qu'il ne peut certes pas donner une note dans le bulletin pour des filles. Au moins, elles s'en rendent compte…

51 | MAO'S LITTLE RED BOOK
Karin Lee

I didn't *become* a feminist, I was raised by parents who encouraged all their children to consider themselves equals in society regardless of gender, race, ethnicity, or class.

My name is Karin Lee. I was born in 1960 and raised in Vancouver, BC. My mother Lillian Mah is a 3rd generation Canadian — her grandparents arrived here from southern China in the late 1890s, settling in Barkerville, BC. My great-grandmother, Ho Shee, had bound feet when she arrived in Canada, but my grandmother Florence, who was five when she came, was spared this signifier of class because she was going to live in the new world.

Florence would marry into the wealthy Chinese family of Mah Bing Kee in Nanaimo, BC, and have seven children — the fourth born was my mother Lillian.

My father's journey to Canada was fraught with challenges. Long before Wally Lee was born, my grandfather, Harry Lee, came to this country in 1903, paid the head tax and opened up a small café in Stoughton, Saskatchewan. But in 1923, the Chinese Exclusion Act came into effect. Harry responded by periodically returning to China where he started a family with his wife Kung Shee, while continuing his business in Canada. It took until 1948 and the creation of the Family Reunification Act before my now 50-year-old grandmother could come to Canada along with her two youngest children. My father Wally, who was still attending university in China, had to wait another year before he could come, because he was over the age of 18.

Kung Shee had spent all of her life in China taking care of the property, the house, and the family, as most "gold-mountain widows" did. Once settled in Canada, she soon found herself relegated to the back of her husband's restaurant while he carried on his affair with his Swedish lover/waitress. Kung Shee was treated like a hired hand, not like the matriarch of the family.

Within a year she committed suicide.

Only after my father's arrival in Canada, did he find out about his mother's fatal demise. Wally turned his attention to the Communist wave in China, and Mao's socialist philosophy. It was around this time that my mother Lillian met my father Wally in Vancouver. She was happy in some ways that he was a "new immigrant" with "new ideas."

By the early 1960s, I was born, and so was my father's new venture: a bookstore in Vancouver that sold goods, literature, and propaganda from the People's Republic of China. Both of my parents worked to support the family. However, my mother was able to boast that her husband did half the housework and childrearing. This socialist practice extended to all the children, including my brother who was often ridiculed by his boy cousins about his equal domestic duties and responsibilities. I was never taught that this was "feminism," and was surprised to learn that so many other families, regardless of race or class, were so backward with regards to gender equality.

In my weekly studies at Vancouver's Chinese Youth Association (a code name for a China Canada Socialist Club) I learned about socialism, gender equality, imperialism and racism through Mao's Little Red Book. Throughout the 1960s and '70s, my parents took me to street protests, political rallies, and community functions. I held up placards and listened to a lot of people talk about societal change. Feminism wasn't an issue within our family, but I became acutely aware of how our family was an anomaly in both the white mainstream and Asian communities. It was the words of Mao Zedong who spoke the truth to me about the inequities of the world, not the North American feminist movement, that my mother noted was primarily white, middle class, and had little to do with our own world and the Chinese community.

I met many white feminists during my youth and early adulthood. I became irritated with them, when time and time again they made assumptions that I came from a patriarchal family and that I needed to be "rescued" from my cultural traditions and Asian roots. What I yearned for was to find a community of women who understood that I didn't experience sexism within my family, but faced rampant "sexism" and "racism" in the larger society, and certainly hidden "racism" within the white feminist movement.

I was perplexed as to why Canadian feminists claimed victory for winning the women's vote in 1918. In reality, all women didn't get the right to vote until 1960 — the year that First Nations' and Aboriginal peoples were granted the vote. Canadian women of Chinese descent were given the franchise in 1948. It was this history that opened my eyes to the problems faced by women of colour within the suffrage movement. It is precisely these details that become edited out of our collective memory that create gaps in our history, and it is important to acknowledge this history in the feminist movement of the past and present.

Women have engaged in acts of resistance and have fought for women's rights for centuries, in diverse ways and in specific circumstances. As for my own daughters — Naiya (age 14) and Sahali (age 10) — they will continue to define their own approach to gender equality, but will realize that there were many women and men who came before them that gave them the privilege to do so.

52 | GRÂCE À SIMONE DE BEAUVOIR

Andrée Lévesque

Dix ans après la publication du *Deuxième Sexe* (1949), censuré par l'archevêque, le livre demeurait introuvable dans la plupart des librairies de Montréal. Heureusement, il se trouvait quelques petites libraires audacieuses, comme La Libraire internationale, rue Sherbrooke, où, discrètement, on pouvait s'approvisionner en livres interdits. C'est là qu'à dix-huit ans je découvre Simone de Beauvoir. Je suis ravie, non seulement de défier les autorités mais de trouver une telle résonance dans les idées de Beauvoir.

J'ai toutefois un problème à cette époque : je ne connais personne avec qui en discuter et je ne vois pas très bien comment le féminisme peut s'appliquer à ma vie d'étudiante en géographie dans un département qui compte très peu d'étudiantes et aucune professeure. Un contexte qui rend difficile de concilier un idéal d'égalité, de non-conformisme avec la réalité de mes études.

Très tôt je me marie et j'abandonne mes études, car « qui prend mari prend pays. » Je suis mon mari dans une ville étrangère (London, Ontario) et j'ai des enfants. Lorsque sort *The Feminine Mystique* de Betty Friedan, je le lis et je me dis qu'il ne m'apprend rien de plus que celui de Beauvoir. Après trois années en Ontario, avec mon mari, nous arrivons en Caroline du Nord où je décide de réorganiser ma vie. Je peux retourner aux études ; l'université a une garderie au moins l'avant-midi ; je peux étudier le soir. Je m'inscris en histoire à l'Université Duke, sans toutefois négliger de taper à la machine les travaux de mon mari.

Je me retrouve une fois de plus avec très peu de consœurs. Il n'y a qu'une seule professeure, Anne Firor Scott, auteure d'ouvrages importants sur les femmes du Sud des États-Unis, mais l'histoire américaine ne fait pas partie de mes champs de spécialisation. C'est seulement beaucoup plus tard (à la Berkshire Conference in Women's History) que j'ai connu Anne et que j'ai pu apprécier ses recherches.

Le mariage s'essouffle et se dissout. Après mes examens de synthèse, je rentre à Montréal. À l'époque où sans doctorat et sans publication on peut décrocher un poste universitaire, je suis engagée au Collège Loyola, qui va bientôt s'affilier à l'Université Concordia. Comme nous sommes deux femmes dans le département, nous partageons un bureau : j'ai ainsi la chance de me lier d'amitié avec Mary A. Hill (alors Mary Porter) qui, en 1980, publiera une magnifique biographie de Charlotte Perkins Gilman. Entre 1967 et 1970, nous vivons, et le savons, en des temps turbulents où tous les espoirs sont permis. Nous discutons beaucoup et lors de longs débats, nous pouvons sérieusement nous demander si nous sommes plongées dans une situation révolutionnaire. Notre enseignement est une action politique, militante même.

Ce doit être en 1968 que Mary me dit qu'elle assiste à un cours, donné à l'Université McGill par l'Américaine Marlene Dixon, sur la libération des femmes. Je l'envie : avec deux jeunes enfants et la préparation de cours, mes sorties sont limitées. Un jour, Mary me parle d'un petit groupe de femmes qui se réunit pour discuter de féminisme. Je me retrouve bientôt dans un cercle de conscientisation sur la libération des femmes. Pour la première fois après avoir lu *Le Deuxième Sexe*, je peux enfin l'analyser et en débattre avec d'autres femmes.

Dans ce petit cercle, la plupart des membres sont Américaines, mariées à des hommes qui se sont établis au Canada pour résister au service militaire obligatoire et à la guerre du Vietnam. Je suis la seule francophone et, par la force des choses, je n'ai aucun contact avec les féministes québécoises pourtant très dynamiques, engagées dans le Front de Libération des femmes du Québec en 1969. Chaque quinzaine, notre petit groupe se réunit pour discuter de nos lectures et nous interroger sur leur pertinence dans nos vies de jeunes profs.

L'inspiration est surtout américaine; on dissèque les brochures des New York Radical Women, des Redstockings et de WITCH. Qui peut oublier l'effet de lire pour la première fois « The Myth of Vaginal Orgasm » d'Anne Koedt ou « The Personal is Political » de Carol Hanisch ? Après avoir lu un article sur la socialisation sexuée des jeunes enfants, nous entreprenons de présenter chacune un exposé sur notre propre socialisation. Autrement dit, d'examiner comment nous avons été construites comme filles. Je réalise alors que je ne suis pas la seule à vivre des contradictions qui semblent insurmontables.

Ces échanges sont pour moi une révélation. Je rédige alors une thèse de doctorat sur la Gauche au Québec, thèse dans laquelle les femmes sont totalement absentes. Je me dis socialiste, mais mes circonstances « objectives », mon éducation et mon salaire, me situent dans la bourgeoisie, une bourgeoisie honnie qu'on ne cesse de décrier. Je me sens souvent en porte-à-faux : écrivant sur la classe ouvrière sans y appartenir, appelant à une révolution surtout au nom des autres, me définissant comme radicale mais agissant en libérale. Cependant, en tant que femme, je n'échappe pas au statut de citoyenne de second ordre, même comme enseignante. Une analyse féministe, la découverte d'une oppression spécifiquement féminine, donnent enfin de la cohérence à mon existence.

Cette période de trépidation s'interrompt brusquement quand, en amour une autre fois, je me retrouve à suivre un autre conjoint jusqu'en Nouvelle-Zélande. Dans une petite ville universitaire, Dunedin, j'établis bientôt des contacts avec quelques féministes et ensemble nous fondons un collectif féministe, The Dunedin Collective for Women. Nous nous battons pour un monde nouveau, nous descendons dans la rue, nous dénonçons le patriarcal sous toutes ses formes, nous sommes radicales.

Entre les enfants et les luttes féministes, je me « recycle » en histoire des femmes : j'ai trouvé le moyen d'intégrer le militantisme et la vie professionnelle. Dans le premier pays à accorder le droit de vote aux femmes, en 1893, je connais l'émerveillement de découvrir les archives encore inexploitées des premières féministes. J'offre bientôt mon premier cours en histoire des femmes au département de l'extension de l'Université Otago. Le privé est devenu politique même dans la recherche historique. Je peux sans complexe enseigner et écrire sur l'oppression séculaire des femmes, sur la contraception, l'avortement, des sujets jamais abordés dans les cours que j'ai moi-même suivis.

Je suis fortement encouragée dans mes nouvelles recherches quand, en 1974, je participe à la Berkshire Conference in Women's History au collège Radcliffe. La rencontre de toutes ces historiennes sérieuses, reconnues, comme Joan Kelly-Gadol, Gerda Lerner et bien d'autres qui ont lancé l'histoire des femmes, m'enthousiasme au plus haut point. Mon but dépasse toutefois l'égalité des femmes dans une société inchangée, capitaliste et patriarcale.

En rédigeant cet essai d'égohistoire, je me suis demandé si mon milieu familial m'avait prédestinée comme féministe. Je suis l'aînée de trois enfants, une sœur puis un frère de dix ans mon cadet, trop jeune pour avoir provoqué des sentiments de discrimination en faveur d'un fils. Au contraire, dans une école catholique de filles, je souhaitais bien avoir un frère aîné qui m'aurait présentée à ses camarades. Ma mère avait travaillé comme secrétaire et en était fière. Tel que prescrit, elle a quitté son travail au moment de son mariage et est devenue une « femme-à-la-maison », souffrant peut-être de cette maladie sans nom décrite par Friedan. Mon grand modèle fut ma grand-tante célibataire, infirmière avant de tenir une maison de chambres. Jamais, à ce que je sache, un homme n'a occupé le centre de sa vie. Elle ne se serait pas appelée féministe, mais elle croyait fermement à l'égalité des droits même si, en catholique fervente, elle n'eût approuvé ni le divorce, ni l'avortement.

Je me suis définie comme féministe assez tôt, mais il a fallu des années pour rapprocher la théorie de la pratique. Depuis, je poursuis mes recherches, surtout sur les femmes qui se situent dans la marge et sur celles qui ont voulu changer le monde.

53 | DAUGHTERS

Florence Gibson MacDonald

Daughters. That's where my feminism began.

I was 30 years old when the first of my two daughters was born and, in many ways, I was born with her. I saw the world for the first time when I saw it through her infant eyes. I had not seen it before because I had lived in a swamp of endless bayous, tangled roots and dark, deep waterways that looped and circled back upon themselves in a confusing maze of options and directions that turned out to be nothing more than opportunities to drown.

Prior to my daughters, I lived a dichotomy of neglect, an absence of self. When my first was born I saw the lie, I saw that my life was not the life I wanted. But I didn't know what I was seeing, so I couldn't name it. All I remember thinking about at that time was fear — a fear that I would never be able to protect her. That she would never be safe. And that my life would never be the same.

I had a very happy childhood. I grew up in a household with three brothers; I ran with the wolves; tomboy, free, muscular, a dreamer. But I was punched in the gut with the arrival of my first period. To be defined a "girl" was a profoundly negative experience for me.

Throughout high school, I didn't know what I wanted to "be." It never occurred to me to just be *me*. I did well in the arts as well as the sciences and I decided, since I could read my favourite books by myself (Tolstoy, Dickens, the Brontës), that I would study science at school and enjoy the arts. So I did an undergraduate degree in genetics and biochemistry at the University of Toronto and then, following in the footsteps of my newly minted husband, I decided I wanted to be a doctor too. I entered medical school at McMaster University in 1974. My medical degree was a ticket to travel and work, something I had always wanted to do.

Over the course of many years, I treated Vietnamese boat people in Hong Kong; wintered in the Northwest Territories flying into native settlements like Tuktoyaktuk and Paulatuk; and worked in the bush in Kenya, establishing a nutrition centre in a polygamous society where the average man had four wives and the average woman had 12 children. While my eyes were opened to the plight of women, still my heart wasn't. It took the birth of my daughter once back in Canada to do that.

Back home, setting up a medical practice was not, in retrospect, something I wanted to do. But I didn't let on, even to myself. At the time, I was devouring *The Second Sex*, *The Female Eunuch*, and the words of Betty Friedan. I was also dieting and obsessing about body image while running an anti-diet program for women, and spouting feminist tracts. And I was (in my new-found, ungrounded feminist way) discovering that I wanted to write.

By the time my second daughter was born two years later, I decided it was time for parallel careers — part-time doctor, part-time playwright, and full-time mother. I was cross-eyed trying to keep my focus, exhausted from the workload, terrified of both my careers, emotionally very alone and isolated within my marriage. One morning I was in front of my house, which doubled as our medical office, on a quiet street in Port Hope, Ontario. I was watching my youngest daughter, still a toddler, charging up and down the street when a woman came by and said, "You shouldn't be here, you should be in the office working."

Wracked with guilt, I gave my daughter over to her sitter when she arrived, only to face the advice of my first patient of the day, a well-meaning, elderly woman who said, "You shouldn't be here seeing me, you should be upstairs with your children, they'll grow up without you." It proved to be a defining moment in my life, and yet it did not take into account the fact that I was in a profession that I was beginning to loath. What I wanted to be was a writer, but I was in the closet.

I didn't believe in myself as a writer. I didn't know what "a writer" was. I had no formal training so I didn't think I deserved the appellation. But in due time, slowly, I made my way up the theatre ranks in Toronto. I would drive into Toronto to get my plays workshopped and produced at the Fringe, and in small independent companies. Slowly but surely I learned the craft from the ground up. I worked on props, painted sets, wrote grants, marketed my work, hung posters, and handed out flyers. I took extensive dramaturgical notes and did exorbitant amounts of research in order to get my plays produced. Gradually, I learned how to please everyone, to garner respect and to gain experience, and I began to win awards.

My work has always, at its core, been an examination of female complicity. This is because I have always been an uneasy member of the feminist tribe — even though I fought, and marched, and signed petitions for abortion rights, women's clinics, eco-feminism and the like, in my heart I was guarded, holding back. Why was that?

At my insistence, in 1991, we relocated as a family to Toronto. I turned forty years old the week of the move and, so stressful was the event, a great swath of grey hair appeared in my jet black hair, just above my left eye, which I proudly swept up and across my head. I began to work part time in women's reproductive health clinics, trying to narrow my medical focus so as to find room for my own vision. Somewhere in the 1990s, exhausted from juggling two professions and parenting my teenage daughters, I opened the door to the writer's closet. There was no defining incident, just a gradual realization of who I was, at least in terms of my profession: I was a writer, not a doctor.

So I stopped practicing medicine.

I see now that my husband never forgave me. Perhaps he was jealous of me, frightened of me, or envious of the power of my voice. Unbeknownst to me, he began to have a string of affairs, creating an even greater emotional divide between himself and his family of women. I, still not an intact feminist, took this as an indicator that I should do more work in order to "save the marriage." Of course all this was subconscious on my part; because all his clandestine activities were just below the surface, I hadn't realized that I had swum back into that swamp and that the water was black and fetid, devoid of oxygen and incapable of sustaining all life forms.

It wasn't until he declared himself gone, clearly stated his emotional absence from the last 25 years of our 37-year-old marriage, that I saw the swamp for what it was. He stepped aside and I saw, not myself, but my complicity, the very subject of my writing: I was a helper, a handmaid, in my own life, a woman whose focus was all about pleasing a man who withheld love. I was complicit in my own half-life. I lived in a shadow. I saw what is hardest for me to look at now: by my example, I have deprived my own daughters of the light of knowledge of who they themselves are. I didn't know who I was

> Spring-summer, 1972

Archives and Special Collections (CWMA), University of Ottawa (PC-X10-1-137)/ Eleanor Gelmo

> Printemps-été 1972

in a lifeless marriage, so I could not provide them with my full self. Daughters.

That's where my feminism begins. That's where it lives and breathes, in making sure that we know ourselves, first and foremost, inside and outside our relationships. Knowing fully who we are, and what we want most, because if we know that, we know the world, and our place in it. Because I am a writer, this is what I will write, as I begin the process of changing my name back to who I was in my mother's house, with the eyes of the newborn, hand-in-hand with my daughters.

54 | MY FEMINIST WALK
Linda MacDonald

I came to feminism by being born into a family where I witnessed and endured violence on a weekly basis. From the age of three I can remember knowing that it was wrong for my father to hit my mother and call her names. As I grew older and tried to stop my father from beating my mother, he directed his misogyny towards me as well, attempting to disarm my assertion by demeaning me with slaps, jeering looks, and calling me names.

The first time he called me "cunt" still rings in my ears. The violence continued my entire childhood, and despite continually begging my mother to leave, she stayed. And thus, even though I knew there was a better way, because my mother did not have the same belief in possibilities that I did, I became stuck in a cycle of violence.

Despite all the ugliness around me I maintained hope for my future. In 1960, when I was just seven years old I remember lying in a field of grass looking up at the blue sky and seeing a vision of my-Self as a very old woman, standing in a room speaking to a large audience. I had a smile on my face and looked very proud knowing that I had helped many people in my life. I tucked that vision away and carried it with me from that time onward, as an image to live my life by.

By age thirteen I decided to stop trying to plan ways to get free from the constant agony of the violence I was living with, and instead made new dreams of a better life for me and any children I might have someday. There were no safe houses in the '60s and even if there were my mother wouldn't have gone. She had too much false pride about what the neighbours would think, and she didn't want to lose her house. I knew the hell of relational violence wasn't worth any secrets, or any house, and vowed to live my adult life as a woman with equality. I buried the agonizing hurt from all the misogyny I endured growing up deep inside, all the while dragging my-Self though my developing years, getting my education and working toward a career.

Over the years, I kept telling my-Self to never put my-Self in the position my mother had, where she felt dependent on a man. I knew with every fibre of my being that such dependence was a deadly trap for a woman and her children.

In the '70s I went to nursing school at a time when student nurses were told that we were equal to doctors, and the birth control pill was easily accessible. I naively thought that the days of inequality were behind me (because I was living away from my family) and that there was a better world out there for women, at least in North America. But I quickly learned that gender inequality was still very present with lecherous male hands grabbing my breasts on numerous occasions, being called a slut when walking home one evening, and even having my vagina grabbed when walking along Barrington St. in the middle of the day.

These men thought they had the right to grab my body simply because I was a woman.

Over time I sadly realized that the world was not a safe place, nor one of equality, but was instead riddled with everyday violations. I continued to add my anger and hurt to the pile I was carrying from my childhood and trudged on, thinking I was stronger than all the hurt of the gender violations that I carried with me.

In the '80s I married and had three children, one boy and two girls, in that order. I was so wrapped up in trying to stay grounded and not let the triggering of my own violent childhood flood into my children's lives I hardly had time to pay any attention to what was going on around me. (I vaguely remember the *Charter of Rights and Freedoms* being passed in 1982.) I worked very hard to bring my children up with equality ever present in their reality, and to never know what it felt like to be trapped in a violent home.

Eventually, the burden of dragging around all my buried emotions became too much and I joined the Self help movement, going to group healing sessions and opening my-Self up to all the hurt and anger that I had buried. My world blossomed, I could feel my-Self growing and I never looked back. Around that time I met another woman whom I knew to be a feminist and I asked her a question that had caused me guilt about why I had often preferred spending time with men rather than women. She talked about oppressed group behaviour and women allying themselves with male power. It was like an explosion went off in my head. The feminist theory had broken the chains on my mind and I could fully embrace my-Self as a woman. On that day I stepped totally into feminism.

In the '90s my children were old enough that I decided to continue my education and fulfill my dream of becoming involved in public education and activism. Knowing that I had learned how to heal from childhood violence, I wanted to help others with the same history. So, along with the feminist woman I had met, we started counselling people who had been harmed as children.

Another key turning point for me was when a woman who was enduring ritual abuse-torture came for help. I was taken to the darkest reality of human evil behaviour and witnessed forms of misogyny that I never knew existed. Since that time I have been standing for the human rights of women and children who are suffering from ritual abuse-torture and have encountered many blockers — the most shocking being misogynist women who call themselves feminists and yet intentionally try to stop other women from speaking their voice about the suffering they are enduring.

Withstanding many discrediting attacks on my feminist activist work has made me a very strong woman and I now consider my-Self a feisty feminist. I have great pride in my work and feel that I am using my best skills of educating others about the ravages of relational violence, showing women ways out so they can live with dignity and respect. On the darkest of days, when I have heard enough about the torture and trafficking of innocent children, I look at my own wonderful adult children and know that I must keep putting one foot in front of another to be a part of the community of very hard working feminist activists who are striving for a better world for all children, both girls and boys.

I keep the vision I had at age seven very close to my heart to remind me how proud I will be as an old woman if I keep true to my goal—to help many women and children live a better life, free from violence. If I succeed I will die a very happy feminist indeed.

55 | A FAILURE AT PHYSICS
Sharon M.H. MacDonald

Because I had the good fortune to be born into a family where a girl child could expect to have all the opportunities that any boy child might have, I grew up oblivious to the fact that gender inequity would one day be an issue in my life.

The first broad hint came in high school when a physics teacher prefaced one of his lectures with, "Girls, you don't need to listen because you won't understand anyway."

I confess that physics was not my favourite subject and, in silent, ineffectual rebellion, I did not listen to or understand what this objectionable man had to say. However, the fact that his remark stands out even now, when everything else that happened in high school has more or less faded from memory, says volumes about the power of negativity. It also reveals my own sense of shock and indignation in encountering the first real misogynist in my life.

I managed to survive high school physics and, with no regrets, said goodbye forever to the subject. But I wonder how many potential physicists among the girls in the school were discouraged from pursuing what might have been their true passion.

In 1967, I moved from the East Coast to the West. It was a glorious time to be young, adventurous, and far away from home.

Not long after arriving, I stopped wearing a bra, but it did not occur to me that I was protesting anything greater than discomfort. If I was aware of "women's lib" I certainly did not relate it to my own life at this time. It is no small irony that a male friend convinced me to cast off the shackles of bra-dom. Looking back, I wonder if, rather than having my comfort in mind, he simply enjoyed the sight of bouncing breasts. With further hindsight, I recognize that this was just one instance among others in which the sexual revolution worked more positively in men's favour. *Quelle surprise!*

I grew up studying and performing ballet and character dance. In Vancouver, I discovered an expressive new world in modern dance and eventually dropped out of university to perform and teach dance full time. Working with musicians, visual artists, poets and actors, I became part of Intermedia — an artists' cooperative. In 1970, Intermedia artists brought their talents together to create The Dome show at the Vancouver Art Gallery. A dynamic time, to be sure, but the great gender divide became evident during the process. With Buckminster Fuller's geodesic dome as the starting point for creative imaginings, we threw ourselves into production. Again, feminist consciousness passed me by, for as a dancer, the exotic "other," working in a predominantly female art form, I was able to avoid the harsh reality that faced the women poets, visual artists and sculptors. Women were not supposed to be artists competing with men on their terrain. It took years before it dawned on me that we, the dancers, were tolerated because we were adornments for the installations of the "real" (i.e., male) artists, and, therefore, did not present a threat.

Years later I returned to the East Coast. Married with children, and living in relative isolation in rural Nova Scotia, it slowly dawned on me that the nuclear family held unexpected pitfalls. I learned that women often had double duty while men had double standards. I reached out for sisterhood among a number of other similarly situated women, and we transformed our mostly unacknowledged frustration and anger into productive projects. We initiated educational programs, community outreach, and support systems for women in more desperate straits than ourselves. For the most part, we considered ourselves privileged. We were articulate, we had a language for our discontent and we were optimistic that we could change the world.

Yet privileged or not, misery or misfortune can arrive and knock us sideways. We discover our lives will not have the storybook endings we unconsciously imagined for ourselves. Nevertheless, if fortunate, we recover and grow, often finding greater freedom and happiness than anticipated because we are not caught up in any story but one of our own making.

Looking back on the 1980s when we were idealistic crusading feminists, I feel a fondness for that time when we doggedly pursued collective action in order to bring about a revolution we passionately believed in. Today I am more solitary and I direct my less overt feminism to uncovering the stories of earlier feminists whose remarkable lives should be acknowledged and celebrated. Muriel Lester, a British pacifist and feminist, said: "Once your eyes get open to… pacifism you can't shut them again… you can't unsee it. You may bitterly regret the fact that you happen to be one of the tiny minority of the human race who have caught this angle of vision but you can't help it."

This is true of feminism. Once viewed and comprehended, you can't "unsee" it. Feminism informs the way you view and relate to the world. For better or worse, I continue to live with and embrace this angle of vision.

56 | MY BEST SELF
Diana Majury

Like many of us, I expect, I like to think that I have always been a feminist. I certainly cannot think of the specific time when I became a feminist; there was no single "aha" feminist moment. Instead, the pieces of feminism all fit for me; they came together, it seemed, naturally and smoothly — the recognition that girls and women were not treated equally and fairly, that we were somehow seen as lesser (as less capable, less smart, less good at sports, less good at most things that mattered); the recognition that many of the things that girls and women were thought to be good at were things not seen as important or valuable. Some of these "truths" I internalized and some I resisted, but as a bottom line, I knew that women are not lesser.

I saw that many of us were pretty damn good at the "boy" things, and that many of the things women were seen to be good at were things that I valued… immensely. So the reality of sexism did not fit my perception, neither my self-perception nor my perception of the girls and women around me. Feminism provided the corrective that made my perceptions fit. Feminism gave me the grounding, confidence, and analysis to believe that we could change this situation of inequality, that we could change the world.

I am to my core a second wave feminist. I participated in consciousness raising; I voraciously read all of the new feminist literature — Greer, Millett, Firestone, Friedan, Morgan, Rowbotham, de Beauvoir, Clark and Lewis, Daly, Griffin, Rich, Lorde — the list was so wonderfully long, and now impossibly so. I was involved in the early days of second wave activism: on the crisis lines for a rape crisis centre, setting up a women's shelter, organizing Take Back the Night and IWD marches, agitating for family law reform and abortion rights, publishing a women's health magazine.

Feminism is my primary self-identification. It is my aspiration and my touchstone. Feminism radicalized white middle-class me and opened my eyes to other forms of oppression and to my role in them. To the extent that I recognize and understand the inequities of race, class, disability, sexuality and gender identity, it is thanks to feminism. My understanding of feminism is that it requires us to work against all forms of subordination. Feminism holds us to high anti-oppression standards and, while many of us as feminists fall short much of the time, feminism evolves and shifts its understanding to constantly demand more and demand better of us. I understand that for some the vision and the push for a better world comes from anti-racism, or from critical disability, or from socialism; it is feminism that drives and pushes me.

My feminism led to my lesbianism. My heterosexual self was having sex with men while all of my emotional, intellectual, and relational energy was with women… But then the lesbian light went on — I suddenly saw the contradiction, and that I had a choice. I could integrate my emotional and sexual selves by dumping the hetero part, by becoming/being a lesbian. Such a gift from feminism!

In the absence of a single, clear feminist moment, I am simply going to list a number of, what were for me, important feminist moments — moments of bonding, aloneness, laughter, tears, pain, joy, intellectual challenge and growth, emotional challenge and growth — moments that I hope will entice other feminists to reminisce with me.

> My first Michigan women's music festival: women everywhere, so many women; amazing women artists singing and performing about women's lives; feeling totally safe walking alone in the dark; seeing the beauty of women's diverse naked bodies — being shocked by how different we are in size and shape; for the first time seeing women with mastectomies — naked, strong, and gorgeous; and, on the down side, the most disgusting porta-janes I have ever encountered.

> Sitting around a table at LEAF, debating, strategizing, arguing about the wisdom of using the word misogyny in a factum, or the strategy of putting forward a feministly controversial argument.

> Silencing lively dinner party chatter with a challenge to a sexist comment, or a racist joke.

> My nieces and nephew whom I adore. I worried about their acceptance of my feminism, of my lesbianism, of me… I worried needlessly. They embraced me and my partner; we discuss, argue, laugh and cry together — as family. I hope to find feminists and even a lesbian/gay among them, but I try not to push them too hard in my direction.

> Spending evenings, days, weekends, with my Healthsharing collective: participating passionately in the most intense and heated, yet amicable, arguments I have ever been part of; laughing hysterically as the linotype machine spewed out a whole article with one word per line; co-writing and co-editing with the whole collective — perhaps not the most efficient but definitely

the most fun. I learned so much — about writing, about editing, about women's health, about the meaning of feminism.

A WAVAW anti-pornography bonfire at Toronto city hall.

My first US NAWL conference: hundreds and hundreds of women involved in the law — lawyers, activists, academics — taking over a downtown hotel in Boston and talking feminist politics and activism for three days non-stop. Feminism writ large in all its energy and potential and all its unevenness and in-fighting — it was totally inspirational for me.

The middle of the night phone call that the Toronto Morgentaler clinic was on fire; rushing to Harbord Street to stand, sing, cry, and shout with hundreds of other feminists.

Marshalling at an IWD march: arm band worn proudly, megaphone in hand, chanting, telling people what to do, feeling a key part of something big and important — I loved being a marshal…still do.

Going out on a feminist limb at a meeting and having a fellow feminist climb out after me to stand with me.

Cringing as I hear one feminist trash another; cringing when I realize myself as the trasher; cringing when I recognize myself as the trashee.

Coming out: my now dear friend Michele's endless patience in answering every one of my many questions about what it was like to be a lesbian, and how exactly you go about coming out, especially how you come out in the abstract — or can you? The "what took you so long" welcome I got from lesbian friends; the love and support I received from heterosexual friends.

Getting the middle-of-the-night phone call that Connie was in labour; many hours later watching my beautiful goddaughter, Bronwyn, pop into the world eyes wide open and ready for life.

Working on a project with immigrant women and learning slowly and painfully that what I initially thought was a chip on their shoulder was in fact a boulder in their path.

Hard and often nasty debates with fellow feminists over pornography, prostitution, and transgender.

Laughing until I cried through years of FemCab (the Toronto Five Minute Feminist Cabaret), and performances of the Clichettes and of Ladies Against Women (L.A.W.) — wicked and delightful feminist humour.

The realization that my mother would have liked to have had a career in the paid labour force, that she felt stifled/unfulfilled as a wife and mother — an "aha" moment that I took a long time to come to, and one that made me question what kind of feminist I was when I had not applied to my own mother's life what I otherwise spouted non-stop.

Endless debates about the role of men in the movement: whether men should be allowed on the march, or in the group at the head of the march; whether men should be invited to the conference, to the potluck, to the classroom.

The opportunity to be a grandmother without having been a mother — which at the moment means being greeted by Madeleine's outstretched arms, big smile, and the squeal of "gwannieee." I look forward to all the rest that it will mean in my life. Thank you, Sarah.

And now… talking with friends about how to cope with aging as a feminist, about where we will find a feminist old age home or whether we will have to create it ourselves, and about what a feminist funeral service might be.

To me, feminism is about negotiating the Scylla of rigid dogma and the Charybdis of mushy liberalism; it is about trying to live up to the ideals of justice and equality. It is a place of ongoing growth and change, challenge and support, disappointment and euphoria. It is who I am, who I aspire to be; it is my best self.

57 | A WOMAN OF AFRICAN DESCENT IN RURAL NEW BRUNSWICK

Mary Louise McCarthy

To tell the story of my path to feminism is to tell my story of understanding equality, or the lack of equality, in a world filled with much potential. Also, to tell my story of my path to feminism is to tell my story of a path to myself and to my inner soul. I will begin by defining and identifying who I am. I am a single female, a single parent of a 22-year-old son. Most importantly, I am a woman of African Canadian heritage.

I was born in rural New Brunswick, the middle child of nine children. My first clear impression or example of inequality was in my childhood home. We were a large family and our roles were defined. As a young child I was poignantly aware of the life roles people played. My mother was the caregiver, the housecleaner, the person who ran the house, and administered all the other people. But my father, though often absent, was the "head."

Growing up, I could not understand why, in the midst of my mother's busy day maintaining a home for nine children and two adults, she would stop all duties to make a cup of tea for my father. I could not understand why it was that whenever I wanted to go somewhere or do some particular activity outside, I always had to defer to permission from my father. I thought my mother ran the house, yet, if my father was present, we would be directed to ask permission from him. My young mind found this so strange. As I matured and took on new roles as an employed person, I finally started to understand various aspects of life and living. I became aware of so much more inequity and systemic oppression, racism, and prejudice.

How can I speak of feminism when I seek to understand all the other "isms" in life? I would say there were a few turning points in my life that led me to proudly state I am a feminist. One major turning point was the birth of my son in Toronto in 1987. To be connected to another person by your DNA, to want to advocate for and support that child, well, the mother bear — complete with claws — came out as I attempted to provide adequate childcare and schooling for my child.

Another clear turning point revealed itself in my search for work. I recall one day in Toronto, shortly after relocating, applying for a position as secretary. I had dropped off my résumé and was called back to a recruitment agency for an interview. The recruiter kept saying, "You are Mary McCarthy?" "*You* are Mary McCarthy?" I later realized that my recruiter's disbelief was not that I spoke with a Canadian accent, or that I had an obviously Canadian name, but resulted instead from my obvious skin colour. The end result of that interview was that there was no interview. I was told by the male recruiter: "The position for secretary was filled. However, we do still have jobs available in the domestic section. Would you still be interested in employment?"

Yet another one of my early "light bulb" moments was when I realized that feminism and equity had everything to do with power. Who has the power and who shares the power? As a woman who has always felt education was the key to empowerment, I have had many experiences that have caused me to realize that regardless of the education levels achieved, success and freedom from inequality in our life, as well as racism and prejudice, still lie in the hands of a few powerful men and women.

I have had much success in my life, yet I still remain a woman who is lacking much power and control due to my skin colour and my geographical location. Specifically, I feel I would have much more power if I had more alliances to support my struggles, and if there were more people who looked like me, and who were sharing similar struggles.

I am, and continue to be, inspired by many strong women whose work I have had the pleasure of reading and studying. I am totally impressed and experience joy with the works of Audre Lorde. Ms. Lorde's work has provided me with truly strong mentorship and teaching throughout my life. I defended my Master's thesis in 2006, and I really felt the presence of her strength and energy around me in that undertaking. It was a wonderful day in my life. I was calm, and when asked to defend some statements, I was filled with Audre Lorde's quotes.

Equality is something we all need — in all aspects of our lives. I struggled for acceptance and equality in my worksite as a woman of African heritage, and I was drawn to the trade union movement to gain support and equity. I am still very involved with the union movement: I sat on national committees, as well as held local appointments via my union local in my home city of Fredericton, New Brunswick.

I am an outspoken equity-seeking woman, or feminist, because I feel I must speak my truths. I cannot let the voices of white women speak my experiences. We are all women struggling for equality, but I know my experiences are very different from white women's experiences, and my voice must be heard. While I choose my battles in life, I must also use my voice. I have been given the gifts of writing, poetry, storytelling, and public speaking, and I continue to use those gifts to educate people about the experiences of racism and prejudice in the life of a rural woman of African Canadian heritage.

58 | FEEDING THE FEMINIST SOUL
Jessica McCrae

I was born in 1972 and my mom was most definitely a feminist. Coming into adulthood in the 1960s with all of the choices and changes that women were facing at the time, she made her decisions and instilled the strength and conviction of those choices in me. I was also born to a father who was, in his own way, a feminist — though he would probably never adopt the label. He instilled in me the belief that I could be anything I dreamed of, and while it may take harder work to crack that glass ceiling, it could be done.

The result was that I was always a feminist. So much so that sometimes I had a hard time understanding how my gender could pose particularly unique challenges in the work force or in society. I grew up in the afterglow of the advances of so many women. I was a feminist in the same way that I was a human being. It was as natural as breathing and something that I rarely considered, except to feel pride over stories of the suffragettes (imagine that at one point women couldn't vote!); and of my grandmother breaking gender roles by working at Fleet aircraft in Fort Erie, Ontario, during World War II (a job which she had to give up when the men returned because they "deserved" it more than the women); and my mother choosing to work after marriage and delaying pregnancy until the time truly felt right for her.

I was ordained in the United Church in 2001. At that time, the ordination of women was a non-issue as we had been doing it for decades. The main debates were reserved for openly gay men and lesbians who sought ordination (still an issue, even though that right was passed by the church in 1988). I never imagined that being a young, unmarried, female clergyperson would bring with it particular challenges, until my first ordained positions that is. I became something of a pioneer as the first female minister to serve these two churches. Add to that the fact that I was unmarried and childless and I found myself serving communities with a very steep learning curve regarding gender bias.

One day before I performed my first funeral service, I received a call from the church women asking how many sandwiches and pickles I would be providing for the reception. When I explained that my time was limited and I was in fact doing the service, I was told simply that it was the minister's wife's job to provide some food, and since I didn't have a spouse that job was considered mine too!

What amazed me most during this time was that the expectation of me being both the minister and the minister's wife was largely imposed upon me by other women.

Again and again, I found myself embracing feminism with a new interest. Feminism, I began to realize, was not just about equal rights and equality, but also the right to choose one's own path. It is about gaining respect for your choices and knowing that it is possible for a woman to choose to marry for love, not security.

One of the biggest challenges to feminism comes from within; we women can be terribly hard on one another. Just as I have come to expect respect for the choices I have made for my life, I have also learned that I need to respect the choices that my Sisters have made for their own lives. Some choose to marry younger, have children, and leave their careers to raise their children. Some choose to find fulfillment in motherhood at all costs, seeking reproductive technology to make that happen. Some came of age in a society very different from the one today. Some have been influenced by religions and cultures vastly different from the ones I knew. And some have made choices similar to my own.

We need to work together to listen to our stories, and try to bridge the divide between generations and the divide between life choices. We need to realize what tremendous strength and support we can find together as women when we find our common ground.

In retrospect, I suppose my understanding of feminism, an understanding that is rooted in the idea that women together can be an awesome force for positive change, came when I was studying in Israel and the Occupied Territories in 1997. I remember watching a group of women — Israeli and Palestinian — who came together for fellowship as a grassroots organization dedicated to finding common ground, and building peace. These women came from different experiences, different backgrounds, and different sides of the political situation. Yet, as they sat together and shared what they had in common, as women and as mothers, and as their children played together on the other side of the room, it was as though a light went on for me. When we take the time to listen and understand and learn from one another, we find our common vision and are a powerful force for change and peace.

But as I write that I wonder, is that something particular to women, or does all of humanity — women and men together — have that potential?

59 | TEACHING SEX EDUCATION

Margaret McCrae

I always knew that I wanted to be a teacher, and chose to go to Hamilton Teachers' College when I had just turned 18. That was in 1962-1963, when teachers were in demand and you had your pick of positions. Women seemed to outnumber men 10 to 1 in the elementary school division and I felt that this was a pity. (Surely there was a need for men to teach in the elementary grades?) Regardless, I soon discovered that the goal of most of the young women in Teachers' College was to get married and quit teaching when, after two years, they received their permanent certificates. I couldn't understand this thinking. I married too, but leave? Not until I retired in 2005.

Teaching marked my entry into feminism. During those early days, I was given the opportunity to teach "Sex Education" to grade 8 girls. Dr. Marion Powell MD, and Medical Officer of Health in Scarborough, Ontario, encouraged this topic in our curriculum. A leader in the field of women's health, she lobbied for wider access to birth control and family planning. She was also responsible for establishing the first municipally-funded birth control clinic in Canada, which served women regardless of age or marital status. When my family learned that I would be teaching sex education, many of my older relations were shocked. They thought I would get in "hot water" for teaching this taboo subject. But Powell's sex-education curriculum for the Scarborough Board of Education became a model for other school boards across Canada.

In 1970 my husband, Nick, and I wanted to buy our first house. It was such an expense! It cost $33,000 to buy a house in Don Mills, Ontario. We wondered how we could ever afford it, but went to the bank to explore our options and find out about getting a mortgage. Imagine my disbelief when I was told by my bank manager that indeed we couldn't afford it! The bank would not count my salary in their assessment of our income. I felt like a second class citizen and to this day I resent the way I was treated. How far we have come.

Some years later, Nick and I shared our greatest joy when we found out that after eight years of marriage we were going to have a baby. We had chosen the time to have our family and we were ready. When I shared the news with my colleagues, my principal expressed relief that my due date was in December. This way I could quit at the end of June and I wouldn't "show" at work.

There was a time when women teachers had to resign when they got married. Now, fortunately, women may carry on working until their due date — if they so choose.

I have been fortunate in my life to have been surrounded by strong women who believed in equal rights for women in all areas of their lives, and by women who sacrificed much in order to help provide an education for younger siblings. My goal has always been to instill these ideals in my own daughter, and I am very proud to say that, in my opinion, she too is a feminist.

As I write this I am impressed by the changes that have come over the years thanks to feminists. I wonder if most young women today ever think of themselves as feminists, or if this is a definition that, according to them, belongs to a bygone era. Regardless, we owe a lot to those that have gone before, and I am proud to count myself as a feminist from the '60s.

60 | INGESTING IT WITH MOTHER'S MILK
Mary McKim

When questioned as to how I became a feminist, the reply is: "I was born one, ingesting it with mother's milk." Feminism was part of my life growing up, a tribute to a Victorian lady, my mother, who was born on a farm in Bruce County, Ontario, in 1887. A second daughter, she was her father's assistant and inherited a love of gardening, and a distaste for housework. I have come to recognize that mother was "First Wave." She attended "Normal School." Teaching in one-room country schools, she saved enough money to register at Queen's University in 1908. Surprisingly for the time, a third of the class was female. (She also owned first editions of two books by Nellie McClung circa 1915.)

Although a whiz at math, mother studied Classics. Following graduation in 1913, she was appointed by the Presbyterian Women's Missionary Society to teach Girls' Secondary School in Honan, China. There she met and subsequently married my father. Later she taught English, Latin, and Greek to Chinese university students. Father, a medical missionary, had a number of women colleagues. Most of the wives in mission communities were university graduates or nurses, and were involved in some aspect of the work. Born there, I returned to Canada to complete high school in 1941. (Father remained until forced out following the Revolution in 1950.) I graduated in medicine from the University of Toronto in 1949, and celebrated a 60th class reunion in June 2009!

Mother commanded great respect from my father and never accepted secondary status. When, as a child, I would admire my dad, she made clear that she was his superior in many areas. Dad was supportive when I expressed a wish to study medicine. Remembering his women colleagues, this did not seem an unusual choice for me in the early 1940s. It was not until university that I experienced male condescension or chauvinism toward women classmates, and found that male students in Arts programs were dismayed when they discovered the faculty in which I was enrolled.

As students in the hospital emergency department we encountered tragic cases of women who had experienced self-induced or "back street" abortions. The inevitable consequences of hemorrhage or infection were often fatal. Abortion was illegal. Any physician providing a safe procedure would risk losing his license and spend time in jail, as Dr. Henry Morgentaler did later.

Internship at Women's College Hospital introduced me to the tragedy of pregnant teens, suffering painful childbirth alone, only to give up their babies to the Children's Aid Society. Surely a cruel punishment for unwise behaviour!

Trudeau's 1969 Omnibus Bill made provision for legal abortion, but strictly defined by hospital abortion committees. Groups across Canada and the US organized to work for repeal of the abortion laws. In 1974, CARAL, an umbrella group for all Canadian pro-choice organizations formed, and I began working for Abortion Rights and Repeal of the Abortion Laws. I served on the National Board for several years. Twice we lobbied federal members of Parliament. Later, I was president of the London, Ontario chapter. This was at the time of the Morgentaler trials in Quebec. It came as a surprise when the laws were finally struck down in 1988. It seemed almost unbelievable after all our years of effort. We hoped that ready access and early termination would avoid Pro Life's "baby killing" accusations, and improve women's health and safety.

My interest in improving the situation for women led to issues surrounding what was then known as "battered women." Energies were directed toward establishing a safe refuge for abused women; London's Women's Community House opened in 1978 on Piccadilly St. (It has now been replaced by two larger shelters.) As "wife beating" was not a criminal offence at the time, we had many meetings with the Crown Attorney and the Chief of Police, and London led the way in criminalization. Later I was on the founding board of the Battered Women's Advocacy Clinic in London, now known as the Abused Women's Centre. The Sexual Assault Line and Centre were also established with rape crisis services. It is a tragedy that shelters are still required.

After obtaining my qualifications as a psychiatrist, I worked in psychiatric hospitals, general hospital psychiatric units, and UWO Student Counseling Services, ending up with thirteen years in private psychotherapy practice. During those years I became painfully aware of the scandalous incidence of childhood sexual abuse and incest, with their long lasting negative effects. My efforts were always directed to raising my patients' self-esteem. For many I provided their first respectful and caring relationship. Throughout my psychiatric practice, I have claimed that no one should have to tolerate abuse, physical or emotional.

Over the years, I have maintained a strong connection with my church. I am a staunch defender of the United Church, which has shown courage in tackling difficult issues. Women have been ordained since 1936; in the '60s they became elders and members of Session. We endured the turmoil over "gay ordination" in the '80s, and survived. We are inclusive and "don't ask, don't tell" no longer applies. We marry same sex couples and the sky has not fallen. And community outreach, both here and abroad, is a very important part of our mission.

In my personal life, after twenty-five years in a somewhat patriarchal relationship, I sought a divorce. I have been lucky to enjoy a truly equal marriage for the past thirty-four years. In 1985, I supported my husband to become an Anglican priest. In 2000, we both retired. Since then I have been a member of the "Women's History Project" in London, with a goal of collecting archival materials and interviews with feminists who were active from 1960 through to 2000.

I am gratified that my sons are respectful of women and in equal relationships. My husband and I now have 16 grandchildren, ready to carry the torch in medicine, journalism, social work, and business.

61 | KNOW THIS: I AM A FEMINIST

Marilou McPhedran

When initially asked to write about how and when I became a feminist, my mind filled with intense sensory memories — of horse sweat and the rustle of tall prairie grass. As a rural child, I benefitted from freedoms that I denied to my own entirely urban sons. From the age of seven or so, my friends and I would pack lunches and set off on adventures far enough away that mothers' calls were a waste of time. And when we got ponies, we ventured even further, testing boundaries forbidden, like trekking across the massive trestle bridge, breathlessly listening for a train and peeking at the water far below. Such physical freedom may have been my first feminist experience: autonomy.

Even earlier in my life, some other physical experiences affected me profoundly for the long term: a lonely young man, trusted enough by my parents for them to leave me in his care, used me sexually. The deep loyalty and jealous affection that I displayed for this man as a little girl were seen as "cute." Only as a mother, did I start to uncover the extent of his betrayal of trust and the ways that our "special relationship" had been obfuscated as family lore.

Growing up, I was often referred to as "melodramatic" or "overly sensitive" — readily upset by depictions of violence or unkindness. This morphed into an early and long-lasting affinity for volunteer organizations that sought to do good things for others on principles of fairness — United Church groups, choirs, school council, and community projects like a book drive for poor kids in St. Lucia. I loved to be "in charge," needed a sense of control and predictability — something that prompted my spinster (I noticed) elementary school principal, Miss Ruth Faryon, to tell my parents that I could be prime minister.

Growing up in that small town — where many of my early role models, like Miss Faryon, were strong independent women, where either my best friend Bev Ann or I got to lead just about everything, and where economic privilege was woven invisibly into our many opportunities — I had a well-developed sense of self, weighed down by a larger sense of duty as the first born child, knowing that it was my task to deliver achievements to bring honour to our family name.

For our final high school year, Bev Ann decided she wanted to edit the school yearbook, so I got to be student president. When, at 19, I decided to run to become the first woman president at my small university, a Winnipeg paper quoted me scoffing that I was not a feminist, that my accomplishments were my own doing. But, as my tumultuous term as student president culminated with being hung in effigy, festooned with sexist epithets, I had come to understand my place in the world quite differently. And yet, I still hesitated to define myself as feminist.

I then followed my socialist boyfriend (whom I unwisely married — briefly — at my mother's urging and against his mother's advice) to the big city, only to discover that women's rights weren't a priority in crafting the thirty-year transformational strategy; wives were still expected to make meals for the meetings, and philandering was still a male prerogative. Having transferred universities as part of following the guy, I pursued my goal of a Ph.D. in Religious Studies. However, I shifted direction on the advice of a favourite professor who informed me that, since it had taken him an hour into a three hour oral exam to detect that I had not read the book being tested, I was a "bullshit artist" and perfect for law school.

In first year criminal law class, with me sputtering in fury over rape cases lauded as "legal precedents," my professor seemed uneasy as I towered over him in my rage. He was a short man with a Beatles cut, who was not a fan of the female influx into law and was heard to say after a class, "girls are for fucking." Thankfully, his diversion technique was introducing me to a senior law student, Barbara Betcherman, who exuded confidence and élan. Proudly declaring her feminism, Barbara recruited me to volunteer in the country's first rape crisis centre. Only then did "feminist" settle into deep places that had been waiting within me.

As the eldest of three girls, with no brothers to compete with, I became a late-night intellectual companion for my father, while my younger sisters were, as my father had been heard to say, "the boys I never had." I think we knew that some of the "house of all girls" jokes held the kind of grievance that Marshall McLuhan warned of. But we also often heard things like, "you can be anything you want, you're my daughter" from both our parents. Mostly, I remember feeling responsible for achieving — to keep my parents proud of me. I had some wonderful teachers, but have no recollection of anything remotely like gender based analysis until women students argued for it in law school — except of course for my mother's complaints about how my father liked to forget who worked as a secretary to put him through vet school after the war, never getting beyond high school, and then working from home to support his practice and raise his children.

Remember the "ranch wife" *Murdoch* case in the 1970s? Mrs. Murdoch had put part of her inheritance into the land in her husband's name. There was evidence of violence in the marital relationship resulting in Mrs. Murdoch having her jaw broken by her husband. Nonetheless, in dismissing her lifetime of work with her husband, the Supreme Court of Canada — with only Justice Bora Laskin dissenting — awarded Irene Murdoch just two hundred dollars a month, agreeing with the trial judge that she had only done the "routine" work of "any ranch wife," not enough to create a legal claim to the matrimonial property. The monthly $200 stipend was later supplanted by a "lump sum" settlement of $65,000, without the monthly payments. Note that when Mrs. Murdoch was asked to describe the nature of her "routine work" at trial, she had replied: "Haying, raking, swathing, mowing, driving trucks and tractors and teams, quietening horses, taking cattle back and forth to the reserve, dehorning, vaccinating, branding, anything that was to be done."

Many identified with Irene Murdoch's humiliating loss — including my irate mother, who called me from rural Manitoba to demand to know what her daughter, the Toronto law student, was going to do to change the stupid law!

Some of my best friends are women in their eighties and nineties. When I was about thirteen, I worked most Saturdays in my father's veterinary office in Neepawa, Manitoba. Our town florist's shop was next door and the florist's elderly mother, Mrs. Parrott, handled their commerce on Saturdays. Neepawa was a small rural town and not that many customers came into my shop or hers, so we left the connecting door open and often chatted between customers or read our books. After many Saturdays, we were friends. I found her scarlet mouth and highly arched, penciled-on brows distracting, but she captured my full attention when sharing town secrets. Mrs. Parrott reserved her fury for the town's disregard of "little Peggy Wemyss" a great author that Mrs. Parrott said I should be studying in school. Mrs. Parrott was convinced that the town of Manawaka, featured in "Peggy's wonderful book," was really our town, Neepawa. That book was *The Stone Angel*, published in 1964, the first of five in the "Manawaka series" by Margaret Laurence — who was known to many in Neepawa as Margaret (Peggy) Wemyss.

As I approach sixty, I have only written one book — *Preventing sexual abuse of patients: a legal guide for regulated health professionals* (McPhedran, M. and Sutton, W., 2004). It demanded to be written to try to give health professionals the information they need to prevent sexual abuse, but I doubt I'll write another. I am in awe of Laurence writing the entire Manawaka series in a decade, as a single mother. But what resonated with me most was when she wrote of Almuth Lutkenhaus' sculpture "Crucified Woman."

It was before this stylized female nude — suspended alone in the quad behind Victoria University on the University of Toronto campus, with her arms reaching out in cruciform — that the first vigil was held the day after the "Montreal Massacre" of fourteen women at the École Polytechnique on December 6, 1989. I had instigated this vigil, phoning friends from the Ad Hoc Committee of Canadian Women on the Constitution at 5 AM because I knew that together, we could have the vigil organized and advertised in just a few hours, much like we organized the women's constitutional conference in less than three weeks in 1981. Ever since, at Easter or Passover, in the years that Toronto was my home, I went with a friend or two, climbed up and wrapped fresh spring flowers into her hand, stood with her, feeling the impact of violence against women and children scouring our world. Know this: I am a feminist; a feminist human rights lawyer, committed to implementing lived rights.

> I see old women dancing
> dancing on the earth
> I see old women singing
> singing children's birth …
>
> I see old women dancing
> dancing through all lands
> foremothers with them
> joining all of their hands
>
> – M. LAURENCE, 1989. "Old Women's Song"
> in *Dance on the Earth: A memoir*

62 | HE ASSAULTED ME

Judy Miller

I was born into the world on December 27, 1953, in the small Canadian town of Paris, Ontario. I was born a white Canadian girl to white, middle-class, English-speaking Canadian parents. These factors played a large part in the options that would be available to me over the rest of my life. I held a privileged status in every category except gender.

My mother told me very early in life what my career options were: social worker, nurse, secretary, or early grade school teacher. She conditioned me to be a social worker so that I could "help people." What we were both to discover was that I would become one of those people that needed help, and I would need that help because I was a daughter and not a son.

I did what was expected of young women at the time — I fell in love with a man and became pregnant. After the birth of our daughter that man abandoned us and I became a part of another minority — the single parent family. I was lonely and overwhelmed and looked for the next man "to take care of us." That next man was charming and promised many wonderful things. After I moved in with him the abuse started.

After three more children, and several more years, this man severely assaulted me in front of my children. That was the turning point. With the assistance of my parents, police, hospital staff, shelter workers, welfare workers, and an Ontario student loan officer, I began my life as a feminist.

It was 1985 and the government provided numerous programs that made it less difficult for a single mom to attend college. The Ontario government provided subsidization for my children's daycare, allowed me to remain on welfare and also receive Ontario student loans, and subsidized my wage for the first year of my employment.

I wanted to become a role model for my children and give them a life free from violence, where gender equality was the norm. I was dedicated to helping my daughters and my sons believe they could be whatever they wanted. I was also dedicated to being a part of women-centred work. I graduated from a social service worker program and have since worked in women-centred feminist organizations for the past twenty-three years; twenty of them have been in feminist organizations centering on support for women and their children who have been victims of woman abuse.

There was a short interruption in my professional career as the Ontario government, led by Mike Harris, withdrew its support and placed obstacles in the way of women-centred feminist-based work. This did not stop my personal career as a feminist but it was a sad time for Canadian society. These cutbacks helped me to realize the strength women have to continue their work against all odds.

I have felt many successes and many disappointments, many exuberating and many painful emotions. As a feminist, I've experienced backlash on both the professional and personal level. But I have no regrets. I have seen and helped many women and children move toward a life free from violence. I have seen and been a part of a family that believes in equality and I've watched my grandchildren be born into homes where equality is a given.

Recently, my seven-year-old granddaughter held up a banner at this year's *Take Back the Night* march, and I realized my feminism has truly been passed on. I watch as my son prepares supper for the family, I hear about my daughter-in-law's latest visits with one of her friends — leaving my son behind to take care of the children. I listen as my daughter encourages her son to be gentle! From these events I know that as my role changes in the family, I am handing the baton on to very capable equality-based hands.

63 | THE OUTSIDER

Renate Mohr

Although the seeds were planted well before my birth, it took me until the night of my law school graduation dinner to blossom. I would say at twenty-six I was a late bloomer, but that would be too generous. I was born a feminist and it took me that long to find my way back.

As an immigrant, I experienced life as an outsider, always the "other." So I learned to take nothing for granted. When the dominant language is not your mother tongue, you understand quickly, and at a fundamental level, that language holds power. Like many outsiders, my reaction to this was a burning desire to assimilate. The only equality I was consciously interested in was entirely self-serving.

When I was young, curfews and allowances were high on the list — I wanted what my non-immigrant (and wealthier) peers had. In high school, becoming a cheerleader was the kind of ambition I was not embarrassed to espouse, and when I succeeded, I came closer to a sense of belonging than I ever thought possible. Born an outsider, I worked damn hard to be on the inside.

There are no excuses for how long it took me to get back to feminism. I had every opportunity to be aware of the politics of my existence — every opportunity to learn from the outsider that I was. But instead I chose the road of denial. It was, so obviously, paved in gold.

My parents were immigrants who, while not wealthy, had had the benefit of university educations. They left Austria after a war and a Holocaust that made Europe too painful to call home. My maternal grandmother, a Catholic who married twice, and who lost her job running an orphanage when she became pregnant with my mother, travelled to the new land with us, and ultimately found work as a live-in maid. My paternal grandmother stayed behind, living alone, having had two children out of wedlock before marrying my grandfather and giving birth to three more. That marriage also ended in divorce, somehow leaving my grandfather with custody of my father and his brothers, who he then raised with his gay partner.

The outsider roots were strong. This meant crafting an even stronger assimilation strategy. Year after year, I worked hard at making friends who were Real Canadians, who lived in houses with rec rooms, who owned colour TV's, and who lunched on white bread sandwiches wrapped in cellophane. I failed miserably. Most of my friends were Eastern European like me, and many were Jewish. Rye bread and salami was our shared fate.

I routinely squandered the opportunities offered by my outsider parents. My father, the first non-lawyer to teach at Osgoode Hall Law School (a philosopher and a philologist who understood the power of language) encouraged me to become a lawyer, so that unlike him, I would not be the outsider who was professionally belittled for not having the right kind of degree. My mother was a painter of abstract art, who, with her exotic fashion sense and disdain for housework, looked and acted nothing like the mothers of my friends. Although she didn't like lawyers (who, according to her, suffered from a lethal combination of snobbery and lack of imagination), she was adamant that both her daughters find "professions" so that, unlike herself, they would never be dependent on a spouse for an income. My sister became a doctor. I became a lawyer.

And yet — I wanted nothing more than to be a cheerleader.

Although I studied sociology and English literature as an undergraduate (I read Joyce to impress boyfriends and spent pocket money on clothes and mascara), it wasn't until law school that I actually lost my identity as an outsider.

I became an alien.

It happened with lightening speed and in slow motion. After only one week of classes, I knew something had gone terribly wrong. I sat alone and bewildered in large classes where discussions were not encouraged, and I listened as professors spoke in a language that was unfamiliar and exclusive. I was assigned readings of poorly photocopied case law that constructed a world of black and white and right and wrong. Issues that I knew in my heart were complex and nuanced were reduced to true or false boxes waiting to be checked. When I raised my hand with a query (before I learned not to), I was told, in no uncertain terms, my questions were irrelevant.

The absence of language that valued women was so blatant, that even I noticed. The judges we read, the lawyers named in the cases, my professors — all were male, as were almost all the litigants and accused. All writing referred to people as men. The reasonable man was the man on the Clapham omnibus — "he" was the legal yardstick by which all was to be measured. Mankind quite simply excluded me. Did I protest, did I howl at the moon, did I chain myself to the dean's desk, did I link arms and lead a march? No. I did nothing. I squandered.

It took three full years for me to understand what was happening. Three full years of opportunities missed. There was, for example, one Women and the Law class offered, but I couldn't understand why I would want to learn about women and the law, when what was clearly needed was an understanding of the law as it applied to both men and women. I didn't sign up. (Apologies to Professor Beverley Baines.)

In second and third year, when we were allowed to take smaller seminar classes with essay assignments rather than exams, I researched what we then called rape law, and read everything I could about how First Nations' women lost their status when they married non-native men. Strangely, I didn't feel the change, but I was in the grips of something big. In seminar classes, I found a few other aliens with similar politics (the only language we had for a shared ideology was "the left") and a few of us got ourselves elected to student council. It was a very small "p" politics, but politics nonetheless. Together we challenged the compulsory recitation of the Lord's Prayer at graduation ceremonies (not insignificant at an institution like Queen's University).

Then we took the unprecedented and radical step of inviting a *female* judge to speak at our graduation dinner. This provoked its share of outrage. Apparently, it was bad enough that we would choose a family court judge (anything less than the Court of Appeal was pathetic), but worse — she was a woman. Where was the prestige in that? I admit to some naiveté. I was shocked at the reactions.

That was Epiphany #1.

The night arrived. The Graduation Dinner. The Last Supper. We sat at round tables with white linen tablecloths, toasted each other for having made it, gave each other awards, and then invited the speaker to the podium. A few minutes after the speech began, I experienced a tingling sensation. It took me a few more minutes to understand what was happening. The pronoun "she" was being used. Exclusively. When referring to a lawyer, our speaker would say "she." Everything was "she." My eyes clouded. A lump lodged in my throat. For three years I had read and heard nothing but "he." Mascara ran down my cheeks. I belonged.

That was Epiphany #2.

The speech finished with an anecdote about a bedtime story she had read to her son the night before. It was a picture book about bus drivers, train engineers, pilots, and truckers — about all kinds of drivers of large machines. At the end of the story, she asked her son what he might want to do when he grew up. He said he didn't know. She offered a suggestion: Maybe you'd like to be a judge. He shook his head in disbelief. No mom, he answered, only *girls* are judges!

Just in case Epiphany #2 was not enough, I was fortified by #3.

I broke down. I blew my nose in the linen table napkin. I stood up and clapped.

It was a profound evening. The same men who voiced their opposition to our choice of speaker, now expressed unbridled anger.

The nerve. "She, she, she." They had been excluded. I was stunned. For three *years* they had been exclusively embraced by language that made them matter, and they didn't even know it. A twenty-minute speech was more than they could bear.

The holy trinity of language, privilege, and power. Busted forever.

After that, nothing was ever the same. And the lowly family court judge whose speech turned my world upside down, was Rosalie Silberman Abella, who twenty-four years later became the first Jewish woman to be appointed to the Supreme Court of Canada.

64 | LEGACIES

Anne Laura Forsythe Moore, Ph.D.

The stairway of the family home on West Street seemed steep. I loved my sunny room and the wallpaper with its faded design. It was a comfort to me as a child to nap in "the big bed" and to awaken with the swish of the street cleaner as it poked its way through the grid of streets in the section of town in which I grew up.

It was here that my transformation as a girl-child began.

In another room of this old house, Gramma Grace sat in her rocking chair. Not saying any words, she rocked all day making eerie creaking sounds on the worn wooden floor: crick crack. Twenty-five years after her death, I discovered what she had been doing in her silence. She had been writing poems in her head and on any scrap of paper she could find. I have a few of those poems still today, written out in her handwriting. The same rocker, now repaired and refinished from its dilapidated condition, sits in our living room. Through her silence and my girl-child understanding of it, I learned to allow my woman's voice to be heard.

She had her first plane ride at age 89 and wrote a letter to Annie, her daughter, who never did get a chance to fly. "It was glorious. We had a cup of coffee and a sandwich. I had no idea that a plane had so much room in them. Live and learn. If I could only afford it, I wouldn't go any other way." Maria Hingley certainly lived and learned. Not only had she learned the Moon System of reading for the blind, she also learned how to write. Blind for twenty-five years before her death at the age of 92, Maria used an apparatus somewhat like a slate, or a present day clipboard, that was equipped with rows of wires for writing her letters. She placed her fingers on them to guide her pencil as she wrote, spacing the words by putting a fingertip down before beginning the next word. This very act inspired me more than any other acts I have heard of in my life. Never give up no matter the challenges. Maria hadn't. Maria's letter written in 1946 using the wired board, or frame, showed evidence of her ever-willing nature to adapt and to survive, to live and learn as she had written in her letter.

Then there was Maria's daughter, Nan Scott, known as Annie by everyone. She stood at the kitchen sink with her hands searching the innards of the Christmas turkey, pulling out what I could barely look at as she scolded: "This bothers you, and you want to be a nurse?" She continued to rinse the turkey and rhythmically moved her hand in and out of the cavity, cleaning and wiping, bump as the turkey was turned, hitting the countertop with each movement. Annie was born on a farm in Pictou County, Nova Scotia. She helped her mother in the kitchen while Lucy helped the boys in the fields and Sadie, the so-called "lady," went off to the nearest town to learn to make hats in the day, circa 1910.

Annie stitched the family together with her handiwork. I learned to appreciate the originality of my dresses. I can't recall wearing a store bought dress until I was 11 or 12. The one I most remember was yellow satin with a scooped collar embroidered with brown butterflies. Annie kept the family together through mince meat and pumpkin pies, scratch pastry, Queen Elizabeth Cake, ginger bread and cream, Waldorf squares. Every recipe includes the name of the woman who had given it to Annie, evidence of a woman's loyalty and commitment to credit someone else's success in the kitchen. On the page dated "Xmas 1949" and included beside "Flossie's white fruit cake" recipe, was scrawled a riddle in red pen: "How do you describe history from beginning of time until now? Adam's rib, Women's Lib."

From Annie I learned how to keep a sense of humour throughout the day to day. I also learned that my identity as a woman reached far into the identity of those around me. And, my gender formation as a woman was inclusive of a critical perspective on relationships with others, both familial bound and community oriented.

Then there was Nan (Laura) Forsythe. I asked my father to write me something about his mother's experiences with a car. The thought stirred me that this woman with all seven children in tow would take them for a ride. What bravado. He wrote: "The Mother's life was not easy in rural New Brunswick. There was the job of cooking, washing, cleaning and getting the children off to school. There was no TV no radio, so there were not many distractions. However, somewhere around 1925 Mother learned to drive our 1922 Model T. Ford Touring car. Then we hit the roads. In those days one took one's children along. I can remember many exciting drives in our old Model T. Mother usually had two hands equal distance on each side of the steering wheel, with each elbow out horizontally and her hair flying in the wind. Open car, you know. The posture gave off the feeling that we were travelling at a high rate of speed. Actually, it was only about 25 miles per hour, but considering that we were only a few years out of the horse and buggy days, I guess one could call it excessive. Every now and then she stopped for a head count. We never departed from anywhere without a head count. Memories."

Then there was my mother, Faye, a child of the Depression, a young mother during the Second World War, a housewife in the '50s.

I am my mother's daughter and she was her mother's daughter. We are our grandmothers. What a legacy.

65 | EDUCATING THE NEXT GENERATION

Eleanor Greig Moore

Women who were, and some who still are, feminists have always been a part of my life. I was born and grew up in Aotearoa/New Zealand. It's often stated that this was the first country to give women the vote in 1893.

My maternal grandmother, although I never actually heard that she called herself a feminist, certainly expected equality in her affairs. She ensured that her only daughter had an education, including a postgraduate degree, so that she would have the means to support herself without a husband.

There was no doubt within my family that my mother was the key decision-maker. In the public space my mother, by virtue of her education and her belief that women were equal to any thinking that men could do, was accorded some leadership role in our community. Interestingly, the minister of our church was a woman, one of the few women in that role, and she and my mother played a formidable role in the church, often taking the male leaders to task.

I cannot ever remember thinking that I did not have equality with men. This of course belies the reality of employment statistics and the roles that women had, but it was ever-present in my being that my gender was not an exclusion from any path that I wanted to pursue.

My husband and I decided that since we both wanted to see more of the world, we would take up his scholarship offer to come to Canada for his Ph.D., and then after travelling we would return home where I would pursue a law degree. But life took over. I found a teaching career, had two children, and we stayed in Canada.

As an adult in Canada, I became interested in many women's issues that passed by me as a student growing up. The constitutional discussions and the development of our human rights legislation and women's rights were of the utmost importance to me. At the same time, in my professional world it was clear that lip service was being paid to women's rights among my students and many of their teachers and parents. All espoused the notion that girls should have a good education, emulating that of the best boys' school education, but I knew this was an education that preserved the status quo and was only available to a fortunate few.

The result of these observations was the development of what would become The Linden School. My colleague Diane Goudie and I wanted to create a "woman-centred" school. What we wanted to do was create a school that espoused feminist principles. We steered clear of the term "feminist" because in 1993 the word was equated with "man-hating" and "lesbian-creating." While both public and private schools in Toronto routinely ostracized us as educators, we were encouraged and supported by tertiary educators both in Canada and in the United States.

Still we were seen as offering an education that was politically motivated — as if public and private schools were not. We encouraged girls to question the status quo and to work to question their assumptions about power and privilege, to work to understand how they might use their education to make a difference. This was "frightening" stuff, often hard to understand, all being explored at a little school that has never exceeded 150 girls in its enrolment.

There has always been a tension between the evolving feminist agenda and the ability for a very small institution which, with the exception of a few key donors, relies entirely on its tuition fees for its funding, to be able to satisfy all the feminisms. Personally, this has also been a difficult position for me; for it is easier to pursue ideals when you know you have a paycheque and when you know your job is secure. At Linden, we never knew for sure that the school could be sustained, especially in the early years, and the financial sacrifice made by us as founders and by our faculty has always been considerable. We are still financially unable to pay into pension plans or to offer salaries which are commensurate with the public board.

The result has been that we have been criticized for not measuring up to our ideals, a painful reality for a founder. Interestingly though, with some exceptions, this reality has not rallied the greater feminist community to offer financial support.

Choice has always been a cornerstone of the feminist movement and yet without the choice of a feminist education within the publicly funded system, it always seemed to me that this was at least the first step in providing that choice.

Living out my feminism in my work place has been a sacrifice for my family and it has taken its toll. Yet, I would indeed do it again, even knowing what a struggle it has been. My feminist work has always kept me in a place of some discomfort, as it has always prodded me to reassess my thinking, to re-examine my assumptions, and to review my own attitudes and behaviours. My pride in creating The Linden School is profound, for it required doing what I believed in and not just talking about it. As I hear from former students I know that we made a difference for them, and they in turn will make a difference for others.

My feminist work has brought me wonderful friendships, new colleagues, contacts with people doing important and interesting work in many communities and, last but not least, it is through my feminism that I found my life partner.

66 | 1968: THE YEAR FEMINISM CHANGED MY LIFE!

Nancy Ruth

It was in Turku, Finland where I became a feminist. The year was 1968 and I was attending the World Student Christian Federation General Assembly. For the first time in my life, women hit the agenda. My feelings of isolation and unfocused anger began to disappear. My immersion into feminism filled me instead with excitement and passion.

The 1960s were a time when protest movements, Nehru jackets, Mao caps, pot, the Age of Aquarius, and folk music flourished in North America. Lesbian singers like Meg Christian achieved acclaim. Liberation theology from South America was hot. And it was the male students from South America who dominated the World Student Christian Federation conference. But in the midst of the vociferous men there surfaced a group of American women who invited the other female participants to come and share their vision.

I went by myself. I was curious.

The American women there had been part of the Black integration struggle, student revolutions on campuses, opposition to the Vietnam War, and the growth of alternative communities. They were resisting the dominance of men in leadership. They protested the limited roles for women. These American women introduced me to feminist ideas and analysis. And feminism changed my life.

For the first time, I felt included in a group that valued me. Feminism caused me to reinterpret history. I began to see how wrong the dominant ideologies and problem-solving techniques were. What I had been taught at university was imbued with patriarchal assumptions. What I had been taught in my family about women's role was stifling. I wanted more.

In Turku I encountered feminism. I was empowered by it, and I became deeply committed to its vision. The latter encompassed many aspirations:

That women are equal;

That we would have equal access to justice and the courts;

That the police would protect us;

That men would stop blaming us, denigrating us, and violating us;

That we are leaders — and have been for centuries;

That we have the right to an education;

That school children would learn about women, and our contribution to Canada, to history;

That women's voices would be heard at all levels of decision-making;

That we could hold good jobs, senior positions, be presidents, and have real power outside the home;

That we would be paid the same as men, have equal access to money, and that poverty would be a thing of the past;

That we would have the same access to health and health research;

That we would have the right to control our own bodies; that is, sexual and reproductive rights;

That we would have fuel with which to cook, clean water to drink, food to feed our children, and land to grow it on;

That industry, governments, and tribal leaders would stop stealing from us, and destroying our environment;

That there would be no more rape, no more violence against women and girls;

That child soldiers and sex slaves would cease to exist;

That the stupidity of war would be a thing of the past;

That the patriarchy of the church, the World Student Christian Federation, and Christianity would fade away; and

That the goddess of the moon would shine upon us.

Well, some progress has been made but we are still far from realizing our vision. I still cherish this dream of worldwide women's equality.

For a decade I worked for the United Church. I was vocal in my feminist critiques of the liturgies and the organization. When I was dismissed in 1979 for various feminist activities, I led a group of defrocked clergy to appeal the Church's decision. The episode allowed me to meet Bertha Wilson, who was on the Judicial Committee, and who would go on to become Canada's first female Justice of the Supreme Court of Canada. We won our case on procedural grounds. The Church had sent us a registered letter dismissing us, instead of giving us our day in the Church court. Therefore we had been denied "natural justice." We were reinstated, but resigned the following year. Who wanted to work for the so called "community of love" when it had caused so many so much pain?

From this experience, I drew several insights. Don't try to put new wine into old wine skins. There are some structures that you cannot change. There are times when the effort of trying to change a patriarchal institution is a poor use of scarce resources. Always work as a group, for there is strength in numbers. You have more rights than you may know. And others need your leadership.

After the fight with the Church, life became sweeter for me as an activist outside that power structure. Nonetheless, the legal battle had taught me valuable lessons, put to use when I co-mothered and worked for a wide range of women's organizations. Let me mention five initiatives of which I am most proud.

The Charter of Rights Coalition was formed in 1982 in response to the government's three-year moratorium on the proclamation of Section 15, the guarantee for women's legal equality in Canada's new *Charter of Rights and Freedoms*. The coalition had two purposes: to educate women from coast to coast to coast on the importance of the equality provisions; and to lobby our governments to bring their laws into compliance. It was my first experience in managing a national lobby, and I had the time of my life. We produced slide shows complete with audio tapes, which we showed across the country. We spoke and spoke and spoke, in school auditoriums, in church basements, to annual meetings, to women's institutes, and on the telephone. In short, we went anywhere a group of women was interested in hearing our message.

The Women's Legal Education and Action Fund (LEAF; www. leaf.ca) took on the struggle of litigating test cases involving discrimination against women. LEAF also intervened in the courts, promoted equality education, and taught teens that "No means No." It was such fun doing something no one else had done, being part of the intellectual creation of feminist legal theory, and making a real difference for the women of Canada. The women I worked with were some of the most fabulous I have ever met and I cherish their friendships to this day.

The Canadian Women's Foundation (www.cdnwomen.org) became Canada's first and only charitable foundation to raise money for violence prevention and the economic development of women in Canada.

The Linden School (www.Linden.ca) was founded as a primary and secondary school dedicated to training young feminist leaders. Linden teaches all its subjects through the eyes of women. When studying English or French literature, the students read women authors. The curriculum includes the great women scientists, mathematicians, and healers, and explores their remarkable contributions. History is taught through the eyes of the women who lived it. Courses on imperialism focus on the experiences of the women who were exploited. Aboriginal history in Canada is seen from the perspectives of Indigenous women.

The Section 15 website (www.section15.ca) was developed as another leadership tool to compile accessible stories of Canadian women's history and activism. It also shares world-wide women's news and women's perspectives, and hopes to inspire young women's leadership.

Then in 2005, my life as a feminist activist changed. My world turned when Prime Minister Paul Martin telephoned and asked me to sit in the Senate as an independent Progressive Conservative. I said yes. I had run for political office twice and failed to get elected; I wasn't going to miss this opportunity.

I sat as an independent for a year, and then concluded that the marginalization attached to being an outsider was overwhelming. So I joined the Conservative party. It's much more productive being part of "the game" — especially being a part of the ruling party, something which facilitates talking to cabinet ministers each week and moving agendas along. From the Senate, I have strategized to push our government to develop a new national action plan on gender equity, and to implement gender-based analysis throughout all its departments and agencies.

One day, the Auditor-General and I were in the same elevator. I asked her if she would consider doing an audit of the federal government's implementation of gender-based analysis. She said that she took seriously any proposal made by a Parliamentary committee. I shared this information with MP Maria Minna, and she moved the idea into the Status of Women Committee in the House of Commons. We managed to get the Committee to pass a motion, supported by all parties, requesting that the Auditor-General undertake such an audit. Sheila Fraser's subsequent report told senior government officials of their failure to consider gender. Gender-based analysis is now getting more systematic attention than it has received in years. The moral of this story is that there is a good reason to get elected or appointed to Parliament. You never know who you will meet in the elevator!

The national anthem has been another hot-button issue. The first (1908) English version of "O Canada" — like the original French version — was gender-neutral. The English words were changed shortly before the First World War from "true patriot love thou dost in us command" to "true patriot love in all thy sons' command." I urged the Prime Minster to restore the 1908 gender-neutral language in order to acknowledge women's active participation in every sphere of Canadian life on an equal basis with men. We have held ramp ceremonies for females killed in Afghanistan, without including them in the national anthem. Canadian women athletes were responsible for winning most of Canada's medals at the 2010 Olympic Games, yet the anthem played to honour their successes did not include them. The Prime Minister accepted the recommendation, and the 2010 Throne Speech pledged to ask Parliament "to examine the original gender-neutral English wording of the national anthem." Sadly, the decision triggered a backlash. The government reversed its position 48 hours after it was announced.

Our struggle is undeniably long-term. However, I urge feminists to recognize that there are politicians who want to work with us. No party is a monolith, and we should be open to all. Feminists should think about becoming politicians, taking the risk of running and losing. When feminists are elected, and become insiders, we must not forget the outsiders. Feminism has given us insights into the power of patriarchal structures. Women's equality takes constant oversight and pressure. Each of us has a role to play.

67 | A NEED FOR STRONG LEADERS
Valerie J. Picketts

After reflecting on my 45 years of life and thinking about how being a feminist has touched my life, I have come to realize that it has been a significant force in shaping who I have become. But I cannot point to any precise moment when I began to live and work as a feminist.

I was born in 1964 and grew up on a farm near Saskatoon. I had three older sisters and a younger brother. The arrival of my brother soon made us notice that he was treated differently. He was expected to take over the family farm, and therefore was given the opportunity to learn much more about the farming operation. My sisters and I were confined to "women's work," including housework, gardening, and the more menial farm tasks, such as cleaning barns and granaries and feeding and bedding the animals. From a young age, I questioned the fairness of this differential treatment. I also questioned the fairness of my parents' traditional marriage where my mother contributed to the work of the farming operation and in addition, did all the household work (with some help from "us girls") and yet seemed to have little say in the decisions, or any control over the money earned. Women were measured by their ability to work but not valued as individuals who could contribute as an equal partner to a farming operation.

Around the same time I began being exposed to a variety of feminist views through books, magazines, and television. I was an avid reader as a youth and liked to read adult magazines and books. One book in particular that I remember reading was based on the life and work of Nellie McClung. I read about her fight for the rights of Canadian women and admired her for how she fought so determinedly. This book, and other readings, led me to think about the roles women play in society and wonder why women had to face such inequalities. I also recall reading about various views on the "Women's Liberation Movement" in women's magazines such as *Chatelaine*. In the 1970s feminism and the women's liberation movement seemed like heated topics to me as I recall the issues being commonly debated in everyday conversations. I also recall hearing women describe themselves as feminists.

I listened to the debates and by my later teen years had decided that yes, I believed in "Women's Lib" and would call myself a feminist.

In 1982, I started university and took general arts classes in my first year. In my second year I decided to enter into the College of Agriculture and planned on becoming a veterinarian. However, after completing my second year, I decided that Economics was my area of interest. In the 1980s, the majority of students in Agricultural Economics were male, and it was a non-traditional area of study for females. With my strong skills in calculus and statistics, I went on to complete a Master's in Agricultural Economics in 1989 and won an award for my Master's thesis from the *Canadian Journal of Agricultural Economics and Farm Management Society*.

While taking my Master's, I noticed that the all-male staff of professors in the Agricultural Economics department at that time seemed to show more interest in working on research projects with male students than female students. However, after entering into the workforce, I was to learn that the university provided a much more level playing field for males and females than working in the Agriculture sector.

I was employed as an Agricultural Economist with the Ministry of Agriculture from 1989 to 1998. During that time I observed that the barriers facing women in a non-traditional field could sometimes be subtle and other times blatantly discriminatory. At the time, the majority of Agricultural Economists were male and the circle of power and influence seemed closed to women in general. There seemed to be a lack of support for young females trying to make their career in the field, while young males were given the support and opportunities they needed. Men were assigned responsibilities that provided them with a higher profile, such as being involved in negotiations at meetings with industry, and sitting on committees that would provide them with the opportunities to network with more senior management.

I suggested there was a need for a women's mentorship program, where women who were experienced in the workplace would provide support and guidance to young females entering the field. However, the idea of a women's support or networking group was not received well and never materialized. There was pressure to conform to the traditional ways; this sector seemed closed to new ideas. While I tried to conform at first, I realized that I wanted to act more in line with my values and beliefs. I joined an employment equity committee, with intentions of improving the workplace for women and other minorities.

I noticed that there was a lot of government support given to the traditional organizations in the agricultural sector that were male-dominated, but little support seemed to be given to those organized by women. I chose to provide some support to a women's agricultural organization called SWAN (Saskatchewan Women's Agriculture

Network). I also began liaising with some staff at the provincial Status of Women Office and provided research assistance for reports they prepared on rural women. I prepared reports that showed the contributions of female farm operators to the agricultural industry. However, this work was not perceived as being important, and I received comments from other staff indicating that this was not the best use of the department's time.

When I came to the realization that it would be difficult for me to have a satisfying career in agriculture, I began considering a career change. I started to take classes in Sociology and Psychology at the University of Regina, and decided I would be interested in working in the area of sociology. In 1998, I was successful in obtaining a policy analyst position with the Saskatchewan Ministry of Justice and Attorney General, and have worked in this position for over ten years. I learned about the Women's Legal Education and Action Fund (LEAF) from other staff who were members. In 2001, I became a member of the Regina Branch of LEAF. The volunteer work I did with LEAF fit well with my feminist lens, and I later served as the Chair of the Regina Branch of LEAF from 2003 to 2006.

My views on feminism have broadened considerably since my youth, when I thought that women simply needed to have the same freedom as men to pursue any career or participate in any activity in order to achieve equality. While women now have better access to education, jobs, and other resources, I see that many barriers to equality still persist in the everyday interactions between males and females in homes, schools, workplaces and other organizations. And when gender intersects with other factors such as race and class, it becomes even more challenging to achieve equality. Government policies, programs, and services can support the status quo of inequalities that women experience, or take corrective action to remove the barriers. There is a need for strong leaders who can make changes in these areas. In addition, strong women's networks (whether formal or informal) are needed to provide support and encouragement to women in making changes that move them closer to achieving equality in their lives.

68 | LEARNING THE FEMINIST VOCABULARY

Ruth Roach Pierson

There's an easy answer to the how, when, where and why I became a feminist: I always was one. The only thing lacking was the vocabulary, the articulated theory. As far back as I can remember I had both the requisite feelings and the will. As a young girl, it upset me that my father wouldn't take me on his fishing and hunting expeditions. In 1960, I was the only one from my circle of high-school girl friends who went on to graduate school after completing a B.A.

The classic works identified with the so-called second wave of feminism are what pushed me from inchoate instinct and intimation into formulated thought and purposeful speech and action. Kate Millett's *Sexual Politics* acted as a particularly strong catalyst. I purchased it in early September of 1970, and read it as I waited for my Ph.D. thesis to be bound for submission to the Yale library. Until I taught Millett's work at OISE (Ontario Institute for Studies in Education) many years later, I believed that the main message of her analysis and exposé of the misogyny and patriarchal assumptions of a number of major male literary figures was that a woman who earned a Ph.D. (me) and then followed a husband to his job (which was where I was headed) was a fool.

Shortly after we arrived in St. John's, Newfoundland, where my then husband had been offered a position in the History Department, I too was offered a job, also in History, although only to teach in what was called Junior Division, designed for first-year students straight out of grade 11. I was so grateful that it took me until my third year of teaching before I gathered up my courage and staged something of a palace coup. In History with a faculty of approximately 25, the Junior Division was staffed by the only women in the department (two others besides me), plus one man with a master's degree and one with a Ph.D. What galled me most was that one of the men teaching in Senior Division was an Austrian who only had a master's degree from Memorial University. (It didn't help that he made jokes about women enjoying rape.) But what really galvanized me into action was learning that the new person hired for a senior position that I was qualified for (and I informed the department head of that fact), not only lacked a Ph.D. but was a close male friend of one of my male colleagues.

I used my power as corresponding secretary for faculty meetings to launch my coup, and inserted into the order of business a motion to abolish the department's Junior/Senior Division hierarchy and regularize all appointments.

When the agenda was distributed, the Head was furious — a stocky man who, when angry, would puff out his barrel chest and bellow — and I remember feeling as though I were being blown back against the wall by the power and volume of his rage. But I held myself together as he took me to task, fuming that a secretary had no authority to change the agenda, and that any and all changes required a week's notice and approval by the Head.

Despite the bluster, he allowed a vote on the motion to go forward and, with the exception of those who held administrative positions in the department, all my colleagues voted in favour. It was my first academic political battle and I had won.

During those first years at Memorial, I continued to read feminist tracts. Between teaching standard courses in European history, I could hardly keep up with the outpouring of feminist works: Betty Friedan's *The Feminine Mystique* (published in 1963 but read by me for the first time in the early 1970s), Susan Brownmiller's *Against Our Will: Men, Women and Rape* (1975), Dorothy Dinnerstein's *The Mermaid and The Minotaur: Sexual Arrangements and Human Malaise* (1976), Lorenne Clark and Debra Lewis, *Rape: The Price of Coercive Sexuality* (1977). In particular, the feminist analyses of rape as a political tool of patriarchy spoke to me. I had suffered a rape attempt in 1966 when doing research for my Ph.D. thesis at the New York Public Library. One male friend at the time intimated I would not have been attacked had I not given the impression of vulnerability. Before leaving St. John's, I became one of the founding members of the city's rape crisis centre.

Already before I read the works on rape, I had experienced another major boost to the development of my feminist consciousness. I attended the second meeting of the revived Berkshire Conference on the History of Women, held at Radcliffe in the early summer of 1974. For me as an academic historian, this was my defining revolutionary moment. For the first time I was at a history conference not dominated by men wearing stern faces and dark suits and carrying briefcases, but women in brightly coloured outfits delivering serious, solid scholarly works. Brilliant women historians like Natalie Zemon Davis.

I still remember seeing Davis stride across the stage to deliver her ground-breaking paper "Women's History in Transition: The European Case," in which she traced a trajectory from the history of "women worthies" toward a social history of women.

Back in St. John's, I pressured my department to allow a course in the history of women to be introduced. By the mid-1970s I was finally allowed to teach a special seminar on the history of feminism, under the rubric "Contemporary Problems in Historical Perspective." In the fall of 1980 I moved away from St. John's to begin teaching at OISE. Eventually I would gain a secure, tenure-track position there, jointly appointed to the Department of History and Philosophy and the Department of Sociology in Education. In my years there, the institute was a hotbed of feminist, gay and lesbian, anti-racist, and post-colonial liberatory scholarship and politics. My feminism was deepened and broadened and made more complicated and inclusive as students and a bourgeoning literature challenged and educated me.

OISE granted me the freedom to teach what I wanted, a freedom for which I am truly grateful, for it enabled me to develop seminars in fields where I was every bit as much the learner as the teacher.

The works that revolutionized my thinking during my twenty-one years at OISE are truly too numerous to cite in full, but I'll end by mentioning a few: *This Bridge Called My Back: Writings by Radical Women of Color* (1981), Makeda Silvera's *Silenced* (1983), Audre Lorde's *Sister Outsider* (1984), Denise Riley's *Am I That Name?* from *Feminism and the Category of 'Women' in History* (1988), and Anne McClintock's *Imperial Leather* (1995) — all works that refused the notion of "women" as an undifferentiated category. Finally I'd like to give a nod to the journal housed all those years at OISE, *Resources for Feminist Research/Documentation sur la recherche féministe*, for providing an important space for feminist scholarship and debate.

69 | FROM THE NECK DOWN

Nancy Poole

Small town Ontario in the '60s. Surely in the "health instruction" part of phys-ed class my high school gym teacher spoke about how one gets pregnant, but I don't remember hearing it. Perhaps pregnancy prevention was in such deep code to meet the school board dictates in Orange Ontario, that I missed it. Perhaps because the practicalities, like birth control pills, weren't legally available in Canada before 1969, I didn't attend to the messaging. Perhaps because I had no prior knowledge to which to attach it, I didn't understand. For my mother came from good Methodist stock, and often declared that proper ladies don't talk about "anything below the neck." When I first noticed menstrual blood in my panties, my mother referred me, without any explanation, to my older sister to get a pad and the suspender belt in which to mount it. I was so naive. I remember filling out an application for Girl Guide camp and the form asked "Do you menstruate?" To me that foreign word looked like it had something to do with music, so I answered "Yes, I play the piano."

We went to camp often, winter and summer, as the leader from my small town enjoyed the companionship of the leader from the neighbouring small town. The latter was a butch, complete with workboots, a red and black check lumber jacket, and a big heart. As campers we enjoyed racing through the fields, swimming for hours, learning to swear, being loved and encouraged by our leaders. I don't remember ever discussing how one gets pregnant; rather, that time was only about being wild girls, away from the constraints of families and small town morality.

Thinking back to that phys-ed class now, I can't help but wonder if I perhaps missed "the birds and bees explanation," as it was then described, because I was overly distracted by the large and shapely calves of my gym teacher. Later, in the '70s when mixing sound for musician Meg Christian, she performed "Ode to a Gym Teacher," and I, like many other lesbians, identified strongly with the lead-in narrative to that song.

I spoke of this interest in my gym teacher's calves when, in the '80s, I was touring with Canadian musician Heather Bishop. We told our life stories to each other, to wile away the hours as we drove together in a van to cities across Canada where Heather would perform. To acknowledge my story, when my birthday came up on the road, the band cut out huge hearts from construction paper, taped them on their calves, lined up, and bent forward — so that when I came to call them onstage, I opened the dressing room door to see a row of heart-shaped calves facing me. To this day, the most moving birthday present received.

Queen's University in the late '60s. I'm still a naive teenager at this point, but now at Queen's University, hiding my naiveté behind a passionate, swaggering emulation of Janis Joplin. Both of us looking for love in all the wrong places. I found myself thinking that perhaps there had just not been enough of a selection of young men in my small town, that I would surely find one of interest in the larger university field. I gave it a good college try.

Interestingly, some years later in Toronto when working on establishing the Lesbian Organization of Toronto (LOOT) older dykes would tell me they had noticed me at Queen's as a potential "member of the tribe." Some of them had been involved in the Queen's Homophile Association at the time. But when I had seen their table at the campus club night, I had no idea what "homophile" meant, and passed it off in my mind as some form of philatelic pursuit.

I gave it a good college try, and I found myself a pregnant teenager at university.

Prior to 1969, abortion in Canada was illegal. But by 1969 our feminist foremothers had fought for, and won, the right to legal in-hospital abortion. In 1969 the Criminal Code was amended by the Trudeau government to include a provision for therapeutic abortion, a right granted with the limiting condition that one had to go before a therapeutic three-doctor committee of hospital-based physicians who considered your need for one. The committee would have to certify that the pregnancy would be likely to endanger the life or health of the pregnant woman. The term health was not defined, and therapeutic abortion committees developed their own definitions as to when a likely danger to "health" would justify a therapeutic abortion.

Pregnant at Queen's. My stern father's best friend is a physician at the campus health clinic, and two other friends of my father are on the therapeutic abortion committee at Kingston General Hospital. No way could I go before them, in privacy — and no guarantee they would judge this situation as a danger to my health. So I find a physician in the Kingston phone book, and ask for help in connecting with a private abortion clinic across the lake in Syracuse, in New York State. I am afraid to tell anyone but the young man with whom I was having sex at the time; I no longer have access to that circle of loving Girl Guide leaders and the pack of wild girls. I am told the abortion will cost $1500, an impossible sum for a university student in 1969. I find two part-time jobs on top of my studies to save for it.

The "father" and I borrow a car to drive to Syracuse for me to have the abortion. We wait in a barren waiting room with other unlucky pairs; some mother-daughter dyads, instead of being accompanied by boyfriends. The clinic, we are told, has an ergonomic flow — wait briefly in the waiting room, speak for 3–5 minutes with the physician while he explains the procedure, have the approximately 10-minute-long procedure, and then briefly rest/regroup before leaving.

I am called in for the physician briefing prior to the procedure. I sit primly as possible, all 110 pounds of me, engulfed in a fancy leather chair facing his massive marble-top desk. Mounted on the wall behind him is a leopard skin, and there are also shelves of leather-bound books, propped up with jade bookends. It is occurring to me that this man is making obscene amounts of money to pay for African safaris, off of women's pain, from women like myself who cannot afford it. Given how fast women are moving through here, he is making $1500 every quarter hour. I am barely following his words, for I am consciously becoming a feminist in this moment.

Marilyn Porter

I came to feminism in Bristol, England, in 1969 with one child in arms, another on the way, and no job.

I heard two women speaking to a group about the new "women's liberation movement" and immediately recognized it as my natural home. I attended my first Women's Liberation Movement (WLM) meeting and realized that for many years, this was just what I had been looking for. I don't remember asking my family if my sudden and complete change of direction met with their approval; I just plunged in, and have never regretted it.

In the Bristol Women's Liberation Group, I learned to name my problems, to see how they interacted with the problems of other women of all classes and races, to share the ferment of theorizing about women's issues, and to become wholly involved in the host of actions and organizing that were taking place.

Those were heady days. We knew we were in at the beginning of something so much bigger than we were, and our commitment to feminism was total. Marriages crumbled, friends who couldn't share our ideals were neglected, other interests and commitments were abandoned. There were conferences and marches and working groups and new publications (with pages run off from women's basements) and impassioned discussions.

In the UK, the women's movement rapidly opened up to all kinds of women and all kinds of interests. It made for passionate confrontations, and it jolted me out of my comfortable white middle-class expectations. Women from all walks of life were soon taking part — including left wing parties and groups like the Communist Party of Great Britain, with its strong working class membership — women who brought a clear, class-based analysis of women's oppression to each discussion. The struggles of women in anti-colonial movements (including women in Northern Ireland), and the influence of the anti-Vietnam War resistance all helped to broaden both the membership and the perspectives of the early movement.

At the same time, lesbian feminists were joining in large numbers and insisting that lesbian existence and thinking were essential and central to the new movement. Thus, two "wings" of the movement came into being — Marxist-feminism (or socialist-feminism, we didn't make a clear distinction), and radical feminism. We didn't give much credence to what came to be known as "liberal feminism" — either as a theoretical approach or as a space that less openly radical women could occupy in the women's movement.

We were, I fear, aggressively radical, mostly young, and rather intolerant. The dress code was not flexible — you could wear denim overalls, scruffy cords, and second-hand sweaters but not skirts, high heels, or makeup. And this was reflected in the way we thought about and treated the more established groups that had been struggling, in a quiet sort of way, for women's equality. We met frequently, in noisy, anarchic "conferences," campaign meetings, or consciousness-raising groups. We remained suspicious of any form of organization, and were downright hostile to women who took "leadership" or who held "positions." We operated on shoestring budgets and relied on ad hoc fundraising for our immediate needs.

Gradually things changed. We founded women's centres in the basements of members' houses. Local groups became aware of the problems of violence against women as battered women started to arrive on their doorsteps, and they set out to lever free houses from local authorities, which they then had to run. Other demands for more substantive action to help women, or to lobby for legislative changes, soon emerged. Theoretical and identity issues threatened to divide us. The last all-inclusive WLM Conference was held in 1978 and ended in acrimony and permanent divisions. As neo-liberalism bit deep in the form of Thatcherism, the movement splintered. Some groups felt they had to address the real needs of women suffering from patriarchy and capitalism; some moved into theoretical or artistic expressions; some became more involved in formal politics and lobbying.

As for me, I went back to university and got a Ph.D. in Sociology. I also divorced, and as a single mother had to compete in an increasingly fierce market for employment. I taught early Women's Studies courses and contributed to the emerging literature in the field, including the first Women's Studies reader in the UK, *Half the*

Sky, written by a collective of eight women.

Universities in the UK in the 1970s were a tough place for feminists and feminism. The trickle of feminists into the academy had to fight every inch of the way. Not only was the institution hostile (or, at best, scoffingly amused at our pretension), but we were working in a vacuum. Eventually we filled that vacuum with feminist books, edited collections, feminist poetry, and fiction. Women's Studies came to life.

All this changed for me in 1980 when the Thatcher cuts deprived me of my hard won position at Manchester University and brought me to Canada. I arrived in Newfoundland as a full-fledged feminist, completely confident in my identity. Within days of my arrival in St. John's to take up a position at Memorial University, I found my way to the Women's Centre on Military Road and went to my first meeting. It was an eye opener. To begin with, it seemed awfully formal to me. They took minutes, had a chair, held formal positions — some even wore makeup.

As I stuttered an amazed protest, the chair (who would become a very good friend) fixed me with a steely glare. "We find we can get more done this way," she said. I began to learn a whole new way of "doing feminism." I learned about the Royal Commission on the Status of Women; I learned about the umbrella organization of the National Action Committee; I learned about local issues and passions, which included the struggles around abortion, legal rights (especially in divorce), and questions surrounding equal pay and equal opportunity at work. With time, I learned too about concerns for embedding equality into the Constitution, and the passion emerging from feminists in Quebec.

I began to work with all sorts of women I would never have considered "feminist" back in the UK: women in all the political parties; church women; even nuns (who seemed to have a better handle on social inequality issues than almost anyone); women from institutionalized organizations, such as the Women's Institute (who had ways of reaching rural women beyond anything I had seen); and even women in business. I traded my political sophistication and theoretical "purity" for effective action and real solidarity. If this was the maligned "liberal feminism," then it had a lot going for it.

As I became increasingly more active in shaping Canadian

feminism in the 1980s, I kept my contacts with UK feminists and kept a running comparison in my mind. Yes, the two movements were different, with different roots, different composition, and a very different way of organizing. Yet both were recognizably and proudly feminist, and both had strengths. As time has gone on, and especially as the UK women's movement has splintered and weakened, I have increasingly come to value the way Canadian and Quebec feminism has kept going. Despite internal struggles and external threats, there is still a distinctive Canadian and Quebec feminism, and that is an achievement worth celebrating.

71 | REBELLIOUS WOMEN

Alison Prentice

The second daughter of a third daughter, I was, like my mother, the youngest in my family. Being the youngest, I've come to believe, led us to take a slightly rebellious attitude to life. This was certainly true of my mother. Born in Wilmington, Delaware, when her mother was 43, she got away with things that had been denied her much older sisters. She always joked, for example, about her attendance at four different colleges, the last chosen when she simply got off the train in Baltimore with her sister Mary and enrolled in Goucher, instead of carrying on to Madison, Wisconsin, where she was expected by her married sister Catherine, and by the University of Wisconsin. She graduated with a course in the history of women under her belt — the text for which she kept all her life (Landon-Davies, 1927). Later she got a lot of fun out of Ashley Montagu's *The Natural Superiority of Women* (1952), hanging onto that book as well. At one level she was something of an iconoclast. Perhaps, especially after our migration to Canada in 1939, she enjoyed seeing things from the margins.

My own sense of margins surfaced soon after our arrival in Toronto. I was five. A girl I walked to school with wanted to know if I was Jewish. I had to ask my parents, and only when my non-Jewish credentials were established was this girl allowed by her parents to be my friend. Difference — Jewish or Gentile, male or female — was palpable in the public schools I attended in Toronto, and in adolescence several of my friends and I were whisked away to a nearby Anglican school for girls. Again, my mother made fun of things: the silly uniforms, white chapel veils, and, especially, the snobbish British head mistress. Four years later, I was sent off to another women's school back in the States. I grew to appreciate Smith College, intrigued by challenging courses and my interesting Jewish friends from New York, one of whom became my roommate. Smith also ran a junior year abroad program which allowed me to study in Europe, in 1953-54.

During that year at the University of Geneva I had friends from many countries, including the various Americans I'd come with, young Europeans studying to be Protestant pastors, translators or interpreters, and older friends of both sexes who were Communists, hailing from California and Southern India. The Europeans among my friends had experienced the Second World War; the Indian had endured the British occupation of his country and civil war. And I became aware, once again, that I was an outsider. In Geneva, there were the international people, the Americans (and some Canadians), and the Swiss. Paths crossed and friendships were made; but the communities were still separate.

Back at Smith I experienced an education free from the distractions of male competition. But it was still a man's world. The college prided itself on its fatherly male presidents and openly sought legitimacy, in those days, by hiring more male faculty. The poet W.H. Auden, writer in residence at Smith during my second year, declared in chapel one morning that our higher education was mainly useful for what we, as mothers later on, could teach our sons. The politician Adlai Stevenson famously said more or less the same thing at our commencement in 1955. Despite these undermining moments, I left Smith keen to learn. And, having experienced many different kinds of teaching and learning over the years, I also came away with a disposition to ask questions about education and its purposes.

Graduation meant going back to Toronto to teach history at my old Anglican school; acquiring Canadian citizenship and an M.A. in order to attend the Ontario College of Education; teaching at a public high school for two years; and, in 1960 when I was 25, getting married and soon giving birth to two sons. Things became difficult at this point. As a young mother living in downtown Toronto, I was isolated and missed the communities I had belonged to as both a learner and a teacher. Happily, the History Department at the expanding University of Toronto needed teaching assistants and I soon landed part-time work outside the home. But one June day as I was scrubbing the kitchen floor, a call came requesting that I teach five tutorials the following fall. I agreed, but inwardly rebelled. It dawned on me that if I wanted some control over my teaching work, I needed the union ticket. By 1967 I had embarked on a Ph.D.

Not everyone applauded. One of my husband's colleagues volunteered that he'd kill his wife if she did that. A favourite professor wondered why I bothered. Why not just write a book instead? But it was the teaching I loved, only learning as I went along that I also loved historical research and writing. My thesis was a critical take on the nineteenth century origins of the public school system in Ontario, a system that by the late 1960s and early '70s was under increasing attack for its profound class and gender biases — biases that were clearly apparent in my children's schools.

All this came together for me in the women's movement. I had become friends with Bonnie Kreps, then married to a physicist colleague of my husband's. Bonnie introduced me to Toronto's New Feminists and probably also to *Sexual Politics*, Kate Millett's riveting study of gender and literary education, first published in 1969. By the early '70s I was beginning to feel that mothers bore the brunt of — and were often blamed for — whatever problems their children encountered at school; that the demanding work of wives and mothers was inadequately recognized and compensated; and that, historically, women teachers had worked as hard but earned less in schools that were mainly governed by men.

In 1972, I had miraculously landed a job at Atkinson College, a wonderful evening school on the margins of York University that was devoted to the higher education of mature students. I soon became aware that, en masse, women faculty at Atkinson attracted attention. When four of us were having dinner together before classes one evening, a male colleague joked that we must be plotting the revolution. On another occasion, the dean of the college popped his head through the doorway of the faculty lounge where a group was having lunch to remark that, if he shot us all, it would finish off the women's movement at Atkinson, wouldn't it!

Stunned? Yes, but not for long. Teaching at Atkinson was transformative. Our rebellious women's gatherings continued and I had the thrill of developing a course on the history of women, the family and education in Canada. While at Atkinson I also had the pleasure of recognizing that the history of women could and possibly should be called "women's history." It might be on the margins, but it belonged to us. We could own it.

Not surprisingly, by the time I left Atkinson in 1975 for a job at the Ontario Institute for Studies in Education, I was a committed feminist.

72 | TEACHING THE PERSONAL IS POLITICAL

Shelley TSivia Rabinovitch

I like saying that I was "born to be an anthropologist." I was born an Anglophone in French-Canada (Montreal), a Jew in Catholic Quebec, and a fat kid who grew up in the Twiggy-era of the late 1960s and early 1970s. I was always liminal — an outsider looking inward. Then my family moved to Arizona, and there, I was again on the outside: a Canadian in the USA, an Anglo in Hispanic America.

My family returned to Canada in 1973, and we ended up in Toronto. I enrolled at York University where I took a first-year course with Dr. Johanna Stuckey. She introduced me to ideas, notions, and concepts that had simply never crossed my mind, including the idea that there was nothing "essential" about the definitions of "male" or "female."

Subsequently, Dr. Stuckey held a fourth-year seminar — that I was given permission to attend — analyzing the ways in which women were portrayed in erotica and pornography. Despite York's reputation as a liberal university (particularly when compared to her older sister, the University of Toronto), we were not allowed to hold the seminar on university property. So about a half dozen women would bus to Dr. Stuckey's home where we would drink tea, eat cookies, and discuss hard-core depictions of women from North America and Europe.

To this day, I use many of the tools I acquired in her analysis of pornography when analyzing the dirty words people use to insult each other, and decoding the underlying metaphors for my students.

While in university, I did some piecework for Toronto-area newspapers, and was actually hired to be a stringer with a major radio station in Toronto. During that time, I met a fellow who worked in the newsroom of CFTR, and one evening, while the two of us were talking, he made a fatal mistake. In his polished pro-radio voice, he intoned to me, "Whatever you do, Shelley, stay in newspaper. Radio is man's work!"

So while he was on vacation, I managed to get an interview with his boss, the news director. By the time my friend returned to work, I was in the newsroom being taught how to edit audiotape. "What are you doing here?" he queried. I replied, "I work here. How about you?" I should have foreseen how difficult my career choice was going to be when, early on, I called to send down some clips and had to deal with an infamous "trash talking" member of the news staff. Making sure I could clearly hear him talking to his colleagues, he asked, "anyone want to f*** Shelley?"

In this cauldron of fire, I learned to talk dirtier and tougher than most of the men I worked with.

After I finished my degree, I was hired directly by a now defunct all news radio-network based in Ottawa. I loved the adrenaline rush, the pressure, and the excitement of the job, and I impressed the heck out of our one senior morning newsreader, a man who had worked as a freelance journalist in Vietnam during the war there. I thought I had it made. I stayed about one year, and subsequently moved to a job in Oshawa, Ontario.

One night, after my evening shift was over, a female technician asked me how I got my on-air job since I "squeaked" when I talked. I looked at her with a confused look on my face. "Squeak?" I asked her. She then did a singsong imitation of my last newscast, over-emphasizing the high notes when I tried to show excitement or concern in the text. "Like that," she said. "I've been told I'll never get on-air because I squeak too much." In those days there were almost no women in professional radio news (or television news, for that matter), and as such there were few voice models for women to adopt. As a result, I looked to my favourite American television reporter, Walter Cronkite, and started to lower my voice so that my "top notes" would be less grating.

The very next day the news director came flying in asking me what I had done to my voice. I was afraid he was angry, but au contraire, he was thrilled at my more modulated tonal quality. It was that self-taught melodious voice (which I still receive compliments on) that earned me a plum job: working with a major radio station in Ottawa. So I relocated back to Ottawa, a city I had come to love, and if the story had a happy ending, that would be that. Unfortunately I landed in a hotbed of misogyny: a news director who hated Jews and a director of news and sports who hated women. I spent nearly a year in radio-hell, having slurs and anti-woman jokes pitched around the entire time I worked there.

About the time I could no longer stand it, I received a phone call from my former boss in Oshawa asking if I was finding it difficult to work where I was. I was surprised, until I found out that at a large industry dinner he had overheard both men holding forth at some length about "damn women" in their industry, naming and insulting me in particular. I was let go by said radio station a few weeks later, and was immediately on the doorstep of both the federal Labour Board and the Human Rights Commission for discrimination on the grounds of sex and religion.

We settled out of court in my favour.

During this time, I called myself an "equalist." I assumed that feminists wanted women to have the upper hand in our society, and I wanted men and women to be truly equal. But somewhere in the 1980s, when I realized that was not what feminism was all about, I turned a corner and embraced feminism as my lifestyle and philosophy.

The lessons from both the university and working worlds radicalized my worldview.

I returned to university in my early 30s to do graduate work. In my third year, I survived a violent sexual assault, and learned that the police don't always listen, regardless of gender. The first officer who received the call would not respond. She merely chided me for being "every man's doormat." The police services board, however, upheld my complaint, and in the end I managed to obtain one of Canada's highest civil suit judgments against a rapist. I also finished my Ph.D.

As the personal is political, I discuss all of these things when I talk to my undergraduates at the University of Ottawa where I teach both Women's Studies and Religious Studies. I survived childhood sexual abuse. I survived an alcoholic father. I survived a career in a misogynist industry. I survived a violent, brutal rape, and still earned my doctorate. I tell my students that it is only when we are silent that we are victims. I am living proof of this, and I am a feminist.

73 | HOW I BECAME A FEMINIST

Arlene Perly Rae

I became a feminist around 1972. I was 22 that year and simultaneously a graduate student at the University of Toronto and a full-time, unionized flight attendant working for Air Canada. Events in both places led to my rapid identification with the women's movement, but it was the union experience that was the most dramatic, and so had the bigger impact; one that would forever influence my views about gender.

On campus, men and women were enrolled in relatively equal proportions in my M.A. program at the Centre for the Study of Drama. Women's enrolment numbers were still way behind in professional disciplines such as medicine, dentistry, and law and there were far fewer women in engineering, architecture, or science — this is still true today, but it's changing. Both men and women were thriving academically, but men more frequently ran for and were elected to student council, wrote more often in the campus newspapers, and held higher status as presidents of clubs and organizers of events. Men also seemed to land all the best jobs after graduation.

The women's movement existed and was growing, though it was still young. Since my off-campus job was as an "air hostess," I tended not to reveal that around the university. Only my best friends knew. Many people made fun of stewardesses (remember "Coffee, tea, or Me?") as easy, too flighty (haha), and too feminine to be activists or liberated women.

Despite liking the hours (evenings/weekends, holidays, summers), and loving the foreign travel and perks (free passes/cheap travel), I worked hard to separate the two spheres. I often changed into my uniform surreptitiously, usually off campus, if I had to rush from school to work a flight. I was afraid that if people knew what job paid for my studies, some of my newer female friends would not respect me, and men might well get the wrong idea as well. This, despite the fact that flying allowed me — a Drama Centre student — to attend cutting edge theatre in London and New York, and to research essays in some of the world's finest libraries. Many books were read, and term papers written while I laboured (unsociably but undisturbed) in quiet hotel rooms, over room service dinners. It worked for me.

I can still remember some heated conversations with friends about women's independence. There I was, fully employed, active in my union and travelling far and wide, arguing about women's independence with friends whose tuition, food, and rent were totally covered by their parents. They attended meetings and consciousness raising sessions about female empowerment; I worked hard on two fronts, at school and in the air, and felt rather strongly that I was the more free and independent. I still believe women have more choice about their living circumstances if they have their own job, paycheque, or income.

In the early years of commercial air travel, at first nurses, and later other young women, were hired by airlines to inspire passenger confidence. They wore paramilitary uniforms, and were not particularly glamorous. They simply showed up and did their jobs. But by the '60s and early '70s, in a highly competitive airline industry, in-flight service became a powerful publicity tool. Air hostesses were all single and under 30; there were restrictions about height and weight, and makeup, hair care, walking, and so on were taught right alongside safety training.

Employees soon became used as part of the ad campaigns. Promotions promised sexily dressed, pretty young women. National Airlines had a "Fly Me" campaign. Braniff's "Air Strip" involved crew members changing outfits mid-flight. Others held en route fashion shows, or dressed their female in-flight crew in uniforms involving low-cut tops, hot pants, or miniskirts. We at Air Canada wore short A-line dresses with bands of bright colour around the edges. To me, the outfits implied we could just as soon be working in an ice-cream shop or selling candy.

But then it all changed. Ahead of our American counterparts, the Air Canada female in-flight crews began to bring our issues to our CALFAA (Canadian Air Line Flight Attendants' Association) union meetings. The meetings grew bigger, more contentious (and more exciting). We fought for many things, including maximum hours, guaranteed rest, parity for meal and cleaning expenses, an end to the restrictions on marriage or age (the "ten year contract") and, most importantly, for something called the integrated seniority list.

As it stood then — in cabin crew terms — all men were Pursers. In other words, a newly hired male was senior, in charge of, and better paid than women who had, perhaps, worked in the air for years. Integrating the lists would, for the first time, allow women to plan on a long-term career with the company. Both men and women, we suggested, should start as gender neutral "flight attendants," and over time, if they wished, apply to become Pursers and Flight Directors (the in-charge person on wide-bodied aircrafts). It sounded fair and reasonable to us women, but not to the company or to the male pursers.

In 1969, we took our allegations of gender discrimination to the Human Rights Commission. In 1973, their Tribunal expressed a ruling that yes, there had been a breach. We had won!

Air Canada was ordered to end the old hiring practices and to blend the male and female lists. The power of that win, that of a determined, organized, fairness-based sisterhood working for, and accomplishing, a multi-faceted victory was heady, thrilling, and memorable. It has forever altered and improved the system.

Not incidentally, this battle and our ultimate success confirmed my belief in the capacity of a dedicated group of hard working and committed people to create real and effective change, politically and in other areas. The male pursers fought us in court. (Bizarrely, it seemed to me, they hired female lawyers to argue that women were unsuitable to serve as "in charges" on flights). It was to no effect. The victory was ours.

Of course, there was an adjustment period. I was one of Air Canada's first "Acting Pursers." We did the same job as male pursers (making announcements, conducting safety briefings and checks, assigning responsibilities, liaising with the cockpit, filling out forms, handling money, etc.), but got paid less (about two-thirds that of a male purser). Then, finally, in 1974, I became part of the first group of true and unrestricted female pursers. By then, I was also a full-fledged feminist.

I still remember one resistant Captain. He persisted, even then, calling me (and other female pursers) "honey" or "sweetie" as he had in the past. We, of course, to show respect, had to call him Captain X. I finally said to him, "Captain, honey, either you and I agree to use first names or last names, or we have ourselves a problem." He reluctantly stopped using diminutives (at least with me).

At Air Canada, new uniforms were issued: navy blue dresses and pantsuits (!) with crisp striped blouses. They were smart, tailored, and looked professional. Eventually, most passengers realized that female flight attendants were not sex objects in the sky but trained individuals who could, if need be, open an aircraft door upside down, in the dark and in a smoke filled cabin. It made us proud.

The US airlines did not follow our lead until the late '70s and early '80s.

I had become a feminist partly through observation and discussions with friends about the numerous inequities in academia and the wider world, but, without a doubt, became more deeply committed through personal experience. Meeting and organizing and working for a just cause tend to have a powerful impact and to stick with you. It was fun to join other young women in the quest for respect and a fairer system. I was not a major player — I was too busy with school and all — but I certainly felt that I was part of a bigger movement, and it was a wonderful feeling.

74 | MOI, LA BATTANTE
Ann Robinson

Je suis née dans l'Outaouais en 1944, quatre ans après l'attribution du droit de vote aux Québécoises et un an avant la fin de la Seconde Guerre mondiale. Alors que je vivais une enfance insignifiante due principalement à la place centrale que j'occupe dans la famille, troisième enfant d'une famille de cinq, les Québécoises, comme toutes les Occidentales, étaient invitées à retourner à leurs chaudrons après avoir soutenu l'industrie de guerre pendant que leurs maris, leurs pères, leurs frères étaient partis à la guerre.

J'entreprends mes études primaires dans un Québec profondément catholique. Après sept années d'école primaire réussies péniblement, je prends le chemin d'un pensionnat à Ottawa. Apeurée, timide, renfrognée, j'en ressors avec un diplôme de douzième année scientifique. Après un été de confrontation avec mon père, je peux enfin m'inscrire dans un externat de filles du côté québécois pour compléter un Baccalauréat ès arts.

Pendant que je m'échine à l'étude du latin et de la philosophie, une première femme est élue à l'Assemblée nationale à Québec, Claire Kirkland-Casgrain. Cette première députée dépose à l'Assemblée nationale la *Loi sur la capacité juridique de la femme mariée* en 1964, connue sous le nom de Bill 16. Jusqu'alors, les femmes mariées au Québec étaient subordonnées à leur mari, quel que soit leur régime matrimonial. Quoique révolutionnaire, cette nouvelle loi n'accordait malheureusement la capacité juridique qu'aux femmes mariées sous le régime de séparation de biens.

C'est dans ce contexte politique et juridique d'ouverture aux femmes que je débute mes études de droit en septembre 1965. Majeure depuis plus d'un an, il est tout de même impensable que je quitte ma famille pour aller étudier ailleurs qu'à Ottawa. Ainsi je continue à vivre sous la férule de mon père qui surveille mes fréquentations, mes allées et venues, mes heures d'études. Dans ma classe, il y a cinq ou six filles et plus de quatre-vingt-dix garçons. Est-il nécessaire de mentionner combien j'ai subi de harcèlement psychologique, moral et même sexuel pendant mes trois années d'études, de la part de mes collègues et aussi de mes professeurs ? La façon de m'en sortir a été de choisir un confrère et d'en faire mon amoureux.

Je décroche ma licence en droit en avril 1968 au mitan des travaux de la Commission royale d'enquête sur la situation de la femme au Canada. Et je me marie une semaine après la collation des grades, sous le régime de la séparation de biens et à l'église, puisque l'institution du mariage civil au Québec ne sera instaurée qu'en novembre de la même année.

Nous nous installons à Québec pour nous préparer aux examens du Barreau et débuter notre carrière. Entre temps, le Parlement québécois se rend aux arguments des groupes de femmes et adopte comme régime matrimonial légal celui de la société d'acquêts. Sous ce nouveau régime, nous achetons notre première maison en 1971. Officiellement, il est le seul propriétaire de la maison parce qu'il est le seul signataire du contrat d'achat et de l'hypothèque. C'était ainsi en ce début des années soixante-dix.

Juriste, je fais carrière à l'Université Laval. J'aime mon mari propriétaire de notre résidence familiale, je veux des enfants. Entre juin 1971 et août 1977, j'ai quatre enfants, deux filles et deux garçons. Un seul, le dernier, naît sous la protection syndicale. Pour l'aînée que j'adopte, mon patron m'accorde deux semaines de congé. Pour la deuxième, née durant l'été, j'ai droit à trois semaines de congé après l'accouchement. Le moment le plus difficile est sans doute l'accouchement de mon premier fils. Incapable de planifier ma grossesse, je me retrouve avec une perspective d'accouchement en janvier. J'enseigne tout le trimestre d'automne, corrige les examens, y compris les examens de reprise tenus en début de trimestre d'hiver. J'accouche fin janvier. Mes patrons m'oublient pendant trois semaines. Puis les pressions sont de plus en plus fortes pour mon retour dans l'amphithéâtre où je dois rattraper le temps perdu, le chargé de cours qui m'a remplacée ayant « figé » devant les étudiants. Hiver mémorable !

Les Québécoises obtiennent en 1971 le droit d'être jurées ; le Centre des femmes de Montréal est créé en janvier 1972. Le gouvernement québécois crée le Conseil du statut de la femme en 1973, et, sous l'égide de l'ONU, on célèbre avec toutes les femmes du monde l'Année internationale de la femme en 1975, année choisie également par l'Assemblée nationale pour adopter la Charte des droits et libertés de la personne. En 1977, la notion de puissance paternelle exercée unilatéralement par le père sur ses enfants mineurs est écartée du code civil et remplacée par l'autorité parentale exercée de concert par les deux parents.

Un an plus tard, alors que le gouvernement du Parti Québécois nouvellement élu annonce la création de cliniques de planification des naissances où il sera possible de pratiquer des avortements, le père de mes enfants commence à montrer des signes d'épuisement. Il se sent exploité à la maison à cause du partage des tâches familiales et ménagères. Après quelques mois de tergiversations, il craque. Il quitte le foyer, incapable de considérer que ses quatre enfants, qui ont alors entre neuf mois et sept ans, n'ont pas de mère à plein temps. La rupture est catastrophique, les lendemains cauchemardesques, mes rêves de conciliation travail-famille tombent dans l'oubli.

Mais je me retrousse les manches, deviens féministe, plutôt féministe égalitariste. « Fais un homme de toi, ma fille. » Voilà qui illustre bien cette période de ma vie. Double et même triple tâche puisqu'en plus de mon travail de professeure à l'université et mes responsabilités monoparentales à la maison, je termine des études supérieures. Deux maîtrises, l'une en éducation et l'autre en droit. Rapidement je me rends compte que le féminisme égalitariste n'est pas l'idéal dans un contexte de monoparentalité. Je dépéris littéralement, mon corps m'envoie des signes. Le médecin me prescrit un long congé de maladie durant lequel je dois prendre des décisions quant à mon avenir et à celui de mes enfants. Ou j'arrête de travailler pour m'occuper d'eux à plein temps, ou je cède la garde à leur père qui, soit dit en passant, ne l'a jamais demandée, ou... je me remarie. Je choisis cette dernière hypothèse. C'est durant les sept années de mon deuxième mariage que ma carrière prend vraiment son essor.

Ce deuxième mariage se déroule sous l'égide de l'égalité totale entre époux, puisque c'est au début des années 1980 que le gouvernement péquiste adopte le Bill 89, dont le but principal est d'établir l'égalité formelle des conjoints durant le mariage. Disparaît alors du Code civil toute trace de la puissance maritale, par l'abrogation, entre autres, de l'obligation pour l'épouse d'habiter avec son mari là où ce dernier établit la résidence familiale.

Comme enseignante, chercheuse en droit, militante féministe, ou dans ma vie privée comme mère, amie ou conseillère des amis de mes enfants, je côtoie de plus en plus fréquemment diverses formes de violence faite aux femmes. Violence en milieu conjugal, agression sexuelle, harcèlement sexuel et sexiste. Je suis confrontée fréquemment à l'intolérance des hommes, que ce soient les collègues, les amis ou les professionnels qui croisent ma route. Un jour, j'en ai assez. Assez du machisme, assez du sexisme, assez du patriarcat, je deviens féministe radicale.

Je commence à dénoncer les inégalités, les injustices faites aux femmes, les diverses formes d'oppression des femmes, le système patriarcal. Je choisis de faire la critique du droit avec une perspective féministe. Je définis des projets de recherche dans ce sens et je bâtis des cours sur l'analyse féministe du droit. Mon deuxième mariage n'y survit pas, je me retrouve célibataire. Une seule certitude alors : plus jamais d'homme dans ma vie. Je suis devenue féministe radicale séparatiste.

En 1988, lors d'un colloque féministe, je suis « frappée par la grâce » de l'amour entre femmes. En 1989, pendant que je fais mes premiers pas comme lesbienne féministe, Chantal Daigle se défend du mieux qu'elle peut dans le système judiciaire canadien afin d'empêcher son ex-conjoint Jean-Guy Tremblay de la forcer à mener à terme une grossesse non désirée. Quelques mois plus tard, Marc Lépine abat quatorze jeunes femmes.

Au retour d'une année sabbatique à l'automne 1993, je participe à la consultation publique sur la violence et la discrimination envers les gais et les lesbiennes organisée par la Commission des droits de la personne du Québec. Je veux rendre publiques les difficultés vécues par les lesbiennes quand elles réclament la garde de leurs enfants nés d'une relation hétérosexuelle antérieure. Je veux dénoncer le sexisme et l'hétéro-sexisme des tribunaux à l'égard de ces mères lesbiennes, le mépris et la complaisance des juges prêts à tout pour défendre l'idée qu'il est dans l'intérêt de l'enfant d'être élevé dans un milieu hétérosexuel. Je veux démontrer que des couples de lesbiennes sont de très bonnes mères pour des enfants mineurs. Ce faisant, j'aborde la question de la conjugalité homosexuelle et, fidèle à moi-même, j'affirme que l'accès au mariage pour les gais et les lesbiennes du Canada est un événement inéluctable. L'avenir me donnera raison.

Je vieillis. Ma première conjugalité lesbienne arrive à son terme. En janvier 1996, je suis à nouveau célibataire, mes enfants sont maintenant de jeunes adultes, ils vont et viennent à la maison au gré de leurs études et de leurs amours. Je travaille toujours beaucoup, je sors peu, je goûte à nouveau les douceurs de la solitude volontaire.

Au détour d'un mandat syndical féministe, l'amour est à nouveau au rendez-vous. J'ai enfin trouvé Ma Grande Lesbienne. Je deviens lesbienne féministe heureuse. Alors que nous vivons nos premières années de bonheur, les divers gouvernements du pays font des pas de géants quant au respect des droits des gais et des lesbiennes du Canada. Dorénavant, les conjoints de même sexe sont considérés absolument de la même façon que les conjoints de sexe différent, que ce soit pour l'accès au mariage ou pour la filiation.

Je suis maintenant à la retraite, j'ai enfin le temps de faire ce qui me plaît et à mon rythme. Vivre. Tout simplement. Plus que jamais lesbienne féministe heureuse. J'ai transmis mon féminisme radical à mes filles ainsi qu'à plusieurs de mes anciennes étudiantes. Mes fils sont maintenant des hommes et je les aime. Cinq petits-enfants, deux filles et trois garçons, sont venus agrandir la famille. Et il y a quelques années, j'ai convolé en justes noces avec Ma Grande Lesbienne.

75 | MY MOTHER CRIED WHEN I WAS BORN
Gurbir K. Sandhu

If some people are born with a strong sense of justice and a yearning for equality, I am one of those people. I was born in March of 1976 in a remote village in the Punjab state of India. I am the middle child and was the second daughter born into a family where everyone was expecting a boy. I am told my mother cried when I was born. My grandparents tried consoling my mother. It was not that my grandparents were happy or content about my arrival; it was probably their spiritual values that influenced them to not be so anti-female — at least not explicitly. I am told that they accepted me as God's gift.

When I try to unravel the process that led to the strong convictions I have, I am sure of only one thing: that my religion played an important role in reinforcing my sense of social justice. I was born into a Sikh family, and my grandparents are strong devotees of their faith. I grew up with stories of how Sikh Gurus and their families sacrificed their lives fighting against oppression of all kinds.

Despite some gaps in theology and practice, I have always been proud of the fact the Sikhism is the only religion that forbids discrimination based on class, caste, and most importantly gender. Sikh Gurus prohibited women from covering their faces. Widows were encouraged to remarry and women were permitted to take part in every aspect of social, political, and religious life.

I am not suggesting that practicing Sikhs have ever been fully successful at incorporating these ideals into their lives, or the functioning of their religious institutions. But, the philosophy is truly radical considering that Sikhism advocated for these values more than 300 years ago, in India, where the country was, and still is, to a great extent plagued by all kinds of social ills.

It also helped that my family was financially comfortable. My sister and I were never denied any opportunity. We were provided with the best basic and post-secondary education available in the area. In fact, there was more pressure on both of us sisters to succeed in education and in establishing our careers because our parents, especially our mother, realized that an established career is a woman's best defence in times of adversity.

My mother herself holds a university degree. And she refused to give up her job in a government school despite pressure from her in-laws, who thought it would be better if she focused more on her home and children. In many ways, my mother unconsciously modelled some of the feminist ideals. She is a very strong and outspoken woman whom I admire and resent at the same time. I admire her for her strength, her career focus, her perseverance through tough times to ensure all her children received good education, and her ability to speak her mind. But I resent her because she still holds the belief that although girls are important, God must grant each family at least one boy. I resent that she cried when I was born. I resent that, although she never denied her daughters an opportunity to access what was important in life, she and my grandmother also showed their special affection toward our brother through subtle ways.

It is interesting how I do not have memories of my father or grandfather exhibiting this subtle bias. I often wonder at what point we, as women, internalize the messages of the sexist society so deeply that we can actually start playing an important, and at times a lead role in sustaining and perpetuating patriarchal structures. When this occurs, men no longer need to work hard to ensure that their position of power stays unaltered.

This reminds me of more recent encounters I have had with some other women in my family about this subject. These well-educated women keep on praying and expecting that my next child will be a boy. When I challenge them on their sexist thinking, their response is, "Well, we just wish this so that you can have a mixed family. Since you already have a daughter, it would be nice if the next one is a boy." Yeah right. The need for a mixed family is a good excuse. I asked one of them the other day if she would have prayed this hard for the second child to be a girl if the first one was a boy. Of course, she had no answer. These are the women who ideologically oppose female feticide in India, but would never admit that they are also responsible for the continuation of this practice. I believe any person who considers the birth of a boy a cause for special celebration is responsible for this practice.

Since I was born with a heightened awareness of unequal gender relations, it felt natural to turn to feminism. It made me understand that I was not alone in my observations, that this feeling of being treated unfairly was not something that was "just in my head," that patriarchy is a phenomenon that is experienced by all women in all cultures.

I was first exposed to an organized movement working towards gender equality when I moved to Canada. This was the piece I was missing back home. Receiving education in social work and working within women's organizations over the past ten years has strengthened my commitment for women's equality. Although my energy for street level activism seems to be dying down, I enjoy teaching women's studies at a local college and hope to fulfill my commitment to feminism by educating the next generation of feminists.

76 | MISOGYNY SEEPING FROM HIS PORES

Jeanne Sarson

Can a toddler be a feminist?

It was December of '45. My mother had just returned home from the hospital having given birth to my brother. As she stood cradling him, I manoeuvred in behind her left leg and holding on I looked up at my father's mother — she had come to look after me while my mother was in hospital — I looked up at her, and called her a bitch.

I knew how to apply the word. I am certain I'd heard my father call my mother a bitch. And as I grew older I realized he fit all women and girls into this classification, including me. Misogyny seeped from his pores, every minute of every day.

It would be years before I knew this Greek term — misogyny. However, I did know that "bitch" applied to my grandmother, but not to my mother.

Protected by my mother, I was seeking my justice, for my grandmother had been guilty of locking me in a room while she "cared" for me. I can still see the light that shone under the door of the locked room. My mother is no longer here with me to confirm the layout of the apartment we lived in, but I recall there was a hallway outside the door and that is where a little friend of mine was; she too lived in the house. We passed paper notes under the door. I'm sure we considered our writings important.

This experience of being locked in a room was the day my flashpoint hit. I don't know how many hours I was locked up, but long enough to feel duress and a strong sense of injustice. I call it a flashpoint because it was as though I was surrounded by light and an internal knowing that if I was to survive I was going to have to do so for myself. I was three years old.

By four I knew that my raving, violent, alcoholic father was a deadly danger, and I kept telling my mother we had to leave. It would take six more years before she permanently left. Her turning point came when she was given an insulin shock "treatment" for her distress — in effect "treating" her for the life-threatening violence my father inflicted night after night. It was the early '50s, when women weren't supposed to leave their husbands. My father's $20.00 bribes to the parish priest ensured my mother heard his sermon that it was her responsibility to stay, a lesson reinforced by the Monsignor who refused her communion because she had broken her vows.

Becoming a single mother meant she had to work. Seeing her walk the several kilometres each way to and from work six days a week brought neighbourhood men with vehicles to the rescue. Offering her a drive initially seemed caring and neighbourly. But then it was payback time — the price to pay came as sexualized advances or no more rides. The rides stopped.

Several neighbourhood women came to visit shortly after my mother purchased a fridge. Their conversation hinted that she must have engaged in prostitution in order to buy a fridge. I watched my mother walk them out the door.

Through these experiences and our talks, I came to realize that both women and men were capable of oppressing the "other." We, of course, were the other, and I was angry!

Sent to a psychiatrist at 15 for "my problems," I told him I would take care of myself. The first and only meeting lasted probably 15 minutes. Years later when I entered nursing, I refused to bow down to the doctors as good student nurses were "trained" to do, and I would not agree to be treated as a lowly student. The result? I was a "problem." Smart, but a problem none the less. Feminism had not reached my Yarmouth Hospital Nursing School; therefore my resistance to the gendered and positional injustices was not well received.

The '60s had just begun. I moved to Canada's Arctic where I worked for 11 years, isolated from the growing feminist movement.

TV didn't exist there until the early '70s, but even in this climate, my gender sensitivity in health care service grew. Providing Inuit women with birth control pills brought misogynist responses when men's procreation was threatened. In Inuvik I became aware that I needed to add race to my gendered concerns. Inuit women were having pelvic exams done in out-patient cubicles with only curtains to shield them from passers-by. This was gendered and racial injustice.

"How would your wife like to have her bottom exposed to the swaying curtains of the passers-by?" was my challenge to the non-native hospital administrator. His compassion saw that permanent walls were soon erected.

Motherhood, with the birth of twin sons, brought unique queries. I wondered how to resist being cast into the domestic sphere of wife and mother. When our sons were six weeks of age, I packed them up for a caribou hunting trip. It would be the next year during moose hunting season when the epiphany hit. I realized that motherhood had made me vulnerable to becoming "just" a man's wife and the mother of "his" children, and that rather than be "left behind" at home, I had instead entered "man's world."

It was the early '70s and it was a struggle to hold on to my cherished individualized personhood — a position of gendered equality that was not automatically granted within the conditioned relational family constructs of Canadian society.

Has my journey to, and with, feminism that began in December of '45 been successful? I suggest so. I have two feminist sons. And in 2009 when presenting at an international conference I was surprised to hear the chair introduce me as a feminist — I had neither discussed nor withheld this aspect of myself from her, she simply seemed to know. Indeed, I am a feminist!

> Women's March Against Poverty, Parliament Hill, Ottawa, June 15, 1996

Archives and Special Collections (CWMA), University of Ottawa (PC-X10-92)/Nancy Adamson

> Marche des femmes contre la pauvreté, Colline parlementaire, Ottawa, le 15 juin 1996

PSAC
Women's
Marche des f
Du pain
et des roses
Des emplois
et la jus
CCA/CT

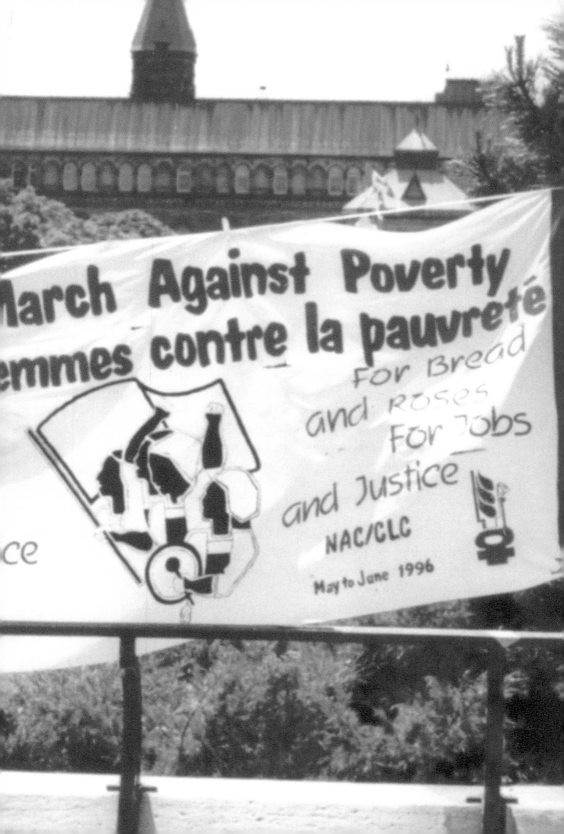

77 | STILL ANGRY

Saima Scally

As a young girl growing up in a small town in Ontario, I thought of myself as equal to anyone, male or female. With this basic belief in equality, I turned easily to feminism when I reached puberty and came up against the barriers that the girls my age faced.

In high school I wanted to take a course in Natural Resources Technology. That was where my heart lay. That was my calling. Girls were not allowed to take it. Already acquainted with feminism, we rebelled. We whispered among one another in the hallways and applied for the course in droves: for the first time, the course schedule was going to be done by computer and we thought the computer would not care if we were male or female. It didn't. As far as it was concerned, a lot of us qualified for admission.

The administrators were furious when they saw what we had done, but they were also powerless — there were too many of us. Instead, they spent countless hours manually reworking the timetables. Not one of us got into the program. Ironically, we were allowed to take the sociology course called "Man in Society" which essentially amounted to a whole course about women's natural role and men's natural role (as superior to women) via our textbook and class discussions of *The Naked Ape*. Perhaps that would teach budding feminists to give up!

In the early 1970s nobody bothered to hide behind a pretense of equality while shafting women. We were boldly told to our faces that the reason we couldn't have a certain type of education, or a certain job was "because you're a girl." That left few options. We would marry and have children and that would be life. If that did not suit us, we could become teachers, nurses, or secretaries — *if* our parents could afford to send us out of town for a year to get this education.

I came of age at the time when the pill was being cautiously introduced, but only prescribed for married women who wished to delay starting a family. The new doctor in town expanded this range to unmarried women, and I was lucky to be one of them. Preventing pregnancy for 12 years permitted me to achieve a living wage. At that point, I married and started a family. It was the wisest time to do so, according to popular wisdom.

It all seemed like the bad days of inequality were behind me. How wrong I was. My marriage turned into a living hell; years of hell. A trusted colleague who had often heard my husband belittle me and order me around, told me she warned him: "If you don't start treating her better, you will pay for it in ways you never thought possible."

Well, in the years after I left him, I was pretty sure that I was the one who paid.

Women who left were punished. Gossip threw the first punch, economics the second. Few women would have or find jobs that paid enough to support a family, so most ended up on welfare which had a system of its own to punish single mothers. And ex-husbands were free to torment their ex-wives in countless way, up to and including murder.

My ex was setting the stage for just such a scene rather nicely. After I left him, he went around to our friends and colleagues and neighbours expressing concerns about my safety considering my fragile and confused state of mind. He was worried about me! One day he picked me up in his car for an appointment downtown concerning the children, and it became quickly apparent that the only way out was to jump. He was speeding toward the highway instead! I escaped unhurt. I told the police and the police told me off for bothering them.

I continued to live in that small town, where my ex still lived, because it was the only way to remain with my children. I stayed, fearful and vigilant for my safety. Another year of struggle bore fruit. My ex, who became increasingly bold in his campaign against me, eventually assaulted me in front of witnesses in a public place. This was something I could take to court. All I needed to back me up was the police report. Unfortunately, the police, who had been at the scene and had supposedly interviewed witnesses, created a report that erased what happened and fabricated something in keeping with the "crazy woman" theme. I handed a copy of it to my lawyer without a word and waited for his reaction. It only took a few seconds for him to burst out: "Bull shit!" He looked at me and added, "They did this on purpose."

My lawyer turned up at court to advise that the police would not protect me. Because of that, he argued, we could not agree to a peace bond as it would be a police job to enforce. And therefore, following the logic, it would not protect me. My safety had to come first. We had to press for probation.

I proceeded to court in the morning with the certainty that I was going to lose the case, but had to go ahead simply because it was my only chance, however slim, of getting peace and perhaps a little justice. After a few dramatic moments, including the testimony of a witness coming out of the woodwork, the judge made his decision. My ex was punished with probation and a fine.

It took me months to realize I was truly freed of further threats of physical violence from him. No longer was my life in danger. But his tormenting didn't stop there. Instead, he moved into the courts to punish me. There would be no divorce until he was ready and that would only be after obtaining full custody of the children, crushing me socially, and keeping me destitute with no hope of leaving welfare.

No local employer would hire me. None, that is, except my lawyer. He hired me on, and we worked together to change things for the women in my town. The end result was greater than I had hoped. The entire District developed a protocol on family violence. The police chief called me into his office and promised that what had happened to me would not happen to any other woman.

One victory was won, yet the battles seemed never ending. A judge decided he would not grant me the right to take the children out of town without their father's permission, even though his history of violence was a proven fact. As such, I could not leave town for work or education.

Finally, my children started school. At the same time, the university established a satellite campus in town to cope with a temporary increase in students. I jumped at the chance to get my education without leaving town and, partly in fear that the opportunity would disappear, I worked hard to earn my degree in two years.

The dumb, stupid ex-wife who didn't know what she was talking about earned first-class standing, and she started having happy times. Thanks to good luck, and many good friends, I did land on my feet.

My belief in equality was not beaten out of me. If anything, opposition strengthened my feminism.

78 | SISTERHOOD IS SISTERHOOD

Donna Sharkey and Arleen Paré

DONNA'S STORY

If you're lucky, a significant historical movement will occur during your lifetime. And if you're really lucky, you yourself become part of that movement. And if you're really really lucky, like I am, you have a sister whose perspective you trust.

When all this comes together, you're in sync, aligned with history. Like the blue fly on the back of a horse, you fly farther and faster than you could have ever imagined before. You cling tight like the fly on the horse, aiming for that utopia somewhere, somehow. This is how I flew onto the back of the horse.

My phone rang. Calling from Montreal, my sister sounded excited. She talked at record-breaking speed. Her consciousness raising group was reading *Sisterhood is Powerful* by Robin Morgan. "Wait, slow down, what book? What kind of group are you involved with? What's going on?" I could tell something big was taking shape. Ten minutes into our conversation I was excited too. My mind was galloping, holding on to her words. My sister talked about something new — women's liberation.

My life took a sharp turn. A day later, I phoned a friend, passing on my conversation with my sister. Together we phoned others and started our own consciousness raising group in Ottawa, meeting for the first time two weeks later. We were thrilled to connect as women, to talk about new and radical ideas, and what these ideas meant for us. We drank cheap wine from cheap mugs and laughed and cried and dispensed advice to each other.

It was the fall of 1971 and I was twenty-two years old. I felt alive, understood; I was burning with hope for women, for the world.

We found other women who had started their own consciousness raising groups and, following a model of women's organizing in other cities, we worked to open the Women's Centre in Ottawa. We kept going. Other groups were formed to support women's lives. I was still a blue fly on a fast-moving horse. We were all blue flies and our lives were moving forward at great speed.

We read and debated approaches, strategies, and pros and cons about various levels and strands of radicalism. We honed our politics and took positions, agreeing or not with what was being put forward. We talked well into the night, debating meanings, relevance, and implications.

I began to speak openly about being a feminist. It felt daring.

I started to work for the Women's Program in the federal government and thanks to my work, connected with feminists across the country. We believed positive change for women was happening. In 1975, International Women's Year, I left my marriage, came out, and soon moved into the famous Lorne Street house in Ottawa with three other women. Our house quickly became a focal point for feminists.

Rarely a day went by without women dropping in; some days many women dropped in. They often stayed for dinner. Some, from other cities, stayed for days, sleeping on couches. The house swelled with women's stories, with laughter, pain, music and dancing. Fun was part of the serious business of building the Revolution.

However, I couldn't help but notice that some women had little truck for the Revolution. For some, it was a mere sidebar to their other interests and concerns. They were what we disparagingly called Normal. Normal normal. It was hard for me to understand why not every woman embraced feminism.

Feminism became my new Normal — a Normal replete with hope, with exciting ideas of liberation, with sisterhood. It fit me well. Thanks to my sister.

ARLEEN'S STORY

And my thanks to my sister. Not that I remember that first phone call, not exactly, the one that flipped Donna's world, but I do remember telling her about the consciousness raising group. It was exciting;

I wanted everyone to know. So I called my sister.

It was *Sisterhood Is Powerful*. I know that. And she didn't tell me I sounded like a fanatic, which I probably did. She didn't tell me to get lost or to get a life. She listened to me calling from Montreal, long-distance and costing money, and she understood, and then started her own group in Ottawa.

And thanks to my husband's sister in Montreal. She too had a friend who was starting a similar group, just like the group described in the *New York Times* article where it said consciousness raising groups first started in revolutionary China, and we all knew what happened there. It led to the Chinese Revolution.

We had high hopes. My sister-in-law and I went together the first night. It was January 1971 and I wore an Army and Navy sweater, navy blue, made from the toughest wool I'd ever worn. No flowers in my hair, no flowing dress, no beads. The navy blue sweater made me feel serious. That first night, a woman from another group came and told us how it worked. She said dying your hair was reactionary and another woman said dying your hair was common, but I didn't dye my hair then, so it didn't matter to me what they said about dying your hair.

I had found my place. What I had been thinking for maybe all my life, the unfairness of women's roles, was considered reasonable. Some of the women in our group were the wives of American draft dodgers and thank goodness for them. They had advanced exposure to the ideas of women's liberation. We met for almost two years.

My sister-in-law and I spent one winter night slapping feminist stickers on offending buildings and cars. We slapped one on the wall of the downtown Playboy Club and another on a Porsche parked outside the club. The owner ran after us, calling out, you can't do that. But we did it anyway.

I started a few other groups in Montreal, joining the first meetings to describe the process, and make sure everything went well — I never said anything about dying your hair. I read and read. I tried to change how the dishes were done in my house. Later, I went back to school and became a social worker.

After two years I moved to Africa with my husband who had a job with CIDA there. I missed the group, but my sister-in-law had already stopped going to the group long before I moved to Africa.

We had disagreements in the group, and for a while she and I argued after the meetings on our way home. We stood on the winter street corners and harrumphed about strategies for change and about anything else too, taking opposite sides. We stamped our feet to keep warm. Our breath froze around the belligerent words as they left our midnight mouths. These were important discussions but we wore ourselves out over them.

Then, eight years later, like my own sister, I came out.

These were years of enormous changes. And as Donna says, we were part of those changes. The way women are included, the way women are treated in any society, indicates the goodness of that society. And the goodness in Canada advanced through those years.

There are still many changes to go. But nothing has ever been quite the same since.

79 | I AM NOT ALICE

Huda Siksek

Who am I?

Well, I am not Alice in Wonderland. She was confused by what she saw; I am not. I see things clearly. Facts opened my eyes when I was a child. My history has not been vocal, dramatic or political. I work quietly in the classroom as a teacher. I have never been arrested, I don't hate men, and I have not burned any of my bras. I have instead been talking about the question of gender equality regularly and consistently for over 35 years.

I cannot escape the reality of living in relation to patriarchy. Much as I try to shake it off and say to myself "please tell me it isn't so!" direct evidence screams to the contrary. My reality is this: I live in relationship to "him" and "his" systems. And "he" controls many parts of my existence.

In Lebanon, where I grew up, Sunday was our favourite day because we got together with all our relatives for a huge lunch banquet. The women would prepare endless dishes of all kinds. The women did everything. They worked collaboratively, had fun, told stories, included us children, and never had to look anything up from a book; they seemed to know how to do everything. It took a lot of effort, planning, and organizing to cook lunch for about 20 people. It was beautiful being a part of that. It was also my first conscious observation of the enablement of gender expectations.

What I noticed is that after a wonderful banquet, the women would get up and begin the arduous task of cleaning. The men, by contrast, would all get up and go for a nap. This astounded me. The women would insist that the men take a nap because the poor things worked so hard and should rest. I never saw the men doing anything that would wear them out physically enough to deserve a nap in the middle of a Sunday. It was the women who never stopped moving.

It would be a few more years before I experienced the injustice of being female, and it happened the day I got my first period.

I was at school playing soccer, which was not traditional for a girl, and noticed the blood when I went to the washroom. I thought I had hurt myself somehow. When I went home, the women explained that I was a woman now, and that I would have to rest and be calmer. I was told not to play sports anymore, especially not on "those days." My girlfriends and I would tell our PE teacher, "Sir, it's the time of the month," and he would say, "ok, go to the library." I was told that sports developed hard muscles which looked ugly on women. Also, sports were for Americans, and who could tell the difference between men and women there anyway? They all wore pants and were flat-chested and had short hair. In our Mediterranean culture men were men and women were women.

But I liked being active. I began to fantasize about becoming an astronaut or an Olympic athlete.

One of the important events each week was going to church on Sundays. I loved the mystery of it all. Especially, I loved the iconography, and wanted to grow up to be an icon painter. But I learned that only men were allowed to paint icons.

I loved watching other children help behind the altar. They appeared to be very important and respected by the community, and I wanted to do that too. But when I volunteered to help with Sunday mass, I was told that girls were not allowed. This was unbelievable to me, I had never thought of it before but sure enough, I took another look and, yes, the helpers were all boys. I asked "why?" and was told that girls are not clean. They bleed every month and so they are impure. They could not be allowed to touch sacred things.

Everywhere I looked these inexplicable contradictions persisted. They seemed to have no logic and yet were followed unquestioned by everyone around me. I felt alienated and in possession of the only questioning mind in the neighbourhood.

Naturally, I wanted to go to university. I was "allowed" to do so by my father, not as a life requirement mind you, but as a whim to pass time before I got married. The expectation was that I would marry as soon as possible and start my own family.

I, however, decided to avoid all that. I would never be married and clean up after a man, unless he was prepared to clean up after me and cook for me as well. Men to me were controlling, almost like prison guards. No thank you, not for me! Instead, I would become a travelling nomad roaming the earth in search of adventurous experiences. I would look for a partner, a friend to share my life with, a man who would be equal with me despite our biological difference. We would both work and support each other and stand on guard for each other against the storms of life.

Instead my parents sent traditional older men my way — always ten to fifteen years older than me. I had nothing to say to them. I was labelled "difficult." I was told not to be so choosy. I was treated with contempt every time I turned down a marriage proposal. I was warned that I would regret it and end up alone and unloved if I didn't marry.

I moved to Canada.

Once here, I began volunteering with local artist and educational groups. For the first time in my life, I let my hair look natural, I did not wear make-up and I went to the gym regularly without feeling the pressure of disapproval from society. It was bliss.

But soon I learned that here too there were divisions. Women in Canada are often paid less than men for performing the same job. I was disappointed. I thought that would only happen back home. I also saw that new immigrant women and men were perpetuating oppressive social and gender behaviour too. What I had thought was specific to me, a condition that I eventually outgrew, turned out to be universal and to affect current generations.

Still, Canada is the only country in the world where I can feel comfortable inside my own skin. I stay in Canada because I know that I can be myself and I can succeed without social judgment. I may never escape the lingering judgments from my family and culture, but I can escape the general and popular social judgments that used to cause me much sadness.

I feel personal liberation in Canada.

80 | A MIND OF ONE'S OWN
Diana Smith

Editors for this publication invited responses to the question: "What made me a feminist?" In my situation, the more useful question is: "What led to the development of a political consciousness?" It was the "aha" moment of seeing the world politically that was pivotal and led me, almost naturally and automatically, to feminism.

This pivotal moment came for me in the 1970s. At 19, with $300 and a suitcase containing my life's possessions, I immigrated to Canada. I was white, female, from a working-class upbringing and an only child, although I was unaware of the significance of these determinants until later on. After renting a basement suite and finding a job as a receptionist at a photographic studio, I went back to school to get the equivalent of a high school diploma. My education in England had been designed to produce a docile worker, with no knowledge, critical thinking skills or opinions. More importantly, I thought I had no entitlement to these. I had left school at 15 to work in the factory where my father worked. Even though I didn't understand this at the time, Canada was a partial escape from the class system I felt trapped within.

Several years later I was tagging along with the back-to-the land movement, living in a small town on Vancouver Island, in a gorgeous old heritage house with two other women, a writer and a painter, plotting to collectively own some land, build a cabin and be a potter. Although one of the women was a passionate and intellectual feminist from a middle-class background, it was not through her that my enlightenment came. Instead it came from David, a male friend with a working-class background.

David was living nearby with his partner (another feminist) and child. It was during our time in his barn, building potters' wheels, that I mentioned to him an incident at the communal house that was troubling me. A cousin of one of my housemates was staying with us and I disliked him almost at first contact. I couldn't understand how or why this was the case. My only means to understand my reaction was psychological. I'd taken a few first year college courses, including psychology, and was reading self-help books, but none of this was helping me deal with my feelings for our visitor. David asked for a few details about this man's life. As I recall he was actually the brother of my housemate but the siblings had been separated when young children. Each went to live with an uncle and aunt but one set was wealthy, one was not; the boy had the less privileged upbringing. With this sketchy information, and a description of our interactions, David gave me an explanation to understand the guest's personality and behaviour that resonated for me. In retrospect, there was much I could have understood about my own internalized class oppression but that developed later, over time.

At the time, I recognized an intelligent and plausible analysis of the social facts of this man's life that explained his behavior. It allowed me instantly to see the individual in a larger context and this helped me respond to him with some amount of compassion and understanding. But more than that, it immediately gave me tools, a framework and a method to interpret not just this but any situation. So much about life, up to this point, had been troubling and mysterious. It also gave me a way to see my own place in the world, to connect my own circumstances to larger factors. What David had done, quietly and unrecognized by me, was provide a class analysis to my situation. What he also did was provide the stimulus for not just a class consciousness to develop but for a general political consciousness. Although I vaguely knew that David was a Trotskyite I didn't really know what that meant. But instead of becoming a comrade with the communist group, I gradually but assuredly became a feminist.

This happened, I think, because the life I was choosing to live was, as usual and seemingly by default, with women. My affinity group had always been based on gender and while I appreciated the political perspective David had provided I was not drawn to the communist fraternity of which he was a part.

Timing was another factor in the choices I made. Soon after the conversation with David I went to a gathering of women at an isolated and idyllic country acreage. It was the first of several annual Country Women's Festivals to be held in the area. Several of the roughly one hundred attendees were from the big city of Vancouver. Their socialist and feminist analysis and ideas, their overall intelligence, blew my mind. The self-defense/karate workshop energized my body. Not incidentally, the sight of a naked, lithe, toned bronze body prancing into the cold, early morning ocean exploded my libido. My fate was sealed. Within weeks I packed up and followed these women back to Vancouver. I joined every volunteer feminist organization going and nervously attended my first lesbian group.

The next 20 years were spent as an active member of the women's movement and the labour movement in Vancouver. In the women's movement, with other working-class women, I periodically tried to address class issues but these efforts never amounted to much. In the class-based labour movement I focused on lesbian and gay issues.

In retrospect I see that, as a working-class person from England, class was the site of my strongest-felt oppression and it was tapping the fragile covering of this source of pain that opened me up to understanding. It was my social reality of primarily and consistently finding emotional satisfaction and comfort with girls, and then women, which meant I felt at home in the women's movement. It was also being in the midst of a feminist revolution at the time of my political awakening, that steered me, much to the disappointment of my communist buddy's comrades, towards feminism. And although I have been a lesbian ever since, the biggest turn-on from that festival was not that beautiful naked body, influential though it was, but the intelligent minds. Becoming a lesbian in a homophobic world was a breeze compared to becoming a person entitled to a mind of her own.

81 | A FEMINIST TEST-CASE LITIGANT

Beth Symes

I had always had an innate sense of fairness. My feminist career took me through law school, into an explicitly feminist, all-female law firm, and into a practice representing clients who were seeking to dismantle discrimination. So, I was a feminist long before 1981. But that is the year that this story begins.

What was different about that year, compared to all my earlier feminist activities, was that 1981 was the year when I chose to put myself forward personally in a sex discrimination claim.

Putting myself forward required me to expose the details of my personal life. I had to put myself on the line and be prepared to be the named plaintiff in an action that had the potential to change childcare in Canada. I launched this litigation because I wanted to make public the professional and financial cost to women of having children, and to try to force the government to respond.

People sometimes ask how it felt to get into this battle. It felt awful. I am an intensely private person. This was not an easy or comfortable thing to do. So why did I do it? Partly out of naivety. I don't think I really, fully understood, thought through, or foresaw all of the implications. Certainly I never anticipated the multiple criticisms that came in response to the case. I think the reason this case stands out so much for me is that although it was done with the best of intentions, it had such a painful outcome.

But let's go back to the launching of the case itself. I had worked for my entire legal career representing workers who struggled in the workplace, facing various forms of discrimination, including sexual harassment, unequal pay, unfair treatment during pregnancy, and so on. I was practising in a small, three-women firm with Liz McIntyre and Fran Kiteley. Having children was the biggest issue for the partnership. Not whether to have them, but trying to schedule them and manage the firm's work around their births was always the most important issue of discussion at our annual partners' conference. We agreed to try to space out the children, so that two lawyers would not be off at the same time.

When I gave birth to my first child, Kate, in 1981, I had to get appropriate childcare to enable me to carry on my practice. I found it to be extraordinarily difficult and very expensive. When Kate was born, I spent over 80 per cent of my income on childcare. I realized that if I, as a lawyer, had this problem, surely the problem would be even more severe for other women. What of women who worked shift work? Sole support mothers?

I returned to work two weeks after Kate's birth. This was a crazy thing to do, but my clients were hospital workers who had led an illegal strike and were fired. I was trying to get them back to work. I ended up renting a room beside the hearing room, and the arbitrator took breaks while I breast fed my daughter. It was clear that I could deduct the cost of the room rental as a business expense. Why could I not deduct the cost of the nanny who cared for my daughter during the hearing? I am very aware that shifts in social or public policy can be brought about by changes in the tax rules. My tax professor had said: if you want to start a revolution, Symes, you'd better learn how to fund it.

So, immediately after Kate was born, I began to deduct the costs of childcare from my business income. Several years later, I was reassessed by Revenue Canada, and the deduction was denied. Right away, I filed a *Charter* challenge against the reassessment. I had a wonderful team of feminist lawyers to launch this challenge to the *Income Tax Act*, with the belief that if successful, it would force the government to change how childcare was funded in Canada. As a self-employed person, my claim was the simplest in law for a working woman to advance. Could I deduct childcare from my business income?

The final answer came in 1993, some twelve years later, in the court decision of *Symes v. Canada*. *Symes* made for very painful reading: the Supreme Court of Canada said that I was an undeserving applicant and that my approach to childcare and tax was unthoughtful. The Federal Court of Appeal said that my arguments risked trivializing the *Charter*. I was criticized for being self-centred: because my victory would only benefit women entrepreneurs, this apparently meant that the income tax deductions I sought would only benefit the rich. Moreover, by having made my choice to have children, deciding to work outside the home, and then claiming that the costs of childcare were a cost of doing my business, the majority of the court suggested that I had somehow attacked the very fabric of Canadian society.

Then and now, I fail to understand how the Supreme Court missed the gender issue. Both the Law Society of Upper Canada and the Canadian Bar Association have conducted surveys that found childcare to be the most significant barrier to women's participation in the legal profession. However, children continue to be seen as a personal "consumption" choice. For example, counsel for the government said: "Mrs Symes, you chose to have children; personally, I chose to have cats." When cats are indistinguishable from children, the costs of childcare are therefore in the private, not the public sphere.

Although my claim for a childcare deduction was disallowed, the majority of the Court went on to characterize me as a rich, white, and privileged woman. The majority said that other women should have brought the challenge. Whoever did they mean? Sole support mothers? Farmers? Women who worked part-time? If I was having difficulty providing childcare for my two daughters, those with even less resources than I had were in a worse position. But that was not even questioned, nor was the issue of whether such women would be able to carry the costs and consequences of a court challenge of test-case litigation. Interestingly, the Supreme Court of Canada and the academics did not condemn Mark Andrews (*Andrews v. Law Society of British Columbia*) or Shalom Schachter (*Schachter v. Canada*) as undeserving litigants, although they were both white male lawyers seeking the equality protections of the *Charter*.

How did this case affect my feminism? It made me painfully aware of the bravery and personal sacrifice that women make when they challenge the status quo. The only real saving grace was that the court split 7:2 on gender lines. The two women, including the current Chief Justice of Canada, wrote a stinging dissent, saying that the evidence had clearly established that the burden of childcare fell disproportionately on women and that this gender discrimination was not justified in a free and democratic society. I was also deeply moved by the extraordinary efforts of my wonderful counsel, Mary Eberts, Wendy Matheson, and Mayo Moran, and struck by the generosity of women and men across Canada who wrote and sent money in support.

The *Symes* case eventually went into the course curriculum for most tax classes in Canadian law schools. Initially, most tax professors were unsupportive of my arguments. They argued that business expenses were meant to cover the traditional activities of businessmen, and the activities of men: golf, business luncheons, and so forth. They said that to extend business expenses into the "personal" realm was impermissible. What they failed to acknowledge was that before a woman could even get to work, she had to put in place appropriate childcare. More recently, the debate has shifted and there is now Rebecca Johnson's book and numerous academic articles, many written by women professors who understand our arguments. People tell me that the case is one that evokes some of the most passionate discussion in law school.

I meet young lawyers who know exactly who I am from studying the case. When I was canoeing the Nahani River, I was asked by a man who had no connection to law: "Are you the Symes from the tax case?" I was astonished. The issues in the *Symes* case resonate with all who have sought or are seeking appropriate childcare.

From the time of the Royal Commission on the Status of Women forward, about every five to eight years or so, government task forces and politicians call for a radical overhaul of the provision of childcare in Canada. We have had numerous election campaigns where political leaders say childcare is one of their key election platforms. Yet time after time, childcare slips off the political agenda and thirty years later, there has still been little progress in addressing this issue outside of Quebec. The problems for my two daughters are as bad if not worse than they were in 1981.

As a feminist, this is still a painful odyssey. But, it has given me such respect for women who find themselves as litigants in equality cases. Without their courage to step forward, court challenges would not be possible.

82 | RIDING THE WAVES

Patty Thille

Do you remember your first exposure to feminism? I do: in the late '80s, as a grade eight student, I decided to write an essay about pay equity for my social studies class. Quite the topic for a thirteen-year-old. I tripped across the concept in a *Maclean's* magazine in my school library. I was astonished to learn that women were not paid as men were for the same or equivalent work. Learning of this inequity disrupted the story I had been told, that people who work hard were rewarded — a story informed by my Catholic, rural, Saskatchewan upbringing.

My pre-existing (and naive) narrative was further challenged by the teacher's response to the essay. While I was given a good grade, my teacher, an older white man with decades of teaching experience, had written a counter-argument against pay equity in every inch of white space on the foolscap. This sudden jarring disconnect, the realization that someone in my immediate circle thought that inequality based on sex was justifiable, brought me to my first association with what is now my ideological home: feminism.

Feminism offered me a narrative thread that could explain my previously noticed but unnamed experiences of sexism. It opened up a worldview by which I could understand my household and school experiences. Even at the age of thirteen, so much more in my world made sense: my father's use of anger to silence my mother's quiet strength; my parents' refusal to fight for me to be allowed to play hockey (when I tried to enrol, I was told girls were only allowed to play ringette, even if I could out-skate most of the boys my age); my physical education teacher's practice of giving the boys more floor hockey playing time than the girls; the town's habit of scheduling the girls' softball games for the potholed field, while the boys got to play on the pristinely maintained diamond. Feminism suggested that equity was a worthy goal but one that would require much work in light of the pervasiveness of sexism in everyday life.

My mother, my rock, my only sense of the notion of "home" was the only woman with whom I could talk with about these kinds of issues. She was a gentle, giving, compassionate and non-judgmental nurse whose emotional insight was well respected by her friends, extended family, patients, and colleagues. Part of her strength to endure my father's wrath came from the church. She understood it as her cross to bear, something she had to endure to keep our family unit intact. My mother never encouraged me to suppress my outrage at the gender-based injustices of the world in the name of being a good woman. She tried to nurture my strong sense of justice and fairness, but she never joined me in identifying as a feminist.

Throughout my teens, I still had much to learn about the spectrum of feminisms. My small Saskatchewan community, pre-internet era, had few resources to help me find my way. Enter my first Women and Gender Studies course, six years after embracing the label of "feminist." Only offered as a "minor" at that time, Women's Studies exposed me to a world of critical thought and a community of activists and academics, each working in her (or his, on occasion) own way to realize a vision of the future that still inspires me. Each class, I would be in awe of my fellow (mostly older) students and the professors. I would burst with energy revisiting the evening's intellectual acrobatics with my then-boyfriend on my way home every week.

This introduction to Women and Gender Studies, and related conversations with older women I admired, pushed me to confront a new disconnect. This time it was an internal one: my feminist, equity-driven vision for our world, and a thread of being "pro-life" (read anti-choice), a remnant of my Catholic upbringing. So my nineteen-year-old self, a great admirer of my mother's way in the world, had to confront the conflict.

The new women-centered vision I was offered understood termination of pregnancy as a centuries-old practice that required accessibility and safety in order to protect women's health. This vision viewed women as something more than incubators, who were to be respected for knowing what is best in light of the complexities of their individual lives. Engaging in a dialogue with pro-choice peers and mentors opened up a vision that placed great value on women's lives, with all their messiness and diversity. This contrasted with the dominant Catholic story I had relied upon to make sense of abortion in the past – that all human life is precious, that the context of women's lives is irrelevant to this issue.

During this time, other women – academics, older coworkers, my boyfriend's feminist Catholic mother – joined my mother in influencing the way I thought about moral issues. My mother had not been replaced entirely but I was learning to listen to more voices and decide for myself.

Over the years, this created an intellectual space for me to understand the misuse and abuse of some and subordination of the majority to protect the greedy and the self-centered interests of a few. These feminist firsts brought to light how I could be unintentionally complicit in maintaining a system that privileges a few at the expense of many.

In the years that have followed, I took additional Women/ Gender Studies courses, volunteered in women's centers, and worked in a feminist sex-positive store. Through these experiences and more, I have met women from a broader range of backgrounds. Each experience produced wave after wave of revelations, each uncomfortable in their confrontation of what I had previously taken for granted. A brilliant essay by Peggy McIntosh called *White Privilege: Unpacking the Invisible Knapsack* led me to question my own racial privilege, and while it is a continual process to unearth the racist ideologies I learned in childhood, I am a better person for it. A peer volunteer at the university women's centre helped me understand her experiences of heterosexism. Working in a sex-positive store, a space that interrupts the story that there is such a thing as "normal" sexuality, has created countless opportunities to learn how to assume less about the people in my life. Over time, I have been humbled into realizing that one could experience both discrimination and privilege. This has strengthened my determination to use my privilege for the benefit of those who are often not given a space to speak.

This is not to say that this has been an easy road; each of these feminist firsts demanded I examine not only my perspectives but my behaviours. My ability to embody masculine behavior traits (competitive speech patterns such as interrupting others, or outspoken confidence even when I knew little about an issue) is likely a function of hailing from such a male dominated family where one had to cut others down to be on top. These traits had helped me be successful in my career, but I sense their destructiveness, how they shut down dialogue, silencing many, fostering a world that rewards arrogance and dominance over cooperation and fairness. I made the choice to confront my own "masculine" tendencies of competitiveness that infiltrated how I interacted with others. More accurately, I continue to choose to confront these dominating speech tendencies that are rewarded career wise, but perpetuate a model that I hope to disrupt.

I have also had to accept that my successes are more than just an embodiment of "good things come to those who work hard." Instead, success is a combination of luck, privilege and only sometimes, determined hard work. I had to come to terms with how to use my privilege to help make this world a better place for everyone, not just those who shout the loudest and think they know better than others.

I did not just happen to be in the right place at the right time, meeting the right people. I was willing to listen, to re-consider everything I thought to be true or important. I have feminism(s) to thank for guidance, and since that time, have been able to share my feminist "firsts" with others. When I can, I attempt to bridge critical, feminist social thought to mainstream health care audiences. I speak about how fat phobia influences care. To give workshops that model how to speak non-judgmentally with patients about sexuality. In each of these types of opportunities, I try to create a space for reflection on how assumptions and privilege jeopardize our ability to provide patient-centered health care. My hope is that I plant a seed, one that can grow into a "first" for another person.

I recognize that my story presents interesting ironies. By embracing the identity label of feminist, I have learned to suspend my reliance on the stereotypes our society uses to denigrate those different from the "norm" (which is not the norm but a hierarchical privileging of white, heterosexual, Christian, able-bodied, middle/ upper class privilege). Paradoxically, I think I behave in ways more consistent with Christianity than I did in the past when I was a know-it-all Catholic.

Feminism offers me strength, a sense of belonging and purpose, one of hope for a more peaceful and equitable world. I cannot foresee what is to come but considering what I have gained through my series of feminist roads less traveled, I welcome the challenge ahead.

> Three women protestors, including Joyce Rosenthal and Elizabeth Smith

City of Toronto Archives, Fonds 111, Series 659, File 12, Id0009

> Trois protestataires, dont Joyce Rosenthal et Elizabeth Smith

83 | THE BROADEST POSSIBLE FEMINISM

D. Gillian Thompson

In high school I became aware of the sexual exploitation of women, and as an undergraduate I became aware of the economic exploitation of women. I wanted to avoid both conditions. And I sought to make the world a better place for all. An idealist and a socialist, I took part in the nuclear disarmament movement in Vancouver, supported the civil rights movement in the USA, and followed the course of the Chinese Revolution with interest. As a graduate student in France, I got caught up in the events of 1968 and, as a university instructor in the American mid-west (1968-70), I opposed the war in Vietnam.

My mother and my teachers encouraged my educational ambitions and my pursuit of justice. In the late 1950s, my free-thinking mother left *The Second Sex* where I was bound to find and read it. Powerful, reform-minded women teachers in my high school encouraged me to be informed about the Middle East, Africa, and Asia. As a university student, I had no women professors in history, but remained independent-minded and aware of injustices to be righted internationally and at home. While I saw no discrimination in the awarding of grades or scholarships (or, in due course, research grants) and did not then question the content of history courses, I knew I did not earn as much money in summer jobs as male students. Acceptance of reality seemed the best policy. As my circle of student friends at UBC lived frugally, my earnings and scholarships were sufficient. Once in temporary university positions, I endeavoured to treat women and men students in the same way, and worked with my most decent male colleagues to encourage others in the almost exclusively male professoriate to do the same.

So it was some years until I worked out my place in feminism. In the mid-1970s, I gained tenure at UNB, where the men of my department had come to accept feminist practices, if not yet feminist rhetoric. My department supported my feminist activity, and may be unique in this regard. I attended meetings organised by women students and faculty, some with community links, whose purpose was to promote feminism and the status of women in the university. When, at last, I recognised the urgency of the cause, I also established myself as a critic of narrow thinking. I resisted suggestions that women are victims, for I knew them in my life and in history to be actors who maintain families and households, overcome or work around the most appalling constraints, and engage in penetrating analyses of the ills of society. I challenged the concept of first and second wave feminism for leaving out too many significant women. I saw only a continuum in the development of feminism. I wanted our own society — and the world — to change. Injustices must be righted so that women may live their lives according to their own choices, under the protection of the law. Education is essential to this process. Feminism's goals should include the creation of societies in which women everywhere may find their voices, speak for themselves, and determine the nature of their own future and that of their societies.

The only woman in my department for 15 years, and one of few women on the faculty of the university, I was soon, like my counterparts elsewhere, involved in making recommendations to improve the status of women at my own university and more widely. I was seconded to organise public consultative gatherings, represent UNB at national meetings on status of women issues, and take part in the preparation of the first *Report on the Status of Women at UNB* (1979). As adviser to the president on matters pertaining to the status of women at UNB, I sponsored a student-organised conference on women's issues in 1984, and, in 1985, presented a hard-hitting summary of the dismal status and remarkable achievements of women at UNB at a public function intended by the upper ranks of the administration only to celebrate the status quo. I was a founder, in 1989, of the women's studies programme at UNB, and a member of the operations committee of the Centre for Family Violence Research through the 1990s. In the 1990s I served on the board of the Canadian Historical Association, with the portfolio on the status of women in the historical profession, so was a consultant to women graduate students seeking to improve their status. And I was an adviser to the New Brunswick deputy minister responsible for publicising and recommending ways to improve the status of women in the province.

By 1987, I was no longer the only woman in my department and, over subsequent decades, my younger women colleagues were committed feminists, several far more distinguished than I. As chair of the Department of History (1996-2002), I stood by women faculty, students and staff. By then all the men in the department were either feminists or did not wish to appear otherwise. Yet I was frustrated in my personal hope to employ more women at the permanent faculty level, a privilege that fell to my male predecessor and successor as chair.

My courses stressed European society and 18th-century France. I offered the first women's history course at UNB (1980) and at St Thomas University, and taught this subject for the last 25 years of my career. My big introductory course examined women's experience and achievements, while challenging stereotypes and encouraging respect for older women, by requiring a report on a focussed interview of a grandmother or woman of similar age. Upper level courses on European women 1200 to 1800 stressed women's experience and achievements, and notably their contribution to the economy and their struggle for education. Natalie Davis's course syllabus and Gerda Lerner's book *The Creation of Patriarchy* were especially useful in planning such courses.

One thread ran through my feminist career at UNB. I am committed to the broadest possible feminism. I have wanted dialogue between women's groups and the generations, and I have made personal sacrifices for this. My greatest joy as a feminist has derived from sponsoring distinguished visiting speakers and enabling students, faculty and others to discuss important issues with such guests and with each other.

How did I come to feminism? By recognising it as the next step for anyone with a social conscience, by building on the foundations laid by good teachers, by responding to the needs of my university. And by recognising that in the search for human freedom for all, we should resist any threat to it, and seek a world in which women, no less than men, may realise their full potential as human beings.

84 | BRINGING THE PARTS TOGETHER
Elaine Meller Todres

Divining the origins of how I became a feminist is much like considering the literature on the psychology of happiness, a combination of influences are involved: part genetics, part doing the appropriate things, and part participating in activities that matter and have intrinsic value.

I was raised by a loving family known for its line of strong women. My grandmother, affectionately known as "the Field Marshall," was a Holocaust survivor, as were both my parents. My grandmother was a businesswoman who was a translator in the Austro-Hungarian army and worked side-by-side with her husband in a remarkably anti-Semitic setting. Her dream for me was that I could do anything I chose to do — preferably become the Prime Minister.

With the full support and encouragement of my family I attended the first-day orientation program at the University of Winnipeg. I entered the Political Science and Economics session to get a better understanding of course offerings. There stood Tom Axworthy, I believe the Senior Stick (the title of Student President, then) and a group of male comrades. When asked what I was likely to study, I offered that I wanted to complete double honours in Economics and Political Science and likely wanted to pursue a doctorate.

The reaction was unforgettable: hooting laughter.

Well, that was that. I completed my double honours with gold medals in each subject, and went on to complete my doctorate in Politics. And in neither area of study — neither Economics nor Political Science — were there any female professors, save one who entered the faculty in my last year.

Throughout my academic experiences, one or two male mentors recognized my talents and nurtured me and offered me guidance. My doctoral supervisor, at the University of Pittsburgh, was a superb teacher of public policy and honed my undying interest in the subject. He was the editor of the most prestigious journal of political science in the United States and had dreams of placing me in the Ivy League schools. However, that wasn't the career path that appealed to me. Upon completing my Ph.D. at the University of Pittsburgh, I returned to Canada where I sought employment with the Ontario public service. I secured my first posting at the Ministry of Revenue.

To paint the picture of my first posting, we are in the late 1970s and there are two female Deputy Ministers, the Chair of the Civil Service Commission, and the Deputy Minister of Community and Social Services. The Ministry of Labour created a Women's Bureau, preoccupied with the stewardship of relevant labour force data. Feeling isolated in the Ministry of Revenue, I worked hard to develop a network of like minded young women, devoted to public policy and to furthering our own careers and the career interests of other women. The Chair of the Civil Service Commission, in her commitment to affirmative action, called a meeting of all the women of a certain rank in the civil service. We were summoned to a dining room at the Westbury Hotel. There was only one man present, the bartender. There we were, awash in a sea of pearls and ultra suede. We were given name tags and two table numbers, one for the entrée, and one for dessert, to maximize networking potential. A feminist speaker was brought in to discuss her book detailing accomplished women in Canada. It was a large room full of hope. Many of the women I met that night rose to become deputy ministers.

Against this backdrop of nascent feminism, the exchange of business cards, and strong feelings of sorority, I concentrated on my work. Back at the Ministry, I sought and secured an appointment with the Comptroller of Revenue, an Assistant Deputy Minister. Mr. Weiers, an austere but fair man, was a corporations tax expert. While sitting in the waiting room before meeting with him, I remember him taking a number of corporate tax auditors to task. I entered his pristine room. He saw that I looked nervous and opined: "It is not hard to provide feedback. It is weak not to do so." He wondered why I wanted to see him. I indicated that I wished him to be my mentor. He asked: "what is a mentor?"

That was the beginning of an extraordinary relationship. Shortly after that conversation, I placed my name in a competition for a Directorship, the first rung in the leadership ladder. I did not win that competition, but Mr. Weiers encouraged me to apply for the second, in the Revenue and Operations Research Branch. I won,

I was ecstatic. The Deputy Minister asked to see me to present the good news. At this meeting he mentioned that I was young and inexperienced and hence would not be paid at the job level, and would be given a lower classification for a year. However, the Ministry was very pleased with the appointment.

Lacking the vocabulary and constructs we now take for granted, it took me a while to integrate the fact that I was "underfilling" and was facing gender-based wage discrimination.

This experience, however, was to help me in the next leg of my journey. So there I was, a thirty-year-old, with four direct reports, all who were in their sixties. We worked together and accomplished much to improve tax administration in the province.

While on maternity leave with my first child, I was courted by Glenna Carr to consider an Economics Advisor position with the newly formed Ontario Women's Directorate (OWD). The Ministry of Revenue had been relocated to Oshawa in the first dramatic economic development move based on ministry locus. My Deputy Minister strongly discouraged me from taking the position, fearing that I would forever be labelled a "bra burning feminist," and indicating ironically that the position classification was below that of a director.

I leapt at the opportunity.

My first assignment was to write a cabinet submission for a plan of action for the women of Ontario. The only instruction I was given was that I must include a section on domestic violence. "What was that?" I queried. Again, no constructs!

And so, I sat with Terry Bisset, my junior economist, closeted in a tiny room writing in effect, a strategic plan to enhance the status of women of Ontario derived in part from our reading of *Chatelaine*, so sparse was the academic literature. On the other hand, I knew that its significance would lie in binding Cabinet Minutes that would hold otherwise uninterested Ministry players to working collaboratively with the OWD to advance a number of areas ranging from domestic violence, to economics, to training and education, and child care. The document was approved by Cabinet and off we were, empowered to proceed.

This was an exhilarating period of my life and the life of my cohort group. I was promoted to Director of Research and later the

Assistant Deputy Minister at the OWD. We began with prima facie matters of discrimination — Ellen Mary Mills went to Cabinet to fight for the inclusion of breast prostheses under OHIP coverage. Denise Bellamy argued for a woman's right to change her name legally. All these matters were prepared by a tiny band of women who would have to joust with entire ministries. And then came the Liberal Minority Government with an Accord calling for pay equity legislation. Suddenly the OWD was headed by a very powerful Minister, the Attorney General Ian Scott, and was given responsibility for the carriage of the private Pay Equity Bill.

The Ministry of Labour was responsible for the public sector Pay Equity Bill. Things were going badly in the Legislature. I sought an appointment with my Minister and asked if he wished to merge the public and private sector bills. He replied: you will not get permission to do that. Worrying that the "noise" regarding the public sector bill would negatively impact our work, I retorted: "I did not ask whether you thought I would be successful, I wanted to know if you would prefer both bills to be combined." He said yes.

Off I went to make the deal. Ultimately, the OWD won the day. The introduction of the Pay Equity Bill, the result of external lobbying, a minority Accord, the furious internal lobbying and painstaking policy development work of a tiny Ontario Women's Directorate, and the political resolve of a powerful and brilliant minister for women's issues, was one of the highlights of my life.

I learned much from that experience. It is difficult to work on policy development and implementation when there are only a very few academics and advocates asking questions about gender and sex. External lobbying is a necessary but not sufficient condition to getting things moving on sensitive and highly divisive issues. Tough issues require internal champions. But mostly I learned the great joy of working with and for women.

Shortly thereafter the Premier asked me to become the Deputy Minister of the Human Resources Secretariat and the Chair of the Civil Service Commission. He told me that now that I had seen the legislation through, it was time for me to negotiate the first pay equity agreement with OPSEU (given that the earlier work was so easy!).

I spent ten years as a Deputy Minister in the Ontario Civil Service. I worked in human resources, culture, communications, tourism, recreation, solicitor general and corrections. I sought to include a gender lens in every setting and policy debate. Over a period of ten years, I was able to see the conceptual frameworks and evidence so hitherto lacking, being developed. I saw the encouragement and development of diversity in hiring. And sadly, too, I saw the dismantlement of some of our landmark policies and frameworks. But in all cases I was there, I was a voice at the table.

The Ontario Civil Service was a crucible for significant policy and program development and an employer that offered tremendous opportunity for women of my cohort group. It also served as a platform for my radicalization as a feminist as I put into practice my training and my beliefs. Many might not imagine civil service as a cauldron for change, but that's precisely what it was for me.

85 | A CLUSTER OF IDENTITY PEGS
Si Transken

Was there a precise turning point in my life? Was there a time before I identified as a feminist? Well, there were certainly many shifting, editing, seeing-hearing-feeling differently moments after which I identified more substantively with what a feminist was, or might be, and how those definitions could be a cluster of identity pegs for me to own. Today, those pegs are associate professor and acting chair of a School of Social Work, published author, and president of the Canadian Women's Studies Association.

But I also define myself as a cranky bitch *and* a cheerful creative eco-feminist Buddhist white trash person being recycled! I am a poet and a published writer. Recently people have been telling me I should do stand-up comedy. Maybe I will.

I grew up in a family where my father abused us in every way possible; I witnessed my mother being abused in every way. One time I thought he'd killed her because he'd been hitting her and then she disappeared for months. He also sexually abused me and pitted the two of us against each other. I ran away from those experiences and began waitressing in greasy spoons and then, as soon as I was old enough, disco bars and strip joints. By the time I was 30 I'd accumulated 15 years of waitressing and a series of experiences in "straight" day jobs. It wasn't until I was 48 that I had a period where I had only one job at a time.

How does all of this relate to my feminist evolution? Someone once joked with me, saying, "If you weren't a feminist before all those shitty experiences — you'd become one because of all those shitty experiences!" Wise words. Feminism, I've often said, saved my life. I'd have ended up as an addicted sex trade worker if feminist theory and feminist role models and comrades had not sparkled up a path of lucidity and meaning before me.

I've had four feminist therapists over the years and been in many groups and consciousness raising events, and been an organizer, activist, researcher, and coordinator in many women's organizations. Feminist voices seemed able to make so much sense out of what had happened to me, why it was that I'd had so much pain and disadvantage, and why the women I made friends with also struggled so much. Feminism helped me break out of the silence and isolation of the violence and degradation I'd been born into.

My first formal contact with feminist energy was at a women's resource centre. At that time, I was incredibly shy and afraid of everyone in the world. I lurked amidst the bookshelves and no one asked me any questions. I could eavesdrop. I could just witness. I could feel safe. Eventually, when I was at university for a social work degree, I ended up doing my placements in that same women's resource centre.

Inspiration to embrace feminism came from unusual places. One of the horribly useful gifts my mother and my gram gave to me was the opportunity to know what mistakes I didn't want to make in life. Relying on a man and his income set women up for disappointment and entrapment. Having babies meant vulnerability and poverty. Add to the mix being a white bush trash woman in a mining town with minimal education, and things were dismal. So I turned to my teachers in grade school, college, and university. I learned from activists and therapists who offered me problem-solving strategies, mentoring, confidence, and communication skills — all things that were absent from my childhood experiences.

I also learned from waitressing in strip joints, just as I was becoming more involved in the women's movement. In a small town it was difficult to keep these lives separate. I had many moments where professors from the university, police officers, political men, or lawyers would come in the strip joint. Later, I'd meet them elsewhere, in contexts like United Way fundraisers, NDP events, or later in my professional life as a social worker. They wouldn't always recognize me because I'd been a nobody with a body in the dark bars, and because I'd dress differently, of course, in these mainstream contexts. Often, as I was introduced to their wives or to their colleagues I'd smile and say things like "of course, we've met many times before, haven't we Mr...?"

This would disturb them, until they remembered. And then it might disturb them even more.

I often laughed during my shifts in the bar knowing that their tips were paying for me to attend feminist conferences, to get a certificate in Women's Studies, to complete two university degrees.

One of the first joyous moments in my life was when I had grown in important ways with my first feminist therapist. At the conclusion of that time I legally changed all of my names and gave birth to a new self: A "sigh" is a sharp cutting instrument, a tired sound. "Si" is also the first two letters of Siamese and the abbreviation for Symbolic Interactionism. Chava was Henry Morgentaler's first wife's name. I'd read an article somewhere about her being a creative person — and I really admired him for what he had done for women's ability to control their own futures. "Trans" can mean to disappear and reappear, and "ken" is my grandfather's first name. He had always been kind to me. Ken can also mean seeking wisdom. I spent $600 on changing my names, and beginning my own life with my own choices; it was the best money I ever spent.

Moments of transformation have taken place over the years as I came to realize how much of our lives are set down around, above, and before us. The sociological/historical/herstorical terrain we're placed in limits our options. Having been born with white skin, in a rural boom-bust town connected only to the mining industry, to parents and grandparents with minimal educations — so much was already taken from me and given to me from the moment I was conceived.

Working as an immigrant settlement worker and being involved for ten years in an antiracist feminist organization I came to recognize more complexly what my privileges were as a Canadian citizen who didn't have an "ethnic" appearance, even though one parent and one grandparent were immigrants who had very limited reading and writing skills in English. Race, class, and geography have each become more and more tangled in their meanings for me.

The feminist movement taught me the core things that I need. Feminist experiences taught me skills in communications, helping others to think differently, public speaking, organizational analysis and curiosities, fundraising, management (woman-agement), how to motivate others, and even how to inspire others.

How were people around me reacting to my new self?

When I waitressed in the bars I was a comedy act or a strange but intriguing creature to some of my women and men peers. The staff would listen to me sometimes. Other times they'd ask me very hurtful questions. Now and then the men would bait me and try to humiliate me. Those same men taught me how to banter, be witty, deflect tension, and sometimes let myself be the person they could safely laugh at or with. Those contexts taught me incredible self discipline. Later when I began teaching at a university I would tell myself: how hard could this be? I've dealt with dozens of intoxicated bikers, lawyers, truck drivers, and business men and managed to get them to not be too rebellious or lewd, but to also have them thank me for it and tip me reasonably well. At least in those contexts I usually knew who wanted to screw me and how badly.

In academia I'm still learning how to read the scripts and make meaning of the body language, gossip, and whispers. Along the way I've had to leave some folks behind, or step away from them. The day after I stopped working in the strip joints was the day I lost contact with everyone from that world. But I am connected with women who are in homeless shelters, and they often feel so comfortable for me to be with. They're the ones who originally "brung me" to the dance, after all. They're usually working poor women, or of ethnocultural minorities, or abused women who have run out of

options at this moment in regards to living independently. I see or hear my mother in many of their stories.

I see or hear who I could have become had I not had feminists to give me a different kind of comprehension, courage, array of choices, and a delicious righteous rage that drives my attendance at protests as potently as it drives my sense of entitlement to stay home on snowy days sometimes and snuggle with my cats and read another book by bell hooks, Adrienne Rich, Lee Maracle, Rita Wong…

86 | MEETINGS BECAME A WAY OF LIFE
Lamar Van Dyke

At the age of eight I helped my crotchety old stepfather build an addition onto our little cement block house, one block at a time. I fabricated elaborate forts out of the doors and pipes and wood that he stashed behind the garage. I took my bike apart and put it back together again. I could do whatever I wanted. My mother told me that, over and over. Life was good.

There were no sex role stereotypes interfering with life, until, at some point, my mother got nervous about her little tom boy and decided it was time for a crash course in make-up, bras, and clothes. That was when everything changed. I hung with my girlfriends. We ironed our hair, wore white lipstick and shaved our legs. We were way more interested in each other than we were in boys. Boys seemed sort of stupid and dull.

By the time social awareness reared its head, the war in Vietnam was in full swing, atrocities pouring out of the television like water over the Hoover Dam. I joined the rank and file, protesting whenever possible — putting all of my energy into trying to stop the War Machine. Meetings became a way of life. It was in those meetings where the men were ego maniacs and women were discounted that a dim glow of light began illuminating the dark recesses of my mind. There I was, gleefully thinking we were all in it together, which we were, but somehow the decision-making process reflected something very different.

Robin Morgan facilitated *Sisterhood is Powerful,* compiling the writings of many women who were feeling the same kind of unease. I devoured that book. It immediately strengthened my ties with other women. We started talking, we started meeting, we started writing. The fog was lifting and I was ready. Women were gathering without men, talking without men, and eventually partying without men. It was liberating.

In an attempt to build a bridge between the gay community and the women's community, I invited Pat Murphy, the coordinator of the Gay Center, to join me and my current girlfriend, Adrienne Potts, for dinner. By the end of the night we'd been arrested for singing "I Enjoy Being a Dyke" at amateur night in the Brunswick Tavern on Bloor St. — history would know us as the Brunswick 4 Minus 1. Our communities were instantly united and much to the surprise and dismay of the judge hearing our case in municipal court, the Honorable Judy LaMarsh defended us.

By now I was with my 3rd girlfriend and we were silk screening t-shirts that said profound things like: "A woman without a man is like a fish without a bicycle." We exhumed famous Canadian women like Emily Carr for the fronts of our shirts. We sold them at women's festivals that were springing up everywhere, and at Toronto's first women's bookstore, "Lettuce Out," which was one little room at the women's center. Women were mobilizing and it was exciting.

I lived in Toronto in a collective that housed the organizers of the Women's Bookmobile, *The Other Woman* newspaper, and me, the coordinator of A Women's Place. Our lives were women, women, women. We ate feminism for breakfast, lunch, and dinner. It was delicious. We really did believe that if women woke up and took themselves seriously the entire structure of society would change for the better. I still believe that. Collectively, we became a loud, irritating and relentless alarm clock without a snooze button.

When *Ms.* magazine popped up it was suddenly and fabulously unfashionable to consider yourself Mrs. Robert Dickson…Mrs. Fred Cox…Mrs. Anybody. Enclaves of feminists were tearing off the scabs of the patriarchy, dancing in the puddles of blood slowly coagulating at its feet. It was party time. The patriarchy had finally been outed.

That marked a major fork in the feminist road. Some women continued to chip away at the monster, and some women decided to make their own world.

After years of slicing and bashing at the barriers in the road, I became part of a group of women who decided to create our own world. We bought a farm outside of Peterborough, where we envisioned a good life full of organic vegetables, hard work, and women. Our escape was not complete, however. The patriarchy was there as well. We couldn't get jobs for more than minimum wage, which meant we couldn't get jobs that were designated as "men's work." We had a difficult time "fitting in." But we felt much better after we made t-shirts proclaiming ourselves "The Cavan Women's Quilting and Bombing Society."

Some of us bought vans and took off in search of dyke heaven. We were convinced it had to be out there somewhere. We drove from women's land to women's land, a caravan of gypsies looking for a place to be. We all changed our last names to Van Dyke, (it only seemed right). We changed our first names to things like Brook (because she babbled), Thorn (because she was scrappy), Sky, and Birch. We changed as much as we could, discarding as much of the patriarchy as possible. We shaved our heads to see what it was like, we became food fanatics just because we could. We smashed monogamy until it smashed us back, and the entire time our world was female, female, female. The adventure made us strong but, of course, in the end it all went wrong.

What made me a feminist? I think I'll credit my mother with that distinction. She loved women and always told me I could do whatever I put my mind to. Little did she know what that would actually look like.

> Cora Bookmobile with (l-r)
Judy Quinean, Ellen Labyris
Woodsworth and Boo Watson, 1974

Archives and Special Collections
(CWMA), University of Ottawa
(PC-X10-1-867)/Amanda Bankier

> La Cora Bookmobile, avec (de g.
à d.) Judy Quinean, Ellen Labyris
Woodsworth et Boo Watson, 1974

87 | A BURNING DESIRE

Gail Vanstone

A deep-rooted pleasure in the stories of women and a circle of remarkable friends are the enduring factors that led me to carve out a feminist life.

In the early '70s, the newly released Royal Commission on the Status of Women fuelled a climate of hope and change, igniting my own burning desire to lead a self-directed life, caught as I was in a series of seemingly insurmountable obstacles — economic, psychological, personal and social. I was young, naive, and trapped in a stifling marriage, my two small children, singular bright lights. A sense of unworthiness and shame, remnant baggage from a teenage pregnancy — the matrimonial spur — was tempered by a stubborn streak that refused to be tamped down.

An elementary school teacher by training, I'd returned to Toronto after a two-year hiatus in Montreal to discover a surplus of teachers in Ontario and an arid job market. I soon found a service position in a major Canadian corporation, work that quickly proved both enervating and diminishing. We "girls" were watched at every turn — even our phone calls were secretly monitored — as though we were errant children. My life was ordered by lean economic circumstances and a raging thirst for a university education.

Then, an epiphany came while reading Margaret Atwood's novel *The Edible Woman* on the subway riding home to a high rise in the suburbs. I was consumed by the story of Marion McAlpine, the central figure of the narrative. Marion emerges from a beauty shop groomed for a party she dreads, hectored by a creeping awareness that forces beyond her are slowly but inexorably devouring her. Her fiancé Peter, a promising young lawyer, is a petulant, self-absorbed tyrant with a penchant for violence. All of the women she knows are trapped variously by their circumstances. Only dimly aware of the dangers the traditional cultural script holds for women, Marion is slowly rendered immobile, relinquishing authority to act on her own behalf.

Likewise, given my own tenuous grasp of "feminist frameworks,"

I held few analytic tools to unravel the knots of my own life. Fiction, however, offered instruction.

At that moment of reading, Marion's plight and my own merged — at least in my imagination.

Several months later the professor in my night course, lecturing on symbolism, asked us to consider the events surrounding the central figure — a significantly unnamed woman — in Atwood's novel *Surfacing* as she dives for the third time deep into a mountain lake searching for clues that might lead to her missing father.

What of the dark, blurry oval floating far below the water's surface, her search, the repeated dives?

His question was met with silence then quizzical responses: the dark mass — her father, her drowned brother, her aborted child? Brow still raised, his eyes scanned the class — what else? Seated motionless, palms sweating, quivering slightly, too timid to raise my hand — my answer might be wrong — I imagined myself saying, "It's the act of surfacing after encountering the sinister in the depths of one's self that's symbolic. The turning point — the act of confronting, of coming to grips with something dark, then rising to the air — is a woman confronting her life and rising to its challenge."

A year later, a single parent, newly separated, I reclaimed the name given to me at birth, thanks to advice from my legal aid lawyer Rosalie Abella, secured serendipitously following a visit to a University of Toronto Women's Crisis Centre. I also entered university studies full-time. For the first time, I remember daring to think about living my life differently, controlling its direction — a radical, unorthodox thought given my strict upbringing. I would not, at that moment, have named myself a feminist. I was too worried about sure censure from my family — parents, brother, children (too young to register protest, but later?) — if I were to strike out in the direction I was contemplating. And I felt I was too lacking in knowledge of feminism as political action to claim the title.

But strike out I did. I continued to read literature written by women — an attraction to feminist literary criticism and to feminist theory were predictable developments, as was a growing interest in films made by women.

Life experience and academic encounters led me to Studio

D, the feminist film studio of the National Film Board, the only government supported unit of its kind in the world. When *Not A Love Story* (Bonnie Sherr Klein, 1981) was released, I watched it as a graduate student in a huge lecture hall packed for the event. Later, as a professor of women's studies, I searched out Studio D documentaries and used them in courses I taught: *A Writer In the Nuclear Age* (Terre Nash, 1985) revealed the activist side of Margaret Laurence; *Firewords* (Dorothy Todd Hénaut, 1986) introduced me to luminous Quebec writers Louky Bersianik, Jovette Marchessault, and Nicole Brossard, particularly Brossard's radical scrutiny of the "patriarchal curse" in Western culture; *Five Feminist Minutes* (1990) celebrated the works of fifteen Canadian feminist independent filmmakers.

I began to think more deeply about the intertwining themes of identity construction, the precariousness of the "emerging" female subject, and the power of feminist documentaries to foster consciousness raising through storytelling. In short, I began to think seriously about the relationship between theory and practice in the understanding and shaping of women's lives.

Pursuing women's stories from a scholarly perspective led me to doctoral studies and, eventually, the publication of a book I would write on the daring enterprise that was Studio D. Throughout these years, I have been buoyed up by a circle of friends, incomparable women and men who espouse feminism — or not. A common thread in many of these friendships, transformative forces in my life, is a love and practice of literature. Among them: Joan Barfoot treasured friend from childhood, "best friend" in high school. We read Freud and Hitchcock together, "psychoanalyzed" each other, secretly depositing our findings in each other's lockers — best friends always knew the other's padlock combination. While our paths diverged, our friendship held, now beautifully embroidered by Joan's skillful fiction.

Dyan Elliott, prodigious scholar of medieval history, first encountered in a Latin class, her beauty, fury, and passion for living, questioning, and writing are infectious qualities that continue to fire me; Leslie Sanders, peerless mentor, agile intellectual, pragmatic friend and wise counsel, introducing me to Toni Morrison's fiction, prodding me into doctoral studies, celebrating afterwards. Miriam

Waddington, poet, English professor, ferocious in her opinions and her affection — sitting up half the night in a cheap New York hotel, watching Eisenstein movies, drinking tea, eating oranges and talking about other Canadian poets. Caitlin Fisher, brilliant, bright spirit, magical teaching partner — our grading sessions, high adventure — creative explorer and mistress of the internet, her celebrated *These Waves of Girls* breaking new ground.

All this, the "pin," as Jeannette Winterson says in her book *Gut Symmetries,* that hurls me past the boundaries of my own life.

88 | MELTDOWN

Tristis Ward

I was raised in a poor, conservative household in a rural area of Saint John, New Brunswick. By the time I was twelve years old I had joined a fundamentalist Christian church. At the same time, I met and fell under the influence of a local man who quickly began to abuse me. In the elastic way that children can be, I continued being both a "fundie" and a follower of this warped man. Driven to escape traps that I barely perceived, I fought my family's disapproval of higher education and graduated from high school. In 1983, I left all that behind to go to university in Halifax — but was still heavily influenced by these combined indoctrinations.

Worse still, my abuser followed me to Halifax. He moved his wife and child there and continued his pursuit. Despite this, the emergence of my true sexuality happened over the next several years. I eventually figured out what my body and subconscious mind were trying to tell me, and began exploring lesbianism. Unfortunately, I confessed all of this to my abuser, and he involved himself in it by taking me to gay bars to "check out the scene."

It was probably a good thing that we hit what I later learned was "the gay wall," where newcomers are completely ignored by gays and lesbians until they find a person on the inside to introduce them to others. I managed to go to the bar alone from time to time, but still did not break through the social isolation I felt was punishment for having first been seen with a man. There were, of course, other means of uncovering support for newly out lesbians, but many of them were connected to social justice organizations that I had not discovered yet. The ones I did discover were all suspect in my paranoid mind. I worried that somebody was monitoring whoever picked up the gay newspapers, and I was afraid to phone the "gay line" in case it was a prank run by a fraternity.

After yet another night sitting invisibly at a table in the gay bar, I finally went up to the bartender and asked if he knew of any person who could answer some questions. When he returned a moment later with the name and number of a woman who agreed to meet with me, I decided it was worth the risk.

That is how I met Dar. She was the first real lesbian I ever had a conversation with, so when I first sat down at the coffee shop table I was almost star-struck. She answered my questions and talked to me about her own life. It was all quite fascinating. She had been one of several lesbian military personnel secretly targeted, transferred to the bunker at Debert, Nova Scotia, then unjustly drummed out. She had come through a lot of public trauma, but was rebuilding her life. I felt a kinship with her and realized a feeling of belonging that had never existed in me before.

Yet all that abruptly fell away when she started to probe my concept of feminism. We were talking about how much I had in common with other women, and she asked me whether I had noticed all the different ways women were oppressed. I had been well versed in identifying "man-haters" by my abuser; and "feminist agendas" by my church. I interrupted her mid-sentence and told her: "Oh, no. You aren't going to turn me into one of those feminists. I'm a humanist! You just want to recruit me!"

To her credit, she accepted my ignorance with grace. She continued to talk to me that day, explaining how to meet other women, that I could trust the gay magazines, and where the women's dances were. I was not so generous with her, though, leaving with a polite thank you and spurious promise to call again. My fear of dealing with the truth of my past and ongoing oppression cut off this connection to the gay community, and slowed my emergence from the closet.

I stopped trying to meet gay people for a year or so.

What broke down my final barrier was a meltdown in a gender studies class. I had been asked to keep a journal during the course. However, at the end, I refused to hand it in. I met with the professor and explained that this was because I had written passages declaring I was a lesbian. She said that since it was now out in the open I could hand it in, but I still refused. The fear was too great to be dealt with logically. In response, she gave me an "incomplete due to illness" and sent me to see a lesbian professor at the nearby Atlantic School of Theology. She helped me make contact with a coming out group headed by the editor of the local gay newspaper, the *Gaezette*.

By this time, I had come to realize how much of my early education was a betrayal of my life. While I had still not broken free of my abuser, I was more prepared to disagree with him and sometimes avoid him.

It is difficult to pinpoint my specific progress along the path toward feminist understanding. But one moment in a sociology class stands out. In class, a film on pornography was being shown. The narrator of the documentary had her own feminist awakening on screen, and I believe I travelled with her in that awakening.

My real movement was in the area of lesbian rights and expression. This was the eighties and it was still very difficult to find information or positive expression on lesbianism. I volunteered with Coming Forward, helping newly emerging GLBTs find safe, effective, alternatives to gay bar cruising. I marched in protests, attended rallies, and distributed petitions.

I think I absorbed feminism by osmosis through all the networking and discussions.

I attended several "Wild Women Don't Get The Blues" weekends in Tatamagouche. They were always amazing adventures for me, full of surprises. The biggest was when I ran into Dar once again. She was still as friendly and as gracious as ever. I managed to get past my embarrassment over my earlier behaviour and approach her. "I need to apologize," I told her, "for the rude things I said. I was wrong and stupid." She told me I had no reason to be embarrassed, that I was young, and had obviously grown. But I insisted, "I work with the same young women as that in Coming Forward, Dar. I know how much it pains to ignore the barbs and try to help them even when they're wrong. And I've still never come across anybody so rude as to accuse me of trying to recruit them."

She accepted my apology. I'm not sure how she felt, but I felt a whole lot better. I still use Dar as my model when dealing with both women and men who are trying — and perhaps momentarily failing — to grasp the huge impact of oppression on individuals as well as the greater whole. I have spent many years teaching radio broadcasting and non-profit administration to thousands of young and fiery university students. There are many times when I have found it pays to gently and firmly present the facts of oppression and be prepared for varying paces along the learning curve.

89 | RESISTING THE (GENDERED) URGE TO MARGINALIZE OUR TRUTH

Rosemary Cairns Way

Reflecting on my own feminist history has been difficult. My instinct is to dismiss my story as insignificant and uninteresting. I recognize that this instinct is gendered, and that this collection is aimed precisely at resisting the urge to marginalize our stories. In fact, the collection is a public and joyful celebration of the multiple and distinct ways that Canadian women have become feminists.

There are two stories from my path that are worth recounting. Both were pivotal to my evolution, and both tell a larger truth about what I now understand about being a feminist.

I am a law teacher and a legal academic. Unlike the committed, passionate, and astonishing feminist students I now encounter, I came to feminism relatively late in my legal training. I was in my early thirties, married, with three young children and struggling to settle on a career path that balanced my personal circumstances with my professional aspirations. I completed my articles at the Supreme Court of Canada where I was a law clerk to the Honourable Justice Gerald LeDain. One of our most important tasks as clerks was to prepare "bench memos." These memos were intended to help the justices prepare for oral hearings. Essentially, the memos summarized the facts and legal issues presented by the case, analyzed the current state of the law, assessed the strength of the arguments made by the parties, and concluded with a recommendation about the appropriate result.

By definition, cases heard at the Supreme Court of Canada involve issues of national significance in which the law is unsettled or evolving. In other words, the legal problems are difficult and complex.

Twenty years later, I recall my clerkship with a mixture of pride and horror. The pride is because I had the opportunity to spend a year immersed in the work of the country's most important legal institution. The horror is at the thought of my recently degree-ed, wet behind the ears understanding of the law, and the fact that I was making recommendations about the resolution of the most challenging legal issues of the day. Luckily, the graciousness of my judicial mentor (and his instincts as a teacher) kept things in perspective. The work felt much like the research I had done in law school, and, with three children under five, I was simply too tired and overwhelmed to worry too much about the critical importance of the issues I was analyzing.

One of the insidious qualities of legal reasoning is how easy it is to lose yourself in abstractions and logical niceties — doing research at this level of decision-making did little to disabuse me of the sense, learned in law school, that law could be abstracted and universalized without sacrificing "justice." Perhaps not surprisingly, it was a sexual assault case that challenged my complacency. The case, *Regina v. Bernard*, concerned the relationship between drunkenness and the crime of sexual assault.

Then, as now, the criminal law on the issue was messy and complex — reflecting an arguably pragmatic balance between theoretical principle and lived reality. Theoretical consistency suggested that drunkenness, just as any other circumstance affecting an accused person's mental state, should be considered in the assessment of whether an accused intended to commit the crime. The question in sexual assault was whether the accused knew that the victim had not consented to sexual contact. Lived reality suggested that a "defence of drunkenness" would be too easily believed in the context of sexual violence. Allowing accused persons to claim that their drunkenness rendered them insensible to the victim's refusal looked like a "license for rape," grounded in stereotypes about alcohol, sex, and gender, which would fail to protect women and children from male sexual violence.

In *Bernard*, the Supreme Court was re-examining the appropriateness of the compromise position adopted in an earlier decision — and reconsidering it in view of the entrenchment of *Charter* rights to a fair trial and fundamental justice. When I began to write my memo, I wrote with the easy and unthinking confidence of a well-trained law student, arguing the position I had learned in law school: theoretical consistency should trump pragmatism and no special treatment should be given to sexual assault.

Somewhere along the way, I began to have doubts.

Perhaps it was because I was actually faced with the consequences of theoretical consistency. Perhaps it was my realization that a change to the law motivated by doctrinal purity could well end up exonerating this, in my view, clearly guilty accused. Or perhaps it was the fact that the *Charter* rights to fair trial and fundamental justice, as applied in the case, seemed curiously indifferent to the realities of sexual assault.

A pre-hearing session with Justice LeDain — a thoughtful and rigorous jurist who insisted on using discussion with his clerks to work through the implications of his decisions — further confirmed my discomfort. With characteristic disdain, he gestured out the window at the silhouette of the Peace Tower, and opined that he would be more inclined to insist on doctrinal purity if he had any confidence that "they" would respond to the problem of sexual assault in the legislature.

In a follow-up memo, which I unearthed and reread while thinking about this piece, I acknowledged my discomfort, confessed to a weekend spent wrestling with the ideas I had carefully internalized in law school, revisited my claim that abstracted universalism was essential to justice, and admitted my relief that it was his responsibility (and not mine) to make a decision. In the end, the case was decided in a jumble of opinions, the law on drunkenness remained mostly the same, and the criminal law of sexual assault continued its halting, awkward, reluctant and sluggish evolution towards equality.

By contrast, my own evolution as a feminist was set in motion by the law of sexual assault. And, later that year, it was pushed further by the various court decisions covering everything from pregnancy and employment discrimination to the famous *Morgentaler* case on abortion rights.

The second story from my feminist path is a simpler, more personal one.

Unlike many Canadian legal academics, I did my graduate work in Canada — at a school that was a two-hour commute from my home, my children's schools, and my partner's work. As a result of the distance, I fulfilled my graduate residency requirements uniquely, but in a manner consistent with the spirit of faculty regulations. Unfortunately, the supervisor assigned to me was a distinguished formalist, who, some months into my program, decided he could not tolerate my unusual situation, and insisted that I comply with the residency requirements in a manner that was patently impossible given my family circumstances.

Shocked by the possibility that I would have to abandon the degree, I stumbled tearfully into the office of a senior feminist faculty member, Beverley Baines, who offered tissues and a sympathetic ear. With compassion, efficiency, and uncanny perceptiveness she arranged for a new supervisor, Toni Pickard. It was my intellectual and personal relationship with Toni, a relationship facilitated by a feminist mentor, and borne of a formalist falling-out, that ultimately propelled me into university teaching; teaching that I am proud to characterize as both critical and feminist.

Having told my two stories, I find myself wondering again about their significance. What strikes me, and confirms my sense that these moments were personal turning points in my evolution as a feminist, is how they reflect larger truths about working as a feminist professor in a law school. My experience at the court was a lesson in context — it was a lesson about the false promise and false premises of universalizing norms, about the importance of accounting for gender, about the need to respond to difference and lived experience, and about the risks of intellectual complacency.

In some ways the experience as a graduate student was also about context — this time my own. I saw how an institution, and the people within it, could respond to individual circumstances with empathy and generosity. I became part of the continuous creation of feminist community because two women with authority were prepared to respond to the reality of my life.

These two experiences and the truths they represent continue to be central to my understanding of my own professional role. I take them into the classroom by challenging my students to think past the comforting abstractions of law, and into the lives of the people who seek justice through law. And I take them into my office, when students, struggling to find their own path, seek my assistance and counsel.

90 | THE WOMAN ON THE TABLE

Liz Whynot

When I graduated from Queen's Medical School in 1972 my feminist awareness was minimal and my feminist credentials were zip. Once on a training rotation in tiny and isolated Moose Factory I had somehow come across the very first issue of *Ms.* magazine. Weird, eh? And I had taken the radical step, driven by lust, of becoming lovers with a woman for the first time, enjoying the thrill of transgression, a term still decades away from common use especially by me. It was she who gave me a copy of *The Female Eunuch,* and — more from romantic passion than an interest in feminism — I followed her to Vancouver where she had been awarded a graduate fellowship. Luckily for the romance, I was successful in obtaining a rotating one-year internship at St. Paul's Hospital.

Through my partner's connections at graduate school, I was introduced in my limited spare time to cultural critiques with impressive names like ethno-methodology and phenomenology. We eventually moved into a co-op (sort of) with her radical feminist professor, Dr. Dorothy Smith, along with Dorothy's sons and dogs and several other graduate students. (In retrospect, I am amazed at Dorothy's courage in doing this!) To keep up, I joined a reading group to study the works of Karl Marx. I read "Women, the Family and Corporate Capitalism." I read *Women and Madness*. I went to my first Ferron concert.

Meanwhile, I endured the trial by fire that was a medical internship year, constantly working beyond my stamina and competence, and quite often feeling that medical school was probably a big mistake. I decided I didn't like hospitals and I didn't like, or couldn't live up to, the constant pressure to compete, which meant there was no way on earth I was going to apply for specialty training, wanting nothing more than to escape.

I left the hospital with some very strong impressions and memories that still creep into my dreams, like the woman who had tried to kill herself with barbiturates. She had been found before dying in her apartment, along with her female lover who had succeeded in her half of the pact. She had two depressions in her forehead, the result of a frontal lobotomy performed twenty years before. Because of what? Being a lesbian? Her brother was a doctor, by the way. I also remember the off-colour sexist jokes told over a sleeping patient in the operating room by a male surgeon to a room full of women — nurses and doctors — all of us expected to laugh. And I remember nights in Emergency where I got my first taste of the misery of people living on skid row.

Yes, I fled the hospital, vowing never to return to such a place, but not before attending the end of year party for interns and staff, a drunken affair at the interns' residence. By the time that year ended, I was alienated from what seemed to be the medical culture of the time: a fraternity that defined itself in terms of what was important to (what I had been taught to believe were privileged and powerful) white men. This feeling was reinforced by the behaviour of several of the staff doctors at the party, for whom alcohol allowed groping of younger females and I'm sure more if the females responded appropriately.

Ironically it was at this sodden affair that the next stage of my life and awareness was decided. Not all of the older doctors were men. In fact there were a few women, among them Dr. Hedy Fry, who approached me with the suggestion that I consider volunteering for the Vancouver Women's Health Collective, something that she and a few other women doctors were doing. She told me they needed licensed MDs to cover their weekly clinics, and now that I qualified for a license, perhaps I'd like to give it a try. I was grateful for her suggestion. The truth was I had absolutely no idea what I was going to do after my internship, or where to do it.

So the next week I braved the bastion of the College of Physicians and Surgeons, obtained a license to practice in BC, and duly signed up for sessions at the Health Collective's Clinic. The Clinic was held weekly in an old house on West Fourth Ave. in Kitsilano, the heart of Vancouver hippie life in those days.

When I arrived for the first time I confronted another irony: the Health Collective volunteers knew far more about women's health, including gynecology, than I. My entire training experience of this area had been three weeks in medical school where contraception and sexual health were not mentioned, as far as I could remember, and a month's rotation on the surgical wards where most women were recovering from hysterectomies or other invasive procedures for incontinence or cervical cancer. I had assisted at a total of three births, usually being elbowed out of the way by obstetrical residents. There was also my personal experience of vaginal exams and brief forays into sex, but as an MD I was exceptionally well trained in compartmentalizing, so I didn't really include that. Women's Health? What's that?

There were other doctors there the first time or two that I worked, thank heaven, but what really saved me were the volunteers who handed me the first Boston Women's Health Collective newsprint pamphlets and talked to me about self-examination and diaphragms. And of course, the "Collective" consciousness. As such a green and self-conscious doctor, embarrassed about what I had come to understand was my undeserved societal power, I was welcomed into the fold and supported to become an equal member of the collective with a very handy medical license.

I quickly figured out that the way to solidify this positive relationship was to complete the main initiation rite, a self-examination. Note that it was a *self*-examination, but not a private one, because it was always done with the assistance or witnessing of others. This was arranged to happen one evening when it wasn't too busy and there was a free examination room and table.

I should say here that the Health Collective evenings were great social affairs. Certainly girls and women came to the clinic for their pap smears and diaphragm fittings, and discussions about all aspects of reproductive health especially. But the Health Collective also welcomed various professional and agency people who visited to see what it was all about. This interaction was part of the political advocacy so important for women's groups. Women, including me, would sit in the comfortable overstuffed chairs in the waiting area and talk about women's health, and visitors would sometimes go upstairs to have a look at the clinic activity. It was there that I heard (for the first time!) about such organizations as Planned Parenthood, and such heroes as Henry Morgentaler.

Anyway, on the evening of my initiation, I took off my bell-bottoms and underwear and climbed up naked from the waist down onto the table. Feminists were proud of their bodies, especially their vulvas, so we didn't have sheets. First there was the external examination: sitting up in a way that I can't manage today, holding the mirror and shining the reflected light on to my flesh. It was amazing, I admit, to actually see a part of myself I'd never seen before. Then I took the proffered speculum and lay back to insert it appropriately, an activity that was quite difficult and required all of my attention for a few seconds. Once I had it in place, I looked up for a moment to reach for the mirror and flashlight only to find myself face-to-face with a formidable older woman, wearing a pearl necklace and skirt, peering into the curtain-free exam room. She looked like Ethel in *I Love Lucy*, only taller and more serious.

One of the Collective members said, "Oh. Um... this is Mary Bishop, from Planned Parenthood." Mrs. B. smiled a little, nodded, and backed out of the room. I really can't remember what my cervix looked like, or how the speculum came out, but I know I got through the next parts really quickly, forgoing the breast self-exam, at least on that occasion.

This unlikely moment has stayed with me for thirty-six years, and it was the first thing that occurred to me when I was asked if I could write a vignette about my emergence as a feminist. Why is that? Certainly I was mortified, fully exposed and embarrassed, so maybe it's not surprising that I remember it so vividly. But I think now that the sudden collision of my doctor self with my woman self, in front of such a witness, a grown-up advocate who was a generation ahead of me, kind of jolted me into an awareness of where I wanted to be in the world. And about how difficult it was going to be to rationalize my professional role with my identification with, and allegiance to, the woman on the table. This challenge has informed my life ever since.

91 | HOW DID THE "F" WORD FIND ME?
Shelagh Wilkinson

As a student nurse in England (beginning in 1945) I bought into the patriarchal status quo and happily accepted it. What else was there? But soon after moving to Canada as a new immigrant — with a husband and three babies under two — I began to realize that something wasn't right. It was 1958, and I was floundering in muddy suburbia (through freezing winters) in a sea of diapers and formula. Was this what I had signed up for? I knew I had to do something to save my sanity, so I began correspondence courses with the Department of Education. I started writing grade 12 papers in English Literature. It seemed to be the answer. I used to get up at night to write my essays and read the texts, often amazed I still had a mind to think with. Now, if only I could share my thoughts with other women, especially about these ideas that Virginia Woolf kept bringing up: Was it better to be locked in or locked out?

The F word had begun to bother me.

It was the 1960s and consciousness raising groups had begun to spring up. The New Feminists, in Toronto, ran some events and I went, meeting other women who were also realizing that, while being locked out was the accepted position, it didn't have to remain that way. Perhaps being conscious of this and challenging it could be the catalyst for change. It was a turning point for me. Claiming the margin meant we could really question the patriarchal centre. It made sense to me. So when Atkinson College opened for part-time students, I went back to school — for the love of literature, but also to learn more about the social and cultural construction of femininity.

Those were exciting days. Just listening to the Vietnam War protestors who flocked up to the college, along with their feminist partners, taught us a lot. Feminist books were now being published, but of course, they were not on the university curricula yet. The critical texts that were being published by feminist scholars taught me how to deconstruct the traditional literature I was reading, and how to begin asking questions. And at the time, even the most basic questions needed to be asked: Why did a course on twentieth century novelists not include a single woman writer? Why, when a new poet was introduced, was it always assumed that a poet was a man? Where was a reading list of Canadian women writers?

Now the F word was ringing in my ears.

In 1973 I went to Oxford. I had won a doctoral fellowship to research the papers of John Locke. My brother was a Blake scholar and Oxford trained. His immediate response was that I could not accept the fellowship; I was married with three children, over forty, and my place was at home. I may have gone back to university, but I was really a nurse, a wife, and a mother and I should think hard about what I was doing. And I did think hard about the decision. It would be a challenge, a girl from Liverpool, thinking she could just walk in to New College, Oxford, where there was so much male privilege and such an intimidating tradition. But imagine actually having my own space…Virginia's "room," what a joy that would be!

And that is exactly what I found. There was more joy in the Bodleian than I could ever imagine. The joy of reading and researching, of having every text you ever wanted available to you, and all of this in a rarefied atmosphere that gave me a freedom I had never felt before. This was an atmosphere quite alien to me — undisturbed, totally undisturbed, by daily demands and 'to-do' lists, someone to even bring my books to me! But life in the colleges was very different. I was inside a bastion of male supremacy. Everyone was very kind to me, but condescending. I was over forty, married with children, reading Philosophy, and a Canadian. I was way outside the centre here. Other fellows may have asked me to tea, (or requested that I make it) but they never discussed philosophy with me. So although I had managed to make it in, I was definitely still locked out. Oh Virginia, how well you had prepared me with your witty observations of Fellows and Bachelors and Masters; and how well you had armed me with your analysis of power, patriarchy, and protectionism.

I did my reading, but was totally ignored by most other fellows, so I joined a group of women at Lady Margaret's who were trying to begin a course in Women's Studies. My research on Locke looked bleak beside my discussions with these women. Even more interesting for me was the fact that I took with me to Oxford a book list I had prepared thinking I would design a new course back at Atkinson, York: "Writing by Women." I had some twenty titles on the list and a bibliography. I took it to one of the meetings at Lady Margaret and it turned out they too had prepared just such a reading list. When we compared the lists, out of the twenty titles on mine only three were different from theirs. Maybe it really was time to start demanding courses focusing on writing by, and about, women.

My brother was at Oxford at that time and one evening I told him how locked out most women felt, how the faculty women at Lady Margaret's did not have salary parity with faculty in the other colleges. Women were marginalized, and it was time to challenge this. His answer shocked me. He said, "If you had a *status quo* like we've had since the 1300s, would you give it up?" (And he is quite a decent, left-wing, tolerant sort of guy.) I knew when I responded with "Then we'll take it from you," that the F word had exploded in my brain. The personal was political and each one of us had to follow it through.

I came back to Canada determined that feminism would be central to any work I do. Within weeks I was hired to run the first Centre for Women at Sheridan College. My new job gave me a budget and I spent it all at the recently opened Toronto Women's Bookstore on Harbord Street. Thinking back to my own solitary studies in the early '60s I knew that what was needed was a Bridging Class that would help disenfranchised women get an education. The community women in Oakville agreed with me, and we began to meet in local libraries. Sheridan College agreed to an admittance scheme, depending on students attaining a B standing.

In the Bridging Class I could actually teach Virginia Woolf and analyze her feminist philosophy. The women arranged their own babysitting system, and helped each other by learning to edit their writing. They began to read, write, and think critically. The classes multiplied and moved to church halls and apartment building recreation rooms. And the women gained back a measure of themselves. Many of them found the necessary time to study, and they enrolled in a course or two.

At some point, the province mandated that colleges and universities should all compile status of women reports, and so I began that useless procedure. I realized it was a "make work" endeavour that would change very little. Regardless, as part of that process I needed to track down information on salary scales. The first dean I went to requesting a copy of the salary scales for new faculty members entering employment simply shook his head at me. No such thing existed. Then how did he assess a starting salary I asked? He tapped his forehead and explained that he just offered salaries that he thought would be acceptable. And women were always grateful… happy with less. Did we women ever need educating on these issues! More importantly, perhaps we needed to start sharing our experiences in the work world as well as in the home. Consciousness raising was a basic and vital tool.

Centennial College was also doing pioneer work in Women's Studies and I left Sheridan to join the faculty there in 1977. President Doug Light was a rare man, a feminist who was not afraid to implement radical change. Centennial was preparing a feasibility study on publishing a new journal in Women's Studies. Marion Lynn was a faculty member; she was a tower of strength in pushing through the concept of this new journal. I was appointed the editor and before we began looking for subscriptions I went to Doris Anderson and asked her if we had a hope of success, and how long she thought such a publication might last. She was honest, as usual, and said (through cigarette smoke) "Oh, about six months!"

But we went ahead anyway, and in October 1978 *Canadian Woman Studies / les cahiers de la femme* published its first issue. Despite her initial estimate about our success, Doris was always totally supportive. She was happy to be the keynote speaker in 1998 when we celebrated our twentieth birthday. We all shared in the unexpected triumph;

CWS/cf is now over thirty years old and has been based at York since 1983. It has morphed into a feminist publisher, Inanna Press, and now has more than thirty titles in print.

By the 1980s I believed that introducing a feminist analysis into as many disciplines as possible, and educating students, would be the catalyst to liberate both men and women from the stifling gender roles that have traditionally bound us all. I became a member of the faculty at York University and in 1983 was appointed to design the Women's Studies Program for Atkinson College, complete with a Bridging Program as a community outreach. The University agreed to monitor the progress of students in the Bridging Program and the Registrar agreed to admit students who attained a B mark, or better, in the thirteen week course.

In March 2010 I was at York giving a seminar on Virginia Woolf's *Three Guineas*. What a joy to still be sharing such a political text with young men and women. But the greatest joy was in having one student come up after class and tell me she was a Bridging student, now in her fourth year and contemplating graduate studies.

Feminism is just a small eight-letter word but it has seen me through from writing alone at the kitchen table (with Virginia looking over my shoulder) to today. Now, I am over 80, happy that the F word found me, and that I am in a country that has honoured me by making me a Person.

92 | GULP! PUBIC HAIR

Karin Wilson

It was the image that drew me in. Thick black curls of ink like Medusa's hair danced across the tan background of a two-page spread enticing me to examine the mystery hidden in the rows of words. Lured in, my naive 10-year-old eyes could barely believe what I was reading, this wasn't about regular hair, this was about … body hair!

The article was among the first in a new magazine called *Ms.* that my mom had been bringing home these last few months. There was the Wonder Woman cover where she was rescuing the world from itself. Then there was the multi-armed woman who looked a bit like my favourite character from the Addams Family, only I don't recall Morticia ever holding a toaster or a baby. But before this moment, sitting quietly on the couch on my own, I don't know if I had ever peaked inside this new magazine. And now, to discover they were talking about something that was growing on my body, something that even my dear progressive European mother wouldn't talk to me about. Well, it was too much to resist.

My cheeks were still burning from that moment when my mom discovered I was on a premature path from childhood to adulthood. Somewhere around my 10th birthday I stepped out of the bath and as usual my mom came in offering to dry me off. Kneeling before me, her hand reached to remove a hair. "Ouch!" I cried. My mother pulled back and we both reeled in shock and embarrassment. Puberty had just slapped me up the front side (I have no idea what I called that part of my body back then). My mom never dried me off again.

So it's no wonder that I was drawn to learn more about this new hair growing on my body. I had seen my mom naked, so I knew it would happen. But what was it for? Why did we have it? And why now?

Rather than answer these questions, the essay prompted so many more. What I inadvertently tapped into was the politics of hair — specifically the North American belief that adult women's body hair was something to be not only ashamed of, but more importantly, removed. The article questioned why the culture of the day demanded that women infantilize themselves. Was this what men wanted? And if so, why? Why did men want their adult women to look like girls? European women let their underarm hair grow, and everything else along with it. They weren't unattractive — they were embracing their maturity.

These were heady things for my young brain to ponder. I sought out ways to talk about them with my friends, but there really was no entry point. As far as I knew, only one other girl in my class had embarked on this rite of passage, and I knew that only because

I spotted the line of her menstruation belt through her sweater one day in class. She would have been a good bet though. She was Italian. My mom told me they had lots of hair.

So I kept my thoughts about pubic hair — the fact that I had some, and what I was supposed to do about it — to myself. Over the next few years, my early maturing body would become an object of ridicule to other girls. One day while discretely changing in a cubicle at the local swimming pool, a group of girls only one year older than me whipped away the curtain to howls of laughter. I didn't know which part of my body to cover first, my vulva or my breasts.

By that time, breasts had become political as well. My mother proudly urged me to hold-off that purchase (although maybe it was just her fiscal prudence). I think word must have reached my prudish English aunt who sent me over a padded bra that Christmas. I received the gift with insult — not just by age, but political persuasion. I was a liberated woman, too young to even own a bra to burn.

But life has a strange way of twisting us in its wind. As women shrugged off their bras, fashion responded by embracing the new look with clothes designed for the boyish woman. It was all nipples and no breasts. Between the empire lines and smocking, suddenly any woman with more than a B-cup was fated to look pregnant. I, feminist that I was, soon realized I would never be in the club. I donned my cross-your-heart bra and hid.

And so it was that in the midst of older women reclaiming their bodies and defining themselves, I became locked in an inner world of contradiction.

Looking back on it now, what I feel is some kind of remorse for a lost childhood. My early exposure awakened in me a depth of questioning many other girls of my time would take years to reach, if ever. But it also set me up in a dichotomy. While feminism was encouraging women to embrace themselves, I was still a girl living in a world of girls who doled out shame like Pez candy. We were morphing before each other's eyes and we didn't like it. We tried to rebel, but we could do nothing to stop the march to womanhood.

Embracing feminism was risky business — it set women apart — but a pubescent girl feminist? Come on. I didn't even know what it was to be a woman, and already it was being defined for me in conflicting ways.

I remained a feminist throughout high school. It inspired me to advocate for gay rights and boycott Anita Bryant's Florida orange juice. In university it encouraged me to join Rape Relief, but every time I tiptoed by the women's group at Simon Fraser University, I shied away from setting foot inside. Rumour had it, they were lesbians, and I wasn't sure I wanted to be one.

Now, at almost 50, I've come to terms with my body, my sexuality, and my feminism. I'm a feminist on my terms. I don dresses, shave my armpits, and wear a padded bra. I love being female, and I no longer feel my femininity contradicts my political beliefs. Feminism made me question the status quo. Most importantly, it gave me the freedom to define who I wanted to be.

And I'm still trying to figure that out. Just like that 10-year-old girl.

93 | FEMINIST — BEING OR BELIEVING?

Linde Zingaro

In the late '70s, when I was engaged in conversations about feminism or "women's liberation" (a term which, at this point, seems impossibly, naively optimistic) one of the problems for me was always the question of what it meant to *be* a feminist. Was it a club? Who decides when you qualify? Given what appears to be the continuation of my life-long resistance to joining any group that threatens to include me, it follows that I came to my identification as a feminist kicking and screaming, or at least making loud and passionate arguments against any formalizing of my part in it. It seems funny to me now, to hear myself as an old broad complaining about how so many young women these days have such a negative view of feminism, when I consider that it took me years to settle for my own version of whatever the word signifies.

At the time that this important conversation was going on in my city, I was a single mother, running a large non-profit agency created to provide residential and support services to people we then called street kids. I was fighting every day against what felt like a very real war on women and children, using my own previous experience of violence and abuse to inform all the policies and practices of an organization endlessly scrutinized by, and in fact almost completely compromised by, our necessary funding relationship with "the system." I have since heard that during that same time many women had very satisfactory and positive experiences, learning about feminism by meeting in private groups, in safe "women-only" spaces, talking about their lives, finding support and understanding and political analysis in each other's stories. Having already been through several years of (bad) therapeutic care from a series of Freudian or otherwise misguided (male) psychiatrists, I was not about to go into any situation that felt so much like those group attacks and confrontations so familiarly imposed on me "for my own good."

So I struggled with childcare, working full-time, and trying to go to school to finish an Arts degree that would make absolutely no difference to my chances of making a living. I felt guilty about not being available for my son, and I felt guilty about wanting to be with him, since the children I was working with had so little, and everything they needed was so urgent, so immediately life and death. I felt guilty about wanting the privilege of going to school, too, and most of what I was studying seemed so irrelevant compared to what my life was that I finally quit. This put a stop to formal opportunities to understand the evolving theories of feminism, and (once again, in character, apparently) I was not satisfied with the simple definitions and discourses that were available to me.

My son was part of my resistance, as well. Having very easily fallen into one of the necessary categories of feminism by starting an intimate relationship with a woman (fortunately or unfortunately one so "out" that I had no choice about being closeted), I was surrounded by the serious discussions going on at the time about "lesbian separatism." Aside from the fact that I had brothers and friends and ex-lovers who were men (and I still do), the idea that anyone would expect me to segregate my son from any part of my life was enough to start me raving again. More kicking and screaming and refusing to feel like this movement had anything to do with me.

And every day I went to work, face-to-face with sexism, racism, homophobia, poverty, addiction, and the very explicit sexual exploitation of children on the street — girls, for sure, but boys, too. If the need for change meant that only violence against girls counted, I just couldn't sign on. But after a few years, the passion and power of my particular style of screaming became a useful tool for a very public advocacy for the philosophical, legal, and policy changes that were beginning to be made in the area of service and support to victims (we changed the term to "survivors" around then) of childhood sexual abuse. In the course of many conferences, workshops, professional dialogues, and what we then called "speaks," I found that my outrage and my intense demand that something be done, and done differently, were met and matched by many others, mostly women, often but not always those who called themselves feminists.

The fact that many of those people around me with whom I had profound and enduring disagreements also called themselves feminists ensured my continued resistance to several of the forms that feminism seemed to take over the years. Having lived in communal houses since my art school days in the mid-1960s, and having been a part of the peace movement and the development of food co-ops in the early '70s, I did not assume that the feminist utopian vision of "community" needed to be limited to women. I had learned that you could live with people you don't like or don't agree with, and that it might actually be easier to do that if you don't have meetings to "process" your feelings all the time. Having worked in a trade where I did a "man's job" for a "man's wages," I didn't see feminism as the source of a decent income — equal work for equal pay always made sense to me. If feminism was either so rigid that it operated like a new fundamentalism, or so soft that it could support those who were dangerous to others because they were part of some politically correct group, I could not *be* a feminist.

So how did I come to agree to call myself a feminist? I actually think of it as a kind of conversion — not so much to a specific ideology, but I came to an understanding of feminism as *practice*. When I finally got back to art school and eventually to graduate school in the late '90s, I was distanced enough from both the visceral battles for political territory and my own defensiveness to be willing to take a theoretical look at the life I had been in for well over a decade. By this time the academic language of post-modernism allowed for the clear articulation of various "feminisms," some of which still rankle. But in the relativist structure of this debate, I was able to find my own version of the word. Shaped by my long-term lesbian partnership, by my son's struggles with having "two mothers" in the homophobia of high school, but most importantly by my work as a counsellor with so many women bravely facing all the difficulties named in any feminist critique of our culture, this construction of feminism has allowed me to claim a space for myself in the practice.

But although I could understand that this practice of feminism includes so many of the things that are most important to me, for a long time I had trouble believing that it could ever embrace some of my earlier incarnations or transgressions. Even with a commitment to expanding the terms of the idea, it still seemed a stretch to assign some of my experiments in identity to an incipient feminism — the raunchy R & B dancer; the sex, drugs, and rock and roll of the hippie days; the work as a cocktail waitress and bouncer at a bar when I was in my 20s. I could probably safely assign to feminism my long-term interest in Gertrude Stein and George Sand, my attraction to cross-dressing, and swaggering female defiance in the face of authority, and my conviction that if you want something done you need to ask a woman to plan it. The idea of a feminist sensibility allows me to understand some of my own art differently, as well. In this light my 1965 "Gorgon" intaglio series of raging female heads could be read as an early indicator of my potential as a feminist, a meditation on the history and the social consequences of the huge power of female anger.

But I finally started calling myself a feminist when I found myself working in Japan with various women's groups, lecturing and teaching what they called "feminist therapy," in a context where there was very little recognition of domestic violence or child abuse. In the effort to talk about my practice through what, in the beginning of my work there, was very sketchy translation, I needed to explain how my philosophy of caring for the vulnerable might be different from what was "normal" or mainstream in the practice of anti-violence or abuse counselling and support. Defining it as "woman-centred," "contexted," or "critical" was too vague, and in the descriptions of what those things meant to me, I found my own articulation of feminist practice, and my own definition of myself as a feminist: a person who does what I do every day, raging.

> Demonstration, 1985

Archives and Special Collections
(CWMA), University of Ottawa
(PC-X10-29-7)/Photographer Unknown

> Manifestation, 1985

NOTES ON AUTHORS /
NOTICES BIOGRAPHIQUES
DES AUTEURES

MARGUERITE ANDERSEN was born in
Germany; she came to Canada in 1958.
She has lived and taught in England,
France, Germany, Tunisia, Ethiopia, the
United States, Quebec, and Ontario.
She has a Ph.D. in French Literature
from the University of Montreal, and
has published about twenty works
of fiction. In 1981, her first novel, *De
mémoire de femme,* received the Prix du
Journal de Montréal, awarded by the
Union des Écrivains québécois. Her
most recent novel, *Le figuier sur le
toit,* received Le Prix des Lecteurs de
Radio-Canada and the Prix Trillium
in 2009. Having taught the first
Canadian interdisciplinary course in
Women's Studies in 1971-72, at Loyola of
Montreal (now part of Concordia), she
edited a collection of texts by Montreal
women in 1971. *Mother was not a person,*
published by Black Rose, sold 6,000
copies. Find more details on www.
margueriteandersen.franco.ca.

M. ELIZABETH (BETH) ATCHESON was
born in Fredericton, NB, and holds
degrees from the University of New
Brunswick and the University of
Toronto. A specialist in the regulation
of financial institutions, she has
practised law in Toronto, and held
policy positions in the Financial

Services Commission of Ontario and
the Ontario Ministry of Finance. Beth
has been a member of the Canadian
Human Rights Tribunal. She is a YWCA
Woman of Distinction, and has been
awarded the President's Award from the
Women's Law Association of Ontario,
and the Law Society Medal from the
Law Society of Upper Canada.

BETTY BABA was born in Northern
Nigeria. She studied in France where
she received her Ph.D. in Women's
Studies at Paris 8, Université Vincennes
in Saint-Denis. In the year 2000, she
immigrated to Canada and taught a
course on "Women, Sexuality and Social
Justice" at the University of Windsor. In
the year 2008, she was appointed as a
lecturer at the University of Ottawa, in
the Department of Women's Studies.

CONSTANCE BACKHOUSE was born
in Winnipeg, and has taught as a
professor of law at the University of
Western Ontario (1979-1999) and the
University of Ottawa (2000-Present).
She has published a number of prize
winning books, including: *Petticoats
and Prejudice: Women and Law in 19th-
Century Canada*; *Challenging Times:
The Women's Movement in Canada and
the United States; Colour-Coded: A Legal
History of Racism in Canada,1900-1950*;
De la couleur des lois; and *Carnal Crimes:
Sexual Assault Law in Canada, 1900-1975.*

CLARE BECKTON is an academic, author
of a book on Media and Law in Canada
and many articles on the *Canadian
Charter of Rights and Freedoms,* a
lawyer, a coach and mentor, a wife and
mother, and a former public servant
serving many years in Justice Canada
and recently retiring as Deputy Head at
Status of Women Canada.

HONOURABLE MONIQUE BÉGIN, PC,
FRSC, OC, is the first Québec woman
elected to the House of Commons
(1972) and former Minister of National

Revenue (1976-77) and National Health and Welfare (1977-1984), a sociologist, and successively the first holder of the University of Ottawa-Carleton University Joint Chair in Women's Studies (1986-90); the Dean of Health Sciences at University of Ottawa (1990-97); and now a Visiting Professor at its Telfer School of Management. A Fellow of the Royal Society of Canada, she has received 16 honorary doctorates for her contributions to human rights and to public policies. She became an Officer of the Order of Canada in 1998. She was a member of the WHO Commission on the Social Determinants of Health (2005-08).

DR. WANDA THOMAS BERNARD received a Bachelor of Arts degree from Mount Saint Vincent University in 1975, a Master's of Social Work from the Maritime School of Social Work at Dalhousie University in 1977, and a Ph.D. in 1996 from the University of Sheffield, England. She has worked in mental health at the Nova Scotia Hospital, in rural community practice with the Family Services Association, and since 1990, has been a professor at the Dalhousie School of Social Work, where she has held the position of Director since 2001. She has had a long and distinguished career in the field of social work and is highly regarded for addressing racial and cultural diversity in social work education and in the community.

JANE BIGELOW graduated from the University of Toronto in 1950, taught in Ottawa and Hamilton, was elected to London City Council in 1969, and was Mayor from 1972-78. She is a YM/YWCA Woman of Distinction (1981), and she volunteers for Women's Community House, Hamilton Sexual Assault Centre, London Sexual Assault Centre, London Second Stage Housing, and My Sisters Place.

JOSÉE BOUCHARD est une avocate bilingue qui a été admise au barreau de l'Ontario en 1989, après avoir complété son baccalauréat en droit à l'Université d'Ottawa ainsi que sa maîtrise à l'Université de Cambridge, en Angleterre. En 1989, Josée a été nommée professeure à la Section de common law de la faculté de droit de l'Université d'Ottawa. Depuis mai 2000, elle occupe le poste de Conseillère principale en équité du Barreau du Haut-Canada.

SOPHIE BOURQUE est née à Montréal en 1961. Diplômée de la faculté de droit de l'Université de Montréal, elle est admise au Barreau du Québec en 1984. Elle pratique pendant 20 ans à titre d'avocate de la défense en droit criminel, puis est nommée à la Cour supérieure du Québec en 2005. Elle est mère de deux jeunes déesses, nées en 2000 et 2002.

LAURA BRANDON is the Historian, Art and War, at the Canadian War Museum. She holds a B.A. (Hons.) in History and Art History from the University of Bristol, England, an M.A. in Art History from Queen's University, and a Ph.D. in History from Carleton University. She is a Fellow of the Royal Society of Arts and an adjunct professor in the School for Studies in Art and Culture at Carleton University. She is the author of the award-winning biography *Pegi by Herself: The Life of Pegi Nicol MacLeod, Canadian Artist* (2005); *Art or Memorial? The Forgotten History of Canada's War Art* (2006); and *Art and War* (2007), a survey of western war art. The curator of numerous exhibitions, in 2000, her exhibition *Canvas of War* received the Canadian Museum Association's Award of Excellence.

CLAIRE BRASSARD est une spécialiste reconnue du droit du travail et de l'emploi, tant en droit québécois qu'en droit fédéral. Membre du Barreau du Québec (1982) et de l'Association du

Barreau canadien (1983), elle détient une maîtrise en administration de l'École nationale d'administration publique (1989). Me Brassard a enseigné le droit du travail de 1981 à 1998 à l'Université de Montréal. Elle siège aujourd'hui au conseil d'administration de diverses corporations, dont la Fondation Léa-Roback, le Théâtre d'Aujourd'hui et Sports Montréal. En 2004, Me Brassard a été nommée membre du Conseil des Montréalaises par le Conseil municipal de la Ville de Montréal.

MARY BREEN started out in adult literacy, moved into oral history, became founding executive director of the Workers' Arts and Heritage Centre, then moved into arts-based work with street-involved youth. She burned out and became a Pilates and Nia dance teacher, then got involved with the Women's Future Fund until cuts to Status of Women Canada shut it down. She is now an entrepreneur, operating a craft shop/gallery/studio called Wise Daughters Craft Market in Toronto. She also provides administrative support to the Feminist History Society.

ALICE BRONA is a retired Public Health Nurse who lives in co-op housing. She blends her interest in wholistic health and Christian faith by writing poetry. And she used to be a Raging Granny.

KIM BROOKS held the position of associate professor and the H. Heward Stikeman Chair in the Law of Taxation at McGill University's Faculty of Law, and has recently become the Dean of Law at Dalhousie Law School in Halifax, NS. She has served as the Chair of the Women's Legal Education and Action Fund, the co-chair of the National Association of Women and the Law, the managing editor of the *Canadian Journal of Women and the Law,* and the Acting Director of UBC's Centre for Feminist Legal Studies. She is currently a member of the Law Program Committee of the Women's

Legal Education and Action Fund and the secretary of the *Canadian Journal of Women and the Law.*

GAIL G. CAMPBELL completed the one-year program at London Teachers College (1964) following graduation from high school. For eight years, she taught elementary school and worked as a school librarian in Middlesex County. She completed her B.A. by extension (University of Western Ontario, 1972) and soon enrolled full-time in graduate studies in History. She holds an M.A. (UWO, 1979) and a Ph.D. (Clark University, 1983). She has been a member of the Department of History at UNB Fredericton since 1989. Her publications focus on the political activities of ordinary people. At UNB, Gail has organized an annual series of public readings to celebrate Women's History Month. In 2003, she was co-organizer of a symposium on the origins of the teaching of women's history in Atlantic Canadian Universities. She has served as editor of *Acadiensis* and is currently Chair of its Editorial Board. She is also a member of the UNB Senate.

MARGARET CONRAD is an Honorary Research Professor at the University of New Brunswick. During her forty-year career as a historian, she published widely in the fields of Atlantic Canada History, Women's Studies, and Humanities and was a member of the collective that founded *Atlantis: A Women's Studies Journal*. She is currently exploring the relationship between historical consciousness and individual and collective identities in Canada.

MAEVE CONRICK is Dean of Arts and Vice-Head of the College of Arts, Celtic Studies and Social Sciences at University College Cork, National University of Ireland Cork and Statutory Lecturer in the Department of French. She has published widely on language issues in English and French. Her books include *Womanspeak* (Mercier Press, Dublin,

1999) and *French in Canada: Language Issues* (Peter Lang, Oxford, 2007).

SHARON ANNE COOK is Professor at the University of Ottawa with a joint appointment in Education and History. She is sole author of eight books in Canadian women's, religious, addictions and educational history, and has edited a collection in women's history, with Lorna McLean and Kate O'Rourke, *Framing Our Past: Canadian Women's History in the Twentieth Century* (Montreal and Kingston: McGill-Queen's University Press, 2001). Currently, she is completing a manuscript on a visual cultural history of Canadian women and cigarette smoking.

HONOURABLE SHEILA COPPS served almost a quarter century in elected political life in Canada. The country's first woman Deputy Prime Minister, Copps was also the first woman to bear a child while in office. As Minister of Environment and Canadian Heritage, Copps was active on the international scene. She played a key role, under the guidance of now German Chancellor Angela Merkel, in the Berlin Accord, a precursor to the Kyoto Protocol. She was also the initiator of a world instrument on cultural diversity, which became a UNESCO Convention in 2005. A strong feminist, Copps introduced laws on pay equity and non-discrimination against gays and lesbians in the Ontario Legislature almost thirty years ago.

ANN DECTER, who is currently Director of Advocacy and Public Policy for YWCA Canada, has worked for women's equality as an advocate, researcher, writer and publisher. Originally from Winnipeg, Ann moved to Toronto to study and settled into Toronto's vibrant women's writing and publishing community, becoming co-managing editor at Women's Press (Canada) and publisher at McGilligan Books. Ann's publications include the reports *Work Isn't Working for Ontario Families* (co-author), and *Lost in the Shuffle: The Impact of Homelessness on Children's Education in Toronto,* as well as the novels, *Paper, Scissors, Rock* and *Honour.*

FRANCINE DESCARRIES est professeure titulaire au département de sociologie de l'Université du Québec à Montréal et coordonnatrice de la recherche à l'Institut de recherches et d'études féministes (IREF) de la même institution. Ses travaux de recherche portent sur le mouvement des femmes québécoises et l'évolution du discours féministe contemporain, de même que sur des questions relatives à la maternité, à la famille, aux conditions de vie des femmes, à l'articulation famille/travail et à la reproduction de la division sociale des sexes et la socialisation

NATHALIE DES ROSIERS est l'avocate générale de l'Association canadienne des libertés civiles. Auparavant, elle a été vice-présidente de la gouvernance de l'Université d'Ottawa, doyenne de la Faculté de droit de l'Université d'Ottawa, section de droit civil, présidente de la Commission du droit du Canada et professeure à l'Université de Western Ontario.

DIANNE DODD received her doctorate from Carleton University in 1988, and has since published on birth control, domestic technology, public health and "women and health care" in Canada. As a postdoctoral fellow at the University of Ottawa (Hannah Institute for the History of Medicine) until 1991, she conducted research into public health and then worked for the National Archives of Canada. In 1996 she joined Parks Canada as a historian. Most recently, she co-edited, with Christina Bates and Nicole Rousseau, *On All Frontiers: Four Centuries of Canadian Nursing,* which was published jointly by the Canadian Museum of Civilization (CMC) and Ottawa University Press.

DIANE DRIEDGER's latest book is *Dissonant Disabilities: Women with Chronic Illnesses Explore Their Lives* (CSPI/Women's Press), co-edited with Michelle Owen. For the last thirty years, she has been involved in the disability rights movement both locally and internationally, with organizations such as DisAbled Women's Network (DAWN) Manitoba and Canada. She recently completed her Ph.D. in Language and Literacy in the Faculty of Education, University of Manitoba.

MICHELINE DUMONT, pionnière de l'histoire des femmes au Québec, a enseigné l'histoire à l'Université de Sherbrooke de 1970 à 1999. Elle a publié plus de dix ouvrages en histoire des femmes, dont le dernier *Le féminisme québécois raconté à Camille* (Remue-Ménage, 2008). L'on trouvera dans l'ouvrage collectif *Minds of our own* (Wilfrid Laurier University Press, 2008), un autre article de Micheline Dumont « Doing Feminist Studies without Knowing it », dans lequel elle explique sa méthode de recherche pour la rédaction de son article pour la Commission Bird. Professeure émérite de l'Université de Sherbrooke, Micheline Dumont est depuis 1993 membre de la Société Royale du Canada.

MARY EBERTS grew up in southwestern Ontario, and attended Western University and the Harvard Law School. After teaching at the University of Toronto Faculty of Law, she joined the litigation department of a major Bay St. law firm, then practiced from 1994 to 2005 in a small specialized firm which she founded. She is a co-founder of LEAF, and writes and speaks extensively on issues of equality. Now conducting a national practice in constitutional and Aboriginal law from a base in Toronto, she is also a doctoral student at the University of Toronto Faculty of Law.

NATHALIE FAVE, artiste polyvalente et mère de trois enfants, dirige à Toronto un centre de services aux femmes. Elle a vécu vingt ans en Afrique avant d'immigrer au Canada. Élève de l'École des Beaux-arts du Parisis dès l'âge de six ans, elle détient une licence de lettres modernes de l'Université Paris X. Coréalisatrice du documentaire *Négritude*, co-fondatrice et rédactrice du magazine panafricain *Découvertes*, elle a reçu le Prix spécial du Jury de la fondation Senghor ainsi que, pour son recueil *Les anges n'ont pas d'ailes* (2002), le Prix de la Maison Africaine de Poésie Internationale.

LOUISE HENRIETTA BARTON FORSYTH is Professor Emerita and Adjunct Professor, University of Saskatchewan, in Women's & Gender Studies, Languages and Linguistics, and Drama. Her administrative positions include: Chair, Department of French (UWO); Dean, Graduate Studies and Research (Saskatchewan); President, Humanities and Social Sciences Federation of Canada. Her friendships in the Hags and Crones in London, Ontario, and her career research on women playwrights and poets of Québec, have made her life meaningful and full of joy.

BARBARA M. FREEMAN is an associate professor at Carleton University, cross-appointed to both the School of Journalism and Communication and the Department of History. She is the author of *Kit's Kingdom: The Journalism of Kathleen Blake Coleman* (1989), and *The Satellite Sex: The Media and Women's Issues in English Canada, 1966-1971* (2001). She is currently completing a series of essays on women media workers in Canada and their social justice causes since 1875.

VERONICA P. FYNN is an advocate of human rights pertinent to vulnerable women and children in Africa. She has a multi-disciplinary educational background: B.Sc. (Hons.) in Zoology/

Biochemistry, University of Ghana; B.A. in Psychology, University of British Columbia; M.P.H. from the University of Nottingham; and Master's in Law (LL.M.), Osgoode Hall Law School. She is currently doing a Ph.D. in Law at Osgoode Hall. She is a Co-Founder/Executive Director of EV Research Inc., the founder of the first ever *Journal of Internal Displacement* and she keeps a blog on the Rights of Women in War. As a former refugee student sponsored by the World University Service of Canada (WUSC), she is a promoter of WUSC Shine the Light Campaign and an avid supporter and mentor to WUSC @ York local community members. She currently works as a research assistant with the Centre for Refugee Studies and the Department of Social Science at York University.

CAROLYN GAMMON was born in 1959 and grew up in Fredericton, New Brunswick. She graduated from UNB in 1981. On completing her graduate studies in English Literature and Creative Writing at Concordia University in Montreal, she refused to receive a "Master's" degree, claiming it was sexist. She requested a "Mistress" degree or gender neutral equivalent and, after a 5-year struggle, the Quebec government approved the changing of degree titles. Carolyn Gammon graduated officially with a Magisterie in Arts in 1994. Since 1992, Carolyn has lived in Berlin, Germany. Her most recent book is: *Johanna Krause Twice Persecuted: Surviving in Nazi Germany and Communist East Germany* (co-authored with Christiane Hemker, Wilfrid Laurier University Press, 2007).

JOAN GILROY is retired from the faculty of Dalhousie University, where she was appointed to the School of Social Work and cross-appointed in Women's Studies. Her teaching, scholarly, professional and community work was focused on feminism in social work education and practice. She coordinated

Dalhousie's undergraduate and graduate programs in social work; and during the years 1990-96, she served as the first woman Director of the Maritime School of Social Work, Dalhousie University. Joan obtained B.A. and M.S.W. degrees from Dalhousie, an M.A. at the University of Toronto, and is doing graduate work in Sociology and Women's Studies at OISE/University of Toronto. She has presented and published articles on feminism in social work and on child welfare. In the 1970s, she and colleagues across Canada pioneered the introduction of feminist theories and practice approaches in social work education. She was a founding member and chair of the Women's Caucus of the Canadian Association of Schools of Social Work (now, the Canadian Association of Social Work Education) and the International Association of Schools of Social Work. Both caucuses were active for many years in promoting feminist ideas and gender analysis in curricula, as well as addressing issues pertaining to sexism in universities and professional organizations. As a volunteer, she was instrumental in developing and managing community based social services for women. Currently, she is an adjunct professor at Dalhousie and is researching the history of feminism in social work education in Canada.

CHARLOTTE GRAY is the author of eight bestsellers of biography and history, including *Sisters in the Wilderness, The Lives of Susanna Moodie and Catharine Parr Traill* and *Nellie McClung*. She is the winner of the Pierre Berton Award for Popularizing Canadian History, and is the Chair of Canada's History Society. She lives in Ottawa.

SHARI GRAYDON is an Ottawa-based communications consultant and the author of two award-winning media literacy books for young people. Her diverse career on both sides of the microphone includes stints as a newspaper columnist, TV producer, broadcast commentator, communications instructor, political press secretary, and the spokesperson for two national feminist organizations. Find out more at www.sharigraydon.com.

LORRAINE GREAVES is an educator, researcher, writer, and speaker. She was the founding Director of both the Centre for Research on Violence Against Women and Children, and the British Columbia Centre of Excellence for Women's Health, and a co-founder of the Battered Women's Advocacy Centre. She laid the foundation for the Women's Health Research Institute at BC Women's Hospital, and received an Honorary Doctorate from the University of Ottawa for her efforts in changing the landscape of women's health in Canada.

SHIRLEY GREENBERG was born in Ottawa but her forebears are all Westerners: Saskatchewan pioneers. She attended university part-time, combining it with motherhood, and began law school at age 40, spurred on by the women's movement and finally realizing that a woman can do anything! She co-signed the lease for Ottawa's first Women's Centre in 1972 and thereafter continued to be guided by feminist principles. At law school she joined with others to form the National Association of Women and the Law, just one of many feminist organizations in which she took part as a founder, a member, and a supporter. She joined with Catherine Aitken (now a judge in Ontario) to form Ottawa's first all-women law firm. Since retiring she has actively supported various causes including endowing a Chair in Women and the Legal Profession, University of Ottawa, and becoming a major patron of the Ottawa Women's Health Centre, part of Ottawa Hospital, named in her honour. She has received an honorary doctorate from the University of Ottawa Faculty of Law, and is a member of the

Order of Canada in recognition of her philanthropy and her efforts to promote the equality of women.

NANCY E. HANSEN is Director of the Interdisciplinary Master's Program in Disability Studies at the University of Manitoba. She obtained her Ph.D. from the University of Glasgow. Her thesis examined the impact of education and social policy on the employment experiences of women with physical disabilities. Her postdoctoral research examined women with disabilities' access to primary health care. She received an Einstein research fellowship to examine Disability Studies and the Legacy of Nazi Eugenics. She is past president of the Canadian Disability Studies Association (CDSA). In June 2006, she was awarded the Ireland Canada University Foundation Sprott Asset Management Scholarship to examine the history of people with disabilities in Ireland. In August 2008, in partnership with Independent Living Canada, Nancy became co-investigator on a Disability, Literacy and Quality of Life Research Project funded by the Department of Human Resources and Social Development.

DR. JEAN D. HEWITT worked in southern Ontario as a teacher and school leader at all levels of education, and as a project officer with the Ministry of Education. In 1969, she became an active feminist determined to end sex role stereotyping in the school curriculum, discrimination in promotional practices, and the tolerance of violence in all areas of society. In 1974 she brought together twenty-eight diverse women's groups to set up and coordinate local initiatives for International Women's Year. She chaired the London and District International Women's Year Committee, and was a Regional Convener for the provincial Status of Women Committee, as well as a founding member of the London Status of Women Action Group. Today, she works as an Educational Consultant with *The Learning Connection*, an organization she founded in 1995. She continues to support various women's projects, including the London Women's History Project. She now resides in Stratford, Ontario. She is married and has five adult children.

AUDREY HOZACK was born in Toronto in 1920. She was widowed in WWII. She has one son, three grandchildren, and four great-grandchildren. She started working at the University of Toronto in 1947. She remarried in 1952. She graduated from U of T as a mature student in 1985, the year of her retirement from Hart House. She studied French, etching, silk screening, figure skating, painting, Italian, yoga, weaving, flying, Spanish, needlepoint, tai chi and writing. She has volunteered with Canadian Friends of Finland, the Royal Ontario Museum, the Textile Museum of Canada, and the Performing Arts Lodges. She has the Chancellor's Award (U of T), the Lt. Governor's Senior Achievement Award, and the Order of the White Rose of Finland, as well as volunteer awards from the University of Toronto and the Textile Museum of Canada.

SYLVIA HUGHES has been a professional writer for over thirty years. Born in Scotland, she attended Business College, but always knew she wanted to be a comedy writer. Over the years she has worked on comedy and dramatic scripts for the CBC, had a comedy column in *Redbook* magazine, published a book on Female Orgasm (Virago Press, London, England) and completed an as yet unpublished novel entitled "Nobody Loves a Lousy Lay" — which was considered for over a year by St. Martin's Press. On another front, she spent twenty-five years working for various international advertising agencies, winning many awards. At the moment she is writing a feature film script, starring her dog, Buster.

TRACY ISAACS is a writer, feminist, and philosopher who immigrated to Canada from South Africa with her family as a child. She writes scholarly articles on collective responsibility and agency under oppression, and writes personal essays on issues ranging from racial identity to getting comfortable with her body by vacationing at a nude resort. She has contributed two shows to the radio program, *Outfront,* which were broadcast on CBC Radio Two. She lives in London, Ontario.

LINDA KEALEY has been a professor of History at Memorial University of Newfoundland (1980-2002) and at the University of New Brunswick (2002-Present). She is the author/editor of several collections in Canadian Women's History, including *Pursuing Equality: Historical Perspectives on Women in Newfoundland and Labrador* (1993; 1999) and *Enlisting Women for the Cause: Women, Labour and the Left in Canada, 1890-1920* (1998). Her most recent publication is "No More 'Yes Girls': Labour Activism among New Brunswick Nurses, 1964-1981," published in *Acadiensis*, XXXVII, no. 2 (Summer/Autumn 2008).

JANICE KENNEDY is a writer and journalist in Ottawa. A native Montrealer and former high school teacher, she spent her 23 years in daily journalism at the *Montreal Gazette* and the *Ottawa Citizen*, from which she retired in 2008. As columnist, theatre critic, senior writer – and mother and grandmother — she has called herself a feminist since the day she first heard the word.

CATHLEEN KNEEN is a retired farmer and currently chair of Food Secure Canada, a national organization working at the intersection of agriculture, environment, health, food, and justice. With her husband Brewster she publishes *The Ram's Horn*, a monthly newsletter of food system analysis (see www.foodsecurecanada.org and www.ramshorn.ca).

PENNEY KOME, an author and journalist, is currently Editor of *Straightgoods. com*, Canada's leading independent online newsmagazine. She has published hundreds of periodical articles, including a 12-year stint as a national columnist, as well as six books: *Somebody Has To Do It; The Taking of Twenty-Eight; Women of Influence; Every Voice Counts; Peace: A Dream Unfolding* (co-edited with Patrick Crean); and *Wounded Workers.*

ANDRÉE LAJOIE est diplômée en droit et en sciences politiques des universités de Montréal et d'Oxford et professeure émérite à la Faculté de droit de l'Université de Montréal. Depuis 1968, elle poursuit une carrière de recherche dans le cadre du Centre de recherche en droit public, qu'elle a dirigé de 1976 à 1980. Axés d'abord sur le droit constitutionnel et administratif, ses travaux ont porté plus récemment sur la théorie du droit (pluralisme, herméneutique). Ses travaux actuels portent en particulier sur les droits ancestraux des Autochtones du Canada.

LUCIE LAMARCHE est membre du Barreau du Québec depuis 1978. Elle a été professeure à la Faculté de science politique et de droit de l'Université du Québec à Montréal de 1988 à 2006. Détentrice d'un doctorat en droit international de l'Université libre de Bruxelles (1994), Lucie Lamarche est aussi récipiendaire du Fellow Jean Monnet de l'Institut universitaire européen (Florence, 1998), du Mérite Christine Tourigny décerné par le Barreau du Québec (2002) et du Mérite CSQ (2006, Centrale des syndicats du Québec). Lucie Lamarche s'est jointe à l'équipe de la Faculté de droit de l'Université d'Ottawa (droit civil et common law) (2007) à titre de titulaire de la Chaire Gordon F. Henderson en droits de la personne. Elle est actuellement la directrice de recherche du Centre de recherche et d'enseignement des droits de la personne (CREDP) de l'Université d'Ottawa.

MICHELE LANDSBERG was a feminist journalist and columnist for 25 years, for the *Toronto Star* and the *Globe and Mail,* and author of three books. After retiring from column-writing, she served as chair of the board of Women's College Hospital in Toronto for four years. Michele is happy to live in a country that rewarded her feminist activism with both a Person's Award and by making her an Officer of the Order of Canada. She is married to Stephen Lewis, and has three grown children and two grandchildren.

LOUISE LANGEVIN est membre du Barreau du Québec depuis 1986 et professeure titulaire à la Faculté de droit de l'Université Laval depuis 1991. En 2010, elle a obtenu le Mérite Christine Tourigny du Barreau du Québec. De 2006 à 2009, elle a été titulaire de la Chaire d'études Claire-Bonenfant sur la condition des femmes de l'Université Laval. Ses champs de recherche et d'enseignement sont en théorie féministe du droit, en matière de droits fondamentaux ainsi qu'en obligations conventionnelles et extracontractuelles. Elle travaille activement avec les différents groupes de femmes du Québec.

KARIN LEE was born and raised in Vancouver, BC. A filmmaker, media artist, and cultural activist, she currently teaches at Simon Fraser University in the Asia Canada Program, Department of Humanities, as well as at the University of British Columbia, in the Department of History, specializing in Asian migration to the Americas as well as cultural identity and media representations of Asians in North America. Her groundbreaking documentary "Made in China" about children from China adopted by Canadians, won "The Canada Award" for best documentary at the 2001

Gemini Awards. She continues to work on films, video installations, and documentaries as well as raising her two daughters, Naiya and Sahali.

ANDRÉE LÉVESQUE est née à Montréal, où elle est revenue après avoir passé plusieurs années à l'étranger. Elle a enseigné six ans à l'Université d'Ottawa avant de se joindre au département d'histoire de l'Université McGill en 1984. Elle est l'auteure, entre autres, de *La Norme et les Déviantes* (Remue-ménage, 1989), de *Résistance et transgression* (Remue-ménage, 1995) et d'*Éva Circé-Côté, libre-penseuse* (Remue-ménage, 2010).

FLORENCE GIBSON MACDONALD is the mother of two astounding and beautiful daughters. She is also a physician and an award-winning writer. Her plays include *Belle*, *Home is My Road*, *Missing*, *Take Care of Me*, *Elevator* and the innovative tap dance show, *i think i can*. Florence has two plays coming up for production: *How Do I Love Thee?* and *Augury*, a play centering around the famed abortion trial of Canada's first woman physician. Florence is currently working on her novel *Stout* and her screenplay, *A Man Like Me*.

LINDA MACDONALD lives with her partner in Nova Scotia. She works pro bono as an expert, activist, and public educator for the exposure of the crime of ritual abuse-torture. Along with a colleague she is presently lobbying for legislative and specific services changes in Canada. Detailed information on ritual abuse-torture can be found on their website www.ritualabusetorture.org.

SHARON M.H. MACDONALD, of Halifax, Nova Scotia, has recently defended her doctoral dissertation in history. Her research interests focus on women's transnational peace networks, social activism, organizational culture, and textile traditions.

DIANA MAJURY teaches in the Law Department at Carleton University. Her areas of teaching, research, and activism include human rights, equality theory and practice, criminal law, violence against women, women's health, and law and literature.

MARY LOUISE McCARTHY received her B.A. in Sociology from York University in 1991 and her Master's of Education, Critical Studies from the University of New Brunswick in 2007. She is currently employed with the Province of New Brunswick as an Employment Counsellor. She divides her time between her community, that of African Canadian heritage, and her ongoing research into their historical graveyards. Her main focus lies with critical mindedness; familiarity with Black feminist scholarship; love of poetry; and her commitment to equity and social justice.

REV. JESSICA McCRAE grew up being told by her parents that she could be anything she wanted to be. She became a minister, with a heavy dose of adventurer on the side. Ordained in the United Church in 2001, Jessica has served rural and urban congregations in Ontario and Quebec. She has also been involved in various international and community development projects, including post-Katrina relief work in New Orleans, and a Palestinian women's cooperative in the Occupied West Bank. She is the author of *In the Middle of Night: Sermons about Courage and Faith in the 21ˢᵗ Century*. She currently lives in London, Ontario, serving two rural congregations. She would be lost without her Blackberry, makes regular updates on Twitter (jess_mccrae), and dreams of one day basking in the glow of the northern lights.

MARGARET McCRAE is a retired teacher having taught many years in the elementary grades of both public and private schools. She has been blessed with many strong women in her family who have been her role models. Volunteering at the Humane Society, reading, church activities, travel, and gardening occupy her time at present.

DR. MARY M^cKIM was born in 1926, in China, where her father was a doctor. She obtained her M.D. from the University of Toronto in 1949; P.G. Fellow of the Royal College of Physicians and Surgeons of Canada, Psychiatry, 1969. She was married in 1950 to Dr. John McKim, Paediatrician, and raised five sons. In 1976 she was married to Rev. A.E. Douglas MacKenzie. Active in the United Church, CARAL, Girl's Group Home, and many feminist organizations, she retired in 1995. On Person's Day, Oct. 18ᵗʰ 2009, she was honoured as one of London's "Famous Five," by London's Women's Events Committee.

MARILOU M^cPHEDRAN is a human rights lawyer and Dean (Principal) of the University of Winnipeg Global College, where she also directs the Institute for International Women's Rights, and teaches her "evidence-based advocacy" and "lived rights" models emphasizing multi-sectoral partnerships and actionable knowledge, as part of the interdisciplinary degree program in Human Rights and Global Studies. She has extensive human rights research, advocacy, and adjudication skills and directed a number of participatory action studies, including the First UN CEDAW Impact Study.

JUDY MILLER is an advocate counsellor at the London Abused Women's Centre and has been involved in feminist based work in the area of violence against women for over 20 years. She has a diverse background ranging from being a program coordinator at London Second Stage Housing, a counselling coordinator with immigrant women, a child care provider with Merrymount

Children's Centre, and a residential counsellor at Women's Community House. Judy was also involved as a research interviewer with the McMaster University women's health study focusing on the impact of abuse on women's health. Judy incorporates into her professional work her personal experience of violence against women and the impact it has had on her and her four children.

RENATE MOHR was a law professor and criminal justice activist for many years before it occurred to her that the best way to get to the truth was to write fiction. Her short fiction has won awards and she is currently writing a novel.

ANNE LAURA FORSYTHE MOORE, Ph.D., completed and defended her Doctoral Dissertation in the fall of 2006 at the Ontario Institute for Studies in Education of the University of Toronto. For "Legacies," Anne draws from her thesis to include snippets of the stories of five generations of Atlantic Maritime women (1826-2006). Her curiosity had been aroused by the archival and primary source materials found in "The Box" that had been collected and saved for over 170 years by her New Brunswick and Nova Scotia grandmothers and then by her mother, who eventually passed the collection to Anne in 1981. These acts of generations of women saving and collecting memories in a box that re-presented lives lived through photographs, letters, lists of names and birth dates, scrapbooks, poetry, recipe books and a variety of household artefacts, became Anne's legacy. The contents of "The Box" called her to search, to define her research question and to study how her Maritime past had informed her education as a girl-child and a grown woman. Dr. Forsythe Moore is a part-time Teacher Educator with the Faculty of Education, York University.

ELEANOR GREIG MOORE, B.A., M.Ed., LL.D., brings over thirty years of experience as a teacher, guidance counsellor and administrator in independent girls' schools. Eleanor was born and earned her first degree in New Zealand before immigrating to Canada. As a co-founder, with Diane Goudie, of The Linden School in Toronto, Eleanor is passionate about making a difference for girls and women. The Linden School practices feminist, girl-centred pedagogy and has implemented a challenging, social justice-based curriculum. In 17 short years, Linden has become known as the leader in girls' education, maturing into what we dreamed of. Now it is time to write down our story, our practice, and our success, and to share this with other educators of girls around the world. On a personal level it is time to mentor others, to develop new skills, and to foster in others the will and the commitment to making a difference.

HONOURABLE NANCY RUTH, C.M., was appointed to the Senate of Canada in 2005. She is an ardent activist for the powerful vision of equality for women embedded in the *Canadian Charter of Rights and Freedoms*. A feminist philanthropist, she leads by example and advocates the need to increase the share of charitable dollars that directly benefit women and girls. Born in Toronto, Nancy Ruth holds a B.A. in Political Science, an M.A. in Applied Behavioural Sciences, and a diploma in Theology.

VALERIE J. PICKETTS is a Policy Analyst living in Regina, Saskatchewan. She grew up on a farm near Saskatoon and has been a Saskatchewan resident all of her life. She has a Master's and Bachelor's in Agricultural Economics from the University of Saskatchewan. She has worked as a Policy Analyst with the Saskatchewan Ministry of Justice and Attorney General for over ten years. She was the Chair of the Regina Branch of the Women's Legal Education and Action Fund (LEAF) from 2003 to 2006.

RUTH ROACH PIERSON, professor emerita of the Ontario Institute for Studies in Education/ University of Toronto, taught women's history, feminist studies, and post-colonial studies at OISE from 1980 to 2001. She is the author, co-author, and co-editor of numerous academic works, including *"They're Still Women After All": The Second World War and Canadian Womanhood* (McClelland & Stewart, 1986), *Canadian Women's Issues*, Vol I: *Strong Voices* and Vol. II: *Bold Visions* (James Lorimer & Company, 1993, 1995), and *Nation, Empire, Colony: Historicizing Gender and Race* (Indiana University Press, 1998). Since her retirement from academe, she has published two books of poems, both with BuschekBooks of Ottawa: *Where No Window Was* (2002) and *Aide-Mémoire* (2007), which was named a finalist for the 2008 Governor General's Literary Award for Poetry.

NANCY POOLE has contributed as an activist with organizations championing abortion rights, lesbian rights, anti-violence programming, and women's health in four provinces. In the '80s she was in demand as a sound mixer with women's music festivals and production companies, and with the Toronto-based women's band Mama Quilla II. Since 1996, she has been engaged in research on women's substance use issues with the British Columbia Centre of Excellence for Women's Health, and she is currently engaged in doctoral studies on virtual communities as locations for feminist action research. References in her text are drawn from the following sources: "Ode to A Gym Teacher" was included in *I Know You Know*, the first album to be issued by Olivia Records, an independent US label devoted to women's music. It can be found on YouTube and *The Best of Meg Christian* compilation (Ladyslipper Music).

"Member of the tribe" is from "Lesbian Code" by Alix Dobkin, included in *Love & Politics: A 30 Year Saga* (Ladyslipper Music).

MARILYN PORTER was born on a farm in North Wales during WWII. She was educated in England and Ireland, with a Ph.D. from Bristol University. She joined the (very new) Women's Movement in Bristol in 1968 and has been an active feminist ever since in the UK, in Canada after she moved here in 1980, and internationally. She works and researches in academic Women's Studies; in and with local feminist activist groups; and in Indonesia, Pakistan, Tanzania and Kenya with feminist colleagues to build and strengthen Women's Studies.

ALISON PRENTICE taught at Atkinson College, York University (1972-75) and the Ontario Institute for Studies in Education (1975-1998), where she directed the Canadian Women's History Project and helped found the Centre for Women's Studies in Education. Her research and writing have explored the history of gender relations in the teaching profession, eventually focusing on the Canadian professoriate. She enjoyed putting together the co-edited collections *Gender and Education in Ontario: An Historical Reader* (1991), *Women Who Taught: Perspectives on the History of Women and Teaching* (1991), *Creating Historical Memory: English-Canadian Women and the Work of History* (1997), and *Education into the 21st Century: Dangerous Terrain for Women?* (1998). In an equally happy collaboration with five others, she helped produce the first overview of Canadian women's history, *Canadian Women: A History* (1988 and 1991).

SHELLEY TSIVIA RABINOVITCH, Ph.D., teaches at the University of Ottawa, where she was named the 2006 Part-Time Professor of the Year. She specializes in the intersection point

of anthropology, religious studies, women's studies, and popular culture. She has also taught at the University of Arizona, Queen's University, and Carleton University. She has two books out (co-authored) on modern Paganism as well as a cd of original music.

ARLENE PERLY RAE is an active volunteer and writer. She is currently a director on several Boards (e.g., World Literacy, Child Poverty, Stratford Festival), and is Co-Chair of the Fundraising Campaign for the YWCA sponsored Elm Centre; a project that will provide housing for 250 women and women-led families, as well as for 50 Aboriginal families. Arlene is a children's advocate, freelance journalist and speaker. She has written adaptations of *The Magic Flute* and *Petruschka* for the Royal Conservatory of Music and has published a guide to children's books called *Everybody's Favourites* (Penguin); she is working on another book.

ANN ROBINSON, chercheuse féministe et professeure de droit à la retraite de l'Université Laval, a écrit de nombreux articles sur l'accès à l'égalité pour les femmes, le harcèlement sexuel, la discrimination envers les lesbiennes et les gais, le mariage pour les couples de même sexe et l'homoparentalité. La forme non conformiste de son écriture, chassés-croisés de textes juridiques et de propos intimistes, l'a conduite à publier quelques essais littéraires pour des revues telles *Arcade* et *Tessera*. Son premier roman, *Et si j'en étais* (2009), a paru aux Éditions Vents d'Ouest.

GURBIR K. SANDHU was born and raised in Punjab, India. She came to Canada in 1998 and finished her Bachelor of Social Work at the University College of the Cariboo in Kamloops, BC, and her Master's of Social Work at the University of Calgary, Alberta. She has worked with many social justice organizations and groups, including the Women's Centre of Calgary. She is presently the executive director of the Calgary Workers' Resource Centre.

JEANNE SARSON lives in Nova Scotia. She is an independent scholar, researcher, supporter and activist working, since 1993, to have torture that happens in the private or domestic sphere specifically criminalized in Canada, and recognized as a global human rights violation that especially impacts on women and children. She shares her work with a colleague. Further information can be found on their website: www.ritualabusetorture.org.

SAIMA SCALLY says, "I lived most of my life in an isolated Canadian town where there were few opportunities for women and I made my way into the 1970s workforce full of the optimism that women were finally getting somewhere. Well, nowadays I look back and see that most of us didn't get much further than the pink collar ghetto and, if really lucky, a shabby little apartment we could call our own. Equal pay remains a dream. Without equal access to many of the human rights that males can take for granted, it appears that the situation for women is worsening all over the world. All my life, I fought my corner, facing both the battles I chose and those that chose me." She now lives in Europe from where she edits an expat magazine, having reached a place of refuge and relief from most of the world's troubles and a new stage in life that brings her peace.

DONNA (MᶜCART) SHARKEY and **ARLEEN (MᶜCART) PARÉ** are feminist sisters. They bumped into feminism almost at the same time, in the early seventies, through consciousness raising groups in their separate cities of Montreal and Ottawa. They have supported each other as sisters, women, and feminists for forty years. Arleen has moved to Victoria, BC, and after a long career in social work, she is now a writer. Donna still lives in Ottawa, where after a long

career in the federal government, she now works as a full-time university professor. They talk on the phone almost every other day. Sometimes they talk about feminism.

HUDA SIKSEK was born in Lebanon to Palestinian parents, a Bulgarian grandmother, and Georgian ancestors. She grew up in Greece, England, and the United States. She is an artist, educator, and transformational life coach. More importantly, she has planted trees. She lives in Toronto. She is currently writing a book, and she asks that you respect our planet's life sources and refrain from buying plastic.

DIANA SMITH is technically retired (from the position of Safety Officer with the federal government) but continues to be a part-time student at Emily Carr University, an art maker, member of a collectively-run art gallery/store and caregiver. She lives in Vancouver, British Columbia.

BETH SYMES is a partner in the law firm of Symes & Street and practices labour and administrative law, civil litigation, and equality rights, including *Charter* litigation. Beth has represented women seeking their equality rights throughout Canada. She is one of the founders of LEAF. Beth is a Bencher of the Law Society of Upper Canada and was awarded the Law Society Medal.

PATTY THILLE was formerly a physical therapist and now works in health services research. She is currently a Ph.D. student at the University of Calgary in the Faculty of Arts. Her award-winning Master's research focused on Canadian women's experiences of weight-based discrimination in health care. Her most recent contribution to the women's health field has taken the form of the co-edited book *Women Who Care*, forthcoming autumn 2010 from Pottersfield Press. She balances her academic work with community outreach as a healthy sexuality educator with Venus Envy. Her essay was previously published in a similar form in (2008) *Back-Story: First time tales by the stranger next door.* J.H.R. Cutler (Ed.) Boston, MA: SoLo Publishing.

D. GILLIAN THOMPSON: born 1943; raised on southern Vancouver Island and in Vancouver; B.A. (University of British Columbia), M.A. (Stanford), graduate work in France, Ph.D. (UBC). Instructor (Purdue University and University of Windsor), Professor of History (University of New Brunswick, 1972-2005), Professor Emerita (2006-Present).

ELAINE MELLER TODRES, Ph.D., is a former Deputy Minister with the Ontario Government who runs a consulting company, Todres Leadership Counsel. Todres Leadership Counsel specializes in governance, strategy, and stakeholdering. Elaine sits on a number of boards and is currently Chair of Women's College Hospital Foundation.

SI TRANSKEN is almost 50. She's doing art, poetry, and annoying public performance pieces — in collaboration with marvellous, funky, sassy, grassroots, punchy feminists in northern BC. She's active with the First Nations' Counselling Centre and the women's homeless shelter doing art therapy on weekends — and social justice activism the rest of the time. Four Siamese "rescue" cats monitor her behaviour. She also writes scholarly things, and teaches in Gender Studies, Social Work, and Sociology. She and her partner are appreciative to have a roof, vegan food, adequate health, creative souls, and comrades who fortify their courage.

LAMAR VAN DYKE arrived in Toronto in the early '70s when A Women's Place was in its embryonic stages, about to blossom into a hub of activity designed to make women stronger, wiser, and more aware of their self worth. She

was the coordinator of the centre and, in a small room on the main floor, put together Toronto's first women's bookstore called Lettuce Out. With her then-girlfriend, Chris Fox, they started Up Front T-shirts, and silkscreened images of Emily Carr, as well as important slogans, like: "A Woman Without a Man is Like a Fish Without a Bicycle" and sold them at music festivals. After driving around North America for a couple of years with the Van Dykes, she settled in Seattle where she writes, tattoos, and paints.

GAIL VANSTONE is an assistant professor at York University where she coordinates the Culture & Expression Program in the Department of Humanities. Vanstone is the author of *D is for Daring* (Sumach Press, 2007), finalist in *Foreword* magazine's 2007 Book of the Year Awards, Women's Issues. *D is for Daring* is the first book length feminist critical history of Studio D, the world's only state-funded feminist film studio, part of Canada's National Film Board from 1974 to 1996. Her main areas of interest are feminist Canadian cultural production, with an emphasis on film and literature. Following a foray into the field of digital media, creating a four-minute documentary film *Remembering Miriam* (2004), an homage to Canadian poet-intellectual Miriam Waddington, Vanstone is currently compiling a digital archive of Canadian feminist filmmakers associated with Studio D.

TRISTIS WARD comes from Saint John, New Brunswick, and completed her studies in English at Dalhousie University, Nova Scotia. She chose a career in her great passion, community access radio, working as an instructor, administrator, and nationally as a lobbyist. Taking early retirement to write, Tristis has been steadily working toward success in this second career. She has written and produced stage and radio plays, and is currently focused on developing both short and long prose projects. Her most recent work, *Bones of the Magus,* will be published by Broken Jaw Press in 2010.

ROSEMARY CAIRNS WAY teaches law at the University of Ottawa where she has been on the faculty for more than 20 years. She graduated as the gold medalist from the law faculty at the University of Western Ontario, after completing both a B.Mus. and M.Mus. in vocal performance. As a professional educator, and an educator of future legal professionals, she encourages her students to use the law as a tool for social justice and equality. Rosemary balances her legal career with a passion for music, performing regularly with Opera Lyra Ottawa at the National Arts Centre.

DR. LIZ WHYNOT retired in November 2008 after 8 years as the President of BC Women's Hospital and Health Centre. After graduating from Queen's University Medical School in 1972, she worked as a general practitioner and as a public health doctor in Vancouver before joining BC Women's in 1998. Liz was a co-founder of Vancouver's Sexual Assault Service and of the Sheway Program. She received the Kaiser Foundation National Award for Leadership in 2009.

SHELAGH WILKINSON was the founding coordinator of the Women's Studies Program at York University (1983, Atkinson College.) She was a founding editor of *Canadian Woman Studies/les cahiers de la femme* (1978). She designed and taught the Bridging Program (for disenfranchised women) at York — now in its 25th year. She was awarded the Governor General's Persons Award in 1992, and in 2009 York awarded her an LL.D. for her pioneer work for women.

KARIN WILSON has been a self-proclaimed feminist since the tender age of 10 when she picked up her first issue of *Ms.* magazine. Throughout her teens she

proudly displayed the 1975 Canadian International Year of Women poster in her room featuring the "why not" slogan which questioned the exclusion of women from many facets of society. Feminism inspired her to publically question the status quo, which she has done throughout her 20-plus year career as a journalist. Today she works for CBC Radio in BC, and her work has also appeared in a variety of publications including *Off-Centre, Okanagan Life Magazine,* and the *Vancouver Sun.* She lives with her next generation feminist daughter in West Kelowna.

LINDE ZINGARO is a mother and grandmother who has maintained a private counselling/consulting practice in Vancouver for the last 25 years. Among various other jobs, she has been Executive Director for 2 large non-profit societies, and a public speaker/ educator, who trains front-line workers, and agency and policy management groups that work with marginalized populations in Canada, the US and Japan. Her recent Ph.D. dissertation was chosen for publication under the title "Speaking Out: Storytelling for Social Change."

> Victoria Status of Women Action Group, November 1988

Archives and Special Collections (CWMA), University of Ottawa (PC-X10-1-381)/Photographer unknown

> Victoria Status of Women Action Group, novembre 1988